# CRIMINAL LIABILITY FOR NON-AGGRESSIVE DEATH

# Criminal Liability for Non-Aggressive Death

*Edited by*

C.M.V. CLARKSON AND SALLY CUNNINGHAM
*University of Leicester, UK*

Routledge
Taylor & Francis Group
LONDON AND NEW YORK

First published 2008 by Ashgate Publishing

2 Park Square, Milton Park, Abingdon, Oxfordshire OX14 4RN
52 Vanderbilt Avenue, New York, NY 10017

*Routledge is an imprint of the Taylor & Francis Group, an informa business*

First issued in paperback 2020



**British Library Cataloguing in Publication Data**
Criminal liability for non-aggressive death
1. Manslaughter - Great Britain - Congresses 2. Criminal liability - Great Britain - Congresses 3. Homicide - Great Britain - Congresses 4. Negligence, Criminal - Great Britain - Congresses
I. Clarkson, C. M. V. (Christopher M. V.) II. Cunningham, Sally
345.4'10252

**Library of Congress Cataloging-in-Publication Data**
Criminal liability for non-aggressive death / by Chris Clarkson and Sally Cunningham, [editors].
p. cm.
Includes bibliographical references and index.
Most of the papers were presented at a conference on criminal liability for non-aggressive death, Leicester, England, April 2007.
ISBN 978-0-7546-7334-7
1. Manslaughter--Great Britain. 2. Criminal liability--Great Britain. 3. Homicide--Great Britain. 4. Negligence, Criminal--Great Britain. I. Clarkson, C. M. V. (Christopher M. V.) II. Cunningham, Sally.

KD7963.C75 2008
345.42'02525--dc22

2008002421

ISBN 13: 978-0-7546-7334-7 (hbk)
ISBN 13: 978-0-367-60345-8 (pbk)

# Contents

# List of Tables

# Notes on Contributors

**Andrew Ashworth** is Vinerian Professor of English Law in the University of Oxford, and Chairman of the Sentencing Advisory Panel. His book *Principles of Criminal Law* was published in a 5th edition in 2006. His other texts are *Sentencing and Criminal Justice* (4th ed., 2005); *The Criminal Process* (3rd ed., with Mike Redmayne, 2005); and *Human Rights and Criminal Justice* (2nd ed., with Alison Macdonald and Ben Emmerson, 2007).

**Chris Clarkson** is a Professor of Law at the University of Leicester. At present he teaches Criminal Law and Conflict of Laws. In 2005 he was appointed Specialist Advisor to the Home Affairs and Work and Pensions Joint Committees of the House of Commons examining the Draft Corporate Manslaughter Bill. He writes articles in Criminal Law as well as two books: *Understanding Criminal Law* (4th ed., 2005) and Clarkson and Keating, *Criminal Law: Text and Materials* (6th ed., 2007). He also writes a book and articles on the Conflict of Laws.

**Sally Cunningham** has been a lecturer in law at the University of Leicester, where she teaches Criminal Law and Criminal Justice System, since 2004. That year she was also awarded her PhD from the same university. Her thesis is entitled 'Criminal Charges Brought in Cases of Road Death Incidents in the East Midlands: Implications for Law Reform' and involved an empirical study of police and Crown Prosecution Service files. Between 1998–2000 she worked on another empirical study of homicide cases at Coventry University with Barry Mitchell, some of the results of which have been published in an appendix to the Law Commission's Report No. 304, *Murder, Manslaughter and Infanticide*. She joined the editorial team on the 6th edition of Clarkson and Keating's *Criminal Law: Text and Materials*, and is currently working on a book to be published in 2008 with Ashgate entitled *Driving Offences: Law, Policy and Practice*.

**Antony Duff** studied classics and philosophy as an undergraduate at Oxford, and philosophy as a postgraduate. He has taught in the Department of Philosophy at the University of Stirling since 1970. His research interests lie mainly in the philosophy of criminal law – both in penal theory (*Trials and Punishments*, CUP 1986; *Punishment, Communication, and Community*, OUP 2001) and in the principles and structures of criminal liability (*Intention, Agency and Criminal Liability*, Blackwell 1990; *Criminal Attempts*, OUP 1996; *Answering for Crime*, Hart 2007). Together with Lindsay Farmer, Sandra Marshall and Victor Tadros, he has just completed an AHRC-funded project on the criminal trial (*The Trial on Trial*, three volumes, Hart 2004, 2006, 2007); with the same collaborators, he is about to embark on a new AHRC-funded project on criminalisation.

**Jonathan Herring** is a Fellow in Law at Exeter College, University of Oxford. He is author of several books including *Criminal Law: Text, Cases and Materials* (OUP, 2008); *Criminal Law* (Palgrave, 2006); *Medical Law and Ethics* (OUP, 2008) and *Family Law* (Pearson, 2007). He has also written widely on issues relating to criminal law, family law and medical law.

**Jeremy Horder** is a Law Commissioner for England and Wales, and Professor of Criminal Law at the University of Oxford. In the 1980s, he read law at both Hull and Oxford Universities, before becoming Porjes Trust Fellow in Law at Worcester College, Oxford. He is a former Chair of the Law Faculty at Oxford, and is currently a member of the Criminal Justice Council. His main academic publications are *Provocation and Responsibility* (OUP, 1992), and *Excusing Crime* (OUP, 2004). As the lead Commissioner, he has to date overseen the publication for the Law Commission of: 'Murder, Manslaughter and Infanticide' (2006), 'Participating in Crime' (2007), 'Conspiracy and Attempts' (2007), and 'Reforming Bribery' (2007).

**Oliver Quick** is a Senior Lecturer in Law at the University of Bristol, where he teaches courses in Criminal Law, Crime, Justice and Society, Medical Law and Public Health Law. In 2002 he was awarded his doctorate on 'Error and the Medical Profession: Regulating Trust' by the University of Wales Cardiff. He is co-author (with Nicola Lacey and Celia Wells) of the 3rd edition of *Reconstructing Criminal Law* (CUP, 2003). His recent research has focused on the subject of patient safety in healthcare and in the notions of risk and trust as they apply in this setting. He has also undertaken research into the exercise of prosecutorial discretion in relation to medical manslaughter which was published in the *Journal of Law and Society* (2006) Vol. 33(3), pp.421–50, and is currently working on a study into the use of expert evidence in these cases.

**Victor Tadros** is Professor of Criminal Law and Legal Theory at the University of Warwick. Prior to his appointment at Warwick he held lectureships at the University of Edinburgh and the University of Aberdeen. He was educated at the Universities of Oxford (BA Hons) and London (PhD).

He has written on criminal responsibility, criminal offences, criminal trials, the presumption of innocence and various aspects of legal and social theory. His book, *Criminal Responsibility* (OUP), was published in 2005. A further book *The Trial on Trial (3): Towards a Normative Theory of the Criminal Trial* (Hart), co-authored with Antony Duff, Sandra Marshall and Lindsay Farmer, was published in 2007. In 2008 he will begin an AHRC funded project, co-directed with Antony Duff and Lindsay Farmer, on criminalization.

**William Wilson** is Professor of Criminal Law at Queen Mary, University of London and a member of the Queen Mary Centre for Criminal Justice. He has written widely on criminal law and theory and is the author of *Criminal Law Doctrine and Theory* (3rd ed., 2007) and *Central Issues in Criminal Theory* (2002).

**Stanley Yeo** joined the National University of Singapore as professor of law in December 2006. Prior to that, he was Professor of Criminal Law at Southern Cross University, Australia, and served for 16 years as co-editor of the *Criminal Law Journal*, the principal specialist journal on criminal law, procedure and evidence in Australasia. He has written extensively on criminal law including major works like *Fault in Homicide* (Federation Press, 1997), *Unrestrained Killings and the Law* (OUP, 1998), and *Criminal Defences in Australia* (LexisNexis, 2005).

# Chapter 1

# Introduction

C.M.V. Clarkson and Sally Cunningham

## I The Subject-matter of this Book

Beyond the core offences of murder and manslaughter, English law has, until recently, only made specific provision for a few other separate homicide offences: causing death by dangerous driving (and its previous incarnations); causing death by careless driving while under the influence of drink or drugs; causing death by aggravated vehicle-taking; infanticide and aiding and abetting suicide. Since 2004, however, yet further such offences have been created: causing or allowing the death of a child or vulnerable adult; causing death by careless driving; causing death by unlicensed, disqualified or uninsured driving and corporate manslaughter. These developments occurred at the same time as the Law Commission was embarking on ambitious proposals for the restructuring of the whole common law of homicide. This prompts an obvious question: are such specific homicide offences needed and justifiable or should such killings be embraced within the general law of homicide (in particular, manslaughter)?

To address such issues a two-day conference was held at the University of Leicester in April 2007.[1] The papers delivered at this conference, with some significant revisions, form the bulk of this book. Jeremy Horder of the Law Commission was unable to attend the conference but we are fortunate that he has produced a significant chapter in this book. The title of the conference and this book is 'Criminal Liability for Non-Aggressive Death'. Most of the specific offences referred to above involve non-aggressive, non-intentional killings. Some of these could sometimes be prosecuted as manslaughter (for example, when death results from dangerous driving). For the remainder, the only charge (prior to the introduction of the new offences) was for an endangerment offence (for example, careless driving). Other chapters address further dangerous activities, which currently can result in manslaughter charges where death results, and where there might be scope for creating new specific offences along the lines of those referred to above.

We are not concerned with those killings that arise from an act intended to cause death or grievous bodily harm. Accordingly, murder and voluntary manslaughter (along with infanticide which has much in common with voluntary manslaughter) have been excluded from consideration. Similarly, while euthanasia and mercy killings can be described as 'non-aggressive' deaths, they involve deaths being intentionally

1 As conference organisers we wish to thank both the Society of Legal Scholars and the British Academy for their funding of the conference.

caused and, particularly given the highly politically-charged and emotive feelings aroused by suggested reforms, are best largely left aside[2] – although they are briefly addressed by Tadros. But neither are we concerned with criminal liability for *all* unintentional deaths. The term 'non-aggressive' is designed to omit killings which take place in the course of an attack, where the defendant has chosen to engage in violence against another person. However, in establishing justifications for drawing lines between different species of homicide, it is necessary to explore what might fall on either side of the line, and attacks are discussed, in particular by Duff, in attempting to establish the role that luck ought to play in the imposition of criminal liability for those who case death. A death falling within the offence discussed by Herring under section 5 of the Domestic Violence, Crime and Victims Act 2004 might be one that is both intentional and aggressive, but in practice the offence is likely to encompass someone other than the aggressor.

## II Specific Homicide Offences

So, the focus of this book is whether killings in specific contexts, where a person is engaged in non-aggressive conduct with no intention to cause harm, should be treated as specific or nominate offences or whether they should fall within the general offence of manslaughter. Five areas of law have been chosen from which to explore this issue. Three of these deal with killings in specific contexts which are, under current law, subject to special treatment with the creation of specific offences.

The first of these is the newly-created offence of corporate manslaughter. Clarkson argues that it is inadequate to prosecute merely for a breach of health and safety offence when someone has been killed by a corporation's dangerous activities. The fact of death needs to be reflected in the offence definition. Rather than simply utilising the general law of manslaughter, he argues that a special offence was needed for two reasons. First, it has proved extremely problematic to adapt the law of manslaughter to cover corporate entities. Secondly, he argues that the context of such killings with deaths occurring within the regulatory setting of health and safety are so far removed from paradigmatic manslaughter that they should be marked by the existence of a special offence.

The second area, examined by Cunningham, concerns the causing of death by dangerous or other bad or prohibited driving. The offence of causing death by dangerous driving was created in 1956 when it was considered that juries were reluctant to convict drivers of manslaughter. Bad drivers who cause death can now face liability for a number of offences, depending on the degree of negligence they display and the way in which prosecutors exercise their discretion in selecting an appropriate charge. These range from manslaughter down to the newly-created offence of causing death by careless driving. Drivers involved in fatal collisions after driving carelessly, when they should not have been driving at all because they

2 The Law Commission has recommended that the Government should undertake a specific public consultation on whether the law should recognise an offence of mercy killing or a partial defence of mercy killing: Law Commission for England and Wales (2006), *Murder, Manslaughter and Infanticide* (Law Com. No. 304) Part 7.

were drunk, had stolen the vehicle involved, or were driving without a licence or insurance or whilst disqualified, have also had homicide offences tailor-made for them. Cunningham argues that neither theoretical nor pragmatic justifications for special vehicular homicide offences stand up to scrutiny, and that death caused by driving should either be prosecuted as manslaughter or the underlying endangerment offence.

The third specific homicide offence, discussed by Herring, is the crime of causing or allowing the death of a child or vulnerable adult under section 5 of the Domestic Violence, Crime and Victims Act 2004. He explains that this offence was created mainly because of evidential problems that arose when a child or vulnerable adult was killed by a carer in the same household, but it could not be proved which carer actually caused the death. After discussing the numerous interpretative problems associated with the offence and the apparently arbitrary distinctions drawn, he suggests that the law could have responded to the problem by simply increasing the maximum penalty for the underlying endangerment offence of child neglect. He concludes that the offence is likely to lead to the prosecution of women who are themselves the victims of domestic violence. Such women might deserve some degree of moral censure, but it is not clear, given their vulnerability and lack of ill-will towards their victims, that they deserve liability for homicide. Instead of prosecuting such women for a homicide offence, the state should recognise its responsibility for providing effective and adequate protection of women and children from violence.

Beyond corporate killings, vehicular killings and killings of children and vulnerable adults, are there any other contexts of killing that might deserve special treatment in the absence of *mens rea* for murder? A doctor or other medical professional whose negligence causes the death of a patient may face liability for gross negligence manslaughter. If it were thought necessary to create an offence of causing death by dangerous driving to apply to drivers who might otherwise be upstanding, law-abiding members of society, why not create a similar offence for professionals who, it could be argued, deserve to be considered separately from other killers because of the fact that their very reason for acting is to help others? This is the subject of Quick's chapter, which in fact takes the opposite view that most medical professionals do not deserve to fall within the scope of the criminal law on homicide at all, and argues that the *mens rea* for manslaughter is in need of reform in order to exclude them. He argues that gross negligence manslaughter, which can currently be used to prosecute medical professionals who cause death, should ideally be abolished and reliance placed on the alternative form of subjective recklessness manslaughter. This would, he argues, allow prosecutions to focus on those doctors who deserve condemnation for the choices they have made, rather than leaving prosecutors with the discretion to bring prosecutions in cases which have resulted from momentary slips and lapses in concentration.

Finally, an issue that has attracted considerable attention is whether a drug-supplier who supplies drugs to another who then dies after consuming the drugs, should be guilty of manslaughter – or whether a new specific offence should be created as has occurred in some states in the USA. Wilson suggests in his chapter that such persons should not be liable for either manslaughter or for a special offence but should be treated more as victims of their addiction than criminal killers.

In evaluating the proliferation of specific homicide offences in England and Wales, it is useful to explore how this issue has been treated elsewhere. Yeo outlines the position adopted in the various Australian jurisdictions. Australia was chosen as a comparator for several reasons. First, while most Australian jurisdictions have rejected calls for the introduction of a special offence of corporate manslaughter (preferring to increase the penalties under occupational health and safety legislation), nevertheless two territories have introduced a special offence with the Australian Capital Territory providing a particularly interesting model that was borrowed, in one respect at least (the corporate culture notion), for the formulation of the new English offence of corporate manslaughter. Also of interest is the fact that the offence there, unlike its English counterpart, only extends to the killing of 'workers'. Secondly, South Australia has enacted legislation not dissimilar to the Domestic Violence, Crime and Victims Act 2004 – although the offence extends to the causing of serious harm while the English equivalent is limited to the causing of death. Thirdly, there has been an increasing questioning in Australia by both judges and law reform commissions of the need to have separate vehicular homicide offences. Also of interest in this context is the position in Victoria where the offence of culpable driving causing death requires the same degree of negligence as is required for manslaughter and carries the same penalty as manslaughter.

## III Relationship of Specific Offences to Manslaughter

It is impossible to address these issues without first questioning the construction of the general offence of manslaughter itself and exploring how it, and any nominate offences, ought to fit within a hierarchy (or ladder) of criminal offences generally. Tadros argues that the present law of manslaughter is too broad and that there should be a separate category of 'culpable killing' to capture the least serious homicide cases. Yeo cites the Model Criminal Code Officers Committee which proposes the introduction of a new offence (alongside manslaughter) of dangerous conduct causing death which would cover existing corporate, medical and dangerous driving cases where death results.

Leaving aside these more far-reaching proposals, a strong objection to the creation of specific homicide offences is that they usually only require a lesser threshold of culpability than common law manslaughter. For example, as pointed out by both Ashworth and Cunningham, causing death by dangerous driving only requires 'danger either of injury to any person or of serious damage to property' whereas for manslaughter there has to be gross negligence as to the risk of causing death. Horder argues that 'such an extrinsic definition of danger renders the link with causing death opaque, and hence makes questionable the moral basis for the offence'. Similarly, as demonstrated by Herring, for the offence of causing or allowing the death of a child or vulnerable adult mere negligence suffices. This lowering of the standard of required culpability is seen most dramatically in the new vehicular homicide offences where, for example, for the offence of causing death by careless driving all that is needed is simple careless driving. Ashworth argues that the minimum fault requirement in relation to death should be the same across all homicide offences.

Cunningham uses a numerical analysis of the fault ingredients of homicide offences proposed by the Law Commission to make a similar point, suggesting that there should be a cut-off point of blameworthiness below which liability for death should not be attributed to a negligent actor.

Ashworth highlights the principle of equal treatment of offences of equal seriousness as being necessary in informing offence structures. Tadros similarly argues that for reasons of equality homicide law should be coherent – which means cases should be 'treated comparatively'. If some context-specific killings are picked out for the creation of special offences, then any other context-specific killings which share the characteristics justifying the special treatment should likewise give rise to specific offences. The implication is that we should either rely on one catch-all offence of homicide in cases of non-aggressive death, or ensure that each context deserving special treatment is catered for by a special offence. Quick, in considering the desirability of a special offence in the context of medical killing, notes that single theories of responsibility which attempt to cater for different forms of behaviour under one umbrella often fail in their objective, and considers whether a context-specific appreciation of responsibility would lead to greater fairness. However, his conclusion is to reject the option of a context-specific offence of medical killing below manslaughter in a hierarchy of homicide offences on the basis that the criminal law should be used as a last resort to achieve some positive benefit and in the context of increased safety in the healthcare environment there is no indication that such an offence would be effective.

The above analysis questions the fact that the specific offences generally employ a lower fault threshold than gross negligence manslaughter. There is, of course, another route to a manslaughter conviction, namely, constructive (or unlawful act) manslaughter. Many of the specific homicide offences implicitly draw on this model. Driving carelessly or dangerously is an unlawful and dangerous act. When the danger materialises and death is caused, the fact of death is marked in the offence classification. The offence of causing or allowing the death of a child or vulnerable adult requires the commission of an 'unlawful act'. Although not a formal prerequisite to the imposition of liability, the offence of corporate manslaughter requires the jury to consider whether there has been a dangerous breach of health and safety laws.

Of course, the fact that these offences are similar to constructive manslaughter begs the highly controversial question: is constructive manslaughter itself justifiable? Should people be liable for a resultant death (whatever the underlying endangerment offence) which could be the result of pure luck? Clarkson argues that for fair labelling and communicative reasons a resultant harm should be taken into account provided the harm flows directly from an unlawful, dangerous activity. A company that operates in a dangerous manner can be regarded as having made its own (bad) luck and should be liable for a resultant death and not merely liable for an endangerment offence (breach of health and safety). Wilson accepts the offence of constructive manslaughter in its paradigmatic form where what is required is danger in a specific context rather than danger 'as a more general social phenomenon'. In its paradigmatic form, constructive manslaughter is a crime of violence involving an attack which disqualifies an offender from saying any consequential harm suffered by the victim is pure bad luck. In contrast, with regard to drug-supply 'where the victim chooses to subject himself to risks and indeed may be the dominant partner in a commercial transaction or exchange of services there is no call for luck to redound to the supplier's discredit'. Tadros also accepts that constructive manslaughter can be justified. Where an actor is engaged in a dangerous criminal action there is 'prospective responsibility' for ensuring that there is no risk of death as a consequence of the criminal act; 'unlawful act manslaughter provides one way of showing that the defendant was reckless in killing'. (However, he concludes that this degree of fault is too trivial to justify a manslaughter conviction and should fall within a new offence of culpable killing.)

Duff argues that our moral response to outcome luck is context-dependent. In the case of attacks which are 'structured by the prospective harm' and where success is the core or paradigm case, not causing the harm (as in cases of attempt) will be seen by the actor as a failure; there will be no remorse, only regret. The issue is then whether that failure makes a penal discount (whether at the substantive or sentencing level) appropriate. In the context of endangerments, on the other hand, where the non-occurrence of harm is the paradigm, the actor can be presumed to be relieved that she has caused no harm or that she will be distressed if she does cause harm. The question is now, not whether there should be a penal discount, but whether the causing of harm should aggravate the seriousness of the offence (again, whether at the substantive or sentencing stage). Because we can assume that the agent will already be distressed by the harm caused the law need not 'induce a forceful attempt to induce such distress in her'. Nevertheless, increased punishment is appropriate to endorse the agent's regret. But, because the agent is already appropriately distressed by the harm she has caused, the increase in sentence should be 'only modest'. Following from this, he argues that the very significant increases in maximum sentence provided by the present English vehicular homicide laws are not justified.

Ashworth rejects all these offences based on the commission of an 'originating wrong that can be connected to the death' on the basis that the 'fatal result lies outside the scope of the foreseeable risk created by the offence D was committing'. Rejecting the familiar argument that a defendant who commits an assault or other unlawful act has 'changed his normative position' (as 'nothing more than an assertion which awaits justification') he argues that the 'moral distance' between the originating wrong and the death in these cases is 'too great' to justify holding such defendants criminally responsible for resultant deaths.

## IV The Case for Separate Treatment

Even accepting the above arguments about the need for 'comparability' between offences, there are still two possible ways forward. First, there could still be a case for the introduction of (some) specific homicide offences with levels of culpability similar to those employed by the common law of manslaughter. Alternatively, rather than employing special homicide offences, it could be possible to adapt the present law of manslaughter to cater for the specific situations that have proved problematic.

### *(i) The case for specific offences*

The following arguments can be adduced in favour of specific homicide offences:

First, the context of the killing is such that it falls outside what is broadly perceived to be a paradigmatic manslaughter. For example, Clarkson argues that corporate activities (even when death results) do not involve attacks on the interests of others. Harming people is not the object of corporate enterprises. Their actions reveal different wrongs (compared to attacks) and show the company's character in a different light. To mark this difference he recommends the specific offence should have been called 'corporate killing' rather than 'corporate manslaughter'. Similar arguments could be adduced in relation to causing death by dangerous driving and causing death by medical negligence. The actors in these cases are engaged in *prima facie* lawful activities with harm to others not being a factor motivating their actions. In a similar vein, Tadros argues that specific homicide offences are only justified if there is a 'sufficiently significant moral distinction which requires separating these offences from killing in other ways or other contexts'. For Tadros, however, there are only two candidates for this: corporate killing ('the fact that the perpetrator is a corporation rather than an individual might have the kind of moral significance that deserves separate recognition in the law') and an offence to cover mercy killing and assisted suicide.

On the other hand, Ashworth doubts whether the circumstances of killing by driving or through corporate activities are so different as to require a special label. Yeo cites the Victorian Law Reform Commission which asks: 'Why should it make any difference that a death occurs in the context of the use of a motor vehicle rather than in the context of the use of firearms or drugs? What justifies the disparity of penalties?' Similarly, Horder challenges the notion that 'the mere identification of a "killing field" with a regulatory backdrop' should lead to the creation of specific offences as this 'undermines the authority of murder and manslaughter'. With regard to the supply of drugs, Wilson rejects the need for a special offence. He cites Peter Alldridge's[3] view that the real wrong in drug-dealing is that it involves a form of exploitation, a wrong 'too far removed from the consequences of death to justify holding the exploiter to account'. He argues that responsibility for the harms engendered by the supply of dangerous drugs stretches too far (starting with the Afghan farmer growing opium poppies) to 'justify singling out individual suppliers and their activities' when death results.

Secondly, and related to the above point, Ashworth (while not supporting specific offences) suggests that nominate offences perform a communicative function: 'emphasising the special duties of citizens in certain roles or positions'. A separately-named offence helps publicise the duty imposed on people in certain types of situation, such as drivers, or to communicate that a duty is owed by an extended class of persons such as 'members of the same household' under the Domestic Violence, Crime and Victims Act 2004.

---

3 Alldridge, P. (1996), 'Dealing with Drug Dealing' in Simester, A.P. and Smith, A.T.H. (eds), *Harm and Culpability* (Oxford: Clarendon Press).

Both Cunningham and Quick consider the practical benefits of special context-specific homicide offences to cater for bad driving and medical killings respectively, only to conclude that any benefits are questionable. Driving and medical practice are both activities sharing the characteristics that they are carried out for positive social reasons but bring with them the risk of death where the actor makes an error or loses concentration. Cunningham and Quick doubt that the existence of special homicide offences can be used to deter bad practice leading to fatalities in these contexts. Cunningham notes that public pressure applied on behalf of victims' relatives has been one of the central triggers for creating causing death by driving offences, and suggests that the needs of such relatives might be better addressed outside the criminal law, perhaps through the coroners' courts. Quick argues that the study of medical error is insufficiently developed and understood to support the creation of a new medical homicide offence (although, interestingly, Yeo in his chapter argues that a special offence of medical homicide should be introduced in Australia).

Horder contrasts the 'common law' view of law ('comprised of accessibly formulated general rules, applicable to all persons largely irrespective of the context in which they act') with the regulatory approach (where offences are specially tailored to the regulatory context) with its 'implication that offenders will be punished in a way substantially more reflective of the need to secure their future compliance with regulations' rather than reflecting public condemnation. These latter offences are context-specific and targeted at particular groups hence distancing such homicides from 'association with the culturally historically rich offence label "manslaughter"'.

Thirdly, in some cases, the legal rules or the operation of those rules make it difficult to accommodate killings within the existing law of manslaughter. As Herring demonstrates, the offence of causing the death of a child or vulnerable adult was introduced mainly because of evidential problems that arose when a child or vulnerable adult was killed by a carer in the same household but it could not be proved which carer actually caused the death. Also, with most criminal law being designed around an individualistic conception of responsibility, the law has struggled to devise appropriate mechanisms to hold corporations accountable. Clarkson argues that the test employed for manslaughter, the identification doctrine, was, quite simply, 'not fit for the purpose'.

Fourthly, with certain types of killings, if manslaughter were the only available charge, there would be the risk of jury nullification (Ashworth). It is well-documented that this was a significant reason behind the introduction of the offence of causing death by dangerous driving in 1956. Ashworth suggests that *if* this problem still exists today, it is 'more a question of convicting a defendant who has hitherto lived a blameless life', a problem that could also apply to doctors charged with manslaughter. Yeo argues that the reason prosecutions of doctors for manslaughter are so rare in Australia is because prosecutors believe the manslaughter label is inappropriate in such cases with many believing that the blame for such deaths lies primarily with the relevant health authorities in failing to provide or maintain adequate healthcare services. Wilson, too, concludes that responsibility for the fatal results of drug misuse 'lies with failed state policies concerning the control of, and treatment available for, drug misuse' – although it is doubtful that this has inhibited prosecutors in England from bringing manslaughter charges (before *Kennedy*).[4]

It is, however, highly debatable whether this risk of jury nullification still exists to the same extent today – particularly in relation to causing death by dangerous driving. Cunningham refers to research conducted in Victoria, Australia, which suggests that the public would be willing to convict drivers of manslaughter in the worst cases, and both Ashworth and Cunningham refer to some work on public opinion conducted by Mitchell which may suggest that attitudes here have also changed.[5] Ashworth notes that one of the principal reasons why prosecutors are reluctant to charge manslaughter is just as much that sentencing practices have changed dramatically in the past 50 years and someone found guilty of causing death by dangerous driving is likely to receive a term of imprisonment no shorter than for manslaughter. This raises the question of whether it is offence label or sentencing which is most significant in determining whether separate offences are desirable. Cunningham rejects arguments that a separate offence of causing death by dangerous driving is justified on the basis of 'situational relevance', since this undermines the underlying message that dangerous driving is a risky behaviour that ought not to be tolerated, and leads to the downgrading of the offence, which Ashworth again notes is something that raises the issue of whether offence labelling, sentencing, or both should be the motivating force in having nominate offences.

### *(ii) Adapting the law of manslaughter*

The alternative approach would be to abolish all (or most) of the specific offences and to 'finesse' (Wilson) the present law of manslaughter so as to capture all cases where a finding of accountability is appropriate. Existing legal rules could be adapted to address the problems involved in securing manslaughter convictions. For example, Clarkson concedes that one possible solution to the problems posed by the identification doctrine could have been a judicial expansion or statutory abolition of the doctrine. With regard to the problem of obtaining a conviction in cases where it is uncertain which of two carers killed a child or vulnerable adult, reform of the law of evidence could have gone some way towards curing the problem.[6] Tadros suggests that special rules of liability or separate modes of proof might be created to assist decision-makers in certain manslaughter cases. For example, there could be special rules of liability to deal with cases involving driving or medical negligence but, crucially, leading to a manslaughter conviction rather than conviction for a separate offence. In a not dissimilar vein, Horder prefers a system of criminal law 'in which common law and regulatory approaches are regarded as mutually reinforcing, rather than as rival claimants'. As an example of this he cites the offence of corporate

4 [2007] 3 WLR 612.

5 Mitchell, B. (2000). 'Further Evidence of the Relationship between Legal and Public Opinion on the Law of Homicide' *Criminal Law Review* 814.

6 Various options were discussed by the Law Commission: Law Commission (2003), *Children: Their Non-Accidental Death or Serious Injury (Criminal Trials)* (Law Com. No. 282).

manslaughter which bears a similar label and involves a fault element broadly comparable to that required for manslaughter.

## V Conclusion

Following the line of analysis above, this book starts with two chapters (Horder and Tadros) examining the general law of manslaughter and how the specific offences could relate to this crime. This is followed by Duff's chapter on the important issue in the law and one which is of particular relevance to many of the specific homicide offences: the role of luck in the criminal law. Following these more general chapters are the five chapters dealing with the specific homicide offences (existing or possible), rounded off by Yeo's Australian perspective on these topics. The final chapter by Ashworth concludes the book by setting out the central issues that need to be addressed in considering whether generic or nominate offences of homicide are to be preferred. His final section raises the issue of enforcement, a practical issue which should not be overlooked in considering the likely operation of any offences in practice.

The conference at which these papers were first presented was the first in-depth look at this particular area of homicide law, and the first to collect together academics to discuss the law of homicide since the conference on homicide in Oxford which led to the publication of the book, edited by Andrew Ashworth and Barry Mitchell, entitled *Rethinking English Homicide Law*.[7] That conference was organised for the purpose of kick-starting fresh debate on reform of homicide at a time when the Law Commission had published its report on *Involuntary Manslaughter* but had yet to consider the reform of homicide as a whole. Despite the Government producing proposals, including a draft Bill,[8] large-scale reform has not been achieved and only the proposals on corporate manslaughter, amended to satisfy the concerns of Parliament, have since been enacted. However, the Law Commission has now set out recommendations for reform of the general offences of homicide.[9] Whether these recommendations go the same way as so many that have gone before (nowhere) is yet to be seen, but what Report No. 304 fails to do[10] is to consider how special offences which have been created to cater for killing in specific contexts should relate to the homicide ladder. It is hoped that the chapters in this volume give food for thought not only in this regard, but in addressing some of the fundamental issues of criminal liability itself.

7 (2000) (Oxford: Oxford University Press).

8 Home Office (2000), *Reforming the Law on Involuntary Manslaughter: the Government's Proposals*.

9 Law Commission for England and Wales (2006), *Murder, Manslaughter and Infanticide* (Law Com. No. 304).

10 This is not a criticism, since other offences were not within its terms of reference.

Chapter 2

# Homicide Reform and the Changing Character of Legal Thought

Jeremy Horder

## I Introduction

I shall try to show how the development of and demand for discrete, specialised and context-sensitive offences of homicide reflects the modern emergence of a distinctive cast of thought about the nature and function of homicide law reform. This is the regulatory or bureaucratic-administrative cast of thought, according to which law is understood mainly as a malleable tool to be fashioned in a way that will promote the achievement of specific ends in a particular context, when the public interest demands this. This cast of thought has come to rival an older tradition of thought about the nature of law that I shall (somewhat misleadingly) call the 'common law' ideal. As we shall see in section II, the common law ideal began to come to prominence over 200 years ago, and since then has influenced almost all formal proposals to reform the law of murder and manslaughter up to the present day. Those who think in a common law style see law reform as involving the retention but also the modernisation of traditional crimes involving *mala in se* (murder; manslaughter; burglary; arson; rape, and so on), through the definition of such crimes in terms of general, readily comprehensible rules and principles applicable to all persons irrespective of the context in which the harm is inflicted.

The regulatory or bureaucratic style of thought is here to stay, and can undoubtedly add an important new problem-solving dimension to reform of the law of homicide. No one should mourn the loss of total hegemony in the field of homicide by the crimes of murder and manslaughter, the crimes that exemplify the common law cast of thought in the domain of homicide. However, I shall argue that something worth retaining may indeed be lost – most particularly in point of legitimacy – by simply abandoning common law styles of thinking, and common law crimes, when shaping homicide law reform. It may sometimes be better to use regulatory forms of law to *support* the application of murder and manslaughter to homicides committed in contexts where the application of the law has proved difficult or controversial. This may enhance the law's legitimacy more effectively than replacing those two crimes with newly minted homicide offences purportedly tailored to suit those contexts more precisely.

## II Homicide Offences: The 'Common Law' View

There have always been competing accounts of the meaning of a 'common law' perspective on law and law reform.[1] Forsaking strict historical accuracy, I want to focus on an account that embodies an *idealised* conception rather than a description of 'common law'.[2] This idealised conception comes to special prominence in the late eighteenth (and early nineteenth) century, emerging as an enduring train of thought as much as anything, as part of a critique of what was perceived at that time to be the haphazard and piecemeal nature of reform effected by statute. It is a largely content-independent account of an ideal of law-making, focused more on the form than on the substance of the law. Most importantly, the view of law-making with which I am concerned was from an early stage regarded by many as better implemented by statute than by incremental judicial law-making; its judicial law-making origins lie in the inductive process of drawing out a general rule or principle from a series of individual judicial decisions.[3] The ideal of law, on this account, is law that is 'common' in the distinctive sense that it is comprised of *accessibly formulated general rules, applicable to all persons largely irrespective of the context in which they act*. Ironically, the essentials of this account of common law form an important part of the reforming ambitions of Jeremy Bentham, in other respects the common law's most trenchant critic. This is because not only does the common law view I will take as my model by its nature seem to require embodiment in statute, but because it is perfectly consistent with – indeed, may exemplify in action – rule utilitarianism of a kind favoured by Bentham. What are the origins of this 'common law' perspective (about which more detail will be given in due course)?

Famously, Bentham caricatured Blackstone as concerned only with the law as it is, he – Bentham – being concerned with the law as it ought to be.[4] Nonetheless, they shared the view that Parliamentary intervention in the law (the Murder Act of 1752 being an example[5]) had to that point been entirely unsatisfactory because of its concern largely for the ephemeral, as opposed to the enduring, and for the particular over and above the general. Encouraging legislators to avoid 'quackery in Government', Blackstone complained that:

---

1 See Postema, G. (2003), 'Classical Common Law Jurisprudence (Part II)' *Oxford University Commonwealth Law Journal* 3, 1.

2 The account would certainly not have been consciously identified as a 'common law' conception of law by all who in fact supported it, like Jeremy Bentham.

3 A seventeenth century expression of this idea is to be found in Sir Francis Bacon (facsimile edition 1978), '*Examples of a Treatise on Universal Justice' De Augmentis Scientarium* (New York: Garland) book 8 aphorism 85, 'It is a sound precept … not to take the law from the rules, but to make the rule from the existing law …', cited by Postema, above n.1, 6.

4 Bentham, J. (1789), 'An Introduction to the Principles of Morals and Legislation', Burns, J.H. and Hart, H.L.A. (eds) (1970) (London: Macmillan), chapter XVII.

5 See, Law Commission for England and Wales (2005), *'A New Homicide Act for England and Wales?'* (Consultation Paper No. 177), para. 1.94.

> To say the truth, almost all the perplexed questions, almost all the niceties, intricacies and delays (which have sometimes disgraced the English … courts of justice) owe their origin not to the common law itself, but to innovations that have been made in it by Acts of Parliament.[6]

With this observation, of course, he coupled the view that it would be 'too Herculean a task' for a popular assembly to replace any 'fundamental point' of common law,[7] a view with which Bentham famously and vehemently disagreed;[8] but Bentham's views on Parliament's record in legislating within the criminal field were strikingly similar,[9] albeit expressed in more lurid terms:

> The country squire who has his turnips stolen, goes to work and gets a bloody law against stealing turnips. It exceeds the utmost stretch of his comprehension to conceive that the next year the same catastrophe may happen to his potatoes. For two general rules … in modern British legislation are: never to move a finger until your passions are inflamed, nor ever to look further than your nose.[10]

Whether – and if so, why – twentieth and twenty-first century homicide legislation suffers from a modern-day version of such vices will be questions addressed in later sections. What did Blackstone, Bentham and others who shared their views, see as the remedy for such 'particularism' in statutory law reform? One theme in particular predominates. For Blackstone, the criminal law, 'should be founded upon principles that are permanent, uniform and universal'.[11] For Bentham, the law must be comprised of, 'written, visible, and intelligible and cognoscible … rule[s] of action and guide[s] to human conduct'.[12] To similar effect, for other commentators, such as Anthony Hammond,[13] what was needed was the, 'substitution of general rules for particular decrees',[14] or, as one commentator put it: 'We would melt down the old, alloyed, and shapeless coin, in order to recast, in a pure and symmetrical shape, the large quantity of precious metal which it contains'.[15]

---

6 Sir William Blackstone, *Commentaries*, Volume I, 10, cited by Smith, K.J.M. (1998), *Lawyers, Legislators and Theorists: Developments in English Criminal Jurisprudence 1800-1957* (Oxford: Oxford University Press) p.73.

7 Sir William Blackstone, *Commentaries*, Volume III, 267, cited by Smith, K.J.M., above n.6.

8 See Scofield, P. and Harris, J. (eds) (1998), '"Legislator of the World": Writings on Codification, Law and Education', in *The Collected Works of Jeremy Bentham* (Oxford: Oxford University Press) pp.20–21.

9 See Smith, above n.6, pp.73–74.

10 Bentham MSS in the library of University College, London, cxl 92, cited in Postema, G. (1986), *Bentham and the Common Law Tradition* (Oxford: Clarendon Press) p.264.

11 Cited by Smith, above n.6, at p.20.

12 Cited by Schofield and Harris, above n.8, pp.18–21.

13 Principal author of the 1824 Report of the Select Committee on Criminal Law: see the useful discussion in Smith, above n.6, pp.80–83.

14 Anthony Hammond (1829), 'On the Reduction to Writing of the Criminal Law', Introduction, xiv–xvi, cited by Smith, above n.6, p.82.

15 Anon (1830), 'On Codification, and its Application to the Laws of England' *Foreign Quarterly Review* VI, 333, cited by Smith, above n.6, p.75. The commentator goes

To be sure, there were great differences of opinion amongst these authors about the content the new model criminal law should have. Should it, for example, be shaped by the existing common law – the 'large quantity of precious metal' – or be determined instead by the new principle of utility?[16] For Sir James Stephen, for example, whose efforts to produce a criminal code comprised of general rules had such great influence on the development of the criminal law in Canada and Australia, 'two things only remain, positive rules, the will of … a legislator, and the principle of general utility'.[17] However, what united this disparate group of commentators was the sense that, whatever the principles governing its content ought to be, law should be comprised of general, uniform, or universal rules.

Moreover, these rules were to take a form such that they were 'intelligible and cognoscible' (in Bentham's words), or as William Eden put it, 'clearly obvious to common understandings and fully notified to the people'.[18] The rules were, in other words, to be addressed (or at least address-able) to citizens rather than just to lawyers. Sir James Stephen argued that reform must take a form such that, 'the old law books and reports must be distilled into a portable and intelligible form, so that the nation at large may have some conception of its rights and obligations',[19] To underline his point, in this respect, Stephen sought to make actions speak as loudly as words by giving a (well-received) lecture on codification to a meeting with the Trades Union Congress, that lasted several hours in 1877.[20] To similar effect, the Attorney-General said, in a speech on 3 April 1879:

> Surely, it is a desirable thing that anybody who may want to know the law on a particular subject should be able to turn to a chapter of the Code, and there find the law he is in

---

on to say, 'Mr Bentham would throw away the whole, silver as well as copper'; but that is an observation on differences of opinion about the content the new rules should have (the point about 'precious metal' supposedly contained in the common law), and not on the form the law should take to accommodate the content.

16 See above n.15.

17 Sir James Stephen (1892), *Horae Sabatticae*, 3rd Series, 210 and 219, cited by Smith, K.J.M. (1988), *James Fitzjames Stephen* (Cambridge: Cambridge University Press) p.50. As it turned out, there was a far from vast gulf between what Stephen took to be consonant with the principle of general utility, and the requirements of the existing common law: see Horder, J. (2002), 'Strict Liability, Statutory Construction and the Spirit of Liberty' *Law Quarterly Review* 118, 458, at 461–462.

18 Eden, W. (1771), *Principles of Penal Law*, 2nd ed. (London: Macmillan) p.312.

19 Sir James Stephen (1856), 'Law Reform', *Saturday Review*, 2 February, 252.

20 For an account of the proceedings, see Hostettler, J. (1995), *Politics and Law in the Life of Sir James Fitzjames Stephen* (Chichester: Barry Rose) pp.165–170. Stephen observed, in relation to the TUC's dislike of common law principles, 'their dead silence when I said anything in its praise and their eager applause when I found fault with it. I felt very queerly towards them' (*ibid.*). Stephen's Code even received the commendation of the normally satirical *Punch* Magazine, which on 20 July 1878 said, 'Punch takes off his cap and bells to Sir James Stephen – Protomendor, and not also, strange to say, as yet, Proto-martyr, of our criminal law' (*ibid.*, at p.179).

search of explained in a few intelligible and well-constructed sentences ... [having] a succinct and clear statement before him.[21]

How should the account, or train of thought, that I am calling the idealised 'common law' account of law-making be understood, in theoretical terms?

## III The 'Common Law' Account Theorised

### *(i) Reform proposals inspired by the common law ideal*

In answering this question, let us take by way of example, the 1878–79 Homicide Bill and its 'successor', the Law Commission's current recommendations for reform of the law of murder. They are both attempts to give effect to a common law view of murder within the law of homicide. The 1878–79 Bill's 'common law' element, as I have explained that notion *qua* the ideal of law-making, can be found in its attempt to define the primary offence of murder (excluding felony murder) through a general rule expressed in ordinary language:

> Culpable homicide is murder...
> if the offender means to cause the death...
> if the offender means to cause to the person killed any bodily injury which is known to the offender to be likely to cause death, and if the offender, whether he does or does not mean to cause death, is reckless whether death ensues or not...

The Law Commission's recent recommendation that there should be created offences of first and second degree murder is a recommendation from the same intellectual stable, a reflection of the same idealised conception of law-making consonant with the common law view. The Commission's recommendation for the offences of first and second degree murder (setting aside the effect of defences), for example, is that they should be comprised of:

> Killing intentionally [first degree murder].
> Killing where there was an intention to do serious injury, coupled with an awareness of a serious risk of causing death [first degree murder].
> Killing where the offender intended to do serious injury [second degree murder].
> Killing where the offender intended to cause some injury or a fear or risk of injury, and was aware of a serious risk of causing death [second degree murder].[22]

21 H.C. Hansard, 3 April 1879, Vol. 245 (3rd Series) col 316, cited by Lord Bingham (1998), 'A Criminal Code: Must We Wait For Ever?', *Crim LR* 694, 696.

22 Law Commission for England and Wales (2006), *Murder, Manslaughter and Infanticide* (Law Com. No. 304) para. 1.67. For a comparison between the 1879 Bill and the Law Commission's recommendations, see Horder, J. (2007), 'The Changing Face of the Law of Homicide', in Horder, J. (ed.), *Homicide Law in Comparative Perspective* (Oxford: Hart Publishing).

These recommendations, like the rules of common law homicide on which they are founded,[23] are a classic embodiment of what has been called the '*gesellschaft*' ideal of law, law that involves: 'pervasive and essentially exhaustive rules of conduct for all relations between individuals, which are to be applied to any circumstances at all'.[24]

As we will see in the next section, it is this – *Gesellschaft* – aspect of common law homicide that has come to be seen as inimical to a primarily regulatory, context-dependent and means-end dominated scheme for the reduction of lethal harm, especially lethal harm caused on the roads.

However, in its dependence on primarily value-laden as opposed to predominantly descriptive labels ('murder' and 'manslaughter', as opposed to, say, 'causing death by dangerous driving'), common law homicide – and the proposals to reform it – also hark back to a pre-modern '*gemeinschaft*' ideal of law, in which: 'the emphasis is on law and regulation as expressing … internalised norms and traditions of an organic society … Here there tends to be no sharp distinction, if there is any formal distinction at all, between … legal issues and moral issues'.[25]

This feature of the common law ideal of homicide remains attractive,[26] even in the regulatory context that (as we shall see in the next section) has come to exercise such an important influence on the law of homicide in relatively recent years. The enduring nature of public identification with an internalised norm such as 'manslaughter', has led reformers to embrace some intermingling of the '*gemeinschaft*' forms of law and administrative-regulatory forms of law, to give the latter greater moral credibility. The creation of an offence of 'corporate manslaughter' perhaps best encapsulates this phenomenon.[27] The new crime involves the adaptation of a general common law crime, with its value-laden and retribution-orientated '*gemeinschaft*' label (manslaughter), to fit a specific regulatory context: that of accident caused by gross breach of a duty of care resulting at least in part from, 'the way in which any of [an] organisation's activities are managed or organised by its senior managers'.[28]

---

23 Such as Coke's famous definition of murder, still in small part good law today: see the discussion in Law Commission for England and Wales (2005), *A New Homicide Act for England and Wales?* (Consultation Paper No. 177) para. 1.52.

24 Kamenka, E. and Tay, A. 'Beyond Bourgeois Individualism: the Contemporary Crisis in Law and Legal Ideology', in Kamenka and Neale (eds) (1975), *Feudalism, Capitalism and Beyond* (London: Edward Arnold) p.139.

25 *Ibid.*, p.136.

26 In its review of homicide, for example, the Law Commission found almost unanimous support for the retention of the terms, 'murder' and 'manslaughter', even if there was less agreement on the wrongs that each should represent: see Law Commission, above n.22, para. 2.2.

27 See the Corporate Manslaughter and Corporate Homicide Act 2007; and www.homeoffice.gov.uk/docs4/con_corp_mans.html for the draft Bill. See further, Sullivan, G.R. (2001), 'Corporate Killing – Some Government Proposals', *Crim LR* 31.

28 S.1(3), and see above n.27. The regulatory dimension to the offence is brought out in s.8(2), where the 'gross' character of any breach of duty is to be determined by the jury in part by consideration of whether – and to what extent – the organisation was in breach of existing health and safety legislation.

### *(ii) The impact of regulatory thinking on the common law model*

There are dangers in seeking to splice together forms of law from such different traditions of legal thought. The creation of the crime of corporate manslaughter can be seen as a classic illustration of what Lacey, Wells and Quick have identified as an important tension within modern criminal law between kinds of law:

> That between the older ideas of crime as public wrongdoing and the modern reality of criminal law as a predominantly administrative system managing enormous numbers of … 'regulatory offences': between the older, quasi-moral and retributive view of criminal law and the instrumental, regulatory aspect of criminal law which has become increasingly dominant under modern and late modern conditions.[29]

The rise of the regulatory state involves challenges – generated by new demands for specialised governance of professions and industries, in the public interest – to the traditional reliance on the impartial application of very general rules of law that cut across any concern for contextualisation:

> [T]he growing concern with and interest in the law of certain areas – broadcasting, fishery, trade practices, the environment – is necessarily one that requires bureaucratic-administrative forms and attitudes: it seeks to regulate an activity and not to adjudicate in collisions between individuals; its fundamental concern is with consequences rather than with fault or *mens rea*, with public need or public interest, or the interest of the activity itself, rather than private rights and individual duties.[30]

In the case of homicide, the process of adjudicating in cases of 'collisions between individuals' comes itself to be shaped by regulatory, public interest-based demands. In some instances – the road traffic context being the prime example – these demands have led to an effective displacement from the relevant legal space of rules of homicide (and of manslaughter in particular) that embody the common law ideal. To replace such rules, offences (discussed further below) specially tailored to the regulatory context have from time to time been created and subsequently reformed,[31] to reflect – amongst other things – the changing demands of that regulatory context.

However, tension of the kind referred to by Lacey, Wells and Quick is not to be found only between the forms of law. It may also be found in the way that each form of law generates different expectations about labelling and punishment, expectations that may prove hard for the state to 'manage' (the management of expectations being yet another emerging task for the modern state). A conviction for 'manslaughter' implies serious wrongdoing and at first blush the need, unless there are exceptional circumstances, for condign punishment. By way of contrast, conviction for a regulatory offence need carry no such implications on its face.[32] So, the severe limitation on punishment for

29 Lacey, N., Wells, C. and Quick, O. (2003), *Reconstructing Criminal Law*, 3rd ed. (London: Butterworths) pp.7–8.

30 Kamenka and Tay, above n.24, pp.138–139.

31 Such as causing death by dangerous driving, or causing death by careless driving.

32 In fact, I shall suggest later that if the labelling is regarded as part of the punishment, then the labelling may be regarded as an integral element in what it means to satisfy legitimate

corporate manslaughter (no sentence of imprisonment can be imposed[33]) creates the appearance of legal paradox: a serious crime without serious penal consequences.[34]

Conversely, consider the effective confinement (just referred to) of criminalisation of death on the roads to the regulatory offences of causing death by various forms of dangerous or careless driving.[35] This way of dealing with homicide arising in the course of regulated activity arguably carries an implication that offenders will be punished in a way substantially more reflective of the need to secure their future compliance with regulations, than of any need to reflect simple public condemnation and demands for vengeance. The implication is reinforced by the presence of such offences in a Road Traffic Act otherwise much taken up with road *safety* issues, rather than in a homicide statute.[36] Yet, the maximum sentence for causing death by dangerous driving has now been increased to the point (14 years) once considered appropriate by the Law Commission as a maximum for the substantive offence of manslaughter itself, a crime whose rationale is focused on the demand for public condemnation rather than on the possibility of future compliance.[37] It has proved difficult, then, for Governments to have their cake and eat it too. It has not been easy to satisfy the perceived need to increase road safety through increasing prosecutions and convictions for causing death on the roads (by taking the administrative-regulatory approach, rather than leaving homicides to be dealt with as potential manslaughters), whilst also satisfying the demand for sentences of a retributive kind that would certainly have fitted the crime, had it remained manslaughter.[38]

Nonetheless, I believe support should be given to the way in which, for example, the corporate manslaughter offence seeks to *combine* forms of law reflecting different legal casts of thought. Seen in a positive light, such a proposal can be regarded as a way of helping traditional ways of thinking and categorising – here, in the shape of a *Gesellschaft* form of law with a *Gemeinschaft* label, manslaughter – to find continued meaning and relevance in a modern regulatory context.[39] The argument may turn out to be, then, that reformers should have adopted such an approach, an approach more supportive of the common law (*Gesellschaft*) and *Gemeinschaft* forms of law, in the road traffic and perhaps also in other contexts. This is a theme to which I will return later.

---

expectations that corporate killing is taken seriously, quite apart from any other element of punishment imposed.

33 Corporate Manslaughter and Corporate Homicide Act 2007, s.1(6).

34 But see section 8 below.

35 To be considered in further detail in ensuing sections.

36 On the appropriateness of the legal 'location' of homicide-related law, see Horder, J. 'The Changing Face of the Law of Homicide', in Horder (ed.), above n.22. On the 'road safety' dimension to dangerous and careless driving, see Cunningham, S. (2007), 'Punishing Drivers Who Kill: Putting Road Safety First?' *Legal Studies* 27:2, 288.

37 Law Commission for England and Wales (1996), *Legislating the Criminal Code: Involuntary Manslaughter* (Law Com. No. 237).

38 Similar problems have been identified in relation to the new offence of causing death by careless driving: see Cunningham, above n.36, pp.297–302 esp.

39 See further, Clarkson, C.M.V. (1998), 'Corporate Culpability' *Web Journal of Current Legal Issues* 2.

## IV Homicide Offences: Common Law and Regulatory Models

In the work of some thinkers, the preservation or pursuit of the common law ideal in law reform has been turned into an ideology of freedom under the rule of law. In F.A. Hayek's writing on the rule of law, for example, he suggests that:

> When we obey laws, in the sense of general abstract rules laid down irrespective of their application to us we are not subject to another man's will and are therefore free. It is because the lawgiver does not know the particular cases to which his rules apply … that it can be said that laws and not men rule … As a true law should not name any particulars, so it should especially not single out any specific person or group of persons.[40]

The idea that there might be a unique association between this view of law (a version of the common law ideal of law-making described in section I above) and freedom under the rule of law was shown to be wrong some years ago.[41] Kinds of law that are very far from embodying the common law ideal may still be perfectly capable of satisfying the demands of the rule of law, properly construed.

Nonetheless, Hayek's exposition of the common law ideal captures something of importance, when applied to the criminal law. It links modern departures from the common law ideal to a wish, through law, to subject people – 'specific … group[s] of persons' – more closely to another's (the legislator's) will. The latter approach is what, building on the analysis in the preceding section, we can call the bureaucratic-administrative or regulatory model of law. This model has (in retrospect, misleadingly) been associated by some with the rise of legal positivist thinking of a kind championed by Bentham, amongst others. So, for example, Richard Tur has suggested that, '[I]deal-typically, positivism may be characterised by such notions as "fact", "will", "power", "instrumentalism", "discretion", "*mala prohibita*", etc.'.[42] To similar effect, Lon Fuller spoke of legal positivism in terms of a 'managerial' or 'top down' one-way projection of power and authority.[43] Whatever the merits of the association of these notions with legal positivism, they are most certainly associated with the regulatory model of law.

Very broadly, some of the contrasting aims and elements of the regulatory model, as compared with the common law model, might be summarised as follows (it is far from an exhaustive list):

40 Hayek, F.A. (1944), *The Road to Serfdom* (London: Macmillan) p.54.

41 See Raz, J. (1979), 'The Rule of Law and its Virtue', in his *The Authority of Law* (Oxford: Clarendon Press), chapter 11.

42 Tur, R.H.S. (1986), 'Criminal Law and Legal Theory', in Twining (ed.), *Legal Theory and the Common Law* (Oxford: Blackwell). It seems rather doubtful that legal positivism can be associated with any particular style of legislation, let alone a particular style of government or administration: see Gardner, J. (2001), 'Legal Positivism: "Five and a Half Myths"', *American Journal of Law and Jurisprudence* 46, 199.

43 Fuller, L. (1969), *The Morality of Law*, revised edition (New Haven: Yale).

COMMON LAW MODEL

1. General applicability (not context specific).
2. Application to all citizens equally.
3. Fault element required.
4. Classical view of responsibility and causation.
5. Comprised of *mala in se*.
6. Legitimacy not tied to consequentialist evaluation.
7. Labels descriptively evaluative.[44]

REGULATORY MODEL

1. Context-specific application.
2. Targeted at particular groups.
3. Fault elements dispensable or watered down.
4. Responsibility and causation elements malleable.
5. Blurring of *mala in se/mala prohibita* distinction.
6. Outcomes law produces crucial to legitimacy.
7. Labels descriptively factual.[45]

The aims and elements of the regulatory model are linked to the rise of a concern – outlined in the preceding section – for the management of sectors of society or specific fields of activity in the 'public interest', understood in terms of the achievement of certain public goods. Nonetheless, in spite of the positive listing of distinctive features of each model, it must be kept firmly in mind that these are ideal-types or casts of thought and not rigid categories that are designed to have normative significance. Not all homicide-related offences fall clearly into one category or other, and not all offences clearly within one category will exemplify all the seven characteristics within that category: they may embody some of the characteristics listed in the other category. I am certainly not claiming, for example, either that the offences of murder and manslaughter have been developed without regard to the consequences of adopting certain kinds of definition (element 6); clearly, they have. It is not part of my plan to seek to place every homicide-related offence clearly within the province of one model or the other (a largely sterile and inevitably ahistorical exercise), but to chart the gradual emergence of the regulatory model as a force within a domain that was previously that of the common law model.

The need for caution in allocating offences firmly to one model or the other is illustrated by modern developments in relation to the offences of murder and manslaughter, offences one might think of as classic examples of homicide offences developed largely in accordance with the common law model or ideal. Each of these crimes has been overlaid with a substantially regulatory covering, in the form of element 6 (making outcomes crucial to legitimacy). In the case of murder, that has

44 In other words they seek not merely to describe an activity, but simultaneously to mark its wrongfulness. Examples are not only murder and manslaughter, but also arson, burglary and rape.

45 So, in contrast to examples given in n.44, examples under this heading would be causing death during unlicensed, disqualified or uninsured driving (Road Traffic Act 2006), or causing the death of a child or vulnerable adult (Domestic Violence, Crime and Victims Act 2004).

come through the introduction of guidance – controlled by the Secretary of State for Justice – on the extent of punishment that should follow conviction for murder in particular kinds of circumstances.[46] Quite clearly, this is an attempt to introduce a degree of direct (regulatory) Government influence on when the punitive outcomes of murder cases are to be regarded as legitimate. Similarly, the classes of person who stand to be convicted of corporate manslaughter have been placed under the control of the Secretary of State for Justice, who may change them by amending the relevant schedule.[47] This provision obviously brings element 2 (is there equality of application, or are some groups (dis)favoured?) into play; but element 6 is at issue, in that there is manifestly a wish to ensure that the new law's legitimacy is not undermined by application in what are regarded by Government as inappropriate contexts. So, even in the heartland of the common law, as Hayek impliedly suggested, the rise of regulatory forms of legal intervention may lead to attempts to subject some groups rather than others more closely to the legislator's will, thus blurring the line between 'purely' common law offences and regulatory offences.

## V The Regulatory Model Exemplified

What might be examples of offences classically regarded as regulatory or bureaucratic-administrative in nature? The most obvious examples are the specific offences concerned with death on the roads, of which more will be said below. As is well known, these offences began with the creation of the offence of causing death by 'reckless or dangerous' driving under the Road Traffic Act 1956, with a maximum sentence (at that time) of five years' imprisonment. By its very nature, this offence fulfils elements 1 and 2 of the regulatory model of law, being context-specific and targeted at particular groups (driving, and drivers respectively). Further, in the way that its wording has come to be reformed – it is now causing death by 'dangerous' driving rather than grossly negligent driving[48] – it fulfils element 3 by watering down the fault requirement (as, *a fortiori*, is the case with the new offence of causing death during unlicensed, disqualified or uninsured driving[49]).[50] This change to the offence also means that it has come to fulfil element 5, in that causing death by dangerous driving now rests on a blurred line between *mala in se* and *mala prohibita,* a development reinforced by the reliance on more descriptive than evaluative labels ('causing death by dangerous driving', as opposed to 'manslaughter'). Element 5 has been further reinforced by the indication from the Crown Prosecution Service that a manslaughter charge should not be brought in a case where death has been

46 Criminal Justice Act 2003, s.269 (schedule 21).

47 Corporate Manslaughter and Corporate Homicide Act 2007, s.21 and s.22.

48 As a result of the changes effected by the Road Traffic Act 1988, s.1.

49 See the Road Safety Act 2006, s.21.

50 It is worth emphasising that the very broad notion of 'danger' that governs the offence under s.1 of the Road Traffic Act 1988 – see text at n.76 below – has not been narrowed (still less has any enhanced fault requirement been introduced) to reflect the fact that the maximum penalty has over time almost tripled to fourteen years' imprisonment.

caused by dangerous driving, even if the elements of that offence may well have been fulfilled, unless it is a 'very grave' case.[51]

More than a hint of element 4 can be found in the offence of 'aggravated vehicle taking' contrary to the Theft Act 1968, section 12A. Broadly speaking, for this offence to be committed, it is only necessary for D, knowing that a vehicle has been taken without authority, to 'allow ... himself to be carried in it', and for it then to be proved that (fatal) injury was caused by the driving of the vehicle. D will be guilty unless he or she can show *inter alia* that he or she was not in or in the immediate vicinity of the vehicle when the driving, or the accident, occurred. When, in such circumstances, death is caused, a sentence of up to 14 years' imprisonment may be imposed. It might be thought hard to imagine, in any criminal offence, a more tenuous connection in terms of responsibility and causation between what D 'did' and any death that occurred.

However, an approach as broad or even broader has been adopted by some state legislatures in the United States to provide a means of securing additional deterrents to, as well as retribution against, those involved in supplying illegal drugs that have killed a user. An example is the creation of the offence of 'third degree murder' in Pennsylvania, defined as follows:

> Section 2506. Drug delivery resulting in death.
> (a) General rule.—A person commits murder of the third degree who administers, dispenses, delivers, gives, prescribes, sells or distributes any controlled substance or counterfeit controlled substance ... and another person dies as a result of using the substance.[52]

This offence, punishable by a minimum of five years' imprisonment, may be committed even when the actions of a third party or the victim him or herself – with no less knowledge of the risks than the accused – have occurred between the act of the accused person who sold, delivered, gave or distributed (and so on) the drug, and the victim's 'resulting' death. The English courts have, of course, taken some faltering steps towards a similar position through manipulation of common law doctrines.[53] The very fact that such developments have been mired in confusion and controversy, is a sure sign that the attenuated forms of responsibility and causation that may connect a drug supplier to an ultimate user's death, whilst capable of being addressed through malleable regulatory forms of law, cannot easily be adapted to fit the principles constitutive of a common law framework.[54]

---

51 <www.cps.gov.uk/legal/section9/chapter_b.html#30>.

52 Pennsylvania Consolidated Statutes, Crimes and Offences (Title 18), chapter 25, section 2506.

53 For analyses of the case law, and opposing views about the direction the law should take, see Ormerod, D. and Fortson, R. (2005), 'Drug Suppliers and Manslaughters (Again)', *Crim LR* 819; Jones, T.H. (2006), 'Causation, Homicide and the Supply of Drugs' *Legal Studies* 26:2, 139.

54 See Ormerod and Fortson, above n.53; It is worth noting, in passing, how the existence of regulatory crimes such as the one under discussion ought to be regarded as casting a significant shadow over the modern demand for a more 'contextual' approach to

It is, however, the emergence of element 6 that is perhaps the most interesting in this context. It has long been a strongly held opinion amongst most lawyers that common law offences, such as murder and manslaughter, should not have their meanings unduly twisted or distorted by judicial interpretation, solely in order to capture particular forms of wrongdoing that might otherwise fall outside their scope. In other words, element 6 of the common law model is an important criminal law principle (even if frequently honoured in the breach[55]). By way of contrast, frequent change in the nature, scope and quantity of offences, in the name of the public interest (element 6 under the regulatory model), can be the accepted and acceptable norm in the regulatory sphere. As is well known, over the years the offences connected with death on the road have multiplied (there are now at least four such offences[56]) as new policy concerns have emerged, such as concern about a rise in the number of unlicensed or uninsured drivers. Further, as I have already mentioned, there has been tacking to and fro between narrower and broader versions of some offences, in response to real or perceived difficulties in prosecuting different versions. So, for example, having begun with causing death by reckless or dangerous driving, in the Road Traffic Act 1956, we moved through its narrower replacement – causing death by reckless driving, in the Road Traffic Act 1977 – to the current offence of causing death by dangerous driving in the Road Traffic 1988.[57]

Let me put on one side the questions whether these changes of policy tack have been effective, and whether they have been motivated more by a wish to placate vocal pressure groups and newspaper editors than by a genuine concern for public policy.[58] What is significant in this context is how an overriding public interest concern (howsoever construed) in enhanced road safety has led to continued experimentation in different forms of offence. We have moved towards what Hayek might have referred to as the greater subjection of the regulated group to the 'will'

---

criminalisation. We can now see how the left-liberal cast to many such demands stems solely from their partisan nature: they typically focus on the contextual circumstances that show up the offender in a favourable light. But if a truly contextual approach is to be taken in a non-partisan way, then law reformers would be free additionally to focus on – perhaps obliged additionally to focus on – circumstances that aggravate the offence, such as secondary or 'knock-on' harms or set-backs to the relatives of victims, to those living in the locality, and so on.

55 A thesis developed with all the indignation he could muster by Williams, G. (1983), *Textbook of the Criminal* (London: Stevens). He said of judicial activism in the criminal law, 'the expansion of the law is unavowed … the judges keeping up the pretence that they are mere mouthpieces of the law … [whereas] … to the discerning eye [a judicial decision] is often no more than … rationalisation accompanied by misdirection and legerdemain' (at 16).

56 See Cunningham, above n.36, p.288.

57 Similarly, having begun with the offence of taking and driving a vehicle away without authority, contrary to the Road Traffic Act 1960, we moved to the somewhat broader offence of simply 'taking' a vehicle without authority, created by the Criminal Justice Act 1982 (amending the Theft Act 1968, section 12), which was then supplemented by the offence of aggravated vehicle-taking, in the Aggravated Vehicle Taking Act 1992, the offence that involves a further 'aggravating element' when death is caused: see text following n.51 above.

58 For discussion on this point, see Cunningham, above n.36, pp.301–302.

of the legislator, in a way that might be regarded by many as unacceptable or dysfunctional had it occurred with the development of a common law offence.[59]

## VI Murder and Manslaughter: The Growing Crisis of Confidence

### *(i) Breaches in the wall: three early examples*

Let me now set the discussion in a broader context. The last 100 years have seen a wide-ranging erosion of the legal 'hegemony' previously enjoyed by the common law crimes of murder and manslaughter in the domain of homicide.[60] Parliament has not (other than in the road traffic context) gone so far as to make 'causing death' an aggravating factor of a whole range of non-fatal offences, in the way that some legislatures have done.[61] Nonetheless, Parliament has intervened to create specific homicide offences of infanticide,[62] 'child destruction',[63] 'assisting suicide',[64] causing death by dangerous driving,[65] and causing or allowing the death of a child or vulnerable adult.[66] In the first three instances (infanticide; child destruction; assisting suicide), the crime of manslaughter could quite easily have been used to achieve one of the effects desired: criminalisation other than through the crime of murder. Instead, an entirely context-specific homicide offence was preferred, henceforth cutting off the homicides in question from association with the culturally and historically rich offence label, 'manslaughter'.[67] The contrast, then, is with the

59 Although, such developments have begun to affect both murder and manslaughter: see section 6 below. The development of the common law is not, of course, immune from 'tacking to and fro' with regard to fault or other elements of offences, or from policy-related changes. The difference lies in the fact that, under the regulatory model, experimentation and (occasionally) 'tacking to and fro' may be intentionally adopted as a medium to long-term *strategy*, whereas this is difficult or impossible in a precedent-based system of case-by-case common law development.

60 See further Horder, J. and Hughes, D. 'Comparative Issues in the Law of Homicide', in Horder (ed.) (2007), *Homicide Law in Comparative Perspective* (Oxford: Hart Publishing); Lacey, Wells and Quick, above n.29, chapter 6. I put on one side here consideration of the old offence, supervening on murder in certain circumstances, of so-called 'petty treason'.

61 See Horder and Hughes, above n.60; Spencer, J.R. and Pedain, A., 'Approaches to Strict and Constructive Liability in Continental Criminal Law', in Simester (ed.) (2005), *Appraising Strict Liability* (Oxford: Oxford University Press), chapter 10. The road traffic context is, of course, the exception in England and Wales: see for example, Road Safety Act 2006, s.20.

62 Infanticide Act 1922.

63 Infant Life (Preservation) Act 1929.

64 Suicide Act 1961.

65 Road Traffic Act 1956. See the discussion of this offence in the next section.

66 Domestic Violence, Crimes and Victims Act 2004.

67 I should not be taken to be saying that manslaughter would have been an equally appropriate label in each instance. On the face of it, that label seems more appropriate in the case of infanticide than child destruction, given the traditional view that neither murder

approach taken in 1957 to death caused as a result of a partly completed suicide pact.[68] In this instance, there was an equally understandable wish to avoid the murder label, even when the survivor or survivors of the pact had intentionally caused the death of another member of the pact.[69] The solution, however, was to treat such killings as manslaughter, consistent with the traditional approach also taken to provocation (and to diminished responsibility),[70] rather than to create a new offence of 'suicide-pact killing' or the like. The often arbitrary nature of the choice,[71] in effecting legal change during the twentieth century, between creating a new specific offence or applying manslaughter, underscores the sense in which it is increasingly no longer seen as morally and legally important to maintain manslaughter's hegemony beyond those homicides appropriately labelled as the greater offence of murder.

*(ii) Vulnerable victims: on the road and in the home*

In the second set of instances (causing death by dangerous driving; causing or allowing the death of a child or vulnerable adult) the practice of charging manslaughter was perceived to be part of the problem, rather than a potential solution.[72] Let me take first the case of causing death by dangerous driving.

It is commonly supposed that it was (at least historically) simple jury reluctance to convict of 'manslaughter' in such circumstances, because of a distaste for the label, that led to *ex hypothesi* unmerited acquittals.[73] However, if that is so, other solutions more supportive of the continued use of the common law offence of manslaughter could have been adopted to address this problem more directly. An example would have been to require (as is the case more generally with trial by jury in France) that the jury in 'motor manslaughter' cases contain a proportion of lawyers, who could be expected – or even required – to exercise influence on lay members in favour of the strict application of the law to the facts.[74]

---

nor manslaughter apply before a victim has been born alive; but there is clearly room for legitimate disagreement on this point.

68 Homicide Act 1957, s.4.

69 For further analysis of the operation of section 4, see Law Commission, above n.5, part 8.

70 Although the pleas of provocation and diminished responsibility are clearly somewhat different in nature to a plea of failed suicide pact, as the latter involves no overt 'subjective' condition in the form of emotional over-reaction or mental disorder: see Law Commission for England and Wales, above n.5, part 8.

71 I do not say that the choice has always been arbitrary. Assisting suicide, for example, seems perfectly appropriately dealt with as a discrete homicide offence.

72 In that, on the typical set facts at issue in such cases, it was thought to be too difficult to obtain convictions for manslaughter.

73 See Ormerod, D. (2005), *Smith and Hogan: Criminal Law*, 11th ed. (Oxford: Oxford University Press) p.1016.

74 I accept, of course, that a judgement whether negligence is 'gross' is a matter for each juror, and not something on which advice about the need to apply the law to the facts will necessarily assist; but the point is that once one has accepted that negligence as to causing

Furthermore, there is no conclusive evidence that tinkering of this general kind to make conviction easier actually leads to higher proportions of convictions in the relevant cases. A case in point, in this context, involves changes to fault requirements. For example, of those charged with causing death by reckless driving, 89 per cent of those prosecuted were convicted in spite of the need to show a high degree of moral fault on the part of the driver;[75] whereas, of those prosecuted for the offence that replaced it, causing death by dangerous driving (involving a wholly objective test), the conviction rate has been 79 per cent.[76] One might seek to argue that the high conviction rate for causing death by reckless driving must reflect the fact that only the worst cases were ever prosecuted; but in fact, prior to the Road Traffic Act 1991, prosecutions for that offence ran at no less than 86 per cent of offences reported, a fractionally higher proportion than has been maintained since 1991.[77]

That brings us directly to the perceived problem that the 'gross negligence' test for liability for manslaughter did not, in any event, cover sufficient ground in this context, because not all 'dangerous' conduct on the roads that may cause death will amount to gross negligence. As Lord Atkin remarked in *Andrews v DPP*:[78]

> [The Road Traffic Acts] … have no direct reference to causing death by negligence … s.11 imposes a penalty for driving recklessly or at a speed or in a manner which is dangerous to the public. There can be no doubt that this section covers driving with such a high degree of negligence as that if death were caused the offender would have committed manslaughter. But the converse is not true, and it is perfectly possible that a man may drive at a speed or in a manner dangerous to the public and cause death, and yet not be guilty of manslaughter.[79]

The existence of this 'justice gap' should be acknowledged. However, it is hard to see how the gap can be regarded as having been filled in a way that adequately respects the interests of drivers, when 'dangerous' – for the purposes of the offence of causing death by dangerous driving – includes not only danger of death, but danger of any injury or even of nothing more than serious property damage.[80] It is hardly a statement of any originality to point out that such an extensive definition of danger renders the link with causing death opaque, and hence makes questionable

---

death was indeed gross, then there should be no shirking the duty to bring in a verdict of manslaughter.

75 It would be pointless to enter here into the old debate whether so-called '*Caldwell*' recklessness (see *Caldwell* [1981] AC 341) really did involve an assessment of moral fault. In factual terms, if not in strict legal terms, it probably did involve such an assessment in most cases.

76 Pearce, L.M. *et al.* (2002), *Dangerous Driving and the Law* (Road Safety Research Report No. 26; Transport Research Laboratory), chapter 4.

77 *Ibid.*

78 [1937] AC 576.

79 *Ibid.*, at 583.

80 Road Traffic Act 1988 s.2A(3). It is, no doubt, the influence of element 3 (fault elements may be watered down) in the regulatory model that provides at least part of the explanation.

the moral basis for the offence as defined.[81] What would have been the difficulty about creating an offence of 'causing death, injury, or serious property damage by dangerous driving', where the meaning of 'dangerous' in relation to each harm means the danger of bringing about that very harm?[82]

So, how should the relationship between causing death by dangerous driving and gross negligence manslaughter have been addressed, given the gap that Lord Atkin rightly saw as existing between them? For what it is worth, the public interest in strong measures being taken against those whose driving poses a danger of death seems to me to justify in law *treating* a death so caused as gross negligence manslaughter.[83] That would be a way of marrying a wish to preserve a common law structure to homicide offences, with the desire – as part of a regulatory scheme – to do justice to the public interest in safety on the roads. Yet, successive governments have shown little interest in supporting the application of manslaughter to instances where death has been caused on the road. Classic recent examples are the creation of the specific offences of (a) causing death whilst driving both carelessly and under the influence of drink or drugs,[84] and (b) causing death whilst driving unlicensed, disqualified or uninsured.[85] In both of these instances, it seems highly likely that D could – and should – be found guilty of unlawful and dangerous act manslaughter.[86] Each involves the commission of an unlawful act – respectively, driving under the influence of drink or drugs, and unlicensed, disqualified or uninsured driving – that may pose a danger of causing some harm, but is not unlawful solely in virtue of involving negligent or careless conduct. As is well known, it is only the latter

81 See, more generally, Ashworth, A. 'Taking the Consequences', in Shute, Gardner and Horder (eds) (1993), *Action and Value in Criminal Law* (Oxford: Clarendon Press).

82 For the view that a correspondence between the nature or degree of fault required and the outcome produced, is defensible where *objective* fault elements are at issue, see Horder, J. (1995), 'A Critique of the Correspondence Principle in Criminal Law', *Crim LR* 759. I leave open the question whether 'dangerous' should be (perhaps in part) defined by reference to engagement in specific acts such as 'tailgating', racing another driver, and so on: see on this kind of suggestion, Spencer, J. (1988), 'Road Traffic Law: A Review of the North Report', *Crim LR* 707; Cunningham, above n.36, pp.307–310.

83 Perhaps subject to a provision that the defendant may raise evidence of an exceptional circumstance, and then show why that should block the inference from dangerousness to gross negligence.

84 Road Traffic Act 1988, s.3A.

85 Road Safety Act 2006, s.21, inserting s.3ZB into the Road Traffic Act 1988: see further Cunningham, above n.36, at p.288.

86 In a slightly different context, see the discussion of this species of manslaughter in Wells, C. (2001), *Corporations and Criminal Responsibility* (Oxford: Oxford University Press) pp.117–120. In the case of causing death by careless driving whilst under the influence of drink or drugs, what is the argument that a jury could not or would not find such a person – on a holistic view – to have driven 'dangerously', and hence to be guilty of causing death by dangerous driving in any event? See the scathing comments of the Royal Commission on Transport 1929 about the Ministry's proposal at that time to distinguish between dangerous and careless driving, cited by Pearce *et al.*, above n.76, chapter 5. 'Dangerous' driving includes driving that poses a risk of serious damage to property, in addition to driving posing a risk of injury: Road Traffic Act 1988 2A(3).

kinds of unlawful act that may not form the basis of an unlawful and dangerous act manslaughter charge.[87]

Turning to the offence of causing or allowing the death of a child or vulnerable adult, this is an offence of simple negligence, by way of contrast with 'gross' negligence manslaughter.[88] I shall focus on the version of the offence that involves 'allowing' a child or vulnerable adult to be killed by another's unlawful act. It is committed if D (a member of the same household as V and having frequent contact with V) ought to have been aware that there was a significant risk of serious harm being unlawfully caused to V, and V's death was so caused by another member of the household in frequent contact with V.[89] D commits the offence if, in such circumstances, D fails to take such steps as could reasonably have been expected to protect V from the risk, and the unlawful act killing V takes place in circumstances of the kind D ought to have foreseen. It is, to say the least, a complex offence. Further, it remains a controversial question whether it should ever be possible to find someone guilty of a homicide offence when they have been guilty of no more than simple negligence.[90] Was the new offence, one that imposes liability on the basis of simple negligence, really necessary?

The Law Commission argued that the offence of manslaughter was inappropriate in this context, because there was doubt whether it could be manslaughter when X – through his or her own carelessness – prevented Y from unlawfully killing V through some deliberate act.[91] It is, though, hard to see how there could be much doubt on that score where X and Y *jointly and severally* share responsibility for V's welfare, and it is not just a case of Y being V's parent but X only having a separate duty towards V in virtue of being, say, V's doctor.[92] Further, we are still left with the question of why the fault element should be simple negligence rather than the more restrictive gross negligence (in some form). To that question it is not easy to find a clear answer in either the Commission's Report or in the Consultative Report that preceded it.[93] Part of the problem may lie with the traditional unwillingness

---

87 See *Andrews v DPP* [1937] AC 576. Again, it has been, no doubt, a relative lack of concern under the regulatory model for evaluative labelling considerations (element 7) that has led to the failure to place prosecutorial emphasis on this route to conviction.

88 See Domestic Violence, Crime and Victims Act 2004, s.5.

89 *Ibid.*

90 This is perfectly possible in France, for example, but the introduction to England and Wales of an offence of causing death by careless driving has been heavily criticised: see Cunningham, above n.36.

91 Law Commission for England and Wales (2003), *Children: Their Non-accidental Death or Serious Injury (Criminal Trials) A Consultative Report* (Law Com. No. 279) paras 5.55–5.62.

92 The Australian courts have found a husband liable for manslaughter when he culpably failed to prevent his wife killing their children: *Russell* [1933] VLR 59. In its evidence to the Commission, the Crown Prosecution Service argued that the law could be adapted in a way that would enable proof of manslaughter in the difficult cases.

93 See Law Commission for England and Wales (2003), *Children: Their Non-accidental Death or Serious Injury (Criminal Trials)* (Law Com. No. 282) paras 6.20–6.27; Law Commission, above n.91, para. 7.18.

of criminal lawyers to recognise any legitimate kind of fault other than subjective fault.[94] Having, thus, no high-profile advocates, 'gross' negligence has received no scholarly – and little judicial – analysis and defence,[95] and has hence been treated by the Legislature and the Law Commission as involving no difference worth attending to from simple negligence.[96]

With these two instances, we see legal change favouring the creation of specific offences, ahead of the provision of support for the application of manslaughter to the supposedly problematic cases. That development has come about, even though there were either ways in which the application of manslaughter could have been better supported, or there is scant evidence that improvements in convictions rates would result from creating a new (lesser) specific offence to displace the application of the more serious offence. Once again, thus, we find evidence of a growing loss of faith in the importance of maintaining manslaughter's hegemony in cases of homicide unintentionally caused.

## VII Pressure Group Politics and Specialised Offences

To some extent, these and other related developments reflect two influences whose growth has been an important factor in twentieth century legal politics. These are the already mentioned increasing significance of the regulatory arm of the state,[97] but also the increasing prominence in legal politics of highly specialised expert or 'single issue' pressure groups.[98] We can detect their influence in more than one legislative change or law reform proposal of recent years that has or would have involved an erosion of the authority or scope of the common law homicide offences.[99]

94 For criticism, see for example, Wells, C. (1982), 'Swatting the Subjectivist Bug', *Crim LR* 209. For continued evidence that the judiciary is still suffering from the effects of being bitten by the bug, see for example, *B (A Minor) v DPP* (2000) 2 Cr App R 65 (HL).

95 See Horder, J. (1997), 'Gross Negligence and Criminal Culpability', *University of Toronto Law Journal* 47, 495.

96 An example from a different context involves sexual offences. Having consistently held out for subjective tests of fault, and been unwilling to defend 'gross' negligence tests in relation to the consent or the age of the victim, 'subjectivist' judges and scholars now find the reformed law of the Sexual Offences Act 2003 centred on tests of simple negligence: Smith and Hogan, above n.73, pp.618–619 and 631.

97 See Lacey, Wells and Quick, above n.29, 6–8; Farmer, L. (1996), 'The Obsession with Definition', *Social and Legal Studies* 64–66.

98 See, for example, observations of the Charity Commissioners for England and Wales in 1969, to the effect that, 'Many organisations now feel that it is not sufficient simply to alleviate distress arising from particular social conditions ... They feel compelled also to draw attention as forcibly as possible to the needs which they think are not being met ... and to press for effective official provision to be made to meet those needs As a result, "pressure groups", "action groups" or "lobbies" come into being', cited in Sheridan, L.A. (1973), 'Charity versus Politics', *Anglo-American Law Review* 47.

99 An important example, not discussed in further detail here, is the influence of the Centre for Corporate Accountability (www.corporateaccountability.org) in getting the offence of corporate manslaughter on to the statute book.

For example, in proposing the creation of an offence of causing or allowing the non-accidental death of a child, effectively displacing manslaughter in the relevant circumstances, the Law Commission said in its 2003 Report:

> Our inspiration for undertaking this project was the work of the National Society for the Protection of Children ('NSPCC') 'Which of You Did It?' Working Group ... We have benefited greatly from their efforts and the generosity with which they have shared their time and their thoughts.[100]

The central concern of the NSPCC was not in fact the question whether any new offence should be created, as opposed to legal support being given to the application of manslaughter to new circumstances. Their concern was the ineffectiveness of the law in attributing responsibility when the death of a child must have been at the hands of one or other of its parents, but there was no or insufficient proof that it was either parent in particular or both acting in concert. Nonetheless, the specialised focus provided by 'single issue' politics in the field of homicide has a tendency to produce proposals eroding the authority of the more generally applicable common law offences.[101]

An example, where an expert perspective has exerted such influence, can be found in the draft Bill that was to legalise assisted dying for the terminally ill.[102] In supporting the Bill at the second reading stage, Lord Joffe (the sponsor of the Bill) said, even before he gave the statistics relating to public opinion:

> Let us *start* with the experts. There is a strong division of opinion among them. For example, the Royal College of Physicians was in favour of neutrality when it gave evidence to the Committee but later, after a consultation process, decided to oppose the Bill. The British Medical Association was against the Bill when it gave evidence, but subsequently changed to a position of neutrality. The Royal College of Nurses was against the Bill, but a survey in the Nursing Times found 60 per cent of nurses in favour of the law being changed.[103]

The balance of expert opinion was clearly regarded by Lord Joffe as a key element in the justification for the proposals: hence his attempts to present the balance as at least neutral, or as marginally favouring the proposals. The importance of this, in

---

100 Law Commission, above n.93, para. 1.8.

101 An example is a recent attempt to introduce an offence creating liability for causing another's suicide. On 18 October 2006, Iain Duncan Smith MP introduced into Parliament a Bill to create a specific offence of causing another to commit suicide, based on a recommendation by Refuge (also supported by Southall Black Sisters). *Hansard*, HC deb 18 October 2006, 877–879. Laura McGowan and I have argued that a context-specific offence of this kind is unnecessary because the conduct in question is adequately covered by gross negligence manslaughter: Horder, J. and McGowan, L. (2006), 'Manslaughter by Causing Another's Suicide', *Crim LR* 1035.

102 Assisted Dying for the Terminally Ill Bill: <www.publications.parliament.uk/pa/ld200304/ldbills/017/04017.1-4.html>.

103 <www.publications.parliament.uk/pa/ld199697/ldhansard/pdvn/ lds06/text/60512-01.htm#60512–01_head2> 12 May 2006, col 1185 (my emphasis).

the present context, is the way that this focus on an experts' perspective is linked to a narrow or specialised approach to the offences that are to hem in or restrict acting on a permission to provide assistance to die to terminally ill people. Under Clause 4 of the Bill, such a permission would not be valid without a declaration given in advance that the patient wished to be assisted to die. Accordingly, clause 11 of the Bill included the following proposed offence:

> (1) A person commits an offence if he wilfully falsifies or forges a declaration made under section 4 with the intent or effect of causing the patient's death. A person guilty of an offence under this subsection shall be liable, on conviction on indictment, to imprisonment for life or for any shorter term.

But, if someone 'wilfully' falsifies or forges a section 4 declaration, 'with the … effect of causing the patient's death', then, under the existing law that must surely be at least manslaughter, and might well be murder. For, such falsification will almost necessarily be done with the awareness that V may, or with the knowledge that V will, be killed in consequence. What compelling purpose, then, is served by the creation of this offence?[104] If a declaration was forged in order to conceal the nature of what was intended to be, and was, an unlawful killing, then there seems to be scant justification for permitting the killer to escape the mandatory life penalty for murder.

There seems little doubt that the adoption of a context-bound approach to criminalisation of homicide, undermining the authority of murder and manslaughter, is more likely to be taken when pride of place in the reform process is afforded to interest or expert groups. This is not, of course, to question the value or importance of such groups. It is simply to observe that such groups now frequently seek not only in practice to enhance the welfare and status of those they represent, but also to secure a discrete legal basis for such enhancement. As the Charity Commissioners long ago observed, speaking of groups representing disadvantaged people:

> Many organisations now feel that it is not sufficient simply to alleviate distress arising from particular social conditions … They feel compelled also to draw attention as forcibly as possible to the needs which they think are not being met … *and to press for effective official provision to be made to meet those needs*.[105]

Activists must all be (would-be) law reformers it seems, in that an attempt to increase the perceived importance in society at large of particular interests would nowadays scarcely be complete without a distinctively *legal* as well as political programme of reform. How should criminal lawyers respond to such developments?

---

104 In a case where D falsifies or forges the section 4 declaration 'with the intent' of causing the patient's death, this would presumably be preparatory conduct falling short of an attempt to kill, and so there is logical space for this part of the section 11 offence.

105 See above n.98 (my emphasis).

## VIII Homicide: Reconciling Common Law and Regulatory Values

Appearances notwithstanding, my argument for homicide reform is not meant to be 'anti regulation' and 'pro common law'. The conclusion I seek to draw from the foregoing analysis and critique is a slightly different one. It is that a wholesale shift from a common law to a regulatory approach in the law of homicide may have few clearly proven advantages, and many real disadvantages, most especially in relation to fault or to punishment, and hence in relation to legitimacy. As we have seen, in these respects a regulatory approach may sometimes be too harsh on accused persons (causing death on the roads; causing the death of a child or vulnerable person), but sometimes also too generous to them (Assisted Dying for the Terminally Ill Bill). The direction of my argument is towards a system of criminal law in which common law and regulatory approaches are regarded as mutually reinforcing, rather than as rival claimants to exclusive occupancy of the relevant legal space.[106] How can such a system be developed?

The offence of corporate manslaughter provides one model, through its use of a '*Gemeinschaft*' concept – manslaughter – to give effect to a regulatory objective: ensuring that a company can in appropriate circumstances be found liable for homicide brought about at least in part by glaring deficiencies in the senior managers' management or organisation of the company's activities.[107] The common law and regulatory approaches are mutually reinforcing in this sense. The powers available to the court upon conviction are classically regulatory in form. The punishment can only be a fine, a punishment well suited, of course, to the special kinds of defendants at which the offence is aimed (profit-making organisations, and public bodies with necessarily deep pockets).[108] Further, the courts are entitled to order specified steps to be taken by a convicted defendant to remedy a breach, a clearly regulatory provision beyond the scope of 'remedy' through punishment at common law.

Most importantly, however, these regulation-orientated powers available upon conviction – probably far less punitive than many groups advocating corporate liability would have liked – are themselves in part reinforced and supported by the way in which the offence takes a common law approach to labelling and fault. Liability is for 'manslaughter', and the fault element – 'a gross breach of a relevant duty of care'[109] – mirrors the common law requirement in manslaughter by gross negligence. In taking this approach, the new offence recognises that the labelling element of conviction for the common law homicide offences (murder; manslaughter) can *itself* be regarded as a part of the punishment, as long as its currency has not been debased by substantial diminution of fault requirements. The contrast, then, is with some of the offences concerned with causing death on the road, and with offences that borrow elements of common law terminology (such as the offence of 'third

---

106 For a broader perspective on the relationship between common law and regulatory approaches, see Brudner, A. (1993), 'Agency and Welfare in the Penal Law', in Shute, Gardner and Horder (eds) (1993), *Action and Value in Criminal Law* (Oxford: Clarendon Press).

107 Corporate Manslaughter and Corporate Homicide Act 2007, s.1.

108 See elements 1 and 6 of the regulatory model of law, in the text following n.43 above.

109 Corporate Manslaughter and Corporate Homicide Act 2007, s.1.

degree' murder[110]) whilst replacing the common law content with elements less sensitive to the common law's concern with fault, responsibility and causation.[111] Here, regulatory law has replaced rather than supported common law offences, with the result that ever-increasing levels of punishment have had to compensate for the absence of a truly condemnatory label for offences (with a fault corresponding to that label) to do some of the punitive work.

An alternative model may be more appropriate where the proposal is otherwise to create specific homicide offences applicable to 'specialists' who kill (typically, through negligence) in the course of their duties when these duties by their nature create risk. Two classic examples of such specialists would be armed police officers, and doctors, who kill through negligence (respectively) in shooting at those considered to be dangerous suspects and in attempting to treat patients. Given that these professionals' execution of their duties necessarily involves subjecting the suspects (and bystanders) or patients respectively to a risk of being killed, the thought may arise that to deal with them through the law of manslaughter is inappropriate for one of two reasons. First (the 'pro specialist' view), some may consider that the risk of conviction for manslaughter when a bad mistake has been made is inappropriate, given that the chance of such a mistake is a professional – and perhaps daily – hazard even for generally competent professionals. Secondly (the 'anti specialist' view), the difficulty of securing a manslaughter conviction – given the stigma attached to conviction – may mean that too many badly incompetent or even uncaring officers or doctors who kill might escape criminal prosecution for homicide altogether. These views may coalesce in a proposal to create an offence of, say, 'unlawful killing in the execution of duty', or the like, that will play something like the same regulatory role as is played by the offence of causing death by dangerous driving in relation to death on the roads.

There is little doubt that the regulatory context in which such killings take place (the conduct of armed police officers and surgeons is certainly regulated by professional codes of conduct) makes specialised and separate treatment by the law of homicide – following the regulatory model – a legitimate possibility.[112] However, the specialists in question may themselves understandably prefer to be judged by the same broad standards – and to stand to be convicted of the same offences – as ordinary people.[113] Further, there is a not inconsequential risk that the way in which they conduct their duties may change, to the detriment of the public, if they are not so judged. Most importantly, though, in this context it is possible to keep faith with the application of common law offences to the lethal conduct of such specialists, *and*

110 See text at n.52 above.

111 See the discussion in section 6 above.

112 See Horder, above n.22.

113 For example, in a discussion of the law relating to self-defence, the Firearms Unit of the Metropolitan Police has indicated to the Law Commission that it would prefer its officers to be judged in accordance with the same basic criteria (such as requirements of reasonableness in all the circumstances) used to judge ordinary citizens, and would not welcome the intrusion of special regulatory offences covering the same ground but applicable only to its officers.

account for the regulatory context, other than through the creation of new homicide offences.

There is more than one way to seek to do this. It would be possible, for example, to ensure that in appropriate cases the jury is given pre-prepared evidence drawn up by the relevant professional bodies (and approved by the relevant Government department) on the frequency with which their members must pose risks of a similar kind, and the conditions of work under which they are expected to do so.[114] More substantially, it is perhaps not impossible to imagine prosecutions in such cases having to be approved in advance – in something like the style of the old grand jury – by a specialised body including (perhaps) members of the relevant professions and their regulators, members of complaints authorities, victims' family groups, and so forth.[115] Whether the current system for prosecuting doctors or armed officers is so defective that a radical scheme of this kind (and *a fortiori* the creation of new offences) is really necessary may be open to doubt, although it is perhaps worth further consideration.

The significant point, in the present context, is that the mere identification of a 'killing field' with a regulatory backdrop to it need by no means lead straight to the adoption of an approach to the application of homicide offences shaped by the regulatory model. As the development of the corporate manslaughter offence illustrates, there is plenty of scope for imaginative solutions that seek to support rather than erode the continued use of the common law model.

114 Naturally, it would have to be possible for the prosecution to seek to show how that evidence has no weight or bearing when considering D's conduct in the individual case in question.

115 Obviously, I cannot here go into how exactly such a body should be constituted, or how it should go about its work.

## Chapter 3

# The Limits of Manslaughter

Victor Tadros[1]

Reform of homicide is best undertaken in a comprehensive way. Different defensible schemes may be adopted, and the justification of any particular scheme will depend not only on arguments with respect to each particular element of the scheme, but on arguments about the coherence and justification of the scheme as a whole. Furthermore, coherence and justification, here, should be understood in their particular institutional and social context. A scheme of homicide offences should provide an appropriate division of labour in determining questions of responsibility and punishment between the legislature and the courts, and it should also provide an appropriate division of labour between different elements of the criminal justice system, crucially the division between questions to be determined at trial and questions suitable for the sentencing stage.[2]

To see this, consider a feature of some killings (*f*) that is under consideration for its moral significance in determining the gravity of those killings. First, there is the question of what the moral significance of *f* is, considered pre-institutionally. That may depend on some things that are universal (directly intentional killing, for example, might be argued to be universally worse than obliquely intentional killing). But there may be other things that are socially dependent (racially motivated killing might be argued to be worse than non-racially motivated killing only in the context of societies with more general problems, current or historic, with racism).

If it is true, on the best moral theory, that *f* is morally significant can that fact properly be recognised institutionally? Perhaps there are some things that may be morally significant on the best account of our moral reasoning but which can't motivate public institutions. To justify our criminal laws, it might be argued, we must seek reasons that are public; that is, reasons that are capable of being endorsed by reasonable citizens in a pluralistic society such as ours.[3] Given that criminal

1 Thanks to the participants at the workshop held in Leicester for a helpful discussion. Thanks also to Jackie Hodgson for her input on an earlier draft of this chapter.

2 See also Wasik, M. (2000), 'Sentencing in Homicide' in Ashworth and Mitchell (eds), *Rethinking English Homicide Law* (Oxford: Oxford University Press). Of course, there is a question of how much can be achieved in the immediate future to achieve coherence and justification. See Lacey, N. (2000), 'Partial Defences to Homicide: Questions of Power and Principle in Imperfect and Less Imperfect Worlds' also in Ashworth and Mitchell.

3 For an influential discussion of this idea, see Rawls, J. (1993), *Political Liberalism* (New York: Columbia University Press), and (1999), 'The Idea of Public Reason' in *The Law of Peoples* (Cambridge: Mass.: Harvard University Press). The extent to, and ways in, which there is a distinctive public morality is undoubtedly controversial, both in criminal law and

offences are best seen as public wrongs, wrongs that can be the proper subject of public condemnation,[4] if there are distinctive restraints on what can count as a public reason, this will be particularly important for the criminal law. Criminal convictions speak in the name of the public, and in that case they must be for offences which the public can endorse as warrants for condemnation. This idea of public reason may also place some restraint on the way in which decisions about the scope and content of the criminal law are taken. Whilst it is important that defendants have a proper opportunity to make claims about their responsibility that are morally significant at trial,[5] the demands of public reason will not be satisfied if the role of the trial, in determining the scope of the criminal law, is too broad. And that requires not only that standards are sufficiently precise, but also that the kind of reasoning to be done by decision makers in the light of those standards is appropriate given their institutional role.

Even if the moral significance of *f* can be recognised in public reason, there is a question about the institutional context in which the moral significance of *f* should be recognised. This is a question of the institutional design of the criminal justice system. Suppose that it is justified to convict the defendant of a criminal offence. There are three kinds of legal method that might be used to provide recognition of the moral significance of *f*. First, and most importantly, there are offence definitions. We might have one homicide offence, or we may have many, and those offences might be distinguished in a number of ways. Currently, traditional *mens rea* terms are used to categorise homicide offences into two main offences: murder and manslaughter. There are also other homicide offences available, which I will mention below, that are distinguished from the main homicide offences by kind. We might consider distinguishing offences according to the method through which the victim is killed, or according to the status or identity of the defendant, the circumstances or identity of the victim, or according to the defendant's motive.

Secondly, there are partial defences. Partial defences are defences that can move defendants who fulfil the *mens rea* of a more serious offence category into a less serious offence category. Most commentators accept that there might be partial excuses, although the law restricts their use to the context of homicide.[6] More contentious is the question of whether there are also partial justifications.[7] For example, consider excessive use of force in self defence. The defendant is attacked,

---

outside, and I don't intend here to take a stance one way or the other. See Ripstein, A. (1998), *Equality, Responsibility and the Law* (Cambridge: Cambridge University Press) for a defence of the importance of public reason, and Gardner, J. (2001), 'The Mysterious Case of the Reasonable Person' *University of Toronto Law Journal* 51, 273 for doubts.

4 See Duff, R.A. (2001), *Punishment, Communication and Community* (Oxford: Oxford University Press) pp.60–64.

5 See Duff, R.A., Farmer, L., Marshall, S. and Tadros, V. (2007), *The Trial on Trial 3: Toward a Normative Theory of the Criminal Trial* (Oxford: Hart).

6 For an argument that partial defences should be available with respect to all serious offences, reducing the offence from the first to the second degree, see Horder, J. (2004), *Excusing Crime* (Oxford: Oxford University Press) pp.143–146.

7 Husak, D. (1998), 'Partial Defences' *Canadian Journal of Law and Jurisprudence* 11, 167.

but uses more violence than is necessary in rebutting the attack and kills the victim. Many commentators would agree that the defendant should have a partial defence, and hence not be convicted of the offence for which he fulfils the *mens rea*, but they may disagree about whether to categorise all or some cases of this kind as partially excused or partially justified.

Thirdly, the law may create aggravations and mitigations.[8] These could be created either to operate at trial (which is uncommon in the law of England and Wales) or with respect to sentencing, and if they operate at the latter stage, they could be more or less formally recognised. Whether the defendant is convicted of the aggravated or mitigated offence or of the offence *simpliciter* might be made a question of proof at trial and determination by decision makers, or the aggravation or mitigation might be determined only for the purposes of sentencing. The law is, in some ways, incoherent about this. For example, there are some offences, such as wounding, assault and criminal damage, which are available in a racially aggravated form, where the racial aggravation must be proved at trial.[9] But in other offence contexts racial motivation is available as a general aggravation to be taken into account at the sentencing stage. If it is so taken into account, the fact that the offence was racially aggravated must be stated by the judge in open court.[10] It isn't clear why racial aggravation is something that must be proved at trial in some offence contexts but not in others.

A range of factors are available to guide judges in determining the sentence that the defendant will receive, and these apply to manslaughter cases. Factors which must be taken into consideration are listed in Part 12 of the Criminal Justice Act (CJA) 2003. There are aggravations for race, religion, sexual orientation and disability. There is an indication that the defendant's culpability in committing the offence is relevant, as well as the harm that he has caused. Beyond that there are facts which are not so much about the act as about the defendant's circumstances (for example, the fact that he was on bail or had previous convictions).

Specific aggravations also apply to the tariff given to those who receive a mandatory life sentence for murder, which are included in the CJA 2003.[11] Some pertain to motives, methods and circumstances of the act (for example, that it was premeditated, that it was racially motivated, or that it involved abduction), some to the status, circumstances and identity of the victim (for example, that the victim was a child or a police officer[12]) and some to the features of the defendant that are unconnected from the particular act in question (for example, that she had a previous conviction for murder).

With respect to all three methods, considerations of equality will be important in determining whether the scheme of homicide offences is coherent. Coherence demands that the scheme of homicide law is justified when cases are treated

8 For a good discussion, see Ashworth, A. (2005), *Sentencing and Criminal Justice*, 4th ed. (Cambridge: Cambridge University Press).

9 Crime and Disorder Act 1988, ss.29 and 30.

10 Criminal Justice Act 2003, s.145(2).

11 See Schedule 21.

12 See further below.

comparatively.[13] If a particular feature or circumstance of a killing is picked out with regard to offence categorisation, partial defence, aggravation or mitigation, other features and circumstances which are similar in salient respects ought to be picked out also. So, for example, if there is a special offence pertaining to a particular kind of victim (say children), and the justifications for picking out victims of that kind apply to another category of victims (say the elderly), that other category of victims ought to be picked out as well. If racially aggravated killings are picked out and the justifications for doing so apply also to killings motivated by sexual orientation, killing motivated by sexual orientation should also be included within the scheme of aggravations.

If recognition is given to one particular feature as an aggravation, it must be possible to say to families of victims where the homicide is not treated as aggravated that there was an important moral difference between the aggravated case and their cases. Coherence may be satisfied if similar cases are treated in a similar way even if justice is not ideally achieved in either case. It may be that a system which created special offences with regard to both child victims and elderly victims would be ideal. It may be that failure to recognise what is distinct about these cases provides strong reasons to distinguish. However, a system which distinguishes homicides of children but not homicides of the elderly may be worse, all things considered, than a system that fails to recognise the special significance of both. Hence, even if we remain uncertain about whether particular features of homicides are morally significant, or whether they are sufficiently significant to warrant recognition in the legal system in some way or other, at least we can perform the more modest (but still ambitious) task of achieving coherence in the law of homicide. Coherence, as noted above, often leaves our options open. In law, we can recognise two features equally, or not recognise either, even if we cannot, for reasons of coherence, recognise one but not the other. There will be other reasons of institutional design that should guide the choice between solutions, each of which is coherent.

Suppose that there are two features of a homicide, *f1* and *f2,* which are similar in terms of their moral significance, and hence require equal treatment for reasons of coherence. *F1* is currently treated as an aggravation at the sentencing stage, for example, and *f2* is not. One solution is to abandon recognition of *f1* as aggravating. This may be the best option where a failure to provide a moral difference between one feature and a host of other features calls into question whether that feature is aggravating at all. So, for example, suppose that killing motivated by religious hatred is morally significant in the same way as killing for any other political or ideological motive. In that case, it may be better to abandon treating religious hatred as an aggravation rather than attempting to recognise the moral significance of the much broader group by creating new aggravations. Another solution is to extend the scope of the aggravation currently provided for *f1*. So, for example, if children and the elderly are picked out because they are both especially vulnerable (I doubt whether this is an appropriate rationale, by the way) there might be an aggravation of killing a vulnerable person, including both children and the elderly. Still another is to

13 For further analysis of coherence and integrity, see Dworkin, R. (1986), *Law's Empire* (London: Fontana) ch.6.

create a new aggravation with respect to *f2*. So there might be different aggravations applying to the children and to the elderly respectively.

There are both principled and pragmatic considerations that will help us to determine which approach should be taken to these questions. Pragmatic concerns include, for example, the simplicity of the law at the point of application in the decision-making process and the complexity and length of provisions, the length and cost of trials, the likelihood of decision makers at both the trial and sentencing stage of applying the rules in a consistent and principled manner and the acceptability of the law to the public. Here, insofar as they can be separated from each other, I am more concerned with outlining the principles of homicide reform rather than its pragmatics. For it is only once we have a grasp of these principles and what they require that we can evaluate the extent to which principled reform should be curtailed, distorted or abandoned for reasons of pragmatism.

In this chapter my main focus will be the proper scope of homicide, and consequently on the scope of the offence of manslaughter. This is a necessary prelude to thinking about how many homicide offences we should have. For if we are to distinguish between homicides in kind, such distinctions should be within the proper scope of homicide as a whole, appropriately differentiated in terms of degree. I will consider the current scope of the offence in England and Wales, and the scope that there would be of the offence if the Law Commission's recent proposals on restructuring homicide were adopted. I will argue that the scope of the offence is currently too large, including those who are trivially at fault as well as those who are seriously at fault for causing a death, as was suggested by the Law Commission's 1996 reform proposals. The Law Commission's most recent proposals for restructuring homicide will ameliorate this problem to some degree, I argue, but not to a sufficient degree.

I will then consider whether we should distinguish offences by kind below the level of murder. I will indicate different features of homicides that might be picked out for this purpose, and suggest that the strongest claims for differentiation concern the identity of the perpetrator (notably if the perpetrator is a corporation) and the value of life of the victim in cases of mercy killing and assisted suicide. Other features of homicide, I argue, might be recognised through independent rules of liability within a single offence of manslaughter rather than through the separation of offences. Beyond that, I doubt that formal rules should be created with respect to morally significant features of killing to operate at trial. The demands of coherence that I outlined above will be unlikely to be satisfied other than through the creation of a very complex set of rules.

## I The Limits in Law

There are a number of homicide offences below the offence of murder, including infanticide,[14] causing death by dangerous driving,[15] corporate manslaughter[16] and

14 Infanticide Act 1938, s.1.

15 Road Traffic Act 1988, s.1.

16 Corporate Manslaughter and Corporate Homicide Act 2007, s.1.

killing of a vulnerable person in one's household.[17] The most general, however, is manslaughter. When investigating reform of manslaughter, one crucial question is what the limits of the offence should be. Manslaughter is what I call a differentiated offence: there are distinct rules of liability, and hence alternative ways of committing the offence. No single test can capture those alternatives.[18] A consequence of this is that there are different limits both at the top and at the bottom of the offence. There is nothing wrong in principle with differentiated offences, although it remains to be seen whether such a broad and variegated offence of manslaughter can be justified.

The top limit of the offence, of course, should not *really* be seen as a limit, in that a conviction of manslaughter is competent for all cases that fall within murder. So the top limit of manslaughter is, in principle, the same as the top limit of murder. However, in cases where a conviction of murder would be warranted, a manslaughter conviction is at least regrettable. Hence, the distinction between murder and manslaughter marks a significant limit of the offence of manslaughter: it determines which cases are *only* manslaughters and *not* murders.

Let us begin by outlining the different limits at the top and at the bottom of the offence. There are six ways of committing manslaughter: three of voluntary manslaughter and three of involuntary manslaughter. Voluntary manslaughter is committed when the defendant has the *mens rea* of murder but has a partial defence of either diminished responsibility or provocation, or kills in pursuance of a suicide pact.[19] Involuntary manslaughter is committed if the defendant kills recklessly, or kills through gross negligence, or as a consequence of an unlawful and dangerous act. Whilst reckless manslaughter is not very important at the bottom end of the offence, as it will probably always be easier to prove gross negligence manslaughter, it is important to retain a focus on reckless manslaughter when considering the top end of the offence.

At the top end of manslaughter are cases where the defendant does not satisfy the *mens rea* of murder because he lacks the relevant intention. As will be familiar, in *Nedrick*[20] and *Woollin*[21] it was decided that the defendant could not be convicted of murder if he recognised that death or serious injury was a highly probable consequence of his actions but not that it was virtually certain. Some of the most serious cases of manslaughter, then, are cases where the defendant was aware that death was a highly probable consequence of his actions, but he did not intend to cause death. Consider a defendant who is escaping from the scene of a crime in a car and being chased by the police. He mounts the pavement on a busy high street at high speed. It is very probable that he will hit a pedestrian with his car and, if he

17 Domestic Violence, Crime and Victims Act 2004, s.5.

18 For more on differentiated offences, see Tadros, V. (2006), 'Rape Without Consent' *Oxford Journal of Legal Studies* 26, 515.

19 I will say almost nothing about this last category.

20 [1986] 1 WLR 1025.

21 [1999] 1 AC 82.

does, very probable that he will kill them. Such a defendant can only be convicted of manslaughter in England and Wales.[22]

The law of voluntary manslaughter provides three further top limits to the offence which I will not have space to spell out in detail. These concern cases where the defendant is at the outer limits of a partial defence to murder. The defence of provocation is very flexible, and if there is sufficient basis to indicate that the defendant lost his self-control, the defence must be left to the jury. This has resulted in the defence being made available in some cases where the provocation was quite trivial.[23] The provocation defence has been regarded by some as inevitably subject to sexist, racist and homophobic interpretation, leading to calls for its abolition.[24] The defence of diminished responsibility includes those suffering from recognised disorders that are of contested legitimacy, and which are regarded by some as examples of badness rather than madness.[25]

Much of the focus at the bottom end of manslaughter in the academic literature concerns involuntary manslaughter. However, the law of voluntary manslaughter sets a distinct bottom limit to the offence. The defendant may suffer from a severe mental disorder that is just insufficient to provide him with the full insanity defence. Given that the insanity defence, in England and Wales, is problematically restricted in scope,[26] we should expect that in some cases of manslaughter by reason of diminished responsibility the defendant will suffer from a serious mental disorder that fundamentally undermines his responsibility, and hence the basis for morally condemning his conduct. Or the defendant may have been provoked by violence that is just insufficient for her to be entitled to self-defence. As will be familiar from the law of provocation, we might find cases where the defendant is provoked by violence and suffers from a very serious mental disorder. The combination of partial excuses cannot combine to provide a full defence to murder.

---

22 Compare Scotland, where such a defendant would fulfil the *mens rea* of murder, which includes defendants who are 'wickedly reckless' as to death. For discussion, see Tadros, V. (2007), 'The Scots Law of Murder' in Horder (ed.), *Homicide Law in Comparative Perspective* (Oxford: Hart).

23 For proposals for reform, see Law Commission for England and Wales (2006), *Murder, Manslaughter and Infanticide* (Law Com. No. 304) para. 5.15. It should be noted that there must be a reasonable rather than a purely speculative basis of the provocative word or act having occurred and the defendant having lost his self control. See *Miao* [2003] EWCA Crim 3486 and *Serrano* [2006] EWCA Crim 3182.

24 See Wells, C. (2000), 'Provocation: the Case for Abolition' in Ashworth and Mitchell, above n.2.

25 The most obvious being the inclusion of sexual psychopathy as a potential basis for the defence in *Byrne* [1960] 2 QB 396. Contrast the position in Scots law where, despite expansion of the disorders that might give rise to the defence, psychopathy continues to be excluded as a basis for a plea of diminished responsibility. See *HMA v Galbraith* 2001 SCCR 551. *Byrne* indicated that irresistible impulse might provide a basis for the defence, something that I think agreeable in principle. See Tadros, V. (2005), *Criminal Responsibility* (Oxford: Oxford University Press) ch.12 for the arguments. There is a question, however, about whether that was appropriate on the facts of *Byrne* itself.

26 I argue elsewhere that it is both too broad and too narrow. See Tadros, above n.25, chs 5 and 12.

Also at the bottom limit of the offence are cases of unlawful act manslaughter and gross negligence manslaughter. The former variety of manslaughter can be committed only if the defendant's act was both unlawful and dangerous. But dangerousness has been interpreted very broadly as an act which a reasonable person would recognise as carrying with it the risk of some (not necessarily serious) harm.[27] The defendant need not have foreseen the risk of any harm, let alone any risk of death. The classic cases of unlawful act manslaughter involve defendants who commit a minor assault on the victim, whose death is then caused by the minor assault, but burglary may become dangerous, for example, if the victim was elderly and frail.[28] The leading case on gross negligence manslaughter is *Adomako*,[29] in which it was held that, where the defendant breached the relevant duty of care owed to the victim,[30] he will be grossly negligent if, in breaching that duty, his conduct fell so far below that to be expected that it should be regarded as criminal.

We can see from this brief outline that the offence of manslaughter is very broad indeed. It includes defendants who are very seriously culpable, but also defendants who, in one way or another, lack a high degree of blameworthiness for killing. The first thing to do is to investigate whether there are cases towards the bottom limit of manslaughter that ought not to fall within the law of homicide at all. We should then investigate how properly to divide up the law of homicide. If the offence of manslaughter is too broad in terms of the degree of fault, we might reform it by bringing down the top level through expansion of the law of murder, or we could divide the offence into a more and a less serious offence, or both.

## II Reform from the Bottom

The bottom level of homicide might be raised by reforming the defences of self-defence, duress, necessity, automatism and insanity, providing some defendants who currently have a partial defence or no defence with a full defence.[31] Other defences might also be made available to restrict the scope of the offence. I do not have space for a proper investigation of those issues here. My main focus will be on reform of the two varieties of involuntary manslaughter.

---

27 *Church* [1966] 1 QB 59.

28 *Watson* [1989] 2 All ER 865.

29 [1994] 3 All ER 79.

30 It appears that the law is in a confused state about this element of the offence. See Law Commission for England and Wales (1996), *Legislating the Criminal Code: Involuntary Manslaughter* (Law Com. No. 237) Part III and Herring, J. and Palser, E. (2007), 'The Duty of Care in Gross Negligence Manslaughter' *Crim LR* 24.

31 It should be noted here, as well, that the range of partial defences is very narrow. That means that with respect to defendants who satisfy the *mens rea* of murder, they are often provided with a full defence or are convicted of murder. That is often unsatisfactory. See further Lacey, above n.2.

*(i) What is the proper lower limit of unlawful act manslaughter?*

Unlawful act manslaughter has come in for a great deal of criticism. It is conventionally treated as an indication of a constructive approach to homicide: the homicide is constructed from full criminal responsibility for a prior criminal act and the fact that the defendant caused death. And that is sometimes seen as an indication of extreme objectivism: that recognition of the risk of death is not required for a homicide conviction.[32] The concern, from this perspective, is that defendants are held responsible for things that were outside their contemplation, and perhaps even outside anything that they *ought* to have contemplated. The defendant, we might think, didn't realise that there was a chance that they would cause death through their conduct, and furthermore we might think that we can't even say that they *ought to have* realised that there was a chance that they would cause death through their conduct. If that is the case, the argument continues, we cannot hold them responsible for causing the death. Is this conventional way of seeing the issue the best way to see it?

One thing to say at the outset is that we should separate out the question of whether a particular defendant should be found guilty of a homicide offence of some kind and whether he should be found guilty of *manslaughter*. In this section I will argue that unlawful act *homicide*, if it was suitably reformed, would appropriately attribute criminal responsibility on defendants for death. The fundamental error of the law is to categorise these cases as manslaughters.

Let us begin by noting that there is at least a sense in holding individuals responsible for death in some social contexts where death is caused through an unlawful act. Leaving aside the criminal law for the moment, there is surely at least some grounds for the family of the victim in such cases to engage D in practices of responsibility and perhaps even to punish him, and not merely for the unlawful act but for the death.

Consider David, who burgles Vernon's house. He is discovered by Vernon who (unbeknownst to David) has a serious heart condition. Vernon has a heart attack and dies. Surely David should at least *hold himself responsible* for causing the death. Furthermore, surely members of V's family can appropriately hold David responsible for the death in this case. They can appropriately call him to answer for the death. And surely he should apologise to the family, and perhaps do more. Finally, they might find ways to punish him for causing the death of the family member. They might shun him, for example. And when asked why they are doing that, it is appropriate for them to say that they are doing so because he killed V.

Now, there are admittedly some practices of responsibility that are appropriate even for pure accidents, where an agent isn't at fault at all. Take John Martin Fischer and Mark Ravizza's example. A person backs his car out of his garage unaware that a tiny kitten is snoozing beneath the tyre. The kitten is squashed. The authors claim that 'it would be odd to judge that the driver is morally responsible for the kitten's

32 See Law Com. (1996), above n.30, part IV.

untimely death, or to insist that he be blamed for the mishap'.[33] But there is surely some practice of responsibility that is appropriate here. The kitten owner says 'you killed my cat!' The car driver responds: 'I'm terribly sorry about that, but it was a pure accident'. Now imagine the alternative response denying responsibility entirely for the kitten's death. That isn't appropriate even though it was a pure accident. Responsibility, then, is at least sometimes strict in ordinary social contexts.[34]

But normally, and at least for serious criminal offences including homicide offences, responsibility ought not to be strict. For the criminal law does more than hold a person responsible for their conduct: it condemns them, and it warrants punishment. So consequently standards of culpability are required in criminal law where they are not required in ordinary social contexts (at least for the purposes of securing apologies). It is difficult to imagine that holding a person responsible for a homicide offence could be justified in circumstances where the person wasn't at fault for the death. In convicting the defendant of any homicide offence, the state implies fault for the death rather than mere strict responsibility. Homicide offences cannot plausibly be seen as regulatory.

So is this the appropriate way to see David's case? David is responsible for Vernon's death. But is this the case of an accidental death, where he is responsible but not blameworthy, and hence he lacks the fault required to hold him *criminally* responsible for it? Or is he criminally responsible for the death?

I'm not sure. But what I am confident about is that the conventional way to approach this question is inadequate. On the conventional approach, we treat these cases as though the central issue is about whether we can hold an individual criminally responsible for the consequences of his actions if those actions were beyond his contemplation. If David contemplated the possibility of Vernon's death, it is sometimes argued, we can hold him criminally responsible for it and consequently convict him of a homicide offence. But if he didn't contemplate, and had no reason to contemplate, the possibility of death, the imposition of criminal responsibility is inappropriate.[35] Others deny that this is the case. They think that a defendant can be held responsible for some things beyond the scope of his contemplation, even what he ought to have contemplated, if (to speak very loosely for a moment) what he intended was in the same 'moral ballpark' as a killer who contemplates the outcome.[36] That is sometimes argued to turn on whether the base criminal

33 Fischer, J.M. and Ravizza, M. (1998), *Responsibility and Control: A Theory of Moral Responsibility* (Cambridge: Cambridge University Press) p.12.

34 See, further, Duff, R A (2005), 'Answering for Crime' *Proceedings of the Aristotelian Society* 106:85, 101–103 and Tadros, V. 'The Scope and the Grounds of Responsibility' *New Criminal Law Review* (forthcoming).

35 See Ashworth, A. (2006), *Principles of Criminal Law*, 5th ed. (Oxford: Oxford University Press) pp.295–296.

36 See generally Gardner, J. (1994), 'Rationality and the Rule of Law in Offences Against the Person' *Cambridge Law Journal* 502, and (1998), 'On the General Part of the Criminal Law' in Duff, R.A. (ed.), *Philosophy and the Criminal Law* (Cambridge: Cambridge University Press); Horder, J. (1995), 'A Critique of the Correspondence Principle in Criminal Law' *Crim LR* 759, and in this context Clarkson, C.M.V. (2000), 'Context and Culpability in Involuntary Manslaughter: Principle or Instinct?' in Ashworth and Mitchell, above n.2.

offence that the defendant committed was in the appropriate family of offences.[37] Committing the right kind of offence, it is sometimes argued, involves a 'change of normative position' with respect to the victim such that one can be held responsible for the unforeseen harms that one causes. Some scholars on either side of this debate exclude criminal responsibility for killing where the defendant's intention was to cause a harm that was very much smaller than the outcome on the grounds of a lack of proportionality between the harm intended and the harm caused.

In my view, that debate has not captured the best way to approach constructive manslaughter cases. The central question in cases such as this isn't concerned with responsibility for consequences that the defendant did not contemplate. And once we realise that, there seems some good ground in thinking that the defendant is at fault for the death in standard constructive manslaughter cases. The remaining question, then, is whether that fault is sufficient to ground criminal responsibility for a homicide offence, and that seems to me a difficult question. But I will present some arguments why, in some standard cases, it is.

Here's what I think is the best way to approach these cases. Unlawful act manslaughter, it will be remembered, warrants criminal responsibility for death where the death was caused in the context of an unlawful and dangerous act. Now, all dangerous action, perhaps even all action, carries with it some possibility that it will cause death. For much ordinary everyday action the risk will be very small indeed, and even for ordinary every day dangerous action, the risk of death doesn't make action impermissible. It doesn't even make it *prima facie* wrong. We can impose some risk of death on others without having to justify that imposition to them. And when we act, we don't have to take steps to rule out all of the risks that our conduct imposes on others. Our lack of prospective responsibility to avoid small risks of death through ordinary everyday actions is reflected by a lack of criminal responsibility for deaths that occur through those actions.

Take driving. Even if I drive with the utmost care and attention, I create some risk of death on the road. But I am not prospectively responsible for ensuring that my driving imposes no risk of death. Driving isn't even *prima facie* wrong, and that is true even though it imposes a risk of death on others. The risk imposed through driving is bound up with the performance of a permissible act, an act that itself doesn't require justification. That is shown by the fact that I don't have to offer any justification for driving. I can drive just for fun, or for no reason at all. It isn't that the risks imposed by driving are justified by the fun that I have in driving. And pedestrians and other drivers consequently can't *ask me* to justify my driving. I don't have to *offer* justifications to them. Consequently if I kill someone through my safe driving, although I may be responsible for the death, and I then have to offer an explanation of how the death came about (accidentally and despite the care that I took), I cannot be *blamed* or *punished* for the death. And as criminal responsibility is concerned with blame and punishment, I cannot be held criminally responsible for deaths that occur as a consequence of my safe driving either.

It should be noted that nothing in this argument turns on my contemplation of the death that occurred. Some drivers, before they go out driving, sometimes think

37 See Clarkson, *ibid*.

that in driving they impose risks on others. But nothing important with respect to culpability turns on whether the driver thought about the risk, either on this particular occasion, or in previous instances. Both drivers who thought about the risk of death that they impose through their safe driving and those who didn't are responsible for the death in some sense. But neither can be blamed or punished for it. And I doubt that there is *any difference at all* in the way that we ought to treat the driver who contemplated the possibility of death and the driver who didn't.

Now compare deaths caused in the course of a dangerous criminal action. Here, in contrast with the driving case, I cannot say that I lack prospective responsibility for ensuring that there is no risk of death as a consequence of my criminal acts. Whereas in the driving case I don't have the responsibility to ensure that my driving doesn't impose any risk of death on others, where my act is criminal I cannot claim that I don't have the responsibility to ensure that my actions don't impose any risk of death on others. Where in the driving case I am permitted to drive, which implies being permitted to impose small risks on others, I cannot say that in the case of a criminal act. Perhaps I can say something else: that the imposition of the risk was only trivial and that imposing trivial risks of death is not wrong, on which more in a moment. But I cannot say what I can say in the case of driving: that the imposition of risk was bound up with, and cannot be separated from, a permissible act.

Now, it might be argued that, in the criminal context, what is important in these cases is the state of mind of the defendant. Consider Doris, who pushes Vera who hits her head and dies. It might be argued that Doris doesn't contemplate the possibility of causing death through her actions. And for that reason criminal liability for a homicide offence ought not to be imposed on her. One question is whether *contemplation* is the appropriate state of mind to be concerned with here. To require contemplation of the outcome for criminal responsibility for that outcome is much too demanding, and rules out criminal responsibility in plausible cases. The central problem is that many criminal offences are committed without a contemplative frame of mind. Defendants don't normally contemplate the outcomes of their actions, and the criminal law must accommodate that fact. Furthermore, the fact that an act is done without contemplation makes no difference to the defendant's level of fault as long as he has a normal set of beliefs and knowledge: that he hasn't made mistakes.

For example, in cases of domestic abuse, some defendants might become increasingly unreflective about the potentially serious consequences of their violent actions. Suppose that a defendant severely beats his wife without thinking about the risk of death in such a case, but death ensues. Are we really to say that he is not responsible for the death because he didn't contemplate the possibility of death at the time of action? Surely it's enough that he *knows* that violent assaults may well result in death, whether or not that fact was 'present to his mind' at the time of acting. Or think about a defendant who stabs another in the stomach with a serrated knife. Does it really make any difference that he did not contemplate that this would cause serious injury, assuming that he had a normal set of beliefs about the possible and probable effects of the stabbing?[38]

---

38 For further discussion, see Duff, R.A. (1990), *Intention, Agency and Criminal Liability* (Oxford: Blackwell) and Tadros, above n.25, ch.8.

But can't we say the same thing about standard unlawful act manslaughter cases? It is not as though defendants in those cases have made some kind of *mistake* with respect to the death. Normally, defendants in such cases have an ordinary set of beliefs about the risk of death that they impose on the victim: the risk is very small but not utterly trivial. Deaths happen through unlawful and dangerous acts, and I take it that most defendants would not be surprised when informed of that fact. If, for some reason, the defendant does underestimate the likelihood that his unlawful act will cause death, perhaps that is a reason not to hold him criminally responsible if death is caused. That turns on the difficult issue of how we should treat responsibility for mistaken belief.[39] But standard unlawful act manslaughter cases aren't cases of mistaken belief at all. The defendants in such cases presumably commonly have the same beliefs as everyone else about the chance of death in these cases: it's very small.

Furthermore, we don't want to treat unlawful act manslaughter cases differently depending on whether we believe that the defendant thought about the very small possibility of death prior to acting. Suppose that the burglar thinks about the very small risk of death before committing the burglary. It isn't *that* that might ground his criminal responsibility for the death. In the absence of an error on the part of the defendant about the risk of death, if the criminal law is wrong in holding individuals responsible for death in cases where the defendant doesn't think about the risks that he imposes through his unlawful and dangerous act then it is also wrong in holding defendants responsible in cases where they think about and take such a small risk. Nothing turns on the awareness of the defendant prior to, or whilst, acting.

Perhaps the argument will be made here that individuals aren't responsible, or at least not criminally responsible, for the outcome of very small risks. The risk needs to be not only unwarranted, but *serious* it might be argued. And in unlawful act manslaughter cases the risk isn't serious. The issue is difficult. Sometimes imposing a very small risk of death on another might be wrongful, and condemnation of the risk taker for the result of that risk (or even for taking the risk) might be justified. Consider the following example. Ian has invented a drug that will cure the common cold. He is almost certain that the drug will not have any side-effects, let alone any lethal side-effects on those that take it. And he has good reason to believe this. But the only way to be absolutely sure is to test it on a human population. He puts the drug in the drinking water in his local town. Unfortunately, due to some very unlikely set of circumstances, one person, Betty, has an allergic reaction to the drug and dies. Surely he has wrongfully tested the drug in this case, and wrongfully imposed a risk, albeit a very small risk, of death on the population of his local town. And surely he can be held responsible, even criminally responsible, for the death of Betty. For, even though the risks were small, putting the drug in the drinking water was reckless.

39 I have attempted to outline the issues in Tadros, above n.25, ch.9. This is one way in which the law is harsh. If the defendant does not appreciate that his act is dangerous, but a reasonable person would appreciate that fact, he may still be liable for unlawful act manslaughter. See *Watson* [1989] 2 All E R 865. That is more objective than it ought to be.

However, perhaps there are other cases where the risk is *so* small that imposition of criminal responsibility for the outcome of that risk is unwarranted. It seems plausible to me that there are cases like this. Some of them are cases which the criminal law currently excludes by restricting unlawful act manslaughter to cases of *dangerous* unlawful acts. For example, if Ray steals Zelda's bag, which, unbeknownst to him, contains her heart pills, and consequently Zelda dies, we might say that the risk of death that Ray imposes on Zelda is too small for us to hold him criminally responsible for her death. In these cases, we can say that the risk is not only very small but *trivial*. Of course, the distinction between very small and trivial risks is not sharp, but that is the distinction that I think ought to help us to distinguish between cases of unlawful act homicide and cases where the defendant is not criminally responsible for the death. By requiring the unlawful act to be dangerous, the criminal law might be attempting to exclude cases where the risk of death is trivial.

The more general *idea* of constructive manslaughter seems right to me, however: that in determining whether a person is guilty of a homicide we should attend not only to the quantity of the risk of death in the defendant's actions, we should attend to whether those risks were attached to permissible or impermissible actions. There are some cases, such as driving, where the imposition of small risks on others isn't even *prima facie* wrongful. There are other cases, such as Ian's, where the imposition of the same degree is wrongful. If an otherwise unlawful act creates a risk of death, even a small risk, there is good reason to see the imposition of that risk as wrongful.

It might further be objected that I have only shown responsibility and fault for the death, not that the *criminal law* should be concerned with *holding* the defendant responsible for the death. But if death ensues through an unlawful act, the criminal law seems the appropriate forum to recognise that the victim was wrongfully killed by the defendant. Imagine the family of the victim, who have lost a relative through D's assault or burglary. If D is convicted merely of assault or burglary, they surely have a legitimate objection that D caused V's death, and not through a pure accident, but by exposing him to a small but unwarranted risk of death. That, they will legitimately claim, should be recognised in law, as part of what D is publicly condemned for.[40]

In other words, I am suggesting that unlawful act manslaughter provides one way of showing that the defendant was reckless in killing. Commonly, an agent is regarded as reckless with respect to an outcome if he takes an unwarranted risk of bringing that harm about. But whether a risk is unwarranted is dependent on the context in which that risk is taken. It is not dependent entirely on the magnitude of the risk. Where the defendant is engaging in an unlawful act, which increases the risk of the death of an innocent person, the risk imposed is unwarranted, not because it is great but because it is in a context where the defendant has no right to impose that risk on others.

That is not to say that D should be *punished* very harshly for causing the death. The fact that D has manifested no worse a vice than other assaulters or burglars should ensure that the difference in the level of punishment between the cases is not

---

40 See also Home Office (2000), *Reforming the Law on Involuntary Manslaughter: The Government's Proposals*, p.10, although the Government also seem to think that deaths in these cases are 'unforseeable'.

too great. This raises difficult issues of proportionality in sentencing: what, exactly, should sentences be proportional to? My suspicion is that sentences for unlawful act manslaughter are often wildly disproportionate given the defendant's limited fault with respect to the death. Furthermore, perhaps the definition of dangerousness in the criminal law is too broad, warranting condemnation of deaths that are not sufficiently wrongful to be criminal; cases where the risk of death was only trivial. But the law may warrant the condemnation of defendants for killing where they have imposed relatively small risks of death on others through their unlawful conduct, and who are therefore not very gravely at fault for those deaths.

What the law gets wrong in a more fundamental way, I think, is the categorisation of these homicides with some much more serious cases that I referred to above, in the category of manslaughter. There are two problems here. First, the degree of fault for the homicide in some cases of unlawful act manslaughter is too trivial to justify inclusion within the same offence as some cases at the upper limit of the offence. The offence of manslaughter, as we have already seen, is very broad, and reform should be aimed at substantially narrowing it. Secondly, the label 'manslaughter' seems inappropriate for cases such as this. The label isn't especially suitable anyway; not all manslaughters have male victims, and very few involve slaughtering. But it is particularly unsuitable for these cases where it implies a much higher level of culpability for the deaths caused than is the case.

But defendants in most cases of unlawful act manslaughter cannot say that they are not criminally responsible for the deaths that they cause at all. They can only say that their level of fault for those deaths was relatively modest. And, if the fault level of the unlawful acts from which manslaughter is constructed is set at an appropriate level, they cannot deny criminal responsibility for killing either.

### *(ii) Recklessness or gross negligence?*

I am more critical of the lower limit set by gross negligence manslaughter. The *Adamako* test has been criticised for its circularity: it defines what is criminal by referring to what should be criminal. But I don't think that this circularity is vicious, in principle at least. We should expect coherence at the outer limits of the criminal law; the distinction between criminal and non-criminal behaviour should be set by comparable levels of fault. Given that, there is nothing wrong in principle with comparing putative gross negligence cases to the line that is drawn between criminal and non-criminal conduct more generally to determine whether the defendant's fault was sufficient to warrant the imposition of criminal responsibility. If the appropriate fault level in other offence contexts is easier to draw precisely, there is nothing wrong with a test that fixes less precise concepts by inviting comparison with the fault level in the those contexts. The problems with the test are otherwise.

First, the criminal law includes a number of offences of strict liability, where there is no fault requirement, as well as a number of offences with 'due diligence' defences. In England and Wales there is no formal distinction between 'true' criminal law and regulatory offences. Manslaughter is obviously a 'true' criminal offence, but in determining the scope of gross negligence what other offences provide appropriate comparisons for determining whether the defendant's conduct was criminal? The criminal law as it stands doesn't provide an appropriate set of standards of criminality in other offence contexts against which gross negligence cases can be compared.

Furthermore, some serious criminal offences can be committed with a trivial level of fault or no fault at all. For example, rape of a child can be committed if the child is below the age of 12, even if the defendant had a reasonable belief that she was over 12.[41] This might be regarded as particularly unfair where the defendant is himself a young person.[42] Inviting another to provide money or property where one 'has reasonable cause to suspect' that it may be used for the purposes of terrorism is an offence,[43] so a naïve person raising money for what she thinks is a charitable organisation, but which turns out to support some terrorist activities, may have committed an offence of terrorism. Is the gross negligence standard to be compared with the standard of fault in offences such as these?

Secondly, juries have the role of determining whether the defendant was grossly negligent. But they lack knowledge of the relevant standards in other contexts to do the comparison in the appropriate way. So they are likely to fall back on their own understanding of what should count as criminal. But the scope of the criminal law is to be determined by public reason, and decisions by juries cannot provide the appropriate kind of public reason for these purposes. In fact, given that juries play a silent and passive role in trials, it is questionable whether their decisions can be regarded as part of public reason at all.[44] If the test in *Adomako* is intended to reflect personal decisions by the jury about the proper scope of the criminal law rather than setting the fault standard by reference to other parts of the criminal law, it will not achieve the desired coherence, and it will not be subject to the appropriate constraints of a public system of law. Of course, it is another thing to say that this problem is sufficiently acute that there is a violation of the human rights of those charged with gross negligence manslaughter.[45] But even if this is not the case, the test can only be seen as inadequate in this respect.

Thirdly, including the duty of care as part of a *mens rea* concept is confusing and unhelpful. There is an important question about the circumstances in which liability might be imposed with respect to outcomes which are caused as a consequence of a failure on the part of the defendant to act where he has a duty to do so. But that question is not obviously dependent on the particular nature of the outcome. There is no obvious reason why the question should be asked in cases where death is caused, rather than cases where the victim suffers grievous bodily harm (GBH), for example. But as gross negligence is the *mens rea* only of manslaughter, and not for assault occasioning GBH, for example, the law is only likely to become incoherent on this issue. The better approach is to treat the question of omissions liability in the general

41 Section 5 of the Sexual Offences Act 2003. For valuable discussion, see Spencer, J.R. (2004), 'The Sexual Offences Act 2003 (2): Child and Family Offences' *Crim LR* 347.

42 See, for example, *R v G* [2006] EWCA *Crim* 821. See also Andrew Ashworth's comment at [2006] *Crim LR* 930.

43 Terrorism Act 2000, s.15. See further Tadros, V. (2007), 'Justice and Terrorism' *New Criminal Law Review* 10:4, 658.

44 See Duff, R.A. *et al.*, above n.5.

45 The test was found compatible with Arts.6 and 7 of the ECHR in *Misra* [2004] EWCA *Crim*. 2375.

part of the criminal law, and that is so even if there is some variation about how it should apply across offence contexts.[46]

Fourthly, to rehearse a claim that I have argued for in more detail elsewhere,[47] in inviting the defendant to be convicted in respect of the standard of conduct shown rather than by reference to any awareness of the risk or failure with respect to his attitude towards others, the test invites convictions in cases where the defendant did not display the kind of vice appropriate to ground criminal responsibility. Arguably *Adomako* was one such case, in that the defendant in the case did everything that he believed to be appropriate to ensure that the victim did not come to harm. He could not be criticised for lack of care for the victim, only for lack of ability as an anaesthetist. A person's lack of ability provides an inappropriate basis on which to convict him, particularly in those institutional settings such as hospitals where others have the responsibility to ensure that workers have the appropriate training and capabilities.

Fifthly, why is gross negligence the appropriate *mens rea* of manslaughter at all? The lower limit of manslaughter should be set by recklessness,[48] and recklessness should be defined in a way that is neither purely subjective (as it has recently been in the context of criminal damage[49]) nor purely objective (which would make it similar to gross negligence). It is not clear that having different concepts of gross negligence and recklessness in different offence concepts helps to ensure that the law is clear and consistent or that convictions are imposed only in deserved cases. Why should recklessness be the appropriate concept to use in criminal damage, for example, but not in manslaughter?[50]

Abandoning the gross negligence standard in manslaughter would substantially raise the bottom end of the offence. Nevertheless, when we reform the law of homicide, we must take into consideration a bottom limit of homicide that involves cases where the defendant's fault for the death is quite limited. I have suggested that cases of unlawful act manslaughter are properly regarded as homicides. And

---

46 For further exploration of the scope and role of the general part, see Gardner, J. 'On the General Part of the Criminal Law' and Lacey, N. 'Contingency, Coherence, and Conceptualism: Reflections on the Encounter between "Critique" and the "Philosophy of the Criminal Law"', both in Duff, R.A. (1998), *Philosophy and the Criminal Law: Principle and Critique* (Cambridge: Cambridge University Press), Tadros, V. (2002), 'The System of the Criminal Law' *Legal Studies* 22, 448 and Horder, J. (2005), 'The Classification of Crimes and the Special Part of the Criminal Law' in Duff and Green (eds), *Defining Crimes: Essays on the Special Part of the Criminal Law* (Oxford: Oxford University Press), and Cane, P. (2007), 'The General/Special Distinction in Criminal Law, Tort Law and Legal Theory' *Law and Philosophy* 26, 465.

47 Tadros, above n.25, 82–85. See also ch.9.

48 It appears from *Adomako* that trial judges *may* refer to recklessness in their directions, confusing matters still further. See the judgement of Lord Mackay. For analysis of distinctions that may be and have been drawn between recklessness and gross negligence, see Halpin, A. (2004), *Definition in the Criminal Law* (Oxford: Hart Publishing) ch.3.

49 *R v G* [2003] UKHL 50.

50 See also Leigh, L.H. (1995), 'Liability for Inadvertence: A Lordly Legacy?' *Modern Law Review* 58, 457.

even if gross negligence manslaughter was abandoned, there would be cases of reckless manslaughter where the defendant's fault for the death is quite limited when compared with the most serious cases that I considered above. This suggests that the scope of manslaughter ought to be limited. The question is how best to achieve that.

## III The Law Commission's Proposals

I have indicated that the offence of manslaughter is too broad. This problem might be addressed either by raising the bottom limit of the offence, excluding some cases where the defendant is not very culpable, or lowering the top limit, categorising as murder some cases where the defendant is seriously at fault. If I am right that the bottom limit of homicide, taken as a whole, should properly include some cases where the defendant's fault for the death is not very substantial, it is natural (though ultimately inadequate) to look towards the latter solution first. Are there manslaughter cases that ought to be murders? If so, it may be that once the law of murder has its proper breadth the scope of manslaughter will be incidentally restricted at the top. Perhaps if manslaughter is then suitably reformed at the bottom in the way that I have indicated, the law of homicide will, overall, be satisfactory.

Reducing the scope of manslaughter by expanding the law of murder is indeed the main solution[51] provided by the Law Commission's current proposals for the reform of murder.[52] The Law Commission recommend that there should be three main homicide offences. In their proposals, they divide the offence of murder into first and second degree murder, and in doing so expand the scope of murder taken as a whole substantially. Reform along these lines would bring within the scope of murder a range of cases currently categorised as manslaughters. Some of those cases would be voluntary manslaughters and others involuntary manslaughters.

With respect to the former, the Commission recommend that cases currently designated as voluntary manslaughter should be categorised as second degree murders. The defences of provocation and diminished responsibility would apply only as defences to first degree murder, resulting in a conviction of second degree murder. The category of voluntary manslaughter would thus be abolished. This would reduce to a degree the number of cases in which provocation and diminished responsibility are pled: those defences would only be used in cases where the prosecution believed that it could prove that the defendant fulfilled the *mens rea* of first degree murder. First degree murder would include intentional killing and killing through an intention to do serious injury with an awareness of a serious risk of causing death.[53] This is

51 They also suggest changing unlawful act manslaughter to 'criminal act manslaughter', including only those defendants who kill another person through the commission of a criminal act that the defendant was aware involved a serious risk of causing some injury. See the Law Com. (2006), above n.23, para. 2.163, more or less following the Government's response to Law Com. (1996), above n.30.

52 Law Com. (2006), above n.23.

53 In the original consultation document, Law Commission for England and Wales (2005), *A New Homicide Act for England and Wales?* (Consultation Paper No. 177), the *mens*

slightly narrower than the present law of murder, including the extra criterion that the defendant must have been aware of a serious risk of causing death.

Restricting the use of provocation and diminished responsibility to the distinction between degrees of murder has pros and cons. On the positive side, it would laudably lower the top limit of the offence of manslaughter by treating some cases where the basis for those defences was weak as murders rather than manslaughters (albeit murder in the second degree). As noted above, there are cases of diminished responsibility, and especially of provocation, where the grounds for a partial excuse are quite weak. In those cases, a conviction of murder will often be appropriate if the defendant has the relevant *mens rea*. This would also ensure that some of the most serious manslaughters are removed from that offence, narrowing it substantially.

On the down side, cases of provocation and diminished responsibility that currently set one bottom limit of the offence of manslaughter would set the bottom limit of the offence of second degree murder! I noted above that there are some cases of provocation and diminished responsibility where the basis for the defence is very substantial, but the defendant is not entitled to a full defence. If the defendant was provoked by violence that was just insufficient to ground self-defence, or if he suffered from a very severe mental disorder that was not sufficient to provide him with the defence of insanity, he may be found guilty of manslaughter. Under the Law Commission's proposals those cases would be labelled as murders. To label cases which are marginally outside the scope of the defences of self-defence or insanity, for example, as murders is unjustifiable.

There are potential solutions to this problem in principle. The defences of provocation and diminished responsibility might be considered by juries as capable of reducing a charge of first degree murder to either second degree murder or to manslaughter depending on the extent of the provocation or mental disorder. Perhaps this is unattractive for pragmatic reasons. It may result in complicated directions to juries which they will find difficult to follow, for example. If such a solution is unavailable, it would be better for the partial defences to reduce either first or second degree murder to manslaughter on the grounds that any inapt labelling should favour the defendant.

With respect to involuntary manslaughter, some cases which are currently labelled as manslaughter would fall within the proposed offence of second degree murder. Second degree murder would include not only cases where the defendant killed through an intent to do serious injury (as is true of murder currently), but also killing where there was an awareness of a serious risk of causing death, coupled with an intention to cause either: a) some injury; b) a fear of injury; or c) a risk of injury. By including cases where there is an awareness of a serious risk of causing death

---

*rea* of murder was defined in a much more restricted fashion as intention to kill. This would effectively have resulted in provocation and diminished responsibility being made issues for sentence rather than for trial, for the reason that it would be very unlikely that first degree murder would be charged in many cases where provocation and diminished responsibility would have been at issue. See Tadros, V. (2006), 'The Homicide Ladder' *Modern Law Review* 69, 601. The final proposals would not have this consequence, however, as the *mens rea* of first degree murder has been expanded.

(coupled with a further intention) the law of murder would be expanded to some degree, although of course in most cases where the defendant intends (in the *Woollin* sense) grievous bodily harm, he will also be aware of a serious risk of causing death. For this reason, we should expect that, under these proposals, most convictions of second degree murder would be cases where the defendant successfully pleads provocation or diminished responsibility to a charge of first degree murder.

Consequently, whilst this would restrict the scope of involuntary manslaughter to a degree, it doesn't go far enough. Cases at the top of the offence of manslaughter would still involve a high degree of fault for the death. Appreciating exactly which cases requires some interpretation of the Commission's proposals. The second part of the *mens rea* of second degree murder is not very clear. As noted, the defendant must have been aware of a serious risk of causing death and also intend injury, fear of injury or risk of injury. It is not clear whether the defendant must directly intend to bring about one of the three consequences (injury, fear of injury or risk of injury) or whether foresight would be sufficient. The most coherent interpretation, I think, is that if the defendant foresaw a high risk of death or serious injury, but did not *directly intend* to cause injury, a fear of injury or a risk of injury, he should be convicted of manslaughter rather than second degree murder.[54] To understand why this is the most coherent interpretation, we need to know something about the definition of intention that the Commission intend to be used in this context.

In general, the Commission seem happy to adopt the *Woollin* direction on intention, potentially including direct intent as well as foresight of virtual certainty.[55] If that is the definition to be used in this context, foresight of some risk of injury would be sufficient to fulfil the second part of the test. But that would also seem to render the first part of the test redundant, for in all cases where it could be proved that the defendant was aware of a serious risk of causing death, he would also have foresight of virtual certainty of causing a risk of injury. To provide any independent restriction on the scope of the *mens rea* of second degree murder, the definition of intention in the second part of the test must be narrower than the awareness that is sufficient for the first part. The obvious conclusion would be to interpret intent in this context as *direct* intent.

If that is right, cases where the defendant was aware that his conduct created a serious risk of death, but did not directly intend to subject others to that risk would be excluded from second degree murder. For example, it would exclude from second degree murder the example considered above where the defendant drives on the pavement in a police chase. Whilst that defendant is aware of a serious risk of causing death through his conduct, he does not directly intend injury, fear of injury or risk of injury. The defendant intends to drive onto the pavement to get away more quickly. We could not say that, had he failed to risk injury or fear of injury, his plan would

54 For a contrasting interpretation, see Ashworth, A. (2007), 'Principles, Pragmatism and the Law Commission's Recommendations on Homicide Law Reform' *Crim LR* 333.

55 Law Com. (2006), above n.23, pt.3. For criticism of this approach first adopted in Law Com. (2005), above n.53, which the Commission respond to in Law Com. (2006) pt.3, see Tadros, above n.53. As will become clear in the course of this discussion, I think that response is unconvincing.

not adequately have been carried out.[56] That case would, then, still be considered at the top end of manslaughter.

One response to this problem would be to expand further the category of murder, ensuring that manslaughter only includes cases where the defendant's culpability is not at the most serious end of homicide. However, the label 'murder' ought to be reserved for the most serious killings. The terms 'murder' and 'murderer' have a social significance that is not easily lost. Expanding the category too far will mark out some less serious killers as murderers socially, and changing the social significance of the terms 'murder' and 'murderer' will obviously be difficult and slow. This is true even if different degrees of murder are introduced as the Law Commission recommend. Furthermore, this social significance of the terms 'murder' and 'murderer' is worth retaining for moral reasons. There is obviously a range of fault levels for killing, and it is difficult to be precise about the proper distinction to draw between different degrees.[57] But there is a profound moral difference between an unmitigated intentional killing and many of the manslaughter cases that we have been considering in this chapter. Restricting murder to the most serious cases is the best way of marking out this profound difference. That is not intended to show that there should not be degrees of murder. Perhaps there should. But if there are to be degrees, they should be degrees within a general category that is restricted to the worst killings.

This suggests that a relatively narrow offence of murder should be retained, and that the offence of manslaughter should be divided into two or three, somewhat along the lines suggested earlier by the Government in response to the Law Commission.[58] There could, for example, be an offence of culpable killing below the offence of manslaughter to capture cases which are not sufficiently serious to be included within the same offence category as some of the most serious instances of manslaughter. I don't have space here for a full investigation of how homicide should be divided up but, along with the Government, I suspect that the category of homicide should be quite wide with respect to culpability, ranging from those who take very small risks of death in the context of unlawful and dangerous activity to intentional killing. Given that, we should expect several rungs on the homicide ladder.

## IV Differentiating by Kind

One way to reform the law of homicide is to develop a better ladder of offences. The central motivation behind the Law Commission's proposals is to have a homicide ladder which grades homicides more effectively in terms of seriousness. In

56 For the failure test, see Duff, above n.38, pp.61–63. The test has come in for some criticism in Simester, A.P. (1992), 'Paradigm Intention' *Law and Philosophy* 11, 235, but those criticisms do not have implications for the discussion here.

57 See Wilson, W. (2000), 'Murder and the Structure of Homicide' in Ashworth and Mitchell, above n.2 and (2007), 'What's Wrong with Murder?' *Criminal Law and Philosophy* 1:2, 157, as well as Tadros, above n.53, for further discussion.

58 *Reforming the Law on Involuntary Manslaughter*, above n.40, responding to Law Com. (1996), above n.30. See also Clarkson, above n.36.

developing tiers of the offence, they reflect the view that homicide has (for the most part) a single *actus reus*, but is distinguished through *mens rea* terms and defences. In this part of the chapter, I consider whether there should be further differentiation of the law of homicide through the *actus reus* of the offence.

Some homicide offences are distinguished through the *actus reus* of the offence, such as causing death by dangerous driving, causing death by careless driving, killing a vulnerable person in one's care and infanticide. The former two offences were created primarily for pragmatic reasons, rather than because of the particular moral significance of the *actus reus*. The offence of killing a vulnerable person in one's household was a response to a perceived problem in some cases where, although it could be proved that the child (or other dependent person) was killed by a carer, it was difficult to prove which carer was the author of the death.[59] The right of silence (even in its eroded state) provides one substantial barrier to discovering the details of what happened in cases such as this. This offence seems to make compromises by allowing the conviction of a lesser offence where it cannot be proved that the defendant was a more serious wrongdoer (by being the principal killer). It seems almost as though a lower evidential basis of wrongdoing can motivate conviction and punishment to a lesser degree, something that may raise concerns derived from the presumption of innocence.[60] But further, if I am right that this offence is a way of circumventing the protections provided by the right of silence, the state should be compelled to make that erosion explicit through procedural changes rather than changes to the substantive law. This is essential in order that the circumvention can be tested for compatibility with human rights and held up to proper democratic scrutiny.

The offences of causing death by dangerous or careless driving were created in a social context where juries failed to appreciate that killing whilst driving could have the appropriate level of culpability for a manslaughter conviction.[61] That is probably no longer the case. But even if it is, the law should resist warranting the failure of juries to convict in manslaughter cases by allowing the defendant to be convicted of what will be perceived as a lesser offence where there is no proper moral discrimination to be made between cases involving driving and other cases.[62] This also creates the false impression that cases toward the bottom limit of the

---

59 See Williams, G. (1989), 'Which of you did it?' *MLR* 52, 179; Griew, E. (1989), 'It Must Have Been One of Them' *Crim LR* 129. It is not, however, being used only, or even primarily, for cases of this kind. See Herring, this volume.

60 At least if my account of the right is correct. See Tadros, V. (2007), 'Rethinking the Presumption of Innocence' *Criminal Law and Philosophy* 1:2, 193.

61 See Law Com. (1996), above n.30.

62 See also Cunningham, S. (2001), 'The Reality of Vehicular Homicides: Convictions for Murder, Manslaughter and Causing Death by Dangerous Driving' *Crim LR* 679 and this volume. Compare sexual offences, where the fact that it is difficult to encourage juries to convict defendants of rape where there is no violence may not be sufficient reason to create a lesser offence. Contrast Schulhofer, S. (1998), *Unwanted Sex: The Culture of Intimidation and the Failure of the Law* (Cambridge: Mass, Harvard University Press) and Power, H. (2003), 'Towards a Redefinition of the *Mens Rea* of Rape' *Oxford Journal of Legal Studies* 23, 379 with Temkin, J. (2002), *Rape and the Legal Process*, 2nd ed. (Oxford: Oxford University

manslaughter offence involve a higher degree of culpability than standard cases of death by dangerous driving. Finally, if the offence of manslaughter were divided into two, there would be even less reason to retain the offence of causing death by dangerous driving.

Similarly, the creation of the offence of infanticide was motivated by sympathy for mothers who kill their children in the first years of life, resulting in a reluctance of juries to convict the defendant of murder in those cases.[63] The real issue here, then, is whether to have a distinct offence or whether to include infanticide claims within the scope of diminished responsibility, resulting in a conviction of manslaughter. Whilst there are undoubtedly cases where sympathy is warranted due to the mental state of some mothers who kill their children, the issue now has to be seen in the light of an increasing social concern for children who are victims of abuse. This concern, for example, was at the heart of the proposal by the Law Commission that the infanticide offence not be extended.

The creation of distinct homicide offences, then, has not primarily been motivated by a genuine concern with fair labelling. What are likely to be the strongest cases for separate recognition in the law? One possibility concerns the identity of the perpetrator. The strongest case here is of corporate manslaughter. The fact that the perpetrator is a corporation rather than an individual might have the kind of moral significance that deserves separate recognition in the law, as has been done through the creation of a separate offence of corporate manslaughter.[64] Are there other perpetrators that we might single out? The offence of infanticide is only available to convict mothers who kill their young children, but particularly given concerns about abuse of young children that might be thought difficult to justify. And that is not so much about the identity of the perpetrator as the relationship between the perpetrator and the victim.

We might distinguish offences according to the mode of killing. Are killing through driving, or through poor medical care, or through supply of controlled drugs, sufficiently distinct to warrant separate offences? It is difficult to see how there is a sufficiently significant *moral* distinction which requires separating these offences from killing in other ways or other contexts. The central problem is that the variety of modes of killing and contexts in which killing occurs seems too great for there to be a realistic prospect of the demands of coherence, as outlined in the introduction to this chapter, to be satisfied. Distinguishing one mode of killing invites claims that other modes of killing are distinct. Distinguishing modes of killing will thus lead to a very great fragmentation of the law of homicide, and it is difficult to see how this could be justified on theoretical, let alone practical, grounds. If that is right, there is less call for separate offences here, but perhaps for separate modes of proof or rules of liability for a single offence of manslaughter. The offence of manslaughter could be

---

Press) and Tadros above n.18, for the debate about whether the offence of rape should be divided and if so how.

63 See Showalter, E. (1987), *Women, Madness and English Culture 1830-1980* (London: Virago).

64 The Corporate Manslaughter and Corporate Homicide Act 2007. See Clarkson, this volume.

further differentiated such that special rules of liability can evolve to deal with cases involving driving or medical negligence, but fulfilling those rules of liability will result in a manslaughter conviction rather than conviction of a separate offence.

We might distinguish offences or aggravations according to the motive of the defendant, for example by separating racially motivated killings from other killings either through specific aggravations to be proved at trial (as is done for other offences) or through the creation of separate offences. But then, for the sake of coherence, we must do the same thing for other kinds of aggravating motivations. I do not completely rule out the possibility that we can achieve coherence here. Perhaps racially aggravated killings are much worse than killings aggravated by other motives which can justify a specific legal aggravation. However, as with modes of killing, there is a great variety of motives that might be at play in homicide cases, and picking out some motives as significant but not others will be difficult to justify in terms of equality. Why should the victim who dies as a consequence of a racially motivated assault be treated differently from a victim who dies as a consequence of an assault motivated by her disability, or by her hair colour, or by her place of residence, or by her gender, or by her sexual orientation, or because she stood up to the assailant? It's not that there is nothing special or important about racial discrimination that can justify treating racially motivated killings as morally significant. It is rather that too many motivations are morally significant in a comparable way for the law to recognise all as distinct through special rules of liability. Furthermore, determining the proper scope of racial aggravation has proved very difficult in the context of assault. Pragmatic burdens, in this context, will, I suspect, outweigh any benefits in terms of fair labelling.

One further possibility is concerned with the value of the life taken. The substantive law of homicide does not for the most part distinguish between victims in terms of the quality of their life. For the purposes of the law of homicide, the value of each life is regarded as equal. And we might think that there is some principle of political equality underpinning this. The state must treat the lives of its citizens as of equal and great moral worth, and that requires treating the killing of citizens as equally and greatly morally wrong regardless of who it is that is killed. Sentences, however, may depend on the value of the life taken. In cases of assisted suicide or mercy killing low tariffs or low sentences are set; in cases of child killing tariffs and sentences are increased. This should invite us to explore the extent to which political equality can motivate differentiation in terms of the quality of the life that is taken.

The issue is obviously controversial, and I won't be able to do full justice to it here. But I think that whether or not one accepts that some mercy killings and assisted suicides should not attract a criminal conviction there is good reason for a partial defence[65] to murder to be available, and for the defendant to be convicted not of manslaughter but of a separate offence. The central idea that motivates this claim is that even in cases where the defendant is not fully justified in killing the victim the defendant, in cases of this kind, normally attempts to respect the rational will of his victim.

65 For reasons of space, I leave aside whether we should see these cases as partially justified or partially excused.

Let's begin with the simpler case of assisted suicide, where the victim encourages the defendant to kill her. The defendant who kills another who encourages her to do so may sometimes show a kind of faulty regard for the rational will of the victim, and thus we may rightly deny her a full defence. But the kind of faulty regard that she shows might, in some circumstances, amount to a partial defence for the killing. Perhaps in order to have this defence available, the defendant will have to provide a plausible explanation of how such a faulty regard has come about, an explanation that will be in part dependent on an account of how a more or less rational agent could see killing as something to pursue, and perhaps in part dependent on the consequences of stress associated with the suffering of the one killed.

The important point here is not just that the defendant's motive is different in a case of assisted suicide from other intentional killings: to prevent the victim's suffering rather than to cause him harm. It is rather that we can understand how the suffering of the victim itself could result in an intentional killing based on that motive, even if the motive is not quite sufficient to fully justify the killing. The victim's consent is significant in that it provides an authorisation for the defendant to consider whether their life has sufficient value to justify their ending it. But the consent alone cannot remove the responsibility on the part of the defendant to consider whether the victim's life has insufficient value to be preserved. This is at least in part because it is possible for those suffering to be mistaken about whether their life is sufficiently valuable to be preserved.[66] The point here is that there may be cases where there is consent and where the death of the victim could plausibly, if wrongly, be seen as an end worth pursuing. The fact that we can come to see it in this way suggests that the defendant may be entitled to a partial defence for killing the victim.

This train of thought can be utilised to give rise to similar claims in cases where the victim cannot consent to the killing: where the victim is in a persistent vegetative state, for example.[67] In such cases we must take into consideration what the victim would have wanted as a way of respecting their rational will over their life, but also the true value of what remains of their life regardless of how they would have come to see it. In order for the defendant to be partially (or perhaps completely) justified in the killing it must both be the case that the life of the victim does not retain its potential value, understood in objective terms, but also that the victim could have come, in the light of their own values and commitments, to see things that way. That shows the proper kind of respect for the rational will of the victim.

Even if it is accepted that in appropriate circumstances the crime of assisting suicide and mercy killing is lesser, however, should we regard it as distinctive or as a part of a more general crime such as manslaughter? I think that there is a strong case for treating these cases as distinctive. What we can say about these cases is that the defendant had a genuine and plausible, even if ultimately faulty, conception of

66 This might work either way. Sometimes it may be that we cling onto a life that is not worth living any more, and in others we warrant an early end that fails to recognise fully the value of our own lives. See Foot. P. (2002). 'Euthanasia' in *Virtues and Vices* (Oxford: Oxford University Press) p.37.

67 Such cases are currently dealt with through a problematic application of liability for omissions. See Tadros, above n.25, ch.7.

how to respond appropriately to the autonomous desires of the victim, and hence a genuine and plausible, if ultimately faulty, conception of respect for the life of the victim. That seems to me fundamentally distinct from, for example, cases of reckless killing or killing with diminished responsibility, where the defendant is insufficiently motivated by respect for the defendant's life, however that is conceived. The form that the law should take, then, is that the defendant, in appropriate cases of assisted suicide or mercy killing, has a partial defence to a charge of murder which reduces a charge of murder to a conviction of a special offence of mercy killing. This, I suggest, preserves the moral significance of the defendant's motive in the light of facts about the victim's life.

## V Conclusion

I have approached the question of the grading of homicide, in this chapter, by beginning with a consideration of the least bad cases that can justify a homicide conviction. Unlawful act manslaughter cases, I suggest, are cases of that kind, along with cases where the defendant was barely short of being entitled to a full defence for their conduct. In some of those cases, the defendant's level of culpability for killing will be quite low. Reducing the scope of manslaughter by expanding the scope of murder, I suggest, is inadequate to ensure that the category of manslaughter is appropriately narrow. This suggests that the only satisfactory way to address the problem is to divide up the offence of manslaughter into two tiers. This, I claim, is more important than restricting the scope of murder. If the label 'manslaughter' is to be retained to capture homicides below the level of murder (and I can see arguments for or against that) I suggest that there should be a separate category of culpable killing to capture the least serious homicide cases. Such an offence should carry a relatively light sentence to mark out the fact that whilst the defendant was criminally responsible for the killing, his level of fault was at the lower end. Beyond the ladder of homicide offences, I recommend that there should be only two further offences: an offence of corporate killing and an offence to cover mercy killing and assisted suicide. Other offences should be incorporated into the homicide ladder. However, special rules of liability might be created to assist decision makers in a range of cases. These proposals, I think, are most likely to improve the coherence and fairness of our law of homicide.

## Chapter 4

# Whose Luck Is It Anyway?

R.A. Duff[1]

Dangerous driving attracts a maximum penalty of a heavy fine or in the most serious cases up to six months' imprisonment; but if it causes death, the maximum penalty is fourteen years' imprisonment. Careless driving attracts a maximum penalty of a level 4 fine; driving whilst under the influence of drink or drugs attracts a maximum penalty of a level 5 fine and/or up to six months' imprisonment: but if someone causes death by careless driving when under the influence of drink or drugs, the maximum penalty is again fourteen years' imprisonment, and for causing death by careless driving it is five years' imprisonment. Driving when unlicensed, uninsured or disqualified attracts maximum penalties of, respectively, a level 3 fine, a level 5 fine, and a level 5 fine and/ or six months' imprisonment; but an unlicensed, uninsured or disqualified driver who causes death faces a maximum penalty of two years' imprisonment.[2] The difference between causing and not causing death in such cases might be purely a matter of luck; we therefore face the familiar question of whether and how it can be consistent with the demands of penal justice to allow 'outcome luck' to make such a dramatic difference to an offender's criminal liability.

My aim in this chapter is, first, to show why the problem of outcome luck in this context is different from the problem of outcome luck in certain other familiar contexts, particularly that of criminal attempts; and, second, to show why, whilst it is appropriate to attach a heavier punishment to dangerous conduct if it actually causes death, the increase in severity should be modest – much more modest than our law currently provides. I will also argue that it is not in the same way appropriate to increase the punishment for a driver who causes death whilst unlicensed, disqualified or uninsured.

### I Justice, Outcome Luck and the Criminal Law

Philosophical and legal theorists too often talk as if there is just one problem of outcome luck in the criminal law – a problem to which there should be a uniform

---

1 Thanks are due to participants in the Leicester conference on Criminal Liability for Non-Aggressive Death, for comments on a previous draft of this chapter – and special thanks to Sandra Marshall and John Stanton-Ife.

2 Penalties as specified in Schedule 2 to the Road Traffic Offenders Act 1988, as variously amended (by, most recently, the Road Safety Act 2006); I leave aside here the mandatory or discretionary disqualifications that such offences also attract.

solution across the criminal board.[3] Crudely put, the problem is: should the actual occurrence or non-occurrence of the harm associated with the offence make any difference to the criminal liability of the person who commits the offence? Slightly more precisely, the problem is: if two people act in a relevantly similar way, with relevantly similar culpability in relation to a kind of harm that properly concerns the criminal law, should the mere fact that in one case the harm ensues whilst in the other it does not ensue make a difference to whether either agent is criminally liable, or to the offence for which each is liable to be convicted, or to the sentence that each receives upon conviction?

Offences that impose 'criminal liability for non-aggressive death' provide familiar examples of this general problem. Two drivers engage in a similarly risky manoeuvre, of a kind that constitutes dangerous, or careless and inconsiderate, driving, and are at similar fault in doing so; one in fact causes death, the other does not; the latter is guilty only of dangerous, or careless, driving, whereas the former is guilty of causing death by dangerous, or by careless and inconsiderate, driving, and likely to receive a significantly heavier sentence. The other familiar example comes from criminal attempts. Two agents attempt to cause some criminal harm (death, injury, damage to another's property) with similar commitment and skill, and with similar chances of success; one in fact succeeds, whilst the other fails; the former is guilty of the completed crime (murder, or wounding, or criminal damage), whilst the latter is guilty only of attempting to commit that crime, and is likely to receive a substantially lighter sentence.[4] Another less often discussed but clearly relevant kind of example comes from offences of reckless harm for which there is no inchoate 'endangerment' version. Two agents create similar risks of damage to another's property, and are similarly reckless as to those risks; one in fact damages the property, the other does not: the former is guilty of criminal damage, whilst the latter might not be guilty of any criminal offence, unless he created the risk in a particular way – for instance by causing an explosion or by starting a fire.[5] In all

3 The label 'outcome luck' is due to Thomas Nagel (1979), 'Moral Luck', in his *Mortal Questions* (Cambridge: Cambridge University Press) p.24. On the significance of outcome luck, see more generally Schulhofer, S.J. (1974), 'Harm and Punishment: A Critique of Emphasis on Results of Conduct in the Criminal Law' 122 *University of Pennsylvania Law Review* 1497; Williams, B.A.O. (1981), 'Moral Luck', in his *Moral Luck* (Cambridge: Cambridge University Press) p.20; Honoré, A.M. (1988), 'Responsibility and Luck' 104 *Law Quarterly Review* 530; Phillips, D.Z. (1989), 'How Lucky Can You Get?', in Phillips, D.Z. and Winch, P. (eds) (1989), *Wittgenstein: Attention to Particulars* (London: Macmillan) p.165; Ashworth, A.J. (1993), 'Taking the Consequences', in Shute, S., Gardner J. and Horder, J. (eds) (1993), *Action and Value in Criminal Law* (Oxford: Oxford University Press) p.107.

4 See for example. Winch, P. (1972), 'Trying', in his *Ethics and Action* (London: Routledge) p.130; Ashworth, A.J. (1987), 'Belief, Intent and Criminal Liability' in Eekelaar, J. and Bell, J. (eds) (1987), *Oxford Essays in Jurisprudence*, 3rd Series (Oxford: Oxford University Press) 1 at 13–20; Jareborg, N. (1993), 'Criminal Attempts and Moral Luck' *Israel Law Review* 27, 213.

5 See Explosive Substances Act 1883, s.2; Model Penal Code, s.220.1(2). On inchoate endangerment offences generally, see Smith, K.J.M. (1983), 'Liability for Endangerment: English Ad Hoc Pragmatism and American Innovation' *Crim LR* 127; Horder, J. (1994),

these examples, a difference in outcome that might be a matter of pure luck makes a substantial difference to the agents' criminal liability.

I will not here rehearse all the familiar arguments for and against allowing outcome luck to play such roles in the criminal law. In particular, I will ignore consequentialist arguments, since I take the question to be primarily one of justice: we must first decide whether justice allows the law to attach such weight to outcome luck, even if we then go on to consider more pragmatic arguments that can guide policy within the constraints of justice. The justice that is at stake here is, clearly, retributive justice: if A is guilty of an offence whilst B is not, or if A is convicted of a more serious offence than is B, or if A receives a heavier sentence than does B, just because A actually caused a relevant harm whilst B did not, does A (or anyone else) have reason to claim that justice has not been done as between A and B? What justice requires here is, in general, that the criminal law treats wrongdoers in ways that are appropriate to their wrongdoing. If the wrong that A commits is relevantly similar, as a wrong, to that which B commits, then either both or neither should, in principle, face criminal liability; they should, in principle, be guilty of the same offence – an offence whose name and definition fairly labels their wrong;[6] they should, in principle, receive similar sentences that are appropriate to the character, including the seriousness, of the wrong that each committed – punishments which in some yet to be clarified sense 'fit' their crimes. Some principle of proportionality is part of that requirement of fit, if only in its modest and negative form as a principle of non-disproportionality according to which those who have been convicted of offences of similar gravity (including both *actus* and *mens* aspects) should not receive sentences that are grossly dissimilar in their severity (although it can be argued that there is more to penal fittingness than proportionality – that we should look for a more substantial fit between the characters of the offence and of the punishment).[7]

Justice-based arguments against allowing outcome luck to affect criminal liability are by now familiar. Criminal convictions and punishments condemn those on whom we impose them as wrongdoers: that is why punishments, unlike other kinds of coercive state imposition (quarantine, taxation, for example) must be grounded in and calibrated to the defendant's culpable responsibility for committing some criminal wrong. But the character and extent of our culpable responsibility cannot

---

'Varieties of Intention, Criminal Attempts and Endangerment' *Legal Studies* 14, 335; Clarkson, C.M.V. (2005), 'General Endangerment Offences: The Way Forward?' *University of Western Australia Law Review* 32, 1.

6 See Ashworth, A.J. (2006), *Principles of Criminal* Law, 5th ed. (Oxford: Oxford University Press) pp.88–90; also Tadros, V. (2005), *Criminal Responsibility* (Oxford: Oxford University Press) pp.103–115.

7 For useful discussions of the proper role of proportionality, see Morris, N. and Tonry, M. (1990), *Between Prison and Probation: Intermediate Punishments in a Rational Sentencing System* (New York: Oxford University Press) ch.4; Tonry, M. (1998), 'Interchangeability, Desert Limits and Equivalence of Function', in von Hirsch, A. and Ashworth A.J. (eds), *Principled Sentencing* (Oxford: Hart Publishing) p.291; von Hirsch, A. and Ashworth, A.J. (2005), *Proportionate Sentencing* (Oxford: Oxford University Press). On proportionality and appropriateness see Duff, R.A. (2001), *Punishment, Communication and Community* (New York: Oxford University Press) ch.4.

depend on factors that are matters of luck or chance, since luck and chance negate the kind of control on which responsibility depends: the lucky fact that your attempt to wound another person failed cannot 'redound to your credit',[8] in that it cannot render you less culpable; the unlucky fact that my careless driving caused someone's death cannot, likewise, redound to my discredit, in that it cannot render me more culpable than one whose similarly careless driving causes no such harm.[9] Such arguments sometimes appeal to philosophically dubious claims about the concept of action (that the agent's action, strictly speaking, includes only what was within his control, and thus does not include outcomes which depended on luck), or about the extent to which luck negates control;[10] but they still seem forceful, when we ask ourselves whether and how it can be just for the criminal law to treat two agents so differently on the basis solely of the fact that, by sheer chance or luck, one of them actually caused a criminal harm whilst the other did not.

I will not tackle such arguments head on here.[11] Instead, I want to take for granted some kind of communicative conception of criminal punishment, according to which a central – if not the primary – function of punishment is to communicate to the offender (and to others) the censure that his crime deserves, and to ask how the content, character and severity of that censure could be affected by the actual outcomes of the offender's action.[12] But I also want to look in a more discriminating way at different kinds and contexts of outcome luck, especially at the difference between outcome luck in the context of attempts (attacks), and outcome luck in the context of endangerment. We will see that outcome luck affects our moral responses to wrongdoers in different ways in these different contexts: the question then will be whether we can or should try to reflect such differences in the criminal law.

## II Attacks, Endangerments and Outcome Luck

An attack is an action that is intended to injure another's interests: it is structured by a direct intention to harm, whether as an end or as a means; it will, from the agent's point of view, have failed if the intended harm does not ensue. Endangerment, by contrast, is a matter of creating a risk of harm as a side-effect of one's intended action: the action is not intended to cause harm, but might do so. An attack necessarily involves *mens rea* (although an attacker might still of course have a defence): if

8 *Carmichael* [1930] 22 Cr App R 142 at 143.

9 See especially Ashworth, n.3 and 4 above; also Ashworth, A.J. (1988), 'Criminal Attempts and the Role of Resulting Harm under the Code, and in the Common Law' *Rutgers Law Journal* 19, 725.

10 For critical discussion see Duff, R.A. (1996), *Criminal Attempts* (Oxford: Oxford University Press) ch.12; Moore, M.S. (1997), *Placing Blame* (Oxford: Oxford University Press) ch.5.

11 Largely because I have little to add to my previous discussion of them, above n.10, chs.12, 13.2.

12 For different communicative accounts (the differences between which need not concern us here), see von Hirsch, A. (1993), *Censure and Sanctions* (Oxford: Oxford University Press); Duff, above, n.7.

harm is not intended, the action cannot constitute an attack. Endangerment need not involve *mens rea*: I can endanger others by my actions not only non-intentionally, but through non-culpable inadvertence or accident.[13]

Although the distinction between attacks and endangerments can be drawn fairly precisely, in relation to any particular criminal harm we can identify a range of different cases along a complex spectrum. At one end we have what can be called a pure attack: the agent acts with the intention of bringing about the very harm specified in the offence definition – death in the case of homicide, or damage to another's property in the case of criminal damage. At the other end we have what can be called a case of pure or mere endangerment: the agent acts in a way that in fact creates some risk (a risk significant enough to be worth taking note of) of the harm in question (death, damage to another's property), but has no intention either to cause any such harm or to create any such risk. In between those two extremes, cases can vary along several dimensions.

As far as attacks are concerned, one kind of variation concerns what is intended. Perhaps the agent intends a harm less serious than, although still related to, the harm specified in the offence definition: he intends to injure rather than to kill, for instance. Or perhaps he intends to create a risk of harm rather than actually to cause harm – to endanger life or property, rather than actually to kill or to damage. Such intended endangerments still constitute attacks, since they are intended to cause at least the secondary harm of risk or danger;[14] the question then is how we should determine the agent's criminal liability if the harm actually ensues. Another kind of variation concerns the agent's chances of success – how certain, or unlikely, it was that he would actually bring about the intended harm: that kind of variation is, however, less significant here than it is in the case of pure endangerment, since the agent is 'intent' on causing the harm, however unlikely it might be that he will succeed. This reflects a larger point: that, at least in the pure case, the action is structured by its relationship to the intended harm. Success is the core or paradigm case, by comparison with which cases in which the harm does not ensue can be seen as the failures that, from the agent's point of view, they are.[15] This suggests that when we ask about the significance of outcome luck, the natural question to ask in relation to attacks is whether the agent whose criminal attempt fails deserves or should receive a condemnation and punishment lighter than he would have received had

13 See further Duff, R.A. (2005), 'Criminalizing Endangerment', in Duff, R.A. and Green, S.P. (eds) (2005), *Defining Crimes: Essays on the Criminal Law's Special Part* (Oxford: Oxford University Press) p.43.

14 See, notoriously, *Hyam* [1975] AC 55, in particular Lord Hailsham's claim that one who intends to expose another to a serious risk of death or grievous bodily harm is guilty of murder if she actually causes death (at 79). See also *Chief Constable of Avon and Somerset v Shimmen* [1987] 84 Cr App R 7: D clearly intended to create a risk of damaging a shop window, when he tried to impress his friends with his martial arts skills by showing them how close he could kick to the window without hitting it. On whether we should see risk as harm, see Finkelstein, C.O. (2003), 'Is Risk a Harm?' *University of Pennsylvania Law Review* 151, 963; Duff, above n.13, at 51–52.

15 There are of course variations along this dimension of success or failure as well: how close to success did the agent come; did he cause some lesser harm?

he succeeded: we ask, that is, whether failure makes a penal discount appropriate, rather than whether success should constitute an aggravating factor.

As for endangerments, the obvious dimensions of variation (if we keep constant the harm that is risked) concern probability, reasonableness and foresight. The risk can vary from very low to near or actual certainty;[16] the taking of it can be wholly reasonable, or utterly unreasonable, or something in between those extremes; the agent might be quite unaware of any risk, or aware of some risk but not of its gravity, or accurately aware of the risk she creates; and if she is unaware of it, that might be a matter of non-culpable inadvertence, or of culpable negligence – which can itself range from minor negligence to gross negligence. There is also of course the key matter of actual harm: does the harm that is risked actually ensue; or does a lesser harm related to it ensue, as when an action that endangers life actually causes some lesser injury; or does no material harm ensue? We can see here one important difference between attacks and endangerments: attacks are structured by the prospective harm in a way that endangerments are not. From the endangering agent's perspective, if the anticipated harm does not ensue, that does not render her action a failure, since the action was not oriented towards that outcome; she can indeed be relieved that she has caused no harm (I will return to this point shortly). From the point of view of a reasonable observer, particularly if the risk was one that it was unreasonable for the agent to take, the risk might be salient: what strikes me about the reckless driver's conduct is not its purposeful character as aimed at getting him to his meeting faster, but the danger it creates to other road users. But the risk is still one that he takes in the course of doing something else; and there is still room for him, as well as for us, to hope that it is not actualised. This then suggests that in asking about the significance of outcome luck in the context of endangerment, the natural question to ask is not whether the agent who does not cause harm should receive a lighter sentence, or should be convicted of a lesser offence, than one who does cause harm, but whether the agent who does cause harm should be punished more severely, or be convicted of a more serious offence, than one who does not: rather than the absence of harm serving to mitigate the seriousness of the wrong, as in the case of failed attempt, the occurrence of the harm (if luck can properly make a difference) aggravates what would otherwise have been an offence of mere endangerment.

(It might be argued that the difference here depends not on the difference between intended and non-intended harm, but solely on differences in the degree of (perceived) probability: the more likely that harm is to ensue, the more we are inclined to see its non-occurrence as a mitigating factor rather than its occurrence as an aggravating factor. But intended actions can be undertaken with only slim chances of success, that is, when the prospective harm is, and is known to be, less likely to ensue than it is in many cases of endangerment; yet we would, I think, still

16 I would count an action that the agent is certain will cause harm as a side-effect as a limiting case of endangerment, not as an attack (so-called 'oblique intention' is not a species of intention); but nothing in what follows hangs on this.

see and respond to such intended actions in the light of success as the paradigm – as we would not do with endangering actions, even when the risk is very high.)

Even if what I have said about the differences between attacks and endangerments, and about the different ways in which questions about the significance of outcome luck figure in each context, is right, it does not yet show that those questions are not, in the end, versions of the same question, to which we should give the same answer – either that outcome luck can properly affect liability, or that it cannot do so – across the board. However, those differences underpin further, more significant differences in the kinds of response that are available to or appropriate for the agent, and others, in each kind of context; and these differences do bear more directly on questions about how such agents should fare in a communicative system of trials and punishments. For simplicity's sake, I will focus in what follows on examples lying at or towards either end of the spectrum: on pure attacks, and on pure endangerments that create only a relatively modest, but still unreasonable, risk of harm, and whose agents are negligent rather than entirely non-culpable in creating them. We certainly should not assume that what applies to these cases will also apply to cases further from the ends of the spectrum along any of the variety of dimensions noted above; but they provide a useful and manageable starting point for discussion.

As 'reasonable' observers, that is as people who share the attitudes and expectations of the 'reasonable person' to whom the criminal law so often appeals as a normative standard,[17] we will feel relieved if the prospective harm does not ensue, both in the case of an attack and in the case of endangerment:[18] 'Thank goodness', we might think to ourselves, 'his shot missed', or 'Thank goodness, there was no car coming the other way'. However, our responses to the agent – both our informal moral responses and thus also the kinds of response that might be appropriate for a communicative criminal process – are conditioned not merely by our own direct responses to the occurrence or non-occurrence of the prospective harm, but by the responses available to the agent: sometimes by his actual response to the occurrence or non-occurrence of the harm, but also and for present purposes more significantly by the responses that his action leaves room for, by the responses that we think he should have – and by the extent to which the former include the latter. These obscurely expressed points should become clearer in what follows.

If an agent engages in an attack, he must see the non-occurrence of the intended harm as a source of regret, frustration and disappointment: that is how we respond to the failure of our projects. There is no room, from within the action as he engages in it, for him to be relieved if it fails: however reluctant he might have been to embark

17 This is not the place to discuss the proper role and meaning of the 'reasonable person' in criminal law. (see generally Moran, M. (2003), *Rethinking the Reasonable Person: An Egalitarian Reconstruction of the Objective Standard* (Oxford: Oxford University Press)). All we need notice is, first, that to ask whether a reasonable person would have acted or reacted as this person did is just a way (sometimes a confusing way) of asking whether this person's action or reaction was reasonable; and, second, that in this context reasonableness is a matter of moral disposition rather than of cognitive competence.

18 I leave aside the complication that, if an attack is justified, we would not feel such relief at its failure; we can focus here on attacks for which there is neither justification nor excuse.

on this course, once he embarks on it, genuinely intending to complete it (as distinct from going through the motions in order to give the impression of someone who intends to complete it), he cannot hope for its failure or be relieved if it fails. After the event he might be relieved; 'Thank goodness', he might then think, 'my shot missed'. But he can think that only if he has undergone a radical change of practical or cognative orientation: he must have foresworn or repented his former intention, for whatever reason, if he is to be relieved at his failure to carry it out.

From the point of view of a reasonable person, however, relief is precisely what the attacker should feel if his attack fails: for that is the normatively appropriate response to the frustration of a wrongful enterprise. What the attacker should feel is, therefore, not something that is available to him, not a response for which there is logical room, from within the action as he engages in it. The relief that he should feel, it is worth noting, is not quite the relief that our imagined reasonable observer feels. The observer's relief is that of a detached, but interested, spectator: she is relieved that the harm or the evil (the death or the murder) did not take place. By contrast, the agent's relief, the relief felt by the repentant agent after the event, is not such a detached response to what happens in the world: he is relieved not merely that V was not harmed (as he might be relieved at seeing someone walk away unharmed from a dangerous situation), but that he did not harm V. Such 'agent-relief' is analogous to the agent-regret that I properly feel when I actually cause harm:[19] I am relieved that I was not the agent of this harm or evil – and, in the case of wrongful actions, relieved that I do not now have that harm or evil on my conscience.[20] The failed attacker should, we think, come to feel such relief: that is what he will come to feel if he repents his attack as he should, and comes to have the kind of regard for his victim that his attack so radically failed to manifest. Our responses to him, at least our informal moral responses, will then naturally be conditioned by that thought: we will condemn his attack; but we will also express our relief at its failure, and we will encourage him to regard its failure as a matter for relief rather than disappointment.

Matters are different in the case of endangerment, since the agent's action does then leave room, as the attacker's action does not, for relief if the prospective harm does not ensue (and regret if it does ensue). There is nothing intrinsic to an endangering action that commits the agent to regarding the non-occurrence of the prospective harm as constituting the action's failure, or as a source of disappointment or frustration; it would be consistent with the attitudes intrinsic to the action as she intends it for her to regret the occurrence of the harm, and to be relieved at its non-occurrence;[21] indeed, her action leaves room, as the attacker's does not, for the hope that the harm will not ensue. It is true that such a hope, or prospective relief if the harm does not occur, is not *integral* to the action of a negligent or reckless agent, in

19 See Williams, above n.3 at 27–31.

20 Compare Winch, above n.4 at 144–150.

21 The attitudes 'intrinsic' to the action are not attitudes that might (or might not) be inferred from it as a matter of empirical discovery – they are not mental states separate from, and only contingently related to, the action. Rather, they are attitudes that are manifested in, and part constituted by, the action as it is intended and carried out: see further Duff above n.13 at 45–47.

so far as it is negligent or reckless: her action is not structured by a concern to avoid causing harm in the way that the action of someone paying due attention and taking due care is structured, such that the occurrence of the harm marks at least the partial failure of the action. A careful agent intends not merely to achieve X (the outcome that gives her action its positive point) but to achieve X without bringing about Y (the harm that it could cause); her hope that the harm will not ensue, and regret if it does, is integral to the structure of her action as she intends it, and to the precautions that she takes in acting as she does. A negligent or reckless agent might of course take some precautions – one can be careless without being without any care at all; in so far as she does take care, such hope and relief, or regret, are integral to her action. But, if she is negligent or reckless, she takes less care or pays less attention than she should; to that extent her action is not structured by, does not itself display, the kind of hope, and the prospective relief or regret, that it should.[22] However, her action does leave room for such hope, relief or regret, albeit as somewhat detached rather than as properly practical attitudes; such attitudes are available to her without abandoning her intended course of action.

As properly concerned, 'reasonable' observers, we will think that a negligent agent should be relieved if the prospective harm does not ensue, and distressed if it does; we will also recognise that whilst those attitudes are not, as we have just seen, integral to her negligent action, they are not at odds with it or ruled out by it. In our response to her, we can therefore address her as someone who, even without any manifest rejection of her own past conduct, can be expected to feel such relief or distress for herself: we can advert to what she has done, or draw her attention to it if she has not noticed it for herself, in the expectation that she will feel and exhibit such responses without the need for further prompting or persuading. 'Look what you have done', we might say when harm is actually caused; or 'Look what you almost did', if the risk was not actualised: once she sees what she did, or what she almost did, such locutions assume, she will be suitably distressed or relieved. Indeed, given the principle of charitable interpretation,[23] whose role in moral life is analogous to that of the presumption of innocence in criminal law, we *should* make such an assumption in our response to her: we should assume that she has such proper dispositions of attitude, unless and until her actions show that she does not.[24]

22 Aristotle claimed that an act is truly 'involuntary' only if it is immediately followed by regret as soon as the agent realises what she has done; in the absence of such regret it is merely 'non-voluntary' (*Nicomachean Ethics* III.1). This reflected his focus on dispositions of character rather than on actions as such, but we can see how the prospect or promise of regret if harm is caused is integral to the actions of the careful agent, in a way in which it is not integral to – though it is not ruled out by – those of the careless agent.

23 Some such principle is, I take it, essential to the possibility of any kind of society: compare Dimock, S. (1997), 'Retributivism and Trust' *Law and Philosophy* 16, 37, on the essential role of trust in social life; see also Davidson, D. (2001), 'Radical Interpretation', in his *Inquiries into Truth and Interpretation* (Oxford: Oxford University Press) on the role of a principle of charity in interpreting others' beliefs.

24 This is, at least, true when we are dealing with relative strangers (which is the moral context most closely analogous to that of the criminal law); matters are more complicated when we are dealing with familiars. I comment on this point below, at the end of this section.

We will also, of course, think that she ought to repent and disavow her own negligent action – a response that is ruled out by the action as she performed it in the same way that relief at failure is ruled out by the attacker's action; and that response can be available to her only through a change of heart – a change that might be induced in her precisely by her clear(er) recognition of the risk that she created or the harm that she caused. When we address an attacker, however, it is not just the repentant disavowal of his own action that we cannot assume he will make; we cannot assume that he will feel a suitable relief at the failure or his attack, or distress at its success, since such responses are not only not integral to, but are ruled out by, his commission of the attack.

These differences between attacks and negligent endangerment – the way in which in attacks success is the paradigm, whereas in endangerment it is the non-occurrence of harm that is the paradigm; differences in the extent to which we can or cannot assume that the agent would react with appropriate distress or relief to the occurrence or non-occurrence of the harm – will in various ways condition the content and the tone of our responses to the agent. The way in which we address a failed attacker, for instance, will be conditioned by our awareness that he was intent on doing the harm that he (luckily) failed to do; by our relief that he failed, and our hope that he will come to share it; but also by our recognition that he will be able to share it only if he repents and disavows his attack. Our response will properly differ from our response to one whose similar attack succeeds, even if there is no relevant difference in the seriousness or competence of their attempts, in their motives or further intentions, or in other culpability-affecting factors, just because it is partly structured by the relief that is appropriate to the attack's failure.[25]

What matters is not just that our relief might incline us towards leniency: it is also and crucially that the attacker *should* be relieved, since he *will* be relieved if he comes to see and repent his attack as he should. To repent his attack is to (re)gain the concern or respect for his intended victim that his attack denied, and such concern or respect will be expressed in relief that the attack failed. The 'But, thank goodness, he failed' that qualifies our own response to the failed attack is therefore not something quite separate from our critical moral response to the attacker as a wrongdoer; if that moral response is intended, as it should be, to elicit from him an appropriate moral response to his wrong, it must include as one of its aspects the 'thank goodness he (I) failed' that is integral to such an appropriate moral response. To be an attempted murderer, fraudster, vandal or whatever is bad enough: but at least – we think, and he should come to think – he did not become a murderer, fraudster or vandal; he did not become the agent of another's death or loss, and although that does not 'redound to his credit', in that he cannot claim it as an achievement, it should condition both our and his response to what he has done.

The way in which we address a careless endangerer will be conditioned in different ways by the occurrence or non-occurrence of the prospective harm, since

25 See further Duff, above n.10, ch.12. The view offered here depends on the further argument, which some would reject, that the actions of successful and of failed attackers are different, as actions on which moral attention focuses: the former murders, or defrauds, or destroys, whilst the latter does not.

we will be able to address her from the start as someone who will – we can assume – share in the appropriate responses of distress or relief (although hers will be an agent's distress or relief, whereas ours is not). In particular, the manifest character of her action does not suggest that we must try to *bring* her to be distressed if it causes harm; we can, rather, expect to be able to share that distress with her (as soon as she realises, if she did not already realise, that she did cause the harm). There is, of course, something else that we might need to persuade her of, as much as or more than we need to persuade an attacker: that she should not have acted as she did. For it is quite possible to regret having caused some harm, or to be relieved that I did not, without seeing the action that caused or that risked causing that harm as being for that reason wrongful – which is to say that it is possible to regret having caused the harm without feeling any remorse for having done so.[26] But in trying to persuade her of that, we could appeal to the reluctance to cause harm that would inform her relief at not causing it and her distress at causing it. There will still be an important difference between 'Look what you have done' and 'Look what you almost did', because there is an important moral difference that both the agent and observers should recognise, and to which they should respond, between actually harming others and only endangering them; if our moral responses to our and others' actions are to be sensitive to morally significant aspects of those actions, they must be sensitive to, *inter alia*, the harm that is or is not caused. My suggestion here, however, is first, that that difference is a different difference from that between our responses to the successful and the failed attacker; and second, that if we can assume that the agent will herself already be distressed by the harm that she actually caused, our response need not include a forceful attempt to induce such distress in her. We will not try to talk her out of such distress – assuming that we agree that her negligent conduct did cause the harm, and that her distress is not disproportionately excessive;[27] but the tone of our response can be one of sharing in the distress that she already feels, rather than of trying to bring her to feel it.

Readers whose main interest is in how the criminal law should deal with outcome luck might by now be a little impatient. Whether or not I am right about these subtleties and nuances in our responses to attackers and to endangerers, it is not clear how they bear on the criminal law, since criminal courts cannot be expected to deal in such niceties. I will argue in the following section that the way in which the criminal law deals – in its offence definitions, in its criminal process and in sentencing – with those who endanger others should be conditioned by the moral differences discussed in this section; but as a final prelude to that argument, I should

26 There might be something else that we need to persuade her to recognise and accept that is less likely to be an issue with the attacker – that she did cause the harm: it is all too familiar a temptation to try to deny (even to ourselves) our own culpable agency in relation to the harm for which others seek to hold us responsible – for instance by denying lack of due care, or by seeking to shift responsibility onto others. But that reluctance to avoid admitting that I caused the harm can itself reflect, in a distorted way, a proper moral attitude to the significance of the harm: I try to deny responsibility for it because to admit responsibility would commit me to a painful kind of agent regret and remorse.

27 I cannot pursue here the interesting questions that arise when we ask what should count as 'excessive'.

respond to a likely criticism from those whose interest is more in our moral lives and dealings with each other than in the criminal law. For I have talked as if we have no knowledge of the agent's own response to the harm she has caused or to the risk she has created – that we have to work on assumptions based on what her endangering action itself did or did not imply; but of course that is very often not the case, since we often have as much information about, as much direct knowledge of, her response as we have about or of her original action. We know whether she is appropriately distressed or relieved – we do not have to make assumptions; we can therefore adapt the tone and the content of our response not merely to her action, but to what we know to be her own response to it. My account of how we would respond might fit some cases in which we are dealing with strangers, but does not fit many of our mutual dealings. Furthermore, it might be said, even when we do not know whether she is appropriately moved, we have no good reason to presume or to expect that she is: her action might not preclude an appropriate response, but surely it undermines any reason we might have had to expect one.[28]

That criticism is apt in the context of our more intimate dealings with our families, friends, colleagues and others with whom we have more or less personal relationships. The point is not merely that in such dealings we are more likely to know, or to be easily able to find out, how the other person in fact responds to the harm that she has caused or risked causing: it is that we have, in virtue of our relationship, a proper interest in how she actually feels about what she has done; that relationship requires a willingness to be in various ways open about our attitudes or feelings, and makes it appropriate to inquire more closely into each others' attitudes and feelings than is proper between strangers. The criminal law, however, is concerned with our mutual dealings not as friends, lovers, family members or colleagues, but as citizens; and in a liberal polity that eschews more ambitiously intimate forms of communitarianism, citizens – at least in their formal and law-governed dealings – preserve a certain respectful distance from each other. That is why privacy is such an important value for liberals: activities, thought and feelings that might be the business of our friends, families or colleagues are simply not the business of our fellow citizens as such, or of the law that regulates our activities as citizens.[29] As we will see in the following section, one implication of this respect for privacy is that the criminal law's responses should depend on what is implied by a criminal action, rather than on what might be known of the agent's subsequent response to it.

## III Endangerment, Outcome Luck and the Criminal Law

I will not pursue the question of whether and how outcome luck should affect the law's treatment of attackers here, since our concern here is with liability for non-aggressive death. All I would claim here, on the basis of the discussion in the previous section,

28 Thanks to John Stanton-Ife for pressing me on this point.

29 Hence the powerful resonances of the Wolfenden Committee's comment that certain kinds of conduct, however immoral they might be thought to be, are 'in brief and crude terms, not the law's business': *Report of the Committee on Homosexual Offences and Prostitution* (1957) (Cmnd. 247; London: Stationery Office) para. 61.

is that we should not assume that the question of outcome luck must be answered in the same way for attacks and for endangerments. One question is whether, why, or to what extent we should reduce the seriousness of the crime for which an attacker is convicted, or the severity of his punishment, in virtue simply of the fact that his attack failed. The other question is whether, why, or how far we should increase the seriousness of the crime for which an endangerer is convicted, or the severity of her punishment, in virtue simply of the fact that she caused the prospective harm. In both cases, of course, what makes the difference is the occurrence or non-occurrence of the harm that was (in the case of an attack) intended or (in the case of endangerment) risked; but I have argued that in extra-legal contexts that difference makes different differences to our moral responses to attacks and to endangerments.

To see what difference the occurrence of harm might properly make to the criminal law's treatment of the endangerer, we should first note the way in which the criminal law of a liberal polity focuses primarily on criminal actions (or omissions), rather than on the motives or dispositions of character from which they flow, or on the perpetrator's responses to them. This is the normative force of the slogan that criminal liability is, or ought to be, for actions. Obscure though the precise meaning and implications of that slogan might be,[30] it expresses a central liberal thought: that whilst the criminal law is properly concerned with the ways in which we make a wrongful impact on our shared social world, it should not seek to intrude too far into the deeper aspects or dimensions of our lives and conduct. It can properly take an interest in those practical attitudes or motives that are directly manifested in our actions, insofar as they make a significant difference to the character and meaning of those actions, but should not seek to explore our moral character more deeply than that.[31] It can properly seek to persuade offenders to repent their wrongdoing; but it should not inquire into the depth or sincerity of any expression of repentance as a determinant of conviction or sentence.[32]

30 See for example, Moore, M.S. (1993), *Act and Crime* (Oxford: Oxford University Press); for a useful critique, see Husak, D.N. (1998), 'Does Criminal Liability Require an Act?', in Duff, R.A. (ed.) (1998), *Philosophy and the Criminal Law* (Cambridge: Cambridge University Press) p.60, see further Duff, R.A. (2004), 'Action, the Act Requirement and Criminal Liability' in Hyman, J. and Steward, H.C. (eds), *Agency and Action* (Cambridge: Cambridge University Press) p.69.

31 This should not be read as implying that we can draw a sharp distinction between action and character: that distinction is to a significant degree flexible, and is negotiated or constructed rather than discovered. Thus to create an aggravated offence of 'racially or religiously aggravated assault' that is committed by someone whose assault 'demonstrates' the hostility towards V's racial or religious group that motivated the assault (see Crime and Disorder Act 1998, ss.28–29, as amended by Anti-terrorism, Crime and Security Act 2001, s.39) need not be to punish motive as distinct from action; its implicit claim is, rather, that such a motive, when demonstrated in the action, makes a significant and relevant difference to the character and wrongfulness of the action.

32 For a development of this idea in the context of punishment and apology, see Bennett, C. (2006), 'Taking the Sincerity Out of Saying Sorry: Restorative Justice as Ritual' *Journal of Applied Philosophy* 23, 127.

If we put that thought together with the values that are reflected in the presumption of innocence, we can conclude that insofar as an offender's attitudes or responses bear on her culpability, or on the character and seriousness of her wrongdoing, the criminal law should make the most favourable or charitable assumptions about her attitudes or responses that are consistent with what her criminal action itself displayed. That is, if her action itself displayed, for instance, a hatred of a particular racial or religious group, that could in principle count as an aggravating factor; similarly, if it displayed an utter practical indifference to the interests of a victim whom she was attacking, she can count in law as being reckless as to the harm that she foreseeably caused to those interests – even if she herself did not advert to the risk that she would cause such harm.[33] If, on the other hand, her action did not display such an utter indifference to the harm that it might cause; if, although it did not display the degree of care to avoid harm that we expect of each other, it left open the possibility that she would be appropriately distressed by the occurrence of the harm (and appropriately relieved by its non-occurrence): then the law should treat her as if she was thus distressed (or relieved).

To put the point slightly differently, the criminal law should assume that those whom it binds, including those who appear as defendants in its courts, are 'reasonable' people unless and until their actions prove otherwise – and when their actions do prove otherwise, it should ascribe only that kind and degree of unreasonableness that their actions irrefutably displayed. ('Reasonableness' in this context is a heavily normative notion: the reasonable person is one who *inter alia* has and displays that modest concern and respect for the interests of others that the criminal law properly requires of us.) Now a defendant's actions might have displayed a criminal lack of such concern and respect – if, for instance, he attacked a protected interest, without justification or excuse; or if he recklessly endangered such an interest; or perhaps if he negligently endangered such an interest: such attacks and endangerments not merely fail to manifest appropriate concern and respect – they are inconsistent with it. However, a central difference between attacks and endangerments that section II highlighted now becomes even more important: that whereas the attacker's action precludes relief at its failure or distress at its success, the endangerer's action does not preclude relief at the non-occurrence of the harm that is risked, or distress at its occurrence. The argument sketched above therefore suggests that the criminal law, and the criminal court in which the attacker or the endangerer appears, should treat them differently in this respect: in particular, whilst it must treat the attacker as someone who is (absent a radical change of heart) frustrated by the attack's failure, it should treat the endangerer as someone who is appropriately distressed by the realisation that she has actually caused the relevant harm.

In moral contexts, especially in dealing with people whom we know, there might well be room to inquire into the agent's actual attitudes and responses: to distinguish the person who is genuinely distressed from one who is unmoved, or not moved in the way or to the extent that she should be, by the harm she caused,

---

33 This is, I think, the best way to understand the way in which recklessness need not always require conscious risk-taking – and the English doctrine of implied malice: see Duff, R.A. (1990), *Intention, Agency and Criminal Liability* (Oxford: Blackwell) ch.7.

and to tailor our responses to her accordingly.[34] But if we take seriously the limits noted above on the scope or reach of a liberal criminal law, we cannot allow the courts to engage in such inquiries: they must work only with what was displayed in and by the defendant's criminal actions. Since the negligent endangerer's action did not rule out a proper distress at the actual occurrence of the harm (or relief if it did not occur), the court must therefore presume that the defendant was in this respect innocent, that is, that she did not lack this proper kind of response. Given proof of an attack, an action structured by the intention to harm, we cannot presume that the successful attacker was properly distressed by the harm that he caused, or that the failed attacker was properly relieved: the presumption that he would have responded in such ways is defeated by proof of his attack. But given only proof of an act of culpable endangerment, we can still presume such appropriate responses in the agent: not because she has given us any positive evidence of them, but because proof of her endangering action does not defeat the presumption that she is in that respect and to that extent innocent. It has been proved that she acted unreasonably, in taking a risk that a reasonable person would not have taken: but proof of that species of unreasonableness in action is not proof of unreasonableness in all her responses to her actions; it should not be taken to defeat the presumption of reasonableness in those responses (I comment later on whether we should treat that presumption as rebuttable or as irrebuttable).[35]

This line of thought suggests that whilst there is good reason for the criminal law to distinguish between mere endangerment that causes no material harm and endangerment that does cause harm (at least when the harm is relatively serious), this need not involve imposing *much* heavier punishments on those who actually caused the harm. I suggested above, and have argued elsewhere, that the difference between causing and not causing harm is a relevant difference in the agents' actions – a difference that should be marked in our moral responses to the agents, and in the criminal law's dealings with them. If my attack succeeds, I have killed, or wounded, or damaged; if it fails, I have only tried to do those things. If my dangerous action causes no harm, I have still endangered others – a wrong for which I can properly be condemned and should feel remorse (of a seriousness appropriate to the kind and seriousness of the risk). But if the risk I take is actualised, my action is one of harming: I have, albeit unintentionally, killed or injured or damaged, and I should see that as a salient, and aggravating, feature of what I did – I have done something worse than I would have done had the risk not been actualised. The moral difference between 'Look what you might have done' as said to a mere endangerer, and 'Look what you did' as said to someone who actually caused the harm can in principle be

34 That is why, as I noted at the end of s.2, the discussion in that section was from a moral point of view very limited, since it did not allow for this possibility; but it was still appropriate to our dealings with strangers.

35 There is an analogous question, which I cannot pursue here, about whether an offender's repentance should constitute grounds for a lighter sentence: see Tasioulas, J. (2006), 'Punishment and Repentance' *Philosophy* 81, 279; (2007), 'Repentance and the Liberal State' *Ohio State Journal of Criminal Law* 4, 487; in partial response see Duff, R.A. (2007), 'The Intrusion of Mercy' *Ohio State Journal of Criminal Law* 4, 361 at 381–387.

properly reflected in the criminal law's definitions and individuations of offences, for instance by distinguishing dangerous driving of various types from causing death by such driving, as distinct offences; the difference in the seriousness of wrong committed can also be reflected in the sentences imposed. I have not defended this claim in enough detail here;[36] but what concerns me now is the suggestion that the increase in sentence should be only modest.

The reason for this modesty is that if the court should assume, as I have argued it should, that the defendant was and is appropriately distressed by the harm they caused, the sentence should aim not to persuade them to be thus distressed, but rather to confirm or to reinforce the distress that they already feel (as well as marking the wrongfulness of taking the risk in the first place, which is an aim common to the sentences imposed on the mere endangerer and on the harm-causer). The point is not that they might, since the event, have come to be distressed as they should be (in the way that an attacker might, given a change of heart, come to be either relieved at their failure or distressed by their success); it is rather that the court must assume that they were so distressed as soon as they realised what they had done, without any change of heart. It is true that, if we focus on the harm that is caused, there is an enormous difference between one whose momentary inattention luckily causes no harm, and one whose similar momentary inattention causes another's death; but the court must assume that the agent themselves marked and responded appropriately to that difference – which suggests that only a modest increase in sentence is needed to mark, as it were, the court's endorsement of that response. If this is right, then the increases in maximum sentence provided by our existing laws are unwarranted: the difference between, for instance, careless driving that fortunately causes no harm and careless driving that tragically causes death does not warrant a difference between a fine and five years in prison, and the same is true of the other ways in which the law takes note of such outcome luck.[37]

Much more work is of course needed to flesh this suggestion out (and to render it plausible), but hope that I have said enough to show that it is worth exploring. I should end, however, with two brief comments.

The first concerns the provisions for unlicensed, disqualified or uninsured drivers who cause death.[38] What justifies increasing the endangerer's punishment if they cause death is that the causation of death actualises the risk that made their conduct wrongfully dangerous: what we say to them is 'Look what you have done by your carelessness'. Now it is true that if the unlicensed (or disqualified or uninsured) driver had not been driving, they would not have caused death (at least in that way); and given that they were unlicensed, disqualified or uninsured, it follows that if they had not been driving whilst unlicensed, disqualified or uninsured they would not have caused death. But it is still not true that they caused death by driving whilst unlicensed, disqualified or uninsured, unless it was their being

36 But see further above n.10, chs.12, 13.2.

37 See at n.2 above for the English provisions in relation to driving. Compare also, for instance, the difference in the Model Penal Code between recklessness-based manslaughter, as a second degree felony, and reckless endangerment, as a misdemeanour (ss.210.3, 211.2).

38 See Road Safety Act 2006, s.21, and text at n.2 above.

unlicensed, disqualified or uninsured that made their driving especially dangerous. Now there is of course *some* connection between being unlicensed, or disqualified, and driving dangerously: under an appropriate system, being licensed gives both drivers and others some assurance that drivers are competent to drive safely, and being disqualified is often the result of driving dangerously or being incompetent to drive safely. However, there is no such connection between being uninsured and driving dangerously, because insurance has to do with paying for harm caused rather than with avoiding causing it; and even in the cases of driving when unlicensed or disqualified it is far from clear that the connection is close enough to treat the causation of death as the actualisation of a risk that made the driving wrongful in the first place.

The second comment concerns a question noted above. The court must presume that a defendant guilty of harmful endangerment was suitably distressed by the harm that they caused: but should that presumption be rebuttable? Suppose that a negligent defendant makes it clear, at the time that they cause the harm, or when questioned by the police or in court, that they are not distressed by the harm they caused (or not in the appropriate way; they might be annoyed that it has now caused them inconvenience): why should the court not be allowed to attend to that fact, as a reason for increasing their sentence? (Given the argument so far, this is the way in which the question should arise – not as the question of whether some suitable display of distress should serve to mitigate the sentence.) It is tempting to say it should, but we must resist that temptation: for the offender's sentence, within the kind of liberal system of criminal law that I am concerned with here, should still depend on the character and meaning of their criminal action; and it remains true of this offender that their action did not itself display the kind of utter unconcern that they now display. If we begin to allow sentence severity to be determined in part by the way in which the offender responded after the event to their commission of the offence, we start down a dangerous road – dangerous not just because of the incentives to dishonesty that such sentencing practices provide, but because they subvert the criminal law's, and the criminal courts', proper focus on the actions that constitute crimes.[39]

39 Compare, again, discussions of whether an offender's repentance should be taken to justify a reduced punishment: see n.34 above; also Nussbaum, M. (1993), 'Equity and Mercy' *Philosophy and Public Affairs* 22, 83; Garvey, S.P. (1996), '"As the Gentle Rain from Heaven": Mercy in Capital Sentencing' *Cornell Law Review* 81, 989; (2004) 'Is it Wrong to Commute Death Row? Retribution, Atonement and Mercy' *North Carolina Law Review* 82, 1319; Tasioulas, J. (2003), 'Mercy' *Proceedings of the Aristotelian Society* 103, 101; Bennett, C. (2004), 'The Limits of Mercy' *Ratio* 17, 1; Murphy, J.G. (2007), 'Remorse, Apology and Mercy' *Ohio State Journal of Criminal Law* 4, 423.

Chapter 5

# Corporate Manslaughter: Need for a Special Offence?

C.M.V. Clarkson

## I Introduction

When someone is killed as a result of unsafe corporate activities, both the company and individual directors or managers can be criminally liable under the special offences contained in the Health and Safety at Work etc. Act 1974[1] (HSWA). Further, it was well-established that corporations, as well as individual managers, could be convicted of the general offence of manslaughter. This common law offence of 'manslaughter by gross negligence' has now been abolished by the Corporate Manslaughter and Corporate Homicide Act 2007.[2] Instead, corporations and other 'organisations' to which the Act applies will now be liable for an offence of 'corporate manslaughter' (in England, Wales and Northern Ireland) or 'corporate homicide' (in Scotland).[3] The question for this chapter is whether such a special offence is necessary. To assess this, two issues need to be addressed.

1. Given the existence of the HSWA offences, why do we need the law to reflect the fact that death has been caused?
2. If that death should be reflected in the crime charged, why was a special homicide offence needed rather than simply relying on the general law of manslaughter?

After each of these issues has been considered, the ambit and nature of the new offence will be assessed.

## II Need to Reflect Death

Corporate activities have long been subject to regulation. The HSWA established the Health and Safety Commission to be responsible for the administration of the Act with enforcement being entrusted to the Health and Safety Executive (HSE). The main focus of such regulation is on achieving safety. The mechanism for achieving this is a compliance strategy: 'the primary purpose of the enforcing authorities is to

1 Ss.2(3).
2 S.20.
3 This Act was brought into force on 6 April 2008.

ensure that duty holders manage and control risks effectively, thus preventing harm'.[4] However, there is a fall-back position of being able to threaten legal prosecution for the endangerment offences under the HSWA. Within such a scheme with its focus on safety, the consequences of lack of safety (for example, death or injury) have traditionally been of secondary importance. While the causing of death is now one of the criteria to be taken into account in the decision to prosecute a company,[5] this has not always been central to HSE policy with the result that criminal prosecutions are only brought in 20 per cent of cases where death has resulted from work-related incidents and in less than 5 per cent of cases where there has been a major injury.[6] It is clear, however, that in all cases (whether on conviction of corporations or individuals) the consequences of the breach of health and safety (particularly, death) are taken into account at the sentencing stage.[7]

Of course, there is nothing new about people being killed at work but it was only when members of the general public began to be killed in the well-documented series of 'disasters'[8] that the mood of commentators and the public began to change. There developed a strong campaign[9] that such deaths should be prosecuted in the same way as when people are killed in other circumstances. Under the general framework of the criminal law, offences are structured in terms of a combination of culpability and harm caused. Pressure mounted for deaths at work to be dealt with in the same manner by the use of prosecutions for manslaughter. The argument was made that simply prosecuting for breach of health and safety offences marginalised the seriousness of such cases.

These developments helped fuel a long-standing debate amongst criminal theorists about the importance of harm and the role of luck. This central issue is explored by Antony Duff in his chapter in this book and so only the briefest outline[10]

---

4 HSC (2002), *Enforcement Policy Statement.*

5 *Ibid.*

6 Bergman, D. (2000), *The Case for Corporate Responsibility* (London: Disaster Action) pp.11–12.

7 *F. Howe & Son (Engineers) Ltd.* [1999] 2 Cr App R (S) 37. In 2005, the two biggest fines ever for breach of health and safety laws were imposed on Balfour Beatty (£10 million) and Network Rail (£3.5 million) following the Hatfield derailment where four people were killed and 70 injured. The fine on Balfour Beatty was reduced on appeal to £7.5 million (*R v Balfour Beatty Rail Infrastructure Services Ltd.* [2006] EWCA Crim 1586).

8 For a list of such 'disasters' see Clarkson, C.M.V., Keating, H.M. and Cunningham, S.R. (2007), *Clarkson and Keating: Criminal Law: Text and Materials*, 6th ed. (London: Sweet and Maxwell, 2007) p.231.

9 Academics (for example, Wells, C. (2001), *Corporations and Criminal Responsibility*, 2nd ed. (Oxford: Oxford University Press) and Trade Unions (for example, UNISON (2002), *Safety Last*) have played a role here but, undoubtedly, it has been pressure groups such as Disaster Action and the Centre for Corporate Accountability (and the work of its founder, David Bergman) that have had the most influence.

10 The following arguments are developed further in Clarkson C.M.V. (2007), 'Aggravated Endangerment Offences' in O'Cinneide, C. and Holder, J. (eds), *Current Legal Problems 2007* 60, 278.

will be sketched here as to why account should be taken of the consequences that flow from culpable activities.

There is a growing literature that distinguishes between 'sheer luck' and 'making one's own luck'. 'Sheer luck' covers situations where a fortuitous result which is unconnected to one's endeavours occurs: for example, a company operates machinery safely in a factory and a worker, disregarding all safety instructions and training, sticks a hand into the machine and the hand is severed. One 'makes one's own luck' when a consequence occurs which is directly connected to one's endeavours. The argument here is that if one is committing a criminal, dangerous activity one has changed one's 'normative position *vis à vis* the risk of adverse consequences of that wrongdoing'.[11] Such a person is engaging in a morally different course of action compared to those who act lawfully. Provided the consequence that occurs flows directly from the dangerous operation, one has 'made one's own bad luck' and ought to be held accountable for the outcome. So, if the machine in the factory is negligently installed without appropriate safety mechanisms, the company can be regarded as operating a dangerous activity and provided the harm flows from that dangerous activity (for example, a chain snaps and injures a worker), the company can be regarded as having made its own (bad) luck and should be liable for the injury caused.

Further, a resultant harm should be taken into account for fair labelling reasons. Criminal offences are generally labelled and structured to reflect the essence of the wrongdoing/culpability and the harm caused. This approach can clearly be seen, for example, in the structure of offences against the person. If the sole focus were to be on the culpability/wrongdoing of the defendant, one could abolish all result crimes such as murder. People who try to kill should be punished for their endeavours irrespective of whether they succeed. The crime of attempted murder could cover all such cases.[12] The result could be dismissed as irrelevant and the possible product of luck. Such an approach would be totally inconsistent with the whole structure of the criminal law. The criminal law has a communicative function: it communicates what conduct is unacceptably wrong. This communication is both to the public (and should reflect widely-held opinions to avoid loss of respect for the law[13]) and to the defendant and the victim explaining the nature of the wrong. It is a formal way of saying: 'look what you did' ... What should be communicated to a successful criminal is not merely that she culpably tried to do some wrongful harm, but that she actually did it ... what she must repent and be grieved by is the harm she has done'.[14]

So when the factory operates the unsafe machinery which kills a worker the fact that a death has occurred should be communicated to the public, the company and the friends and relatives of the deceased. It is revealing that of the 150 respondents to the Government consultation on the Corporate Manslaughter Bill 2005, and the 29 organisations and individuals who gave oral evidence to the Joint Home Affairs

11 Horder, J. (1995), 'A Critique of the Correspondence Principle in Criminal Law' *Crim LR* 759 at 764.

12 Duff, R.A. (1996), *Criminal Attempts* (Oxford: Clarendon Press) pp.350–351.

13 *Ibid.*, p.124.

14 *Ibid.*, p.352.

and Work and Pensions Committees who considered the draft bill, there was near-unanimity that the fact of death should be reflected by the law at the substantive stage.[15] The only controversy was over how this should be achieved.

## III Need for Special Offence

Assuming that a resulting death needs to be reflected in the offence charged, the next question is: why not simply apply the general law of manslaughter? Why should it matter whether a person was killed at work or by a car or in the course of a fight?

Special homicide offences tend to be introduced when:

1. They cannot be easily accommodated within the existing offence of manslaughter, and/or
2. The context of the killing is such that it falls outside what is broadly perceived to be a paradigmatic manslaughter. Each of these issues will be considered in turn.

### *(i) Manslaughter not fit for purpose*

Most of the special homicide offences have been introduced largely as a result of problems in accommodating them within the law of manslaughter – whether in terms of the legal rules themselves or because of the operation of those rules. For example, the offence of causing death by dangerous driving was introduced largely because of the difficulties in obtaining manslaughter convictions in such cases: many juries were not prepared to convict on a 'there but for the Grace of God, go I' basis.[16] Similarly, the offence of causing the death of a child or vulnerable adult was introduced mainly because of evidential problems that arose when a child or vulnerable adult was killed by a carer in the same household but it could not be proved which carer actually caused the death.

Imposing liability for manslaughter on corporations has presented its own distinctive problems. Most criminal law is designed around an individualistic conception of responsibility. Special mechanisms have been needed to hold corporations accountable. The simplest method that could have been employed is vicarious liability. Such an approach has been rejected as being both under-inclusive (one needs to pin-point an individual who committed the crime when in many cases the crime is a result of systems failures) and over-inclusive (a company could be held liable for the actions of a maverick employee even though it has clear policies and systems to achieve maximum safety). Vicarious liability has also been felt to be inappropriate for an offence of manslaughter: a highly stigmatic offence associated

15 House of Commons Home Affairs and Work and Pensions Committees (2005), *Draft Corporate Manslaughter Bill, First Joint Report of Session 2005-06*, Vols I–III.

16 MacKenna, B. (1970), 'Causing Death by Reckless or Dangerous Driving: A Suggestion' *Crim LR* 67.

with a high level of culpability.[17] Accordingly, vicarious liability has largely[18] been restricted to offences of strict liability (such as pollution offences) or mixed-offences involving due diligence defences.

Instead, the law opted for the notorious identification doctrine under which it is necessary to establish that the offence was committed by a person sufficiently senior in the corporation as to represent the controlling mind of the company.[19] In such cases the corporation can be identified with such action and held responsible. The problems associated with the identification doctrine are well-documented and will not be rehearsed here. In essence, this test can only be applied to very small companies. With larger companies where decision making is delegated to various persons it is almost impossible to pin-point any individual senior enough to be regarded as part of the directing will and mind of the company who themselves committed the *actus reus* of an offence with the appropriate *mens rea.*

Of course, these problems could have been met head-on. Building on ambiguous statements in *Meridian*[20]and the approach adopted by the Scottish courts in *Transco plc v HM Advocate*[21] the courts could have expanded the doctrine to include a broader range of managers including, for instance, those responsible for health and safety. However, this route has not been adopted with *Attorney-General's Reference (No. 2 of 1999)*[22] slamming the door shut and insisting on the application of the strict *Tesco v Nattrass*-style identification doctrine for the offence of manslaughter. An alternative solution could have been legislative intervention to abolish the identification doctrine in much the same way as the year-and-a-day rule was abolished by the Law Reform (Year and a Day Rule) Act 1996. However, this would have left a huge gap in the law. With no identification doctrine to latch on to, on what basis would corporations have been found accountable? Put simply, the courts would have been operating in a vacuum and having to make up law as they went along.

Apart from these difficulties with the identification doctrine, there are other reasons why so few manslaughter prosecutions were brought in these cases. As seen above, the HSWA is enforced by the HSE which adopts a compliance strategy and regards advice and assistance to companies as being more important than prosecution. The HSE's regulatory practice is underpinned by three concepts: self-regulation,

17 'The special characteristics of corporations do not insulate them from the stigmatising and penal consequences of a criminal conviction'. (Colvin, E. (1995), 'Corporate Personality and Criminal Liability' 6 *Criminal Law Forum* 1 at 8).

18 In *Seaboard Offshore Ltd v Secretary of State for Transport* [1994] 2 All ER 99 it was stated in the House of Lords that whether vicarious liability applies or not is a matter of statutory interpretation, taking into account the policy of the law and whether vicarious liability will assist enforcement.

19 *Tesco v Nattrass* [1972] AC 153.

20 *Meridian Global Funds v Management Asia Ltd* [1995] 2 AC 500.

21 68 JCL 118 (2003).

22 [2000] 2 Cr App R 207.

cooperation and compliance seeking.[23] Where a death has resulted, since 1998[24] the police have also been involved but are working hand-in-hand with the HSE with its very different culture.[25] Given the paucity of manslaughter prosecutions, it would appear that the investigating and prosecuting authorities (the HSE, police and the CPS) do not conceive and construct most of these cases as manslaughter. Between 1992 and 2005, 3,425 workers were killed at work.[26] It has been estimated that in some 70 per cent of cases where death has resulted from corporate activities, the company involved is to blame.[27] Yet there have only ever been 34 prosecutions for manslaughter brought against companies.[28] While there is evidence that the HSE is more prepared to resort to prosecution than was previously the case,[29] the reality is that most prosecutions are for HSWA offences. Most HSE inspectors have never been involved in a fatality case leading to a manslaughter prosecution. Their experience and training relates to the enforcement of the HSWA. [30] The police also have little experience of investigating work-related fatalities. They do not generally get involved in cases involving workplace injuries[31] and so when they become involved in a workplace fatality they are operating in unfamiliar territory. The HSE is fairly dismissive about the role of the police in such cases. As one HSE inspector put it: 'The police ... don't know anything about health and safety'.[32] The result of this uneasy collaboration was a relative dearth of manslaughter prosecutions and continued reliance on the HSWA offences where the HSE is operating within its comfort-zone.

*(ii) Context of killing*

Special homicide offences are perhaps needed when there is something distinctive about the context in which the killing occurred that justifies labelling the offence as something different from manslaughter.

The first problem is to determine what the label 'manslaughter' should cover. This involves identifying the paradigmatic manslaughter which is difficult because under present English law it is simply a catch-all category for all those non-intentional homicides where blame is felt to be appropriate (or intentional homicides where blame is reduced because of the existence of a partial defence). Nevertheless,

---

23 Almond, P. (2006), 'An Inspector's Eye View: The Prospective Enforcement of Work-Related Fatality Cases' *British Journal of Criminology* 46, 893 at 896.

24 The HSE, ACPO and the CPS jointly agreed a Protocol: HSE (1998), *Work-Related Deaths: a Protocol for Liaison*.

25 Almond, above, n.23.

26 Health and Safety Commission (2005), *Statistics of Fatal Injuries, 2004/05*.

27 HSE (1988), *Blackspot Construction*, p.4.

28 Home Office (2005), *Corporate Manslaughter: The Government's Draft Bill for Reform*, Cm 6497.

29 Almond, above, n.23.

30 *Ibid.*

31 Gobert, J. and Punch, M. (2003), *Rethinking Corporate Crime* (London: Butterworths LexisNexis) p.297.

32 Almond, above, n.23.

empirical examination suggests that it is an offence largely used in cases of violence. In a survey of 56 involuntary manslaughter sentencing appeals between 1994 and 1999, 46 of the cases involved an attack amounting to at least an assault.[33] Amongst the main non-violent situations where this offence is employed are those where death is caused by medical negligence or by the supply of drugs, both areas explored in chapters in this book to ascertain whether such killings should be removed from the ambit of manslaughter.

Where a death has been caused in the context of corporate activities, the killing is far removed from the paradigmatic manslaughter. Duff[34] distinguishes attacks from endangerments and argues that there is a significant moral difference between them. Attacks manifest 'practical hostility' towards people and their interests. An attack involves being guided by the wrong reasons: I attack you because I want to harm you; this is not a reason by which I should be guided. Endangerment involves not being guided by the right reasons.

Corporate activities do not involve attacks on the interests of others. Harming people is not the object of corporate enterprises. Such activities are widely regarded as acceptable and beneficial: we want to buy and use the goods made by companies; we want to live and work in the buildings constructed by companies; we want trains and boats and planes for our everyday public transport needs. But if a company allows dangerous machinery or operations it is not being guided by all the reasons against allowing danger at work. These different actions reveal different wrongs (compared to attacks) and show the company's character in different lights.

In many workplaces, buildings and modes of transport there are inherent risks. What we want is for these risks to be managed to ensure maximum safety. And that is the function of the Health and Safety legislation and the HSE which enforces that legislation. For reasons outlined earlier, we want to hold corporations accountable, not simply for operating unsafe practices, but also for the resultant harm, such as death, that materialises. But wanting to take account of the resultant death does not alter the basic fact that that death occurred within the regulatory context of health and safety. When the harm is less than death (say, injury) many seem content to regard the offence as simply breach of health and safety[35] with perhaps greater punishment

---

33 Clarkson, C.M.V. (2000), 'Context and Culpability in Involuntary Manslaughter: Principle or Instinct?' in Ashworth, A. and Mitchell, B., *Rethinking English Homicide Law* (Oxford: Oxford University Press).

34 Duff, R.A. (2005), 'Criminalising Endangerment' in Duff, R.A. and Green, S. (eds), *Defining Crimes* (Oxford: Oxford University Press).

35 In 2003–4 while 235 people were killed at work, 30,666 workers sustained serious injuries and 129,143 people suffered injuries at workplaces. When someone is seriously injured at work it is extremely rare for the police to conduct an investigation into the incident (Bergman, D. (1991), *Deaths at Work: Accidents or Corporate Crime*, p.17). In 1996/97, even the HSE only investigated 4 per cent of the 50,000 major injuries at work (Trotter, 'The Paddington Rail Crash' (1999) *NLJ* 1505). For an argument that there should be a special offence (or offences) where serious injury (or injury) has been caused, see Clarkson, C.M.V. (2005), 'Corporate Manslaughter: Yet More Government Proposals' *Crim LR* 677. However, it is clear from evidence presented to the Joint Committees that such a solution is not a political priority.

to reflect the causing of injury. Whether someone dies after being seriously injured can, of course, be pure chance but the law and society accords special significance to the value of life and to the killing of another. But, like injury, death is still the product of a lack of health and safety measures. It is very far-removed from manslaughter and so should be marked by the existence of a special offence. To underwrite this difference, it can be strongly argued that the label 'corporate killing'[36] would have been more appropriate than 'corporate manslaughter'.

This argument gains strength when one examines again the enforcement of the law in cases where people are killed at work. Non-corporate manslaughters are investigated and prosecuted by the police and the CPS. The position with work-related fatalities is different with the police working alongside the HSE. In 2000 the Home Office recognised this difference and proposed that fatalities at work should be investigated and prosecuted by the HSE without needing police involvement.[37] This was largely on the basis of the expertise and experience of the HSE but also is a recognition of the very different context of such killings.

The Home Office, in publishing the Corporate Manslaughter Bill 2005, abandoned this proposal and opted for a continuation of the joint role of the HSE and the police. The police should continue to be involved because the new offence of corporate manslaughter would be 'a serious offence under the general criminal law, rather than an offence that might be characterised as regulatory'.[38] The involvement of the police has a symbolic value signifying that the death in question may involve a serious criminal offence.[39] But the continued role of the HSE in the investigation and prosecution of such offences is a recognition that such offences need to be approached differently – but with police involvement to underwrite the seriousness of the offence. In short, when a death has occurred as a result of corporate activities there is an amalgam of two competing ideologies: police involvement representing the desire to bring such killings within mainstream criminal law (meaning the law of homicide for this purpose) – and HSE involvement recognising the different way and context within which such deaths have occurred. Workplace deaths 'contain their own unique sphere of actors and effects in which to engage traditional punishment versus compliance regulatory debates'.[40] Breach of health and safety is a regulatory offence. Causing death as a result of such a breach is a quasi-regulatory crime. So, inasmuch as it is not pure or paradigmatic homicide, the offence deserves special treatment.

---

36 This was the terminology favoured by the Law Commission (1996) (Law Com. No. 237, *Legislating the Criminal Code: Involuntary Manslaughter* and by the Government in its consultation paper in 2000 (Home Office (2000), *Reforming the Law on Involuntary Manslaughter: the Government's Proposals*).

37 Home Office (2000), *Reforming the Law on Involuntary Manslaughter: The Government's Proposals*, paras 3.3.1–3.3.5.

38 Home Office (2005), *Corporate Manslaughter: The Government's Draft Bill for Reform* (2005) para. 58.

39 Gobert, J. and Punch, M. (2003), *Rethinking Corporate Crime* (London: Butterworths LexisNexis) p.305.

40 Gray, G.C. (2006), 'The Regulation of Corporate Violations: Punishment, Compliance, and the Blurring of Responsibility' *British Journal of Criminology* 46, 875 at 876.

## IV Individual Liability for the Special Offence

Once the decision to introduce a new offence of corporate manslaughter had been made, a crucial question needed resolution. Who should be liable for this offence? Should the offence be restricted to companies and other similar organisations or should the offence be extended to embrace individual directors or managers?

Individual officers of a company can be prosecuted for gross negligence manslaughter if their own grossly negligent conduct causes death. Since 1989, 22 directors and business owners have been convicted of manslaughter. Further, when a corporation has been convicted of a health and safety offence, individual directors and managers within the corporation can also be found guilty of the same offence under section 37 of the HSWA if the offence was 'committed with the consent or connivance of, or [was] … attributable to any neglect on the part of any director, manager, secretary or other similar officer of the body corporate'. This offence is punishable with a fine and convicted directors can be disqualified from being a company director.[41] Since 1999, 16 company directors (mostly of small companies) have been convicted of this offence and eight directors have been disqualified on this ground. One of the most controversial issues in the debate leading up to the enactment of the 2007 Act was whether such directors and managers should also be guilty of the new offence of corporate manslaughter.

At first sight such an approach would seem a distinct oddity involving a misnomer. 'Corporate' manslaughter is an offence designed for corporations, not people. However, the term 'corporate manslaughter' could equally be employed to convey that the unlawful killing took place within the context of corporate activities and so could cover both corporations and individuals. Indeed, this is how the term is widely used by the media – although it is probable that much of this usage is attributable to journalists having little understanding of the legal intricacies of this area of law. Without a firm grasp of the concept of legal personality and how an artificial entity can commit a crime, it is perhaps understandable that there should be widespread confusion in the public mind between the liability of corporations and that of individuals. Nevertheless, and albeit based on such misunderstandings, the term 'corporate manslaughter' has taken on a broader meaning as encompassing all killings taking place within the context of corporate activities. The offence need not be the sole preserve of companies. Indeed, the 2007 Act expanded the new offence beyond 'companies' and make it applicable to various Government Departments and partnerships and trade union or employers' associations. Some of these bodies have no corporate personality. Nevertheless, they all constitute 'organisations': groups of people. Accordingly, if the new offence had been applied to individuals there would have needed to be a special mechanism to achieve this.

In the debate leading up to the introduction of a special corporate manslaughter offence, views were split as to whether individuals should be liable for the new offence. Those opposed to the liability of individuals tended to argue that it would

41 Company Directors Disqualification Act 1986, s.2(1).

discourage managers from taking up positions that involved directly managing risks, especially in high-risk industries.[42] As Lord Justice Judge put it:

> I think that it would be very difficult to persuade anybody to take on the responsibility of senior manager ... if he were going to be liable to be found guilty for the inadequacy of the operation as a whole ... [Such a person] will be the fall guy .. responsible for everything that goes wrong in the organisation.[43]

It was also argued that the object of a new offence is to close gaps in the application of the law, not to create a new, wider offence.[44]

On the other hand, there is a strong case that individuals should be capable of being liable for the new offence. The essence of the case here is based on deterrence. People are more amenable to deterrence than corporations. Whilst directors do not want their company to be convicted of a serious offence, they might nevertheless still be prepared to take risks that they might not take if they knew they could be personally convicted and sentenced to imprisonment. It is revealing that in evidence given to the House of Commons Joint Committees it was employer groups that were most opposed to the introduction of personal liability. Further, it was argued that if a new corporate manslaughter offence were introduced without personal liability, this could well result in even fewer individual manslaughter prosecutions being brought as holding a corporation liable for the new offence could be regarded as the easier option.

If individuals were to be held liable, there are three ways in which this could have been done. The first method would simply be to utilise the rules of accessorial liability (aiding, abetting, counselling and procuring) to hold individuals, along with the company, liable the offence. There are, however, problems with such an approach. If the *Powell; English*[45] test were to apply, it would need to be proved that the individual director foresaw that the company would commit the crime with the appropriate *mens rea*. Such a test is devised for secondary parties who are separate from the principal offender. Such a test would be difficult to apply where the secondary party's actions or omissions will usually be 'part of the overall management failure, rather than separate from it'.[46] Such difficulties could have been surmounted but it would probably have been easier to bypass the antiquated rules on accessorial liability that are currently being examined by the Law Commission with a view to their reform. The second alternative would have been to follow the Australian Capital Territories model where there are two offences of Industrial Manslaughter: the 'employer offence' and a 'senior officer' offence.[47] As there are major problems with the way this senior officer test is framed,[48] one could draw on

42 Above, n.15, para. 303.

43 *Ibid.*, para. 305.

44 The Institute of Directors, cited *ibid.*, para. 303.

45 [1999] 1 AC 1.

46 Joint Committee's Report, paras 308–309.

47 Crimes Act 1900 (ACT), ss.49C and 49D.

48 Clarkson, C.M.V. (2005), 'Corporate Manslaughter: Yet More Government Proposals' *Crim LR* 677.

the better proposal that was contained in a failed Victorian Bill that an officer would be 'organisationally responsible' if she had materially contributed to the offence by performing or failing to perform his or her organisational responsibilities knowing that this involved the company engaging in high risk conduct.[49]

The third solution was that devised by the House of Commons Joint Committees. The legislation creating a corporate manslaughter offence should contain a provision similar to section 37 of the HSWA that if the offence was committed with the consent or connivance of any manager or director, and so on, or was attributable to the neglect of such a person, that person would be liable for corporate manslaughter along with the company.[50] This approach was recently adopted in the Terrorism Act 2006, section 18.

With regard to the penalty for the offence, it was felt that it needed to carry a lesser maximum sentence than manslaughter. In the worst cases manslaughter could be charged. An analogy was drawn with causing death by dangerous driving. In the worst cases where a driver kills, there can be a charge of manslaughter but in lesser cases the charge will be causing death by dangerous driving carrying a maximum penalty of 14 years' imprisonment. Following this example and on the basis that these are offences of comparable seriousness, the Joint Committee Report proposed that the new law should be extended to individuals and should be punishable by a maximum sentence of 14 years' imprisonment.[51]

As shall be seen in the following section, however, the Government rejected the proposal that individuals be capable of being liable for the new offence of corporate manslaughter.

## V The Introduction of a Special Offence

### *(i) History*

In 1996 the Law Commission, as part of its recommendations for reform of the law of involuntary manslaughter, proposed the creation of a new offence of corporate killing.[52] Soon after the Labour Party came to power in May 1997 it was announced that the Government would implement this recommendation.[53] In 2000 the Home Office published a consultation paper endorsing the Law Commission's views,[54] the most significant difference being that, unlike the Law Commission proposals, the Government recommended that individuals should be liable for aiding, abetting counselling or procuring the offence of corporate killing. The Labour Party manifesto

---

49 Wheelwright, K. (2004), 'Prosecuting Corporations and Officers for Industrial Manslaughter – Recent Australian Developments' 32 *Australian Business Law Reveiw* 239.

50 Above, n.15, para. 312.

51 Para. 314.

52 Law Com. No. 237 (1996), *Legislating the Criminal Code: Involuntary Manslaughter*.

53 *The Independent*, 2 October 1997.

54 Home Office (2000), *Reforming the Law on Involuntary Manslaughter: The Government's Proposals*.

of May 2001 committed itself to the introduction of the new offence. There followed a long period of delay allegedly caused by intense opposition from business leaders to the notion that individual directors or managers could be liable for the new offence.[55]

In 2005 the Corporate Manslaughter Bill was eventually published and, after consultation, was subjected to pre-legislative scrutiny by the Home Affairs and Work and Pensions Joint Committees in the House of Commons. One of the most controversial aspects of this Bill was the exclusion of potential liability for individuals. In December 2005 the Joint Committees published a Report[56] to which the Government responded in March 2006.[57] The Government rejected the Committees' proposal that individuals should be liable. Finally, in July 2006 the Corporate Manslaughter and Corporate Homicide Bill was introduced. The Bill passed through all its parliamentary stages in the Commons but in February 2007 the Government was defeated in the House of Lords and an amendment was carried covering deaths in custody. The Government finally conceded on this point (although a date for implementation on this specific issue has yet to be set).

*(ii) Corporate Manslaughter and Corporate Homicide Act 2007*

The Act abolishes the 'common law of manslaughter by gross negligence' in its application to corporations and other organisations covered by the new offence.[58] A new offence, corporate manslaughter,[59] is created. Individuals cannot be liable for aiding, abetting, counselling or procuring the new offence[60] but can still be liable for the common law offence of manslaughter.

*(a) The offence* The offence is committed if an organisation owes a duty of care to the deceased and 'the way in which its activities are managed or organised by its senior management is a substantial element'[61] of 'a gross breach of the relevant duty of care'[62] and this breach causes a person's death. A breach is 'gross' if the conduct 'falls far below what can reasonably be expected of the organisation in the circumstances'.[63]

In assessing whether there has been a gross breach of the relevant duty, the jury must consider whether the organisation failed to comply with health and safety legislation or guidance and how serious that failure was and how much of a risk

55 *The Independent*, 10 November 2003; *Financial Times*, 27 December 2003.

56 House of Commons Home Affairs and Work and Pensions Committees (2005), *Draft Corporate Manslaughter Bill, First Joint Report of Session 2005-06*, Vols I–III.

57 The Government's Reply to the First Joint Report from the Home Affairs and Work and Pensions Committees (2006), 2005-06 HC 540, *Draft Corporate Manslaughter Bill.*

58 S.20.

59 S.(1)(5)(a).

60 S.18.

61 S.1(3).

62 S.1(1)(b).

63 S.1(4)(b).

of death it posed.[64] The jury may also consider whether the organisation allowed a corporate culture to develop which encouraged or tolerated the failure to comply with such legislation or guidance.[65]

*(b) Organisation* Despite the nomenclature of 'corporate' manslaughter, the offence can be committed by any 'organisation' which is defined as '(a) a corporation; (b) a department or other body listed in Schedule 1;[66] (c) a police force; (d) a partnership, or a trade union or employers' association, that is an employer'.[67]

The provision in (d) was a late amendment which had been strongly recommended by the Joint Committees who were concerned that there would be a gap in the law where a death resulted from the activities of large unincorporated bodies such as big partnerships of accounting and law firms.

While the lifting of Crown immunity and the extension of the offence to the police is significant, there are various exemptions from liability specified by the Act. These include public policy decisions by public authorities and things done in the exercise of an exclusively public function.[68] In relation to the police there is an express provision that no duty of care is owed in relation to 'the carrying on of policing or law-enforcement activities'.[69]

*(c) Relevant duty of care* Neither the Law Commission nor the Joint Committees thought that it was appropriate to apply the civil law concept of 'duty of care'. Rules for liability for damages under the civil law are driven by different policy considerations from rules that should apply in the criminal law.[70] However, the Government was fearful about the potential liability of bodies carrying out public functions, particularly with the lifting of Crown immunity.[71] It was concerned that the new offence should not apply in wider circumstances than the current offence of gross negligence manslaughter under *Adomako*.[72]

The organisation must owe a 'relevant duty of care' under the law of negligence in relation to any of the following duties:

---

64 S.8(1).

65 S.8(3).

66 For example, the Crown Prosecution Service, the Department of Health and Her Majesty's Revenue and Customs.

67 S.1(2).

68 S.3.

69 S.5(2)(b).

70 *Wacker* [2003] 1 Cr App R 22.

71 The Government Reply to the First Joint Report from the Home Affairs and Work and Pensions Committees Session 2005-06 HC 540, *Draft Corporate Manslaughter Bill* (2006), pp.10–11.

72 *Ibid.*, p.16.

(a) a duty owed to its employees or others working for the organisation or performing services for it;
(b) a duty owed as occupier of premises;
(c) a duty owed in connection with the supply of goods or services, the carrying on of construction or maintenance operations, the carrying on of any other activity on a commercial basis, or the use or keeping of any plant or vehicle;[73]
(d) a duty owed to anyone detained in custody.[74]

The inclusion of the duty owed to anyone detained in custody was the hotly-contested (by the Government) amendment carried in the House of Lords which caused the Home Secretary, John Reid, to announce immediately that the Government would abandon the whole Bill. This petulant decision was revoked less than an hour later with a revised statement that the Government would consider its position. After several further defeats in the Lords, the Government finally gave way on this issue.

Whether a relevant duty of care is owed is a question of law.[75] In *Wacker* it was held that the civil law doctrine of *ex turpi causa non oritur actio* had no application in the criminal law. This decision would not have survived under the Act as it is the civil law of negligence that is applicable and this doctrine is part of that law. However, to preserve the effect of *Wacker* and also to ensure that the civil law rules on *volenti non fit injuria* do not apply, the Act specifically provides that neither doctrine applies for the purposes of corporate manslaughter.[76]

The extent to which a duty of care is owed by public authorities, the military, police and law enforcement agencies, emergency services, child-protection and probation agencies are severely limited by sections 3–7. In essence, all these bodies do not owe a duty of care in relation to their operational activities. So, for example, if a fire authority acts negligently while rescuing people from a fire, there will be no liability. However, if the fire authority negligently fails to maintain its fleet of fire engines with the result that a death is caused, the fire authority can be liable for the new offence.

It has to be questioned whether it is appropriate to employ the civil law concept of duty of care here. The concept has been developed and refined in the totally different context of claims for compensation. It is also a complex legal concept that is still evolving through judicial decisions; its application here 'provides ample opportunity for all the legal pedantry'[77] associated with the concept.

Given the special context of the new offence, it might have been better not to have followed the contours of the law of gross negligence manslaughter and instead to have recognised that the focus of the new offence should be on breaches of health and safety that cause death. As shall be seen, such breaches form a critical component in the assessment of whether an organisation is liable. Several bodies

73 Ss.2(1)(a)–(c).

74 S.2(1)(d): an extended definition of this is provided in s.2(2).

75 S.2(5).

76 S.2(6).

77 Evidence by Mr Antoniw of Thompsons Solicitors, Joint Committee Report, above, n.56, para. 101.

giving evidence to the Joint Committees recommended that the offence should not be based on the civil law concept of duty of care but should instead be based on breaches of duties owed by statute, such as the HSWA and the Merchant Shipping Act 1995. Such offences are specifically designed for regulating corporate conduct and are clear and well-established:

> Companies do not get prosecuted for breaches of duties of care, generally, so in our view it makes much more sense for the new offence to be grounded on statutory legislation which is broader and is also better understood than civil law duties of care.[78]

The Joint Committees accepted this view and recommended a return to the Law Commission's original proposal that the offence should not be limited by reference to any existing duties of care. The 2007 Act rejects this view.

*(d) Senior management failure* An organisation will be liable for the new offence 'only if the way in which its activities are managed or organised by its senior management is a substantial element'[79] in the gross breach of the relevant duty of care. 'Senior management' is defined as persons who play significant roles in making decisions or actually managing or organising the whole or a substantial part of the organisation's activities.[80]

Along with the matter of individual liability, this was a highly controversial issue during the progress of the legislation. The Home Office justified the senior manager test on the basis that this is the most effective way to identify true corporate fault in the management of risk rather than criminalising purely local acts of negligence. The insistence in the Act on fault by senior management is a response to critics of earlier proposals who argued that because companies are purely creatures of law, crimes can only be committed by people and not companies and so the real issue is one of determining when the acts of these people should be attributed to a company.[81] This insistence on identifying the 'senior management' seems unduly restrictive and threatens to open the door to endless argument in court as to whether certain persons do or do not qualify as part of the 'senior management'.

Further, there is the real danger that such a test could encourage companies to delegate health and safety responsibilities to non-senior managers so as to shield the company from criminal liability.[82] In anticipation of the Act, there was evidence that some companies were already delegating health and safety responsibilities down to more junior employees.[83] A further obvious problem with this approach is that it replicates one of the main problems with the previous law in that it could apply

78 Evidence by Centre for Corporate Accountability, cited *ibid.*, para. 103.

79 S.1(3).

80 S.1(4)(c).

81 Sullivan, G.R. (1996), 'The Attribution of Culpability to Limited Companies' 55 *Cambridge Law Journal* 515; Glazebrook, P. (2002), 'A Better Way of Convicting Businesses of Avoidable Deaths and Injuries' 61 *LQR* 405.

82 Joint Committee Report, above n.56, para. 133.

83 *Ibid.*, para. 135.

inequitably to small and large organisations.[84] It will clearly be easier to identify senior management failings in small companies. In essence, this senior management test is little more than a broadening of the identification doctrine in that, instead of identifying one senior directing mind, one aggregates the actions and culpability of several senior persons. It is unfortunate that the Law Commission approach was not adopted whereby the definition of a management failure removed the need to identify persons representing the senior management and placed the emphasis on the *activities* of the company: 'the way in which its activities are managed or organised'. This would have placed the focus where it should be: on the activities and organisational practices of the company.

*(e) Gross breach: factors for the jury* A breach of duty is gross if 'the conduct alleged to amount to a breach of that duty falls far below what can reasonably be expected of the organisation in the circumstances'.[85] It is for the jury to determine whether a breach of duty is a 'gross breach'. In response to criticisms that the Law Commission's proposals were too vague in this respect, the Act provides a range of statutory criteria for assessing this:

(i) Failure to comply with health and safety legislation

In deciding whether there has been a gross breach of duty, the jury *must* consider whether the organisation failed to comply with any health and safety legislation that relates to the alleged breach, and if so – (a) how serious that failure was; and (b) how much of a risk of death it posed.[86]

This provision is to be welcomed. Companies are expected to comply with the health and safety legislation. Their failure to do so raises at least a prima facie case of a gross breach. Equally, it is right that not every (perhaps trivial) breach of health and safety laws should give rise to liability for the new offence. The jury must go on to assess how serious the failure was and how much of a risk of death it posed.

Of course, there is an inevitable circularity in asking whether conduct falls far below a standard and then measuring this by 'how serious' is the failure to comply with the law. However, making these decisions in relation to something tangible (the breach of health and safety laws) is a helpful step compared to the current law of manslaughter where, under *Adomako*, the jury simply has to assess the broad, open issue of whether the conduct was 'so bad' that it deserves to be labelled manslaughter.

(ii) Corporate culture

As a result of the Joint Committees' Report, the 2007 Act introduced a new, additional, test for the jury in determining whether the conduct 'falls far below what can reasonably be expected of the organisation in the circumstances'. The jury may also 'consider the extent to which the evidence shows that there were attitudes, policies, systems or accepted practices within the organisation that were likely to

84 *Ibid.*, para. 150.

85 S.1(4)(b).

86 S.8(2).

have encouraged'[87] the failure to comply with health and safety laws or to have produced tolerance of such a failure.[88]

This is drawing upon the corporate culture test applied in the Australian Capital Territory which has tried to escape from the notion that corporate acts must be linked to individual human beings' choices and acts. It has adopted an organisational model with the focus being on corporate structures and systems and on practices and policies and whether the corporation has allowed a 'corporate culture' to develop which facilitated the commission of the crime.

In assessing whether a relevant corporate culture exists academic commentators[89] have suggested that the following factors could be relevant in establishing a corporate culture:

- hierarchy of corporation: does the Board make efforts to comply with the law? Is the management structure organised in such a way as to encourage non-compliance (for example, insulating certain officers from responsibility)?
- corporate goals: are these realistic or do they encourage unlawful behaviour?
- monitoring compliance: monitoring systems/internal audits/channels of communication for employees to report concerns?
- circumstances of offence.
- reactions to past violations.
- incentives and indemnification.

It should be noted that the Joint Committees' Report proposed this corporate culture test as a *substitute* for the senior management test. This Australian approach has, however, been strongly criticised as being too vague.[90] Accordingly, the Act has preserved the senior management test but has invoked the corporate culture test as one that may be utilised as an *additional* test to the breach of health and safety laws test in determining whether there has been a gross breach of a relevant duty of care. It is only when there has been a breach of health and safety laws that the jury *may* go on to consider the corporate culture within the corporation. The provision specifically relates to how the corporate culture encouraged the failure to comply with the health and safety laws. This is a far more focused issue than the rather unstructured and broad test from Australia.

(iii) Any other relevant matters

Neither of the above two provisions prevents the jury from having regard to 'any other matters they consider relevant'.[91] It is difficult to see that this provision will be much utilised. It is unthinkable that a jury could conclude that there had been no breach of health and safety laws and yet because of 'other matters' there was a gross

87 S.8(3)(a).

88 The jury may also have regard to any health and safety *guidance* that relates to the alleged breach s.8(3)(b).

89 Cited in Clough, J. and Mulhern, C. (2002), *The Prosecution of Companies* (Melbourne: Oxford University Press).

90 *Ibid.*, pp.140–147.

91 S.8(4).

breach of duty. So the relevance of this provision must relate to the issue of 'how serious' was the failure to comply with the health and safety laws. Such issues would normally fail to be determined by the corporate culture test.

*(f) Relationship to health and safety legislation* Under section 19 an organisation may be charged with both corporate manslaughter and a health and safety offence. The jury may return a verdict on only the lesser charge. This serves to highlight that the new offence of corporate manslaughter is, in reality, an aggravated breach of health and safety offence. It is an offence straddling two families of offence: homicide and health and safety offences. Accordingly, as it does not fall fully within either family of offence, it deserves a special offence category. To underwrite this special nature of the offence, it was suggested earlier that corporate killing would be a better offence label than corporate manslaughter.

## VI Conclusion

This chapter has argued that when a death has been caused through negligent corporate activities it is inadequate to deal with the matter purely under the HSWA. Such an approach leads to the marginalisation of the seriousness of such wrongdoing. Such deaths are not merely the result of 'pure luck' and for fair labelling reasons there should be a prosecution for an offence reflecting that a death has been caused. It was argued that manslaughter prosecutions under the old law were doomed to fail in most cases. Further, it was argued that the particular context of corporate killings should be marked by the creation of a special offence. On the other hand, the refusal to extend the offence to individual directors or managers is a matter of regret, as is the continued commitment to the senior management test. Nevertheless, despite these shortcomings, the introduction of a new offence of corporate manslaughter is, in principle, to be welcomed.

Chapter 6

# Vehicular Homicide: Need for a Special Offence?

Sally Cunningham

## I Introduction

Under the current law of England and Wales a driver who causes death may face prosecution for a number of offences signifying the homicide, depending on his or her blameworthiness. These range from murder, where *malice aforethought* can be proven, to the new homicide offence of causing death by careless driving (CDCD) under the Road Safety Act 2006.[1] In between these offences fall the common law offence of manslaughter and the statutory offence of causing death by dangerous driving (CDDD).[2] In addition, there also exist homicide offences to penalise drivers who should not have been driving at the time that a fatal collision occurred: causing death by careless driving whilst under the influence of drink or drugs (CDCDUI);[3] aggravated vehicle taking causing death;[4] causing death by unlicensed, disqualified or uninsured driving.[5]

The question for this chapter is whether such specific offences are needed, or whether the general homicide offence of manslaughter suffices to punish drivers whose bad driving causes death. The focus of the chapter will be on the offences of CDDD and CDCD, although some consideration will also be given to the other statutory offences. I have chosen to focus on these offences since they penalise drivers who kill because of their negligence, rather than because of some additional factor used to justify the creation of separate offences. My approach on this occasion is to use the Law Commission's recent proposals for reforming the general law of homicide to explore the justification for and desirability of preserving the special homicide offences. There appear to be two main reasons for the creation of the special offences: those that are pragmatic, and those that are theoretical. To start, however, the current law on the special offences will be summarised briefly.

---

1 Road Safety Act 2006, s.20, inserting s.2B into the Road Traffic Act 1988. The offence is triable either way with a maximum penalty of five years' imprisonment when tried on indictment. The section had not entered into force at the time of writing, however.

2 Road Traffic Act 1988, s.1. The maximum penalty is 14 years' imprisonment.

3 Road Traffic Act 1988, s.3A. The maximum penalty is 14 years' imprisonment.

4 Under the Theft Act 1968, s.12A, the offence of aggravated vehicle taking carries a higher maximum sentence (now 14 years) where death is caused.

5 Road Safety Act 2006, s.21, inserting s.3ZB into the Road Traffic Act 1988. The offence is triable either way with a maximum penalty of two years' imprisonment when tried on indictment.

## II Vehicular Killing – The Current Position

Of the special vehicular homicide offences, CDDD is arguably the most serious.[6] Section 1 of the Road Traffic Act (RTA) 1988 states that:

> A person who causes the death of another person by driving a mechanically propelled vehicle dangerously on a road or other public place is guilty of an offence.

According to section 2A of the Act, a person is to be regarded as driving dangerously if:

(a) the way he drives falls far below what would be expected of a competent and careful driver, and
(b) it would be obvious to a competent and careful driver that driving in that way would be dangerous.

Under subsection 3, 'dangerous' means a danger of injury to any person or of serious damage to property. The offence under section 1 is a constructive crime in that all that is needed to be made out is the offence of dangerous driving under section 2A plus the aggravating factor that death was caused thereby. The key to proving a charge under section 1 is, therefore, in establishing what is expected of the 'competent and careful' driver. The Association of Chief Police Officers (ACPO) and the Crown Prosecution Service (CPS) have attempted to give guidance to police officers and Crown prosecutors as to the meaning of such terms in their *Driving Offences Charging Standard.*[7]

If a driver is suffering from any impairment or disability which she knows could result in creating an obvious and serious risk, this acts as evidence of dangerous driving.[8] The competent and careful driver test is an absolute one because if a driver does not comply with the standard she is more likely to be a risk to other road-users and so her position cannot be supported, irrespective of how much control she has over her own ability. The test is entirely objective.[9]

---

6 Although in terms of sentencing it is on a par with CDCDUI and aggravated vehicle taking which all carry a maximum penalty of 14 years' imprisonment following the enactment of the Criminal Justice Act 2003, s.285. In terms of blameworthiness, however, CDDD is arguably more serious than either of these offences.

7 The Charging Standard was first published in 1996. The hard copies of this document were replaced in November 2004 by a revised electronic version, available on the CPS' Legal Guidance Website: http://www.cps.gov.uk/legal/section9/chapter_b.html. The CPS has conducted a public consultation exercise with a view to amending the Charging Standard following the enactment of the Road Safety Act 2006.

8 *Marison* [1996] Crim LR 909.

9 Despite this being the accepted position, the High Court recently held that it should be possible to take into account the fact that a driver has special skills when applying the test. In *Milton v CPS* [2007] EWHC 532 (Admin) a police officer's conviction for dangerous driving was quashed because the District Judge failed to take into account the fact that the officer was a Grade 1 advanced police driver when he drove at speeds of up to 148mph on public roads. It is submitted that the case was wrongly decided and that the District Judge in

Driving is not only 'dangerous' because of the manner in which the task is carried out; it may also be 'dangerous' due to the dangerous condition of the vehicle which is being driven:

> s.2A(2) A person is also to be regarded as driving dangerously for the purposes of sections 1 and 2 above if it would be obvious to a competent and careful driver that driving the vehicle in its current state would be dangerous.

This covers both the mechanical state of the vehicle and the way in which anything is attached to or carried on the vehicle.[10]

CDCD is another constructive crime based on the less serious driving offence of careless driving. Again, all that is required is that the prosecution prove that the defendant drove carelessly (the term used in statute is 'without due care and attention') according to the definition of that offence, and that death was caused thereby. The Road Safety Act 2006 placed the definition of careless driving on a statutory footing for the first time.[11] Section 30 of the 2006 Act inserts a new section 3ZA into the Road Traffic Act 1988:

> (2) A person is to be regarded as driving without due care and attention if (and only if) the way he drives falls below what would be expected of a competent and careful driver.
> (3) In determining for the purposes of subsection (2) above what would be expected of a careful and competent driver in a particular case, regard shall be had not only to the circumstances of which he could be expected to be aware but also to any circumstances shown to have been within the knowledge of the accused.

The alternative form of the offence is inconsiderate driving, which now has the following statutory definition under s. 3ZA of the Road Traffic Act 1998:

> (4) A person is to be regarded as driving without reasonable consideration for other persons only if those persons are inconvenienced by his driving.

In the past it would seem that this form of the offence of inconsiderate driving has very rarely been used.[12] It would be unfortunate if prosecution policy altered so that this version of the offence was used to prosecute drivers for CDCD, since it is not clear from the statutory definition what is the level of blameworthiness required.

---

the case, DJ Wallis, who is general editor of *Wilkinson's Road Traffic Offences*, was correct in his application of the law at trial.

10 S. 2A(4).

11 Prior to this, although careless driving was itself a statutory offence the term 'driving without due care and attention' was not defined in statute but was interpreted as meaning driving falling below the standard of a driver 'exercising the degree of care and attention that a reasonable and prudent driver would in the circumstances' (*Simpson v Peat* [1952] 2 QB 24).

12 The author conducted an empirical study of charges brought in fatal road traffic collisions occurring in 1999–2000 for the purpose of her PhD thesis. In over 300 cases studied, none were prosecuted on the basis of inconsiderate driving.

One thing to note in relation to careless driving is that the statutory definition lacks an equivalent explanation of the meaning of 'dangerous' under section 2A, that is, that it would be obvious to a competent and careful driver that driving in that way would be dangerous and that 'dangerous' refers to a danger of injury to any person or of serious damage to property. Thus in relation to careless driving no risk of harm to others need be created by the driving for the offence to be made out.

The three other statutory offences which punish drivers who kill are again constructive crimes. CDCDUI is now an aggravated form of CDCD where the fact that the defendant drove carelessly having drunk enough alcohol to make them over the limit, or was under the influence of drugs when they drove carelessly, results in an indictable only offence and increases the maximum penalty from five to 14 years' imprisonment where death is caused. For aggravated vehicle taking it must be proven that the defendant took a vehicle unlawfully and either drove it dangerously or was involved in an accident. If death was caused a higher penalty is provided. Thus, it is possible to prove the offence without reference to the standard of driving involved. This is also true of the new offence of causing death by unlicensed, disqualified or uninsured driving, which could be described as a strict liability offence. All that is needed to be proven is that the defendant was driving when they ought not to have been because they did not have a valid licence or insurance or had been disqualified from driving, and was involved in a fatal collision. Even if the defendant's driving was impeccable and the collision was the result of a drunken pedestrian dashing out in front of their car in circumstances such that no driver could have avoided them, they can be convicted of the statutory homicide offence.

In addition to the above, the common law offence of manslaughter remains a possible charge in cases of fatal road traffic collisions. Indeed, following the enactment of the Road Safety Act 2006 it is now possible for the Crown to charge manslaughter with the safety net that a jury can return a verdict of guilty of CDDD if they decide that the elements of manslaughter are not made out.[13] Manslaughter could take the form of either constructive (unlawful act) manslaughter or gross negligence manslaughter, depending on the circumstances. Whenever a vehicle is used as a weapon of assault, for example when the defendant has driven their car at the victim in order to frighten them and has killed the victim, manslaughter will be the appropriate charge.[14] It must be noted, however, that the unlawful act upon which liability is constructed can only be assault; acts which amount to driving offences, such as dangerous or careless driving, speeding or drink-driving cannot form the basis of a manslaughter charge. This rule goes back to the case of *DPP v Andrews*[15] in which Lord Atkin stated:

---

13 Road Safety Act, s.33, amending the Road Traffic Offenders Act 1988, s.24. The CPS has indicated that it does not intend to alter its approach to charging decisions significantly by prosecuting routinely for gross negligence manslaughter in cases which are currently prosecuted as CDDD, and that the view is that in the majority of cases CDDD will remain the appropriate charge: CPS (2007), *Prosecuting Bad Driving – A Consultation on CPS Prosecution Policy and Practice: Response to Consultation*, p.14, available from <www.cps.gov.uk>.

14 This is acknowledged in the CPS *Driving Offences Charging Standard*.

15 [1937] AC 576.

> There is an obvious difference in the law of manslaughter between doing an unlawful act and doing a lawful act with a degree of carelessness which the legislature makes criminal. If it were otherwise a man who killed another while driving without due care and attention would *ex necessitate* commit manslaughter.[16]

It could be argued, however, that the law regulating drivers has changed to such a great extent in the past 70 years, that the reasoning in *Andrews* might no longer apply. *Andrews* was decided shortly after driving competency tests were introduced,[17] and driving seems to have been viewed as a right rather than a privilege. Corbett notes that in the early days of the motor vehicle, only the elite could afford to engage in what was then an exciting pastime, and the dangers involved in this new-found pursuit may have been overlooked.[18] Writing in 1968, Elliott and Street argued that those who drive on public roads are exercising their public rights, not some withdrawable privileges.[19] This argument seems to have been based upon the fact that the generality of people are entitled to hold a licence to drive if they are over a prescribed age, have no health problems which impair their driving, and have passed their test.[20] In addition to this, however, they note that unlike the days when cars were first introduced, by 1968 a large proportion of the population had come to rely on their own vehicles, meaning that public transport was no longer needed, falling into disuse and thereby causing people to become even more dependent on their own transport. They stated that: '[i]n this kind of milieu it is ingenuous to talk about the privilege of driving a car'.[21]

Lord Atkin's statement in *Andrews* may derive from an attitude which still, to some extent, persists today: that driving offences are not real 'crime' and so cannot constitute an 'unlawful act' for the purposes of manslaughter. It is arguable, however, that contrary to this view driving is indeed a privilege, rather than a right. If an individual gets behind the wheel of a car and sets off to drive, such an act is only lawful if certain conditions are met. The driver must not be under the influence of drink or drugs, must have a valid driving licence, must be insured to drive the vehicle in question, and the vehicle must be in a roadworthy condition. However, following *Andrews*, if any of these legal conditions are not met this is not an unlawful act for the purposes of manslaughter. If the position in *Andrews* were to be altered then there would be no need for offences such as CDCDUI or the new offence of causing death by unlicensed, disqualified or uninsured driving.

That such a change might occur is not, it seems, beyond the realms of possibility. In the case of *Willoughby*[22] the defendant was prosecuted for manslaughter following a fire at his pub in which the deceased died. The Crown's allegation was that the defendant had enlisted the help of the deceased to burn down his pub in order to collect on the insurance, but the plan went wrong. In this case the prosecution, much

16 *Ibid.*, at 585.

17 Motor Vehicles Regulations 1935.

18 Corbett, C. (2003), *Car Crime* (Cullompton: Willan Publishing) p.30.

19 Elliott, D. and Street, H. (1968), *Road Accidents* (Harmondsworth: Penguin) p.153.

20 *Ibid.*

21 *Ibid.*

22 [2005] 1 Cr App R 29.

to the court's dismay, chose to base its accusation on gross negligence rather than constructive manslaughter. The conviction for manslaughter was upheld on appeal, but the court pointed out that the case could have been argued more simply on the basis of constructive manslaughter, and Brown J. gave the following examples of cases which could fall under both constructive manslaughter and gross negligence manslaughter:

> First, an employer travelling with an employee driver, whom he has required to deliver goods at high speed, through a built-up area, causing the death of an innocent pedestrian; secondly, a doctor who dangerously waives a scalpel (as the defendant did a [*sic*] R v Larkin 29 Cr App R 18), cutting the throat of a patient. Both employer and doctor could be guilty of manslaughter by both routes.[23]

The reasoning behind both of these examples is rather dubious. In the second instance, for the doctor to be liable under constructive manslaughter 'dangerously waiving' a scalpel would have to be done with the intention (or recklessness) to cause the patient to apprehend immediate unlawful force, if it were to be established as an assault. In the driving example it is unclear how Mr Justice Brown's argument can be reconciled with the decision in *Andrews*, since the only unlawful act committed is that of procuring speeding or dangerous driving. It is difficult to evaluate such an *obiter* statement, or to suggest that it might indicate that the common law is ripe for change in this matter. At present, however, cases of vehicular homicide will have to be argued on the basis of gross negligence manslaughter unless an assault can be proved.

When the case of *Andrews* was decided, Lord Atkin rightly noted that 'the law of manslaughter has not changed by the introduction of motor vehicles on the road'.[24] Accordingly, the case of *Bateman*[25] setting out the law in relation to gross negligence manslaughter was held to apply in that case. Lord Hewitt CJ in *Bateman* laid down the following test for gross negligence: 'in order to establish criminal liability the facts must be such that, in the opinion of the jury, the negligence of the accused went beyond a mere matter of compensation between subjects and showed such disregard for the life and safety of others as to amount to a crime against the state and conduct deserving of punishment'.[26] Although it is still true today that the introduction of motor vehicles on the road has not changed the law of manslaughter, since *Andrews* was decided the criminal law has undergone various relevant changes. Significantly, a new statutory offence of causing death by reckless or dangerous driving was introduced in 1956. Unrelated to this, the common law of manslaughter has undergone a number of changes.

The introduction of a specific offence dealing with drivers who kill has not replaced the possibility of a driver who kills from being guilty of 'motor manslaughter'. 'Motor manslaughter' is merely a term used to denote that a particular case of involuntary manslaughter has been committed through the use of a motor

23 *Ibid.*, at [19].
24 At 583.
25 (1925) 19 Cr App R 8.
26 *Ibid.*, at 11–12.

vehicle. In *R. v. Governor of Holloway Prison, ex p. Jennings*[27] it was held that motor manslaughter had not been impliedly repealed by the Road Traffic Act 1956, and, following this, the case of *Seymour*[28] addressed the question of the necessary *mens rea* to be proved in such cases. It was held in this case that in cases of manslaughter, including motor manslaughter, the jury should be directed in terms of objective *Lawrence*[29] recklessness.

*Adomako*[30] reversed the decision in *Seymour* by replacing the test of objective recklessness with one of gross negligence. In *Prentice*[31] the Court of Appeal had held that the ingredients of involuntary manslaughter involved proving a breach of duty which had caused death, coupled with gross negligence. However, the court made motor manslaughter an exception to their ruling, based on the decision in *Seymour*, and suggested that for motor manslaughter the test of objective recklessness remained. The House of Lords subsequently was given the opportunity to clarify the law in *Adomako*. Lord Mackay approved of the cases of *Bateman* and *Andrews*, and gave his view that the law as stated in *Seymour* should no longer apply and that motor manslaughter should be dealt with in the same way as other forms of involuntary manslaughter. In doing so he set out three questions which must be answered in order to prove manslaughter by gross negligence.[32] First, the defendant must have breached a duty of care towards the victim who has died. Secondly, that breach must have caused the death of the victim. Thirdly, the jury must consider whether that breach of duty should be characterised as gross negligence and therefore as a crime.

Lord Mackay noted that as a result of applying this test, cases of motor manslaughter might become rare.[33] In a case of manslaughter involving motor vehicles it can be argued that all drivers owe a duty of care to other road users, whether they are pedestrians, cyclists or other drivers, and thus the first part of the test will always be met. The second part of the test is a simple question of causation. It appears, then, that it is the final part of the test which led Lord Mackay to suggest that motor manslaughter would become rare. In such cases he opined that juries should be instructed to consider the extent to which the defendant's conduct departed from the proper standard of care incumbent upon him, having regard to the risk of death involved. This test is one which bears a strong resemblance to the test required to prove dangerous driving and CDDD. One of the ways in which the tests can be distinguished is that whilst the jury must have regard to the risk of death involved in a case of manslaughter, for CDDD the relevant risk is that of serious injury or damage to property.

Although rare, prosecutions for motor manslaughter do occasionally take place. From looking through the sentencing reports it is possible to get a flavour of the type of case that comes before the court on such a charge. Cases involving death

27 [1983] 1 AC 624.
28 [1983] 2 AC 493.
29 [1982] AC 510.
30 [1995] 1 AC 171.
31 [1994] QB 302.
32 Above, n.30 at 187.
33 *Ibid.*

caused by a motor vehicle which do not take place on a road or other public place will normally be charged as manslaughter,[34] such as the case of *Barker*.[35] It remains possible, however, for a death on a public road to lead to a conviction for gross negligence manslaughter, as in the case of *Attorney-General's Reference No. 14 of 2001*,[36] in which an offender with defective vision drove in darkness without spectacles and was involved in a fatal collision. In recent years there appears to have been a small increase in the number of motor manslaughter cases.[37]

It may be that the possibility of juries returning verdicts of CDDD on a manslaughter charge will encourage prosecutors to charge the common law offence in future and increase the number of motor manslaughter cases further. However, this will be dependant on prosecutors' views of there being a realistic prospect of conviction in such cases. CDDD was first created in 1956, when the offence was causing death by reckless *or* dangerous driving. It was created because it was feared that many drivers who killed whilst driving badly escaped liability altogether, as juries were reluctant to convict them of manslaughter. This reluctance stemmed from a feeling that it could just as easily be the jurors themselves who were in the dock, and luck was between them and the label of 'manslaughterer'. This mentality of 'there but for the grace of God go I' was to be cured by creating a new offence, bearing a succinct description of what the offender had done. However, although the new legislation may have been more acceptable to jurors, some academics were less than impressed.[38] Over the years, several bodies have suggested reform of the law,[39] and a number of statutes have made various alterations to the law, including the Criminal Law Act 1977. This statute abolished the offences of dangerous driving and causing death by dangerous driving, but preserved the offence of causing death by reckless driving. The law changed again in 1991 when, on the recommendation of the North Report,[40] the Road Traffic Act 1988 was amended to replace reckless driving with dangerous driving.

The question that is yet to be answered is whether public attitudes have remained the same or changed in such a way as to make it more likely that jurors would be

---

34 CDDD can only be committed on a road or other public place.

35 [2003] 2 Cr App R (S) 22.

36 [2002] 1 Cr App R (S) 25.

37 See, for example, *AG's Reference (No. 134 of 2004)* [2005] Crim LR 321; *Attorney General's Reference (No. 111 of 2006)* [2007] 2 Cr App R (S) 26; *Cambray* [2007] RTR 10. The cases of *Rule* [2003] 1 Cr App R (S ) 47, *Parfitt* [2005] 1 Cr App R (S) 50 and *Dwyer* [2005] Crim LR 320 all involved defendant drivers who pleaded guilty to manslaughter but it is not clear from the reports whether the basis of the plea was gross negligence manslaughter or constructive manslaughter.

38 For example, see MacKenna, B. (1970), 'Causing Death by Reckless or Dangerous Driving: a Suggestion' Crim LR 67.

39 For example, both the James Committee on the Distribution of Criminal Business between the Crown Court and the Magistrates' Courts (1975) (*Report*, Cmnd 6323), and the Criminal Law Revision Committee (1976) (*Working Paper on Offences Against the Person*) recommended that the offence be repealed.

40 Department of Transport and Home Office (1988), *Road Traffic Law Review Report* (North Report) (London: HMSO).

willing to convict of manslaughter in cases of vehicular homicide. There is a dearth of evidence available either way,[41] although what little evidence there is suggests that attitudes may have changed. Twenty years ago Brook carried out a survey of attitudes to road traffic law.[42] He found that when he asked a representative sample of the public to rank eight traffic and non-traffic offences in order of seriousness, injuring a pedestrian whilst driving carelessly was ranked the most serious of the eight offences, while driving after drinking too much was placed second. The non-traffic offences of burglary, vandalising and shoplifting were placed in third, fifth and seventh place respectively. Speeding (driving at 50mph in a 30mph limit) was seen as the least serious of the eight offences, and driving whilst disqualified and driving through a red light were placed fourth and sixth.

Elsewhere in the British Commonwealth there is an indication of public attitudes to drivers who kill. In Victoria, Australia, a public attitude survey was conducted in 1991 in order to inform reform of the law in this area.[43] Respondents were given three scenarios and asked whether the appropriate charge in each would be manslaughter or some lesser offence.

The first scenario was of a drunk-driver knocking down and killing a pedestrian on a pedestrian crossing. Nearly 90 per cent of respondents responded that the appropriate charge was manslaughter. In the second scenario a person who is running late for work overtakes near the crest of a hill, without thinking and ignoring the double white lines, and kills the driver of an oncoming car. In this case 68.1 per cent thought that the driver should be charged with manslaughter, whilst 28.5 per cent thought that a lesser charge would be appropriate. The final scenario was a non-vehicular homicide involving a person who jokingly points a gun at another person without first checking to see if it is loaded. By accident, the gun goes off and the other person is killed. Over 56 per cent of respondents thought that manslaughter should be charged.

---

41 Barry Mitchell has carried out some research on public attitudes to homicide. In his original study none of the scenarios included in his study involved cases of vehicular homicide: Mitchell, B. (1998), 'Public Perceptions of Homicide and Criminal Justice', *British Journal of Criminology* 38:3, 453–472. In a follow-up survey, however, he reports that the responses of interviewees suggest that traffic homicides ought to be placed on a par with 'traditional' murders and manslaughters, with many interviewees of the opinion that a drunken motorist who kills a pedestrian should be convicted of manslaughter 'at least': Mitchell, B. (2000), 'Further Evidence of the Relationship Between Legal and Public Opinion on the Law of Homicide' *Crim LR* 814 at 823–824. In addition, in his more recent survey of public opinion relating to sentencing for the Law Commission, he reports that one of the issues raised by some participants was that of drink-drivers who kill. Some participants suggested that a mandatory sentence of indefinite disqualification from driving would be appropriate in such cases: Mitchell, B. (2005), 'Report on Public Survey of Murder and Mandatory Sentencing in Criminal Homicides', Appendix A to Law Commission for England and Wales, *A New Homicide Act for England and Wales?* (Consultation Paper No. 177).

42 Brook, L. (1987), *Attitudes to Road Traffic Law*, Transport and Road Research Laboratory CR 59.

43 Law Reform Commission of Victoria Report No. 45 (1992), *Death Caused by Dangerous Driving*, Appendix 3.

The Victorian Law Reform Commission took the following conclusion from the survey: 'the community appears to take a more punitive view of people who are grossly negligent in the use of motor vehicles than those who are grossly negligent in the handling of firearms'.[44] The Commission did recognise, however, that it is difficult to equate responses given in public opinion surveys with verdicts likely to be returned by juries at criminal trials, but pointed out that the only way of being sure is to implement change and monitor jury response.[45] It therefore recommended that the statutory offence of 'culpable driving causing death' be abolished and that all such cases be charged as manslaughter.

As noted by Yeo in his chapter of this book,[46] abolition did not take place but the penalty for culpable driving causing death was increased to ten years' imprisonment, and now stands at 20 years' imprisonment. The proposal for abolition was backed not only by the public opinion survey used to rebut arguments of pragmatism in favour of the special offence but, perhaps more importantly, arguments pertaining to legal theory in punishing drivers. The Commission argued that a driver who causes death because she is reckless, grossly negligent, or does an unlawful and dangerous act, deserves to be charged with manslaughter. She should not be charged with a lesser offence simply because a motor vehicle was used.

This combination of pragmatic and theoretical arguments relating to the need for a special offence will be explored throughout the rest of this chapter, starting with the question of whether it is theoretically preferable to retain special vehicular homicide offences. The issue at the heart of this discussion is the idea that homicide is a unique harm which may or may not require the law to provide special offences for different ways of causing the harm. Why is it that causing other harms by dangerous driving does not amount to specific offences but can be catered for by the endangerment offence of dangerous driving?

## III The Uniqueness of Homicide

Because of the uniqueness of homicide, Fletcher notes that the starting point for determining criminal liability is different to that of other harms. He states:

> What makes homicide unique is, among other things, the uniqueness of causing death. While all personal injuries and destruction of property are irreversible harms, causing death is a harm of a different order. Killing another human being is not only a worldly deprivation; in the Western conception of homicide, killing is an assault on the sacred, natural order.[47]

Fletcher later explores the implications of this:

> There are three prominent starting places for thinking about criminal liability. In the pattern of manifest criminality, the point of departure is an act that threatens the peace

44 *Ibid.*, p.10.

45 *Ibid.*

46 Yeo, S., in this volume.

47 Fletcher, G. (2000), *Rethinking Criminal Law* (Oxford: Oxford University Press) p.235.

> and order of community life. In the theory of subjective criminality, the starting place is the actor's intent to violate a protected legal interest. In the law of homicide, the focal point is neither the act nor the intent, but the fact of death. This overpowering fact is the point at which the law begins to draw the radius of liability. From this central point, the perspective is: who can be held accountable, and in what way, for the desecration of the human and divine realms? The question is never where to place the point of the legal compass, but how far the arc should sweep in bringing in persons to stand responsible for the death that has already occurred?[48]

The Law Commission of England and Wales has recently considered this question in detail, and provided recommendations for creating a new 'ladder' of homicide offences.[49] This provides for general homicide offences, with specific existing offences, which are the subject of this book, falling outside the scope of its terms of reference.[50] The question of what specific offences should exist beyond the recommended ladder, and how they should fit into the ladder, requires examination. If we are to have a hierarchy, or ladder, of homicide offences (which we should do), how far down the ladder do we go before we reach the limits of Fletcher's radius? This may depend on how we construct the ladder to begin with.

The Law Commission, like Fletcher, recognises the uniqueness of homicide in its Consultation Paper on homicide.[51] I will be using the Law Commission's proposals to help explore this question of how far the arc should sweep in permitting liability for homicide, taking as the starting point their ladder of offences of first degree murder (Murder 1), second degree murder (Murder 2) and manslaughter. Should the ladder (and thus the arc of liability) be extended to include more specific offences on lower rungs to accommodate death caused in specific ways, particularly by driving? Is there a need or even a justification for building such an extension?

## IV The Homicide Ladder

The Law Commission's proposals have been fairly well received and they do, it seems, create a logical hierarchy of offences dependant on the blameworthiness of the killer. I want to explore the structure of the different rungs of the ladder for 'killers' before addressing the question of whether existing or alternative vehicular homicide offences should be added to the bottom rungs of this ladder for 'causers of death' by driving. The difference between a 'killer' and a 'causer of death' is worth considering here. Fletcher explains that whether homicide amounts to 'killing' or 'causing death' depends on whether we take the 'harm-oriented' approach or the 'act-oriented approach' in analysing the *prima facie* case of homicide.[52] The harm-oriented approach, as expressed by Blackstone, supposes that killing amounts to

---

48 *Ibid.*, p.341.

49 Law Commission for England and Wales (2006), *Murder, Manslaughter and Infanticide* (Law Com. No. 304).

50 The exception here is that reform to the law of infanticide was considered.

51 Law Commission (2005), above n.41.

52 Fletcher, above n.47, p.238. A similar distinction is made by Gardner, who argues for the importance of distinguishing 'outcome reasons' from 'action reasons' not to kill:

murder unless justified or excused. The starting point is always death. Whereas, with the act-oriented approach, it is necessary to consider *mens rea* as a component of the *prima facie* case of homicide. One of the implications of the distinction is that a theory of negligence must be developed only if the act-orientated approach is adopted.[53] This, in turn, explains why the law on negligence has developed in recent history, as the law has taken a more act-oriented approach.[54] Here, in considering whether drivers should be liable for homicide, we must necessarily take the act-oriented approach, and consider them as 'causers of death' rather than 'killers'.

I will in fact be using the Law Commission's initial proposals for its ladder of homicide offences, rather than the recommendations published after consultation. The reason for this is that, unlike many consultees, I prefer the original proposals to the recommendations. This preference is explained by the analysis of the proposals which I provide below. The proposed ladder is for three general homicide offences:

> 'First degree murder' (mandatory life penalty):
> (1) Intentional killing.[55]
>
> 'Second degree murder' (discretionary life maximum penalty):
> (1) Killing where the offender did not intend to kill but did intend to do serious harm.
> (2) Recklessly indifferent killing, where the offender realised that his or her conduct involved an unjustified risk of killing, but pressed on with that conduct without caring whether or not death would result.[56]
> (3) Cases in which there is a partial defence to what would otherwise be 'first degree murder'.
>
> 1.40 Manslaughter (fixed term of years maximum penalty):
> (1) Killing through gross negligence;
> (2) Killing through an intentional act intended to cause injury or involving recklessness as to causing injury.[57]

How do the rungs of the ladder fit together to create a true hierarchy of blameworthiness, with Murder 1 at the top, Murder 2 in the middle and manslaughter at the bottom? Since the harm in homicide is constant (death), everything turns on the level of blameworthiness demonstrated, and I have therefore attempted to take a logical

---

Gardner, J. (1998), 'On the General Part of the Criminal Law' in Duff (ed.), *Philosophy and the Criminal Law* (Cambridge: Cambridge University Press).

53 Fletcher, above n.47, p.239.

54 *Ibid.*, p.240.

55 The recommendations in the Report add to this the alternative form of *mens rea* of intention to do serious harm being aware of a serious risk of causing death.

56 This was replaced in the Report by a clearer test of 'killing where there was an awareness of a serious risk of causing death, coupled with an intention to cause either (a) some injury; (b) a fear of injury; or (c) a risk of injury': Law Commission (2006), above n.49, para. 1.36.

57 Law Commission (2005), above n.41, paras 1.38–1.40.

approach to this by allocating points to the elements of blameworthiness. There are two elements of blameworthiness here: first, what we traditionally think of as *mens rea* terms such as intention and recklessness; secondly, what I shall term the *subject* (in terms of harm) of that *mens rea*.

First, each level of *mens rea*, representing one supporting side of the ladder, must be allocated a seriousness score. I have chosen to use a scale with a maximum of 5, and with each rung of the ladder set apart from the next at an equal distance or value, but any scale could be used. Although I have provided five anchoring points on each side of the scale the Law Commission's ladder only uses the top three. The bottom two points of each side of the scale have been added to help contribute to a discussion of whether further offences ought to be added to the ladder.

| | |
|---|---|
| Intention | = 5 points |
| Reckless indifference | = 4 points |
| Gross negligence | = 3 points |
| Negligence/carelessness | = 2 points |
| Blamelessness | = 0 points |

On the opposite side of the ladder the second support is made up of a scale of different levels of harm forming the subject of the *mens rea*. So was it death that was intended or foreseen, or some lesser harm?

| | |
|---|---|
| Death | = 5 points |
| Serious harm | = 4 points |
| Some harm | = 3 points |
| No physical harm but harm to property | = 2 points |
| No harm | = 0 points |

Having established these scores for the anchoring points it is then possible to add each side of the ladder together to determine where the rung is situated in the hierarchy and, as a result, what level of offence is achieved as a result of the sum of the two elements of blameworthiness. Thus:

| | |
|---|---|
| Intention (5) + Death (5) | = Murder 1 (10) |
| Reckless indifference (4) + Death (5) | = Murder 2 (9)[58] |
| Intention (5) + Serious harm (4) | = Murder 2 (9)[59] |
| Gross negligence (3) + Death (5) | = Manslaughter (8) |
| Intention (5) + Some harm (3) | = Manslaughter (8) |

58 Under the Law Commissions recommendations following consultation this could amount to first degree murder, which includes 'killing where there was an intention to do serious injury, coupled with an awareness of a serious risk of causing death'. I prefer the original proposal that first degree murder could only be committed with an intention to kill. This analysis should explain why.

59 Other than these two examples of Murder 2, this level of the ladder can be reached where D has successfully pleaded one of the partial defences to Murder 1. Thus each of these partial defences (provocation, diminished responsibility and possibly duress) should be given a score of -1 which would bring the mark of 10 for Murder 1 down to the required mark for Murder 2 of 9.

If the rules of this scale are to be followed then any combination resulting in a score of 8 should be manslaughter. This would, in addition to the Law Commission's proposals, include:

Reckless indifference (4) + Serious harm (4) = Manslaughter (8)

The importance of this schema[60] is that it suggests that any combination of the blameworthiness elements with a score of less than 8 is insufficient to lead to liability for the general homicide offences of murder and manslaughter. Gross negligence must relate to the risk of *death* involved, and if a person were only grossly negligent as to serious harm they would not be sufficiently blameworthy to warrant conviction for manslaughter (3 + 4 = 7). If someone intended to harm the victim's property by stealing or damaging it then they too would not face liability under this schema (5 + 2 = 7).

In relation to vehicular homicide, a driver who killed and met any of the requirements within the proposals should, no doubt, be liable for the corresponding offence. Tadros gives the example of D who drives his car at 70mph down a busy street, pursued by the police. If D was to drive up onto the pavement without caring about the consequences and a pedestrian were killed this would amount to reckless indifference as to death and therefore second degree murder.[61] What must then be established, however, is whether we should have more specific offences below the rung for manslaughter which would penalise those who cause death with a score lower than 8. Should we solely punish those who kill and fall within the general homicide offences or should we also punish those who are less blameworthy on the scale, but are involved in some activity (in this chapter, driving), which for various reasons might warrant liability for death at a lower rung of the ladder?

Under the current law those with a score of 7 or even as low as 5 can be liable for the specific statutory offence of CDDD. For CDDD the defendant's level of *mens rea* must be 'dangerousness' which I will, for the sake of simplicity, equate to gross negligence worth 3 points (particularly since the test of falling 'far below' the standard of a competent and careful driver has now been adopted elsewhere to indicate that negligence was gross)[62] and the subject of that *mens rea* is either 'injury to any person or serious damage to property'[63] worth 3 or 2 points, totalling 6 or 5. This demonstrates the difference between the current offences of CDDD and

60 This schema resembles an analysis of criminal liability provided in an old edition of Clarkson and Keating: Clarkson, C.M.V. and Keating, H.M. (1994), *Criminal Law: Text and Materials*, 3rd ed. (London: Sweet and Maxwell). Clarkson and Keating set out levels of blame and harm in a numerical hierarchy and proceeded to create a table from the conjunction of the two offence elements. This related to fatal and non-fatal offences against the person, and resulted in certain homicide offences equating in seriousness to certain non-fatal offences, since the authors were of the opinion that both elements of harm and blame 'should generally be equally weighted' (at p.812).

61 Tadros, V. (2006), 'The Homicide Ladder' *Modern Law Review* 69:4, 601–618 at 613.

62 Both the Law Commission's proposals for manslaughter in the Consultation Paper and the Corporate Manslaughter and Corporate Homicide Act 2007, s.1(4)(b), use this test.

63 Road Traffic Act 1988, s.2A(3).

manslaughter, given that the latter offence requires a risk of death but CDDD does not.[64] CDCD moves even further down the ladder, scoring 5 and below (remember that the definition of careless driving in the Road Safety Act does not relate to any risk at all – there is no equivalent to s.2A(3) RTA 1988).

This schema has one weakness which is that it fails to accommodate aggravating features which form a supplementary element to the blameworthiness assessment under current law. Thus someone guilty of CDCDUI would have the same score as for CDCD but could receive a far longer sentence (maximum of 14 years rather than five) because of the fact that they were under the influence of drink or drugs at time of the offence.[65] Some might argue, however, that the doctrine of prior fault comes into play here in that a drink-driver who drives carelessly and kills is more blameworthy than a sober careless driver because his carelessness is the result of driving under the influence. This, however, is not the rationale behind the offence of CDCDUI – there is no requirement that the carelessness be caused by the fact that the defendant was under the influence.

Providing more of a problem is the fact that the new offence of causing death by unlicensed, disqualified or uninsured driving is really a strict liability offence (there is no requirement that D drove dangerously or carelessly), and so D should be allocated a blameworthiness score of 0. However, the Government has decided (with the approval of Parliament) that driving without insurance or a licence or whilst disqualified warrants punishment for a specifically tailored homicide offence. It might be true that someone who is unlicensed, like someone who is drunk, is more likely to drive badly. However, if such a driver has driven badly he could be liable for CDCD or CDDD depending on the gravity of his driving and so there is no need for such an offence.

Perhaps the fact that these factors cannot be accommodated by the schema is not a weakness of the schema itself, but an indication that such offences punish those whose level of blameworthiness does not justify such punishment. The question that needs to be considered is whether offences with a low blameworthiness score (7 or below) ought to lead to liability for the harm caused – death? Or have the outer reaches of the arc or radius of liability been met at a score of 8?

---

64 I have, however, argued elsewhere that in most cases of CDDD there will have been a clear risk of death so that in practice there is little to distinguish CDDD from manslaughter: Cunningham, S. (2001), 'The Reality of Vehicular Homicides: Convictions for Murder, Manslaughter and Causing Death by Dangerous Driving' *Crim LR* 679. On that basis manslaughter could and should be charged in such cases. Here I am questioning the need for an offence which, on paper at least, punishes for death caused as a result of a lower level of blameworthiness.

65 In Clarkson and Keating's analysis the highest level of blameworthiness was 'intentionally bringing about the harm in aggravated circumstances': above, n.60, p.810. I am not proposing such an approach, since it would imply that Murder 1 would, as is the case in many states in the USA, be committed where the identity of the defendant (prisoner) or victim (child) was significant, or where the murder was committed using a particular method or in certain circumstances (torture; felony murder). However, it might be that further down the ladder, where negligence is aggravated by a factor reflecting greater blameworthiness (for example, drinking and driving), a higher grading in the schema ought to be attached.

The answer to this question will involve several additional issues. This assessment may bring to mind von Hirsch and Jareborg's Living Standard Analysis.[66] However, it should be noted at this stage that my starting point is different to theirs. Because we are dealing with homicide and, as Fletcher noted, the question of liability is determined differently to other kinds of harms because the starting point is always the fact of death, the ladder is determined by *mens rea* and blameworthiness rather than the level of harm caused, because this is consistent (death). It might, though, be possible to incorporate this ladder into the criminal law as a whole, to help determine proportionality in sentencing as the living-standard analysis attempted to do. Von Hirsch and Jareborg start with a harm analysis on which to construct a hierarchy of offences. We are starting with a blameworthiness analysis. So far the harm caused has been consistent – death. Would it then be possible to expand the analysis to combine the blameworthiness analysis with one of harm?

We can start off with a very simple ladder of harm:

Death = 10 points
GBH = 8 points
Some physical harm = 6 points
Harm to property = 4 points

I have used a higher ranking of points so that the score for the worst harm equates to the score for the worst level of blameworthiness. So someone who commits Murder 1 has a score of 20 (10 + 10). Someone who attempted to commit Murder 1 but failed and instead only caused serious harm would have a score of 18. This would rank some cases of attempted murder at the equivalent rung of a general offence ladder as manslaughter (blameworthiness score of 8 + harm score of 10).

This latter example might be attractive to some. This will depend, however, on the person's view as to what role luck should play in determining criminal liability. Those who think that luck should not determine D's level of offence might argue that because D has a higher blameworthiness score than someone who has committed manslaughter, and has no control over the outcome of his actions, he should receive a higher overall score. Thus it might be necessary to include within the ladder of harms those harms that have been risked, not just those that have been caused. Otherwise, an offence such as attempted murder would carry a different score depending on the particular circumstances of the case and whether any physical harm had been caused at all. If there was an objective risk of death but luckily the victim escaped with some lower level of harm, or indeed was unharmed, what score should that second order harm of risk of death attract? The answer to this question will probably be one of the most controversial issues to be discussed and is the subject of a separate chapter.[67]

66 Von Hirsch, A. and Jareborg, N. (1991), 'Gauging Criminal Harm: A Living Standard Analysis' *Oxford Journal of Legal Studies* 11, 1.

67 Written by Antony Duff. An in-depth discussion of this issue is beyond the scope of this chapter. I have recently addressed the issue: Cunningham, S. (2007), 'Punishing Drivers Who Kill: Putting Road Safety First?' *Legal Studies* 27:1, 288–311. One of the main arguments in favour of allowing 'moral luck' to play a part in determining liability is that once D chooses to break the law she changes her normative position and in doing so should accept

I support the view of Ashworth that, as a censuring institution, the criminal law should censure people for wrongs not misfortunes,[68] meaning that luck should not play a determinative role in establishing criminal liability. I might thus give a maximum harm score of 10 to a case in which death was risked. Alternatively, if, contrary to the argument here, the consensus is that luck should play a role in liability, it would be possible, as suggested by Von Hirsch and Jareborg, to apply a discount for the fact that the harm of death did not materialise,[69] and so it might warrant a score of 9.[70]

But why venture into these difficult waters if we are only concerned with the harm of death and the question of how far the arc of liability for homicide should reach? The answer is that if I am correct to suggest that luck ought not to determine liability, then those who risk death by driving but fortunately do not cause death should be liable for no lesser offence than those who risk death and *do* cause death. Additionally, those who cause death (by driving) but whose blameworthiness falls short of gross negligence as to death should not face liability for the harm caused. Can this be reflected numerically? Someone guilty of CDDD has an overall score of 17 at most (7 for blameworthiness + 10 for harm). Someone guilty of dangerous driving where death is risked but not caused will have the same score for blameworthiness but their overall score will depend on the number we allocate to the harm of risking death. If we give it a 9, the overall score will be 16 – only one less than CDDD and 2 less than manslaughter. Without a discount for the risk not materialising the overall score would be the same (17) and there would be no need for separate offences of CDDD or CDCD. An objection to this might be that, as we have seen, the definition of dangerous driving does not require a risk of death to have been created. All that is needed is a risk of injury (or serious damage to property). In many cases, however, a risk of death will have been created by dangerous driving. The lack of correspondence

---

the consequences (Horder, J (1995), 'A Critique of the Correspondence Principle in Criminal Law' *Crim LR* 759). I would counter that by questioning whether the argument can be applied to offences where there is no conscious choice to break the law. Offences of negligence such as dangerous driving and CDDD do not require any awareness on the part of the defendant that an offence is being committed or that a risk of harm has been created, unlike offences of violence such as assault which require the defendant to intend or be reckless as to at least causing the apprehension of unlawful force. Thus, unlike cases of constructive manslaughter where engaging in a crime of violence might justify imposing liability for death where that violence proves fatal, in the case of driving the role luck plays is to alter the family of offence under which the defendant is convicted (a driving offence becomes an offence of violence), without the subjective *mens rea* requirement that that would normally require. My argument is that this stretches the role of luck too far and a driver who drives badly has not changed her normative position in the same way as a defendant who chooses to engage in violent behaviour.

68 Ashworth, A. (1993), 'Taking the Consequences' in Shute, Gardner and Horder (eds), *Action and Value in the Criminal Law* (Oxford: Clarendon Press).

69 Above n.66, p.30. Von Hirsch and Jareborg did not provide a formula for such discounts, but suggested that the more remote the risk of death, the higher the discount should be.

70 This may or may not satisfy those who view harm as important and argue that we make our moral luck. They might call for a greater discount to be applied.

between the risk that must have been created and the risk caused in a case of CDDD is something which itself suggests that CDDD is illogical.

There might be further theoretical issues to be taken into account when deciding whether to do away with the specific offences, however. One justification put forward for having a separate offence of CDDD is that of 'situational relevance'. For example, Clarkson[71] argues that drivers who kill should be treated differently to other killers because driving is such a widespread activity that we identify with their actions more than with those of, for example, expert surgeons displaying gross negligence. Their wrong is 'situationally relevant'[72] to ourselves. This has echoes of the reasoning behind the introduction of the offence in the first place and the mentality of 'there but for the grace of God go I'. Having a method of killing more readily at one's disposal and realising that one could also cause death if one does not pay attention when driving, however, does not justify retaining a separate offence to cover such eventualities. It merely perpetuates an undesirable attitude towards driving (we would not fear the results of our dangerous driving if we did not drive dangerously). Whilst 'accidents will happen', it is very rare that road traffic collisions cannot be explained by either human error, to a lesser or greater degree, or else a mechanical defect or some other outside influence.[73]

A further issue to raise in relation to the idea of 'situational relevance' is that even if the public can, to some extent, identify with those drivers who cause a collision due to a momentary lapse of attention (which would certainly not lead to liability for CDDD), the same may not be true of identifying with HGV drivers, who having breached the rules on drivers' hours subsequently fall asleep at the wheel and plough into the rear of a queue of traffic on the motorway, causing multiple deaths.[74] Can we really draw a line between professionals, such as surgeons, with whom the public are not expected to identify, and professional drivers, who may operate machinery quite alien to members of the public who hold licences to drive cars?

Fletcher[75] suggests that in assessing the acceptability of risk-taking which leads to death the social value of an activity is an important factor in addition to gravity of risk and the actor's awareness of the risk being run. He argues that some risks can be offset by counterbalancing benefits, for example carrying out a dangerous operation to save a life. At present, doctors who perform dangerous surgery and do so with gross negligence, killing their patient, may be liable to be convicted of manslaughter. To contrast this with a driver who drives negligently and causes a fatal collision

---

71 Clarkson, C.M.V. (2000), 'Context and Culpability in Involuntary Manslaughter: Principle or Instinct?' in Ashworth and Mitchell, *Rethinking English Homicide Law* (Oxford: Oxford University Press).

72 A term first coined by Lloyd-Bostock: Lloyd-Bostock, S. (1979), 'The Ordinary Man, and the Psychology of Attributing Causes and Responsibility' *Modern Law Reivew* 42, 143–168 at 156.

73 This is the reason why the police are attempting to do away with the word 'accident' in their documentation and replace it with words such as 'collision' or 'road death incident'. The CPS similarly now prefers the term 'collision' to 'accident'.

74 Such a scenario is a fairly common cause of death on the roads and occurred in several of the cases studied for the purposes of my PhD.

75 Fletcher, above n.47, p.260.

shows that we do not apply theories consistently, as such drivers are liable to be convicted of CDDD, an offence which carries less stigma than manslaughter. Yet which is the most socially valuable of these two activities? It would be difficult to argue that driving is considerably more socially valuable so as to deserve a separate offence, whereas surgery does not. This is implicit in the fact that dangerous driving in itself is an unlawful activity, whereas negligently performing surgery is no crime at all, unless the doctor causes death with gross negligence. Distinguishing between activities by saying that the average man on the street carries out one (driving) and not the other (surgery, which is only carried out legally in the course of employment) is to make an immaterial differentiation. Such activities of social value which lead to death should be treated consistently and, if it is necessary to make them criminal offences, should all lead to the same level of criminal liability if carried out with the same degree of negligence.

This concept of 'situational relevance' brings nothing to the debate. The situation in which killings take place will always be relevant when determining whether negligence ought to lead to liability for death. The reason being is that in many cases of negligent killing it is an omission, rather than a positive act, which causes death. In order to establish whether someone can be liable for an omission it must be established that a duty of care was owed to V by D. This will depend on the situation in which D was acting. If it is in the situation of a doctor treating a patient then D will owe V a duty of care. If it is in the situation of a parent or guardian caring for a child then D will owe V a duty of care. If it is in the situation of D having assumed responsibility or created a dangerous situation, then D will owe V a duty of care. If it is in the situation of one road-user causing the death of another through diving, then D will owe V a duty of care. This does not assist us in deciding if any of these situations ought to lead to liability for a separate homicide offence rather than manslaughter.

Thus far my approach has attempted to apply logic to the question of whether there should be a special offence of vehicular homicide. The schema described above may be useful in establishing a hierarchy of offences according to blameworthiness, and where the bottom of the ladder begins can be determined by a numerical score. This in turn will help to promote proportionality in sentencing, as was the objective of von Hirsch and Jareborg's Living Standard Analysis. A ladder of offences anchored to a scale of blameworthiness allows the law to achieve its most important aim, and the one aspect of criminal law that distinguishes it from other branches of law: to express censure in relation to wrongdoing. To kill or to cause death is wrong, but there are degrees of wrongdoing that can be rationally demarcated. However, this discussion started by acknowledging the unique nature of homicide. Given the enormity of the resulting harm it may be that criminal offences could be created to help prevent that harm. Another important consideration is that it is not always possible for those involved in the administration of justice in such cases to remain rational and logical and there is arguably a need for the law (but not necessarily the criminal law) to acknowledge and accommodate more emotive concerns. The next section will discuss how that might be possible without interfering with the logical schema developed in this part.

## V Practical Concerns

One of the pragmatic issues in prosecuting vehicular homicide has already been addressed: the concern that juries may be reluctant to convict drivers of manslaughter. Beyond this there are two further pragmatic issues to consider. One of these relates to using the criminal law to do more than just censure wrongs, but to achieve utilitarian goals. The other relates to the perceived need of bereaved relatives for drivers to be punished for the harm they have caused. Whilst it is not suggested that victims ought to have a role to play in dictating the substance of the criminal law it may be naïve to think that their views can be ignored completely, especially given the likelihood that politicians will base their policies on popular opinion.[76]

### *(i) Utilitarian goals of the criminal law*

With the proposed ladder providing a rational basis for determining the seriousness of homicide offences and suggesting a possible cut-off point in terms of blameworthiness for liability for killings it might be said that this only deals with one aspect of criminalisation (censuring wrongs/just deserts/retributivism). It fails to recognise that there are also utilitarian reasons for punishment and we might want to punish those who kill but whose blameworthiness score is less than 8, albeit to a lesser extent, in order to achieve some utilitarian goal of punishment. In relation to those who kill whilst driving it could be argued that even where a driver's blameworthiness falls below the requirement of gross negligence in relation to death they ought to be punished in order to promote road safety goals. This was indeed one of the arguments put forward by the Government for introducing the new vehicular homicide offences within the Road Safety Act 2006. However, such a goal is unlikely to be achieved through the creation of serious homicide offences for the following reasons.[77]

In relation to deterrence, those who take risks do so because they hope that the risk will pay off. A driver who drives dangerously may not do so consciously, since it is possible to drive below the standard of the competent and careful driver without realising that one is so doing. One reason for this is that psychologists and criminologists have found that drivers usually self-appraise themselves highly, and would class their own driving as 'better than average'.[78] The test for dangerous driving is an objective test for good reason, but it does cause problems in terms of its capacity to deter drivers from committing the offence. If a driver views their driving, however risky, as better than average, they will often discount the possibility of having a collision because of their perception that their greater skill will allow them

76 For a discussion of the contribution of populist politics see, for example, Johnstone, G. (2000), 'Penal Policy Making: Elitist, Populist or Participatory' *Punishment and Society* 2, 161–180.

77 This argument no doubt deserves greater consideration than that given to it here. I have developed my arguments in a more comprehensive manner in Cunningham, above n.67.

78 See, for example, Svenson, O. (1981), 'Are We All Less Risky and More Skilful Than Our Fellow Drivers?' *Acta Psychologica* 47, 143–148.

to avoid the risk materialising. If they believe this, and are willing to risk their own life in the process, they are unlikely to be deterred from taking the risk by the threat of punishment for CDDD or CDCD. It is thus misguided to use deterrence as a justification for special vehicular homicide offences.

*(ii) Emotional involvement of victims' relatives*

It is often the case that relatives of homicide victims, when interviewed by the press following a criminal conviction and sentencing, will express a view that justice has not been done. Whatever the state of mind of the causer of death at the time of the death and the level of blameworthiness established by legal advocates, relatives will unavoidably feel that the result of a criminal trial in the form of a prison sentence should relate to, or even equate to, the harm of death caused. They have suffered the worst loss known to humans, and will be grieving long after the trial has ended and the public announcement as to culpability made. Often the sentence passed is seen to be woefully inadequate in reflecting that loss, and relatives may feel that insult has been added to injury by the sentencing judge. This may be so whatever the level of blameworthiness demonstrated by D. The relative of a victim of a careless driver may feel the same loss as a murder victim, and view any penalty as derisory. But we cannot expect relatives to remain rational and objective on the issue of exacting justice; that is the role of the State. The law should at least recognise their needs but should not alter D's fate in doing so.

Whilst the victim should not be entirely forgotten in any trial, it must be remembered that the criminal justice system exists in order, first of all, to determine the guilt of any suspect and, secondly, to decide upon a fit punishment if a conviction is obtained. Any victim of crime has suffered wrongdoing, but it is important that wrongdoing is not suffered by the defendant at the hands of the criminal justice system if that system is to avoid falling into disrepute. The criminal trial remains a dispute between the State and the defendant, not between the victim and the defendant. It may be possible for the victim of any wrongdoing to sue for damages in the civil courts, but in the criminal courts whilst the victim may have an emotional interest in seeing that justice is done it is the State which has a vested interest in seeing that punishment is brought to bear on any wrongdoing. As noted by Tadros, criminal conviction carries public moral condemnation in two senses: the condemnation is both *in public* and is expressed *to the public*.[79] It is not expressed solely to the victim.

Recent initiatives have attempted to temper the brutality of this truth by showing some recognition that the relatives of homicide victims are secondary victims who often want their loss acknowledged by the criminal courts. The Labour Government has said much, and done a substantial amount, to implement its policy that the criminal justice system ought to be rebalanced in favour of the victim.[80] In 2001 Victim Personal Statements were introduced, allowing victims of crime (including relatives of homicide victims) to put how they feel about the crime into words as a statement which is then available to decision makers within the criminal justice

79 Tadros, V. (2005), *Criminal Responsibility* (Oxford: Oxford University Press) p.2.

80 Home Office (2003), *Justice for All* (Cm. 5563).

process, and can be used by the judge in sentencing.[81] More recently the Victim's Advocate initiative has allowed bereaved relatives to use publicly funded advocates to help them at various stages of proceedings in cases of murder and manslaughter.[82] Advocates can be used as a way of imparting information to relatives about the law and procedure, to increase their understanding of the trial process. Advocates may also liaise with prosecutors on the case to put forward the relatives' views prior to trial and, perhaps more importantly, inform the relatives of any decisions made in relation to the case. Relatives are able to give a verbal statement of the impact of the homicide on their lives in court, with the assistance of the advocate if required. At the sentencing stage the advocate may advise the prosecution on the victim's behalf of any perceived inaccuracies in the defendant's plea in mitigation. This scheme was piloted in five areas in England and Wales from April 2006.

This initiative has attracted opposition as well as support. It has been pointed out that the purpose of the victim's advocate's address to the court at sentencing stage is unclear and is likely to raise false hopes that a severe sentence will be passed.[83] There is a question over whether any cathartic experience it provides for bereaved relatives will justify the court time it will take up.[84] There is also the danger that it may lead to inconsistency in sentencing.[85] Despite such concerns, however, the scheme has been extended to all courts in England and Wales and now includes cases of CDDD.[86]

Some victims' gripe with the criminal justice system is not only, if at all, with the sentence handed down by the judge following a conviction, but with the process as a whole. Respondents to the CPS consultation on prosecution policy in cases of bad driving expressed a feeling of lack of empathy or respect on the part of the CPS for victims' relatives.[87] Relatives of victims may have hoped that many questions would be answered during the course of the criminal trial, shedding light on the reasons for their loss so that they can better come to terms with it. But in some cases, particularly where a guilty plea is accepted by the prosecution avoiding the need for a trial, such questions remain unanswered.

If the criminal justice system is to maintain its role in bringing the defendant to justice whilst keeping the focus on the defendant rather than the victim, is there any alternative resolution for victims' relatives who have to endure the stress of a court case from the sidelines? Is there potential, perhaps, for a different type of court to meet their needs? The coroners' court system is currently undergoing major reform. This reform was sparked by the murders by Harold Shipman, who was able to kill dozens of his patients before any suspicion was laid at his door. However, the

81 *Practice Direction* issued on 16 October 2001 by Lord Woolf CJ: [2001] 1 WLR 2038.

82 Department for Constitutional Affairs (2005), *Hearing the Relatives of Murder and Manslaughter Victims*.

83 *The Times*, 24 April 2006.

84 *Ibid.*

85 Spencer, J. (2006), 'Victim Advocates and Victim Care – the Place of the Victim in the Criminal Process' *Magistrates' Court Practice* 10:4, 10.

86 *BBC News Online*, 1 October 2007: <http://news.bbc.co.uk/1/hi/uk/7021290.stm >.

87 CPS, above n.13.

reforms now extend beyond the need to ensure inquests take place in appropriate cases. Could coroners' courts in fact provide the forum in which relatives' victims have their emotional needs met following an unlawful homicide?

The uniqueness of homicide is still recognised by the existence of the coroner's court and the need to hold an inquest. Indeed, it may be the potential for an inquest, as much as that of a criminal prosecution, which is at the forefront of police officers' minds when investigating a fatal road traffic collision, and may explain the resources provided for the investigation of such cases.[88] Under current law an inquest will be opened whenever a death appears to be unexplained.

Here too, it seems that victims' relatives fail to have their emotional needs met under the current system. Unlike a criminal prosecution, the inquest is an inquisitorial process which seeks to establish the facts surrounding the death and does not seek in any way to apportion blame. The conclusions[89] open to the coroner or coroner's jury in a case of road death are those of accident/misadventure, unlawful killing[90] or an open verdict. In most cases the conclusion will be one of accident or misadventure, which according to Matthews are interchangeable terms, with no distinction between the two being observed in practice.[91] He notes, however, that it is sometimes suggested that: '"accident" connotes something over which there is no human control, or an unintended act, while "misadventure" indicates some deliberate (but lawful) human act which had unexpectedly taken a turn that leads to death. Thus misadventure, apparently involving the taking of a risk, is seen as morally more blameworthy than accident'.[92] Victims' families may well feel a sense of injustice, then, in a case in which they feel that some blame lies with a driver but the coroner's conclusion is one of accident.[93] Wells has suggested that the question posed at an inquest, that of explaining the cause of a sudden death 'cannot always be answered without playing

88 See Cunningham, S. (2005), 'The Unique Nature of Prosecutions in Cases of Fatal Road Traffic Collisions' *Crim LR* 934.

89 The word 'verdict' is used by the layman to refer to the answer on the form of inquisition which relates to the 'conclusion' of the coroner. 'Conclusion' rather than 'verdict' is the correct term in the legal sense: Matthews, P. (2002), *Jervis on the Office and Duties of Coroners*, 12th ed. (London: Sweet and Maxwell) para. 13–03.

90 'Unlawful killing' should be returned as a finding only in cases where the road death is likely to amount to murder or manslaughter, rather than CDDD or CDCDUI – see text to footnote 92 below.

91 Matthews, above n.89, at para. 13–26.

92 *Ibid.*

93 This was recognised in the Luce Report, which recommended that the current findings should be replaced by narrative and analytical findings but that for the purpose of collecting statistics such findings could be categorised in some way. The suggested categories include 'traumatic road death as passenger/pedestrian/driver' to replace 'accident' in cases of road death and 'traumatic death at the hand of one or more other people' to replace 'unlawful killing' in cases of assault. This would ensure that the findings remain as far as possible from determining liability: Luce Committee (2003), *Death Certification and Investigation in England and Wales and Northern Ireland: The Report of a Fundamental Review* (Cm. 5831) Chapter 8.

a part in allocating blame'.[94] This may be because historically allocating blame was part of the inquest's remit, and piecemeal reform has failed to establish a true rationale for the inquest: 'What is strange is that the different forms and functions of inquests and inquiries should be so varied, under-explored and rarely questioned'.[95]

This may be particularly true in relation to deaths caused in circumstances which may lead to liability for homicide offences which are fairly modern constructs, such as those under discussion in this chapter. Matthews submits that a conclusion of unlawful killing is not appropriate in cases of CDDD or CDCDUI, and is confined to the offences of murder, manslaughter and infanticide.[96] In practice, however, this question should rarely be raised, since in a case where CDDD or CDCDUI is charged, the coroner must adjourn the inquest until after the conclusion of criminal proceedings.[97] In most cases the inquest will never be resumed,[98] unless the accused pleads guilty to the charges and a trial is avoided.

Howarth notes that bereaved relatives can be bewildered by the conclusion of the inquest because there is a common expectation that 'something' will result from the inquest in the form of an explanation of *social cause* and an assignation of *blame*, as a way of making sense of their loss.[99] Even more incomprehensible is the fact that the conclusion of unlawful killing is intended to be a purely neutral conclusion as to fact,[100] and does not equate to a finding of guilt. In a recent consultation process by the CPS about its charging policy in cases of bad driving, 68 per cent of respondents were individuals, many of whom were relatives of victims of road traffic collisions.[101] When asked about how the CPS could offer an enhanced service to bereaved families, 'closer involvement by the CPS in inquests' was mentioned, and 28 of 40 responses to the question 'do you think it would be beneficial for the case prosecutor to attend the inquest?' were positive.[102]

It is not proposed that victims should receive an assignation of blame at the end of an inquest, although it may be appropriate that the social cause of death is discovered. Changes under the Draft Coroners Bill may, however, address many of the concerns that bereaved relatives have, and help them in providing a public and official explanation of the death. Under the Draft Coroners Bill[103] bereaved relatives will, according to the Lord Chancellor, be given a clear legal standing with rights

94 Wells, C. (1991), 'Inquests, inquiries and indictments: the official reception of death by disaster' *Legal Studies* 11, 71 at 77.

95 *Ibid.*, at 82.

96 Matthews, above n.89, para. 13–34.

97 *Ibid.*, para. 10–53.

98 *Ibid.*, para. 10–55.

99 Howarth, G. (1997), 'Death on the Road: The Role of the English Coroner's Court in the Social Construction of an Accident' in Mitchell (ed.), *The Aftermath of Road Accidents* (London: Routledge) p. 151.

100 Matthews, above n.89, para. 13–31.

101 CPS, above n.13, p. 10.

102 *Ibid.*, p. 11.

103 Cm. 6849 (2006).

of appeal against 'decisions which concern them'.[104] There will be a 'Charter for Bereaved People', similar to the Victims' Charter, providing standards of service that can be expected and rights of participation. There are also reforms relating to the organisation of the coroners' service, which requires modernisation, with the appointment of a Chief Coroner and the creation of a national Coronial Advisory Council.

If bereaved relatives were given access to documents relating to the death this might help them. Under the Charter for Bereaved People, relatives will have a right to view reports of any post-mortems and any other investigations.[105] However, this right may be of limited value given that the coroner can deny it in cases where the information must be kept confidential in order to protect the rights of third parties. Such a limit is unavoidable. However, more could be done in relation to the outcome of an inquest. Under the Draft Bill a jury will only be needed in cases involving the death of someone in custody.[106] It is already the position in practice that in the vast majority of cases a coroner will sit without a jury and return a finding on their own. It is also recognised by the explanatory notes that coroners are increasingly making use of narrative findings,[107] providing a few sentences rather than a simple finding of, for example, 'accident'. The Draft Bill would expand this to more cases, with Clause 12(2) giving the coroner:

> the power to make a report to a person who may have the power to prevent similar events happening in future. This power could, for example, be used by the coroner to report to a local authority the fact that several deaths have occurred in similar circumstances on the same stretch of road. It would then be up to the local authority to consider what action, if any, they should take.[108]

It is suggested that the reforms could go further. It might be preferable to allow the coroner to conduct a full investigation over a period of time, at the end of which they produced a written report setting out their findings in detail.[109] This might help

104 Foreword to the Draft Coroners Bill by Lord Falconer and Harriet Harman. The rights of appeal are provided for in Clause 60 of the Bill.

105 *Draft Charter for Bereaved People Who Come Into Contact with the Coroner Service*, para. 14.

106 Clause 13.

107 Explanatory Note to Clause 12.

108 *Ibid.*

109 It was recommended by the Shipman Inquiry that public inquests should only be held in cases where there was a 'public need to know' about the causes of death. In most cases there would be no public inquest but the coroner's investigations would result in a written report for bereaved relatives: *3rd Report of the Shipman Inquiry, Summary*, para. 113. The Luce Report similarly recommended that public inquests should only take place in limited circumstances, with road traffic deaths not automatically resulting in public inquests: Luce Committee (2003), above n.93, Chapter 7. The Shimpan Inquiry's suggestion was adopted by the Government in February 2006 in relation to specific deaths such as child deaths and suicides: Department for Constitutional Affairs (2006), *Coroners Service Reform: Briefing Note*, p.1. Following opposition from coroners this was dropped before the Draft Bill was published.

bereaved relatives gain 'closure'. They could examine the report at their leisure, and be provided a greater explanation than a simple finding or short narrative finding. If this means that their expectations in relation to the criminal courts are reduced this may be beneficial as it could prevent the Government feeling the need to introduce new legislation to placate the relatives of homicide victims, which seems to have been one of the main driving forces behind the creation of the new CDCD offence.[110]

The difficulty with this is that in most cases in which criminal charges are brought, it is unlikely that an inquest will take place. The law could be amended to allow for an inquiry by a coroner resulting in a written report even in cases where a criminal charge is brought. Difficulties with this approach are envisaged, however, in that it would be difficult for a coroner to return their finding before the trial took place as this could prejudice the case in the criminal court. However, the suggestion perhaps warrants further consideration since the role of the coroners' court would remain quite distinct from that of the Crown Court. Whilst a criminal court establishes whether punishment is necessary to express censure where it is appropriate to blame a causer of death, a coroner undertakes to establish the facts leading to death which could possibly enable what was once referred to as 'tainting'.

Returning to the work of Fletcher, he notes that historically there was a distinction between blaming a killer and tainting a causer of death: '[t]he tainted person is not necessarily to blame for causing death; he is to be shunned and separated, rather than punished'.[111] Because of the superstitious view that causers of death were contaminated with evil, the practice of tainting was left behind. Fletcher suggests that this was misguided: 'our concern for distancing ourselves from "pre-rational" legal forms camouflages the contemporary influences of these modes of thought'.[112] Since tainting does not amount to blaming, it may be that what bereaved relatives seek, albeit subconsciously, is not always to blame the driver who caused death but perhaps to taint them. Should the law seek to reinstate this tradition by providing a mechanism for tainting?

## VI Conclusion

There are various arguments in favour of maintaining special statutory offences dealing with vehicular homicide. The oldest is the pragmatic argument that juries will be reluctant to convict drivers for manslaughter. Doubt has been cast on the residual validity of such an argument. Other pragmatic arguments relate to using law enforcement to promote road safety and allowing the public to influence the content of the criminal law in a modern democracy. Again, it has been argued that such pragmatic goals are unlikely to be achieved by the substantive criminal law. Whilst it might be foolish for Parliament to ignore the pleas of bereaved relatives that the justice system is failing to reflect their bereavement, it would be more appropriate to use some process other than the criminal justice system to satisfy such demands.

110 See Cunningham, above n.67.

111 Fletcher, above n.47, p.345.

112 *Ibid.*, p.347.

They alone should not be used to support the creation or ongoing existence of special homicide offences.

Given that the most important function of the criminal law is to express censure for wrongs done it is the need to assess wrongdoing in a rational and logical manner that has been the focus of the arguments here. The wrong in causing death by driving is the same as the wrong in causing death in a negligent manner by any other means. Where gross negligence can be proven, there is no persuasive argument why causing death with a car in breach of the driver's duty of care to other road users should be treated in law any differently to causing death in breach of any other duty. Under current law and under the Law Commission's proposed ladder that amounts to liability for manslaughter.

It has been argued that the homicide ladder should not be extended to attach to the bottom of the ladder specific offences where the blameworthiness falls short of gross negligence as to death. I have used a numerical schema to illustrate this. It may be that, as suggested by Ashworth,[113] punishment for the underlying offences of dangerous driving should be punished more harshly under current law, to reflect the gravity of the harm risked but not caused due to luck. In any case, unless the charge of manslaughter can be made out in relation to a fatality resulting from dangerous driving, there is no convincing reason, either ideologically or pragmatically, to charge a driver with anything other than the underlying endangerment offence of dangerous driving.

113 Ashworth, above n.68, p.123.

Chapter 7

# Mum's Not the Word: An Analysis of Section 5, Domestic Violence, Crime and Victims Act 2004

Jonathan Herring

## I Introduction

'Parents "get away with murder"' screamed the newspaper headlines.[1] Something must be done agreed the Law Commission, the judiciary,[2] lawyers,[3] academics[4] and the Government. Hence, the new offence in section 5 of the Domestic Violence, Crime and Victims Act 2004 came to be born.

The source of all of this concern was a problem neatly summarised by the Law Commission:

> A child is cared for by two people (both parents, or a parent and another person). The child dies and medical evidence suggests that the death occurred as a result of ill-treatment. It is not clear which of the two carers is directly responsible for the ill-treatment which caused death. It is clear that at least one of the carers is guilty of a very serious criminal offence but it is possible that the ill-treatment occurred while one carer was asleep, or out of the room.[5]

As the Law Commission noted, following *Lane and Lane*[6] in such a case there would be enormous difficulties facing the Crown. At the close of the prosecution case each defendant to a murder charge could claim there was no case to answer in that there was insufficient evidence that they (rather than the other defendant) had killed the victim and each would have to be acquitted.[7] This could be avoided if the prosecution

1 Dyer, C. (2002), 'Parents get away with Murder' *Guardian*, 1 November 2002.

2 Rose, L.J. is reported to have said '[t]he present position is wholly unsatisfactory'. Law Commission (2003), *Children: Their Non-Accidental Death Or Serious Injury (Criminal Trials) A Consultative Report* (Law Com. No. 279) para. 2.27.

3 The Criminal Bar Association in its detailed response to the Law Commission Consultative Report began with the statement that 'doing nothing is not an option' (Law Commission (2003), *ibid.*, para. 2.27).

4 Cobley, C., Sanders, T. and Wheeler, P. (2003), 'Prosecuting cases of suspected "shaken baby syndrome" – a review of current issues' *Crim LR* 93.

5 The Law Commission (2003), above n.2, para. 1.1.

6 (1992) 94 Cr App R 180.

7 See *Studwick* (1994) 99 Cr App R 32; *S and C* [1996] Crim LR 346.

could prove that both were either the principal or the accessory to murder.[8] The mere fact that a person was present in the room at the time of the killing would not be sufficient to show they were accomplices.[9] In all of this it must be remembered that the prosecution must prove its case beyond reasonable doubt when it has been shown to be notoriously difficult to prove child abuse on the civil basis, let alone the criminal one.[10]

Section 5 of the Domestic Violence, Crime and Victims Act 2004 was created to deal with such cases. It enables the conviction of a defendant who ought to have known that their partner posed a serious risk to the child, even if they could not be proved to have been a principal or accomplice to a crime. The offence is not limited in its drafting to the 'which of them did it?' cases. It can also be used even where it is clear who did the killing, but the prosecution wish to punish the killer's partner for failing to protect the child from the danger posed.

The offence which was created is complex and controversial. This chapter will be in two halves. First, it will look at some of the complex issues involved in the interpretation of the offence. It will be suggested that the offence is replete with ambiguity and that it requires the drawing of distinctions which are hard to justify. Secondly, it will be argued that once the offence is put in its broader social context it becomes hard to justify in cases where the defendant has been the victim of domestic violence. This chapter will not discuss the enormously important procedural changes that are effected by section 6 of the Act, which raise important issues about the compatibility of the procedures with defendant's rights to a fair trial under Article 6 of the European Convention on Human Rights.[11]

## II The Background to the Offence

At the heart of the new section 5 offence is a desire to protect children and vulnerable adults from abuse. The statistics are disturbing. Infants under the age of one are more at risk of being killed than any other age group in England and Wales.[12] The average number of children under the age of 16 killed per year between 2000 and 2005 was 77.[13] Where a child under 1 was killed the parents were the principal suspect in 78 per cent of cases.[14] A major NSPCC study found that between 1 January 1998 and 31 December 2000 more than three children per week under the age of 10 were killed

8 *Marsh and Marsh v. Hodgson* [1974] *Crim LR* 35.

9 Griew, E. (1989), 'It must have been one of them' *Crim LR* 129 and Williams, G. (1989), 'Which of you did it?' 52 *MLR* 179.

10 Colby, C. (2006), 'The quest for truth: Substantiating allegations of physical abuse in criminal prosecutions and care proceedings' *International Journal of Law, Policy and the Family* 20, 317.

11 See for example, Hoyano, L. and Keenan, C. (2007), *Child Abuse* (Oxford: Oxford University Press) pp.163–166.

12 Home Office (2006), *Violent Crime Overview 2004/5* (London: Home Office).

13 *Ibid.*

14 Creighton, S. and Tissier, G. (2003), *Child Killings in England and Wales* (London: Home Office, 2003).

or seriously injured by their parents or carers.[15] Sixty-one per cent of these cases did not reach the courts and even where proceedings were brought in only 27 per cent was there a conviction. So for every one hundred children killed, in only 16 cases was there a successful prosecution. The report explained that a common reason was the difficulty in proving which of two individuals in the house with the child at the time of the killing had caused the death.[16] The problem on the ground was neatly summarised by the evidence of one police officer:[17]

> If you have a victim without a voice then you have got to prove that whoever had responsibility for that child is the person who caused that injury. ... The CPS will not prosecute a case where there is a possibility someone other than the offender has caused that injury.

The difficulty is, as the Court of Appeal has recently acknowledged, child abuse cases often involve a complex factual matrix: the adults involved often lie; the expert evidence can be equivocal; and the victims are unable to provide accounts of what happened.[18] As Lord Nicholls explained, in hearing a case concerning child abuse 'the court is frequently unable to discover exactly what happened ... the judge is unable to penetrate the fog of denials, evasions, trusts and half truths which all too often descend in court at fact-finding hearings'.[19]

## III Section 5

Section 5 of the Domestic Violence, Crime and Victims Act 2004 creates the offence of causing or allowing the death of a child or vulnerable adult. The section reads as follows:

> (1) A person ('D') is guilty of an offence if-
> (a) a child or vulnerable adult ('V') dies as a result of the unlawful act of a person who-
> (i) was a member of the same household as V, and
> (ii) had frequent contact with him,
> (b) D was such a person at the time of that act,
> (c) at that time there was a significant risk of serious physical harm being caused to V by the unlawful act of such a person, and
> (d) either D was the person whose act caused V's death or-
> (i) D was, or ought to have been, aware of the risk mentioned in paragraph (c),
> (ii) D failed to take such steps as he could reasonably have been expected to take to protect V from the risk, and

---

15 Creighton, S. (2004), *Child Protection Statistics* (London: Home Office).

16 Judge I. Plumstead, *Papers for the NSPCC 'Which of you did it?' Conference*, 2 November 2002.

17 Davis, G., Hoyano, L., Keenan, C., Maitland, L. and Morgan, R. (1999), *An Assessment of the Admissibility and Sufficiency of Evidence in Child Abuse Prosecutions: A Report for the Home Office* (London: Home Office) p.43.

18 *Re W, S and C* [2005] EWCA Crim 1095.

19 *Re H and R* [1996] AC 563.

(iii) the act occurred in circumstances of the kind that D foresaw or ought to have foreseen.

(2) The prosecution does not have to prove whether it is the first alternative in subsection (1)(d) or the second (sub-paragraphs (i) to (iii)) that applies.

(3) If D was not the mother or father of V-

(a) D may not be charged with an offence under this section if he was under the age of 16 at the time of the act that caused V's death;

(b) for the purposes of subsection (1)(d)(ii) D could not have been expected to take any such step as is referred to there before attaining that age.

(4) For the purposes of this section-

(a) a person is to be regarded as a 'member' of a particular household, even if he does not live in that household, if he visits it so often and for such periods of time that it is reasonable to regard him as a member of it;

(b) where V lived in different households at different times, 'the same household as V' refers to the household in which V was living at the time of the act that caused V's death.

(5) For the purposes of this section an 'unlawful' act is one that-

(a) constitutes an offence, or

(b) would constitute an offence but for being the act of-

(i) a person under the age of ten, or

(ii) a person entitled to rely on a defence of insanity.

Paragraph (b) does not apply to an act of D.

(6) In this section-

'act' includes a course of conduct and also includes omission;

'child' means a person under the age of 16;

'serious' harm means harm that amounts to grievous bodily harm for the purposes of the Offences against the Person Act 1861 (c. 100);

'vulnerable adult' means a person aged 16 or over whose ability to protect himself from violence, abuse or neglect is significantly impaired through physical or mental disability or illness, through old age or otherwise.

(7) A person guilty of an offence under this section is liable on conviction on indictment to imprisonment for a term not exceeding 14 years or to a fine, or to both.

### *(i) The central idea of the offence*

This is a complex offence. It will be explored by answering several central questions about its scope. Then some of its elements will be considered in more detail.

*(a) Who can be the victim of this offence?* The victim must be a child or a vulnerable adult. A child is defined as a person under the age of 16 and a vulnerable adult as 'a person aged 16 or over whose ability to protect himself from violence, abuse or neglect is significantly impaired through physical or mental disability or illness, through old age or otherwise'.[20]

*(b) Who can be guilty of this offence?* For a defendant (D) to be guilty of the offence they must have been a member of the same household as the victim (V) and 'had frequent contact with him' at the time of the act which killed the V. Section 5(4)(a)

20 S.5(6).

states that 'a person is to be regarded as a "member" of a particular household, even if he does not live in that household, if he visits it so often and for such periods of time that it is reasonable to regard him as a member of it'. So even if a person is not living in the house where the victim lives they can be regarded as a member of the household if they are a regular visitor.

*(c) What is the actus reus of the offence?* The offence can be committed in two ways:

> (a) D did an act or omission[21] which caused the death of the victim; or
> (b) D 'failed to take such steps as he could reasonably have been expected to take to protect V from the risk' of significant physical harm by the unlawful act of a person living in the same household as V and having frequent contact with V.[22]

There is no need for the prosecution to prove in which of these two ways the offence was committed as long as the jury are convinced it was one or the other.

*(d) What is the mens rea of the offence?* Where D's act or omission caused the death it appears that no *mens rea* is required, except that the act must be an 'offence'. The only *mens rea* requirement would therefore be for the offence which D is said to have committed when they killed V.[23]

Where the unlawful act of someone else caused V's death then it must be shown that D knew or ought to know that there was a significant risk of serious physical harm being caused to V by the unlawful act of a person living in V's household.[24] It must also be shown that the act which caused V's death occurred in circumstances of the kind that D foresaw or ought to have foreseen. This is notably an objective test.

*(ii) The ambiguities within the offence*

This offence oozes ambiguities. The rest of this chapter could easily be taken up with exploring them. But to leave space for a consideration of some of the broader issues only some of the key ones will be examined.

*(a) Household* In order to be guilty of the offence it must be shown that D 'was a member of the same household as V' and 'had frequent contact with him'. The Act does not offer a definition of the word 'household'. Presumably the existence of these two requirements indicates that it is possible for D to be in the same household as V, but not have frequent contact with them. Given the additional requirement that there is contact, it is suggested that 'household' is best regarded as a description of

21 S.5(6) makes it clear that an act includes an omission.

22 S.5(1)(d).

23 This version of the offence has a substantial overlap with constructive manslaughter; although it is narrower because (unlike constructive manslaughter) it requires proof there was a risk of serious physical harm.

24 It does not need to be shown that the risk is posed by the person who ultimately kills V.

physical residence. In other words that the defendant must live in the same house as the victim, but need not have any mutual life with the victim. This is reinforced by section 5(4)(b) which states that a person can be 'regarded' as a member of the household for the purposes of section 5 if they visit the household often enough that it is reasonable to regard them as a member of the household. Such a provision would only be necessary if co-residence was not normally seen as an essential element of a household.

It must be admitted that this interpretation is not consistent with that used where the term 'household' is used in other statutes. In the Inheritance (Provision for Family and Dependants) Act 1975 the word 'household'[25] has been taken to include those who were living together, but have since separated but are still in a relationship.[26] In *Kotke v Saffarini*,[27] it was held that the notion of a household in the 1975 Act was a 'concept somewhat elusive of definition, combining as it does both the physical connotation of a place i.e. a particular house or home and personal connotations of association i.e. the family or household resident within it. Both aspects are covered by the various dictionary definitions available'.[28]

In the light of such uncertainty over the meaning of household it would have been better to provide a statutory definition.[29] The context appears wide enough to include those living in the same household as the child and having regular contact with the child, even though the person has no especial responsibility towards the child. It may, therefore, include a lodger or family friend who is staying in the house for a reasonably long period.

Notably the Act does not cover relatives who are not a member of the child's household. If a close relative was present at the time when the child was killed it is not obvious that they should escape liability. For example, if a father who no longer lives with the child and has only occasional contact with the child is present at the time of the killing why should he not be expected to protect the children from a serious danger?[30] All will depend on whether his visits to the household are 'so often and for such periods of time that it is reasonable to regard him as a member of it'.[31] It is far from clear what frequency of contact will do that. And what of a father who sees the child very regularly but not at the child's house? Could that be such as to make it 'reasonable to regard him as a member of the household'? It might be stretching it too far to say that a father who has never entered the house is a member of the household. In dealing with such cases a court may be persuaded to reject the view suggested above that 'household' should be understood as a description of physical location, but rather as a description of a group of people sharing their family life. This does throw up the question of the theoretical basis for imposing

25 S.1A.

26 *Gully v Dix* [2004] 1 WLR 1399; [2004] EWCA Civ 139.

27 [2005] 1 FCR 642, para. 8.

28 Para. 8.

29 In the House of Lords debates (Hansard, H.L., 21 Jan 2004: Column GC362) Baroness Scotland stated that there had been a deliberate decision to leave the definition to courts.

30 Hayes, M. (2005), 'Criminal trials where a child is the "victim": Extra protection for children or a missed opportunity' *Child and Family Law Quarterly* 307, 317.

31 S.5(4)(a).

this obligation. Is it imposed on those who have a special responsibility towards the child? If so it appears too wide (it includes a lodger living in the same house as the child); but also too narrow (it does not include a father who is not living with the child and does not see the child very regularly). It might be argued that the limitation of household is based on the argument that only those living with the child are likely to know of the danger. This does not explain why it should not apply to those not living with the child, but who are aware of the risk to the child, such as a neighbour who regularly hears the child screaming.

One final point on the use of the term 'household' and that is that it does not include those working or residing in a care home or a nursery.[32] The Home Office circular states that such cases are dealt with by 'professional safeguards and standards and professional duties of care'. Is there a good reason why a care worker in a care home who is aware that a resident is being abused by a colleague is not under a criminal law duty to intervene, while an informal carer working at home, aware that a relative is abusing an older person would be?[33] Baroness Scotland explained the restriction of the offence to those in the same household as the child in these terms:

> As we have said, our proposed offence is confined to members of the household. It is drafted with the idea that members of the household will know enough about the activities of the other members that they can be expected to be aware of the risk to the victim and take action. They are 'complicit' in the offence, either directly or by proximity, through standing by during the preceding abuse or neglect and doing nothing. Therefore, in this context, if one were to ask, 'Am I my brother's keeper?', the answer would be, 'Yes'.[34]

These arguments would appear to apply equally in the residential home context as in a domestic setting.

*(b) Child or vulnerable adult* It is interesting that the age of 16 is used in this statute as the definition of a child. Generally in the law age 18 is the end of minority. It might be argued that the statute is designed to protect vulnerable people and it can be assumed that those aged 16 and over are no longer vulnerable. This leaves the question of vulnerable to what? In the definition of vulnerability the Act defines a vulnerable adult as one whose 'ability to protect himself from violence abuse or neglect is significantly impaired'. The statute appears to suggest then that although 16 and 17-year-olds may be vulnerable in some ways, they are not vulnerable to this particular danger unless they suffer from a physical or mental disability or illness so as to render them a vulnerable adult.

There is an interesting distinction that exists between the treatment under the offence of victims aged under 16 and vulnerable adults where the prosecution's case is that D failed to protect V from the risk of neglect at the hands of another. The distinction arises because it is necessary to show that at the time V was at a significant risk of serious physical harm from an *unlawful* omission. In the case of children this

---

32 *Home Office Circular 9/2005, The Domestic Violence, Crime and Victims Act 2004*, at para. 15.

33 Collinson, A. (2004), *Tough Love* (London: Policy Exchange).

34 Baroness Scotland, *Hansard, House of Lords*, 21 Jan 2004, Column GC361.

requirement poses no difficulty due to the offence of child neglect.[35] However, in the case of vulnerable adults there is no equivalent offence. Therefore, in a case involving a vulnerable adult, even though D may know that another person in the household is neglecting V and V is therefore liable to suffer serious harm, it will be difficult to show that this harm was caused by the *unlawful* act of another person. The prosecution might seek to rely on the offence of gross negligence manslaughter and claim that the vulnerable adult was at risk of being the victim of that offence. Or in a case where the neglect is intentional or reckless and a duty of care can be established between the D and V then it may be possible to argue there was a risk of an offence of inflicting grievous bodily harm under section 20 of the Offences against the Person 1861 being committed.[36] But neither of these arguments is without difficulty. It is not clear whether Parliament intended there to be this distinction between cases involving children and vulnerable adults in such cases.

*(c) The meaning of 'significant risk of serious harm'* The offence is committed where at the relevant time there was a significant risk of serious physical harm being caused to V by the unlawful act of a person in the same household as V and in frequent contact with him or her. Significant harm is defined in the 2004 Act as 'harm that amounts to grievous bodily harm for the purposes of the Offences against the Person Act 1861'.[37] That would cover any really serious injury. Under the 1861 Act grievous bodily harm would include a really serious psychological illness,[38] but section 5 limits the offence to 'serious physical harm'. Presumably that is intended to exclude risks of psychological harm, although it is not clear why they should be excluded. Consider a case where a mother is aware a father is engaging in sexual abuse of a child. Should there be any room for an argument that sexual abuse does not involve 'physical harm'?[39]

Another issue here is the meaning of 'significant'. In particular does this require it to be shown that the harm is more likely to occur than not; or is it sufficient to demonstrate that there is serious possibility? The Act provides no clear guidance on the meaning of 'significant risk'. One might argue that whether a risk is significant or not depends on what the risk is of. A low risk of death is significant; while a moderate risk of minor harm may not be. If that is right, given that we are talking about a serious harm, even a small risk may be regarded as significant.[40] On the other

35 Children and Young Person Act 1933, s.1.

36 The difficulty with lesser offences against the person is that if there is no positive act and only neglect, there will be no evidence of an assault or battery.

37 S.5(6).

38 *R v Burstow and Ireland* [1998] AC 147.

39 Notably, the concept of harm in s.5 is narrower than the notion of significant harm in the Children Act 1989. The Children Act 1989, s.31(9) defines harm as 'ill treatment or the impairment of health or development'. Health is defined to include physical or mental health. The statute also explicitly states that 'ill-treatment' embraces 'sexual abuse and forms of ill treatment which are not physical'. Significantly the Children Act 1989 also makes it clear that harm includes 'impairment suffered from seeing or hearing the ill-treatment of another' (s. 31(9) as amended by the Adoption and Children Act 2002, s.120).

40 The Law Commission, above n.2, para. 6.22 had preferred the phrase 'a real risk'.

hand, the use of the word significant is surely meant to add something to the idea of risk and so may be said to require proof that there is more than a mere possibility of serious harm. The Court of Appeal in *Stephens and Mujuru*[41] held that 'significant' in section 5 should carry 'its normal meaning'. A judge should not offer any guidance on the meaning of the word. That is, with respect, not very helpful, especially as a jury may seek the guidance from a judge in determining the meaning of 'significant risk'. It seems, however, the judiciary are unlikely to provide any further guidance on the meaning of the phrase.

*(d) The role of the requirement of 'significant risk of serious harm'* An essential element that must be proved for a conviction under section 5 is that there was a significant risk of serious physical harm being caused to V by the unlawful act of a person in the same household as V. This can produce some peculiar consequences. If a father was charged under section 5 and it became clear at trial that he had killed the victim, it would be a defence for him to claim that the killing was completely out of character and unpredictable and so there was no significant risk that he (or anyone else in the household) would cause the child serious physical harm. Even more oddly, this defence would not succeed if it could be shown that even though he did not pose a risk of harm to the child, his wife did. In a case where it is found that D killed the child why must it also be shown that there was a significant risk that D would cause the child serious harm? And why should it be relevant whether there was someone else who posed a risk of harm to the child?

*(e) Act/Omission* There are two ways D can be convicted of the section 5 offence following an omission. First, if D's act or omission causes the death of the victim *or* where D failed to take such steps as they could reasonably have been expected to take to protect V from the risk of significant physical harm by the unlawful act of a person living in the same household as V and having frequent contact with V. The fact that the alternative is provided must mean that the defendant can be liable for failing to intervene to protect V from an act in circumstances in which D would not be liable under the general law based on omissions. Under the general law on omissions if a defendant owes the victim a duty of care (as a parent will towards their children) and the defendant fails to act reasonably in accordance with that duty and as a result the victim dies then the defendant can be said to have caused the victim's death. The Act therefore must envision that D could be guilty even though it could not be shown that their breach of duty directly caused the death. An example of that would be where D is aware that her partner is a violent man who poses a risk to her children and yet she does not leave him or summon help. One evening he kills the children in circumstances in which she could not have intervened to protect the children. The section 5 offence means that although at the time of the killing she had not breached her duty and therefore would not be liable based on the usual rules on omissions liability, she would be liable if at some earlier time she would have been able to protect V from the risk, but failed to do so. Given the criminal law's general

41 [2007] EWCA Crim 1249.

reluctance to criminalise omissions, it is, perhaps, surprising that section 5 is willing to extend criminal liability for omissions in this context.

*(f) Where D is under 16* Generally an under 16-year-old cannot be charged with the section 5 offence. However, if the under 16-year-old is the parent of a child she can be convicted. Mary Hayes has expressed the concern that this could mean that a girl who has been brutally treated by a family member could face prosecution for failing to protect her baby from a fatal assault by that same family member.[42] Of course the jury could take the circumstances, including her age, into account and conclude that there were no reasonable steps that she could have taken to protect the child. The Home Office circular supports the conviction for under 16s on the basis that such parents will have had access to the advice and support of GPs, social services and health visitors and therefore will have access to assistance if they had concerns about their child. This may present a rather idealised view of minor parenthood and the degree of support available.

*(g) Sub-section 3(b)* Section 5(3)(a) states that a defendant may not be charged with an offence under the section if they were under the age of 16 at the time of the act that caused the victim's death, unless they were the mother or father of the victim.[43] Section 5(3)(b), however, then states that when considering what steps could be expected to take to protect the child 'D could not have been expected to take any such step as is referred to there before attaining that age'. The reference to that age must be the age of sixteen referred to in sub-section (a) immediately above. The problem is that as (a) has already said that a defendant cannot be charged with an offence if they are under 16 it seems unnecessary then to state that in considering whether an under 16 non-parent committed the offence that they are not expected to have taken any steps to protect V from the risk of harm. Sub-section (b) therefore appears at first sight to be redundant.

One explanation may be that sub-section (a) states that because an under 16-year-old non-parent cannot be charged with the offence this does not mean that they have not committed the offence. Section 5(1)(d)(ii) is telling us that in effect an under 16-year-old non-parent does not commit the offence where the basis of the charge is an omission.[44] The significance of this arises where an adult is charged with being an accessory to an offence committed by an under 16-year-old. Where the principal has not committed the *actus reus* of an offence then no one can be charged as an accessory.[45] The effect, then, of sub-section 3(b) is that an under 16 non-parent cannot commit the offence where the charge is based on an omission and nor can anyone be charged as an accessory for their failure to protect. An alternative, and perhaps more convincing explanation is that where D at the time of the killing is just

42 Hayes, M. (2005), above n.30 at 319.

43 I am grateful to Prof. Stanley Yeo for bringing the complexities of this provision to my attention.

44 *Home Office Circular 9/2005, Domestic Violence, Crime and Victims Act 2004*, para. 21.

45 *Loukes* [1996] Crim LR 341.

over 16, the prosecution cannot rely on their failures to protect V which took place before D's 16th birthday.

*(h) 'Ought' to have been aware* The defendant can be liable if they were, or ought to have been, aware of the significant risk of serious physical harm being caused to the child by a member of the child's household. This use of an objective test is, of course, controversial in the criminal law, especially in relation to serious offences. In *R v G and R*[46] the House of Lords famously asserted the importance of a requirement of subjective *mens rea* in English criminal law. That said, gross negligence manslaughter and rape[47] both use an objective test; although it might be replied that these both involve rather special situations. For manslaughter negligence *per se* is insufficient, it must be gross. In relation to rape it is very easy for the defendant to ensure that they have reasonable grounds for their belief, namely asking the complainant. In relation to section 5 mere negligence is required, and to have a reasonable belief in this context is not as straightforward as it is in relation to rape.

There is a particular difficulty in that behaviour which may obviously pose a significant risk of serious harm to some people will not to others. Let us say that the mother is aware that the father is regularly giving the child fierce corporal punishment. She, however, believes that this is an appropriate way to raise a child (say, because of her religious beliefs). Is she to be taken to be unaware of a risk, if most people would regard this conduct as indicative of a significant risk?

*(i) The defendant failed to take such steps as he could reasonably have been expected to take to protect the child from risk* This objective test is the standard one used in relation to omissions. Where a duty to act is found in criminal law the defendant will be liable if they did not act as a reasonable person would have acted. As always with any 'reasonable person' test there is the question of which, if any, characteristics of the defendant are to be taken into account.[48] Would a mother who produces evidence that she is suffering from 'battered women's syndrome' only be expected to act as would a reasonable woman suffering from that syndrome? Is low IQ a relevant factor?

The Home Office circular on the Act states that 'the circumstances of the person and their relationship to the victim'[49] should be taken into account in assessing what the reasonable person would have done. This is interesting for two reasons. First, it suggests that the defendant will be able to rely on their own particular characteristics and circumstances. Secondly, it suggests that less might be expected of a person whose relationship with the child is remote. The Home Office guidance states:

> For example, if the defendant is a foster-child of 16, the steps which he or she could be expected to take to protect a younger member of the household might be limited. If

46 [2004] 1 AC 1034.

47 Sexual Offences Act 2003, s.1.

48 See for example, *Bowen* [1996] 4 All ER 837 (on the use of the defendant's characteristics in relation to the defence of duress) and *Holley v A-G for Jersey* [2005] 3 All ER 371 (in relation to provocation).

49 *Home Office Circular 9/2005, Domestic Violence, Crime and Victims Act 2004*, para. 18.

> one of the defendants has themselves been the victim of domestic violence, the steps that defendant could have reasonably taken may be more limited than someone not suffering that violence. Depending on the facts of the particular case the court may find that the defendant may have been too frightened to take some of the steps which in other circumstances might have been available to them.[50]

However, shortly after that passage there is the following:

> The fact that the defendant may be young and uncertain, feel intimidated or have suffered violence, will not in itself be conclusive evidence that it was reasonable for the defendant *not* to take any steps to protect the victim. In most cases (although not necessarily all) there will be steps, however limited, which the defendant could have taken.[51]

This indicates that even where there has been violence or defendants are young they may still face difficulties in showing they could not have taken steps to protect the victim if they did nothing at all. The difficulty in relation to the omissions-based liability is that it is difficult to show that at no point in time could the defendant not have helped the victim. One might, for example, be willing to accept that a battered woman at the time of the killing was not responsible for her failure to intervene, but to be persuaded that there was never a point in time earlier when they should have intervened will prove much harder.

The Home Office guidance gives indications[52] of what steps could be taken to protect a child in these kinds of cases:

- Reporting suspicions of abuse to the police.
- Contacting social services. Most local authorities have websites and helplines for those seeking further advice.
- Making sure that the child or vulnerable person is treated promptly and appropriately for any injuries or illnesses which they may suffer.
- Explaining concerns to their family GP or health visitor.
- Contacting their teacher, head teacher or school nurse.
- Contacting organisations such as the NSPCC or Childline.
- Ringing one of the other voluntary agencies that support families, such as Home-Start.
- Contacting grandparents, an aunt or uncle, or another responsible adult member of the family.
- Exploring concerns with neighbours or others who may have contact with the person who is at risk.
- Making sure that alcoholism or drug dependence in other members of the household are acknowledged and appropriately treated.
- Attending anger management or parenting classes if appropriate, or ensuring other members of the household attend such classes.[53]

50 *Ibid.*, para. 18.
51 *Ibid.*, para. 24.
52 The list is not exhaustive: *ibid.*, para. 26.
53 *Ibid.*, para. 25.

To show that it was not reasonable for you to do anything may prove a Herculean task. The Home Office guidance notes that several of these could be done anonymously, if the victim feared domestic violence.[54] This is true, but if there is official intervention the abuser may well suspect that D had informed the authorities. Any suggestion that anonymity means that reporting the abuser is safe is naïve in the extreme. Further, the defendant is guilty if they 'failed to take such steps as' could reasonably be expected. This indicates that although D may have taken some steps to protect V, these may not be sufficient. How many of the things on the Home Office list should D do to avoid a conviction?

*(j) Why must the death be in circumstances of the kind that D foresaw or ought to have foreseen?* The wording of section 5 makes it clear that even if D was aware that V was at risk of significant physical harm from another and does not protect V, D will not be liable if the death occurred in circumstances of the kind that were not foreseen or ought to be foreseen. So, imagine a case where the mother knows the father tends to play very roughly with their baby, throwing them up in the air in a dangerous way. However, she fails to supervise him, comment on his conduct or inform any authorities. One day the father deliberately kills the baby by stabbing. Just because the method of killing was not that foreseen by D should that provide a defence? If D had acted as she 'should' and supervised the father or sought outside help then V may not have died. How is the fact that the way the father killed was not foreseen relevant? The essence of the offence is the failure not to protect V from the risk of serious harm as a result of which V died. That culpability is the same whether the form of killing was foreseen or not.

*(k) Only death* It should be noted that the offence is only committed where death results. Where V is not killed but suffers other serious harm D cannot be liable of an offence under section 5, even if they ought to know that the victim was at risk of suffering the harm and did nothing to protect the victim. Where death does not occur in the case of a child a charge still lies for the offence of child neglect.[55] Where V is a vulnerable adult there is no provision analogous to that relating to children and unless it is possible to establish liability under the general rules of omissions liability no charge can be laid.

Indeed one way the law could have responded to the problem of failure to protect cases is simply to increase the maximum sentence for child neglect (which is currently two years). That way the focus of the offence would be on the degree of the neglect, rather than the outcome of the act of someone else which would be outside the control of the defendant.

54 *Ibid.*, para. 26.

55 Children and Young Person Act 1933, s.1.

### *(iii) Conclusion on problems with statutory definition of the offence*

From this discussion two points in particular emerge. First, there are plenty of aspects of this offence that are ambiguous. This could be said to create 'rule of law' problems in particular because it is insufficiently clear when the obligation to ensure the child is protected under section 5 kicks in and what needs to be done by a defendant to attract liability. This is especially because there is no need to show that D was aware that V was suffering significant harm nor that they were aware they had failed adequately to protect the victim. Secondly, there are some arbitrary distinctions. Whether a person is a member of a household or not; the method of killing; whether the victim is a child or a vulnerable adult can all play a role in rendering a defendant guilty or not guilty and yet it is far from clear whether such distinctions should make such a difference in criminal liability.

## IV Policy

Turning now to look at some of the policy issues behind the offence. The motivation behind the creation of this offence is understandable. To acquit two parents knowing that one of them at least has committed murder or manslaughter is hard to stomach.[56] At worst it appears to provide an easy way of committing murder and being able to get away with it: just ensure that there are two of you present in the building at the time of the killing and both keep quiet.[57] The offence is useful even if the case is not of the 'which of you did it?' variety. Where one parent knows the other poses a threat to the child the law should protect children by requiring the other parent to take steps to avoid the danger. The most basic obligation of a parent is to protect the child's life. Children's rights to life deserve as much, if not more protection, as adults under the criminal law. The fact that so few child homicides are prosecuted could mean that children's right to be protected by the criminal law is being violated. The offence, Mary Hayes claims,

> aim[s] to achieve a proper balance between protecting the fundamental human rights of the child victims against the rights of those allegedly involved in a child's killing to receive a fair trial.[58]

The offence manages to protect children without resting on the fiction that because both carers were present and it was unclear who committed the offence that both are guilty of it. Instead it pinpoints the wrong in failing to offer sufficient protection to the child.

Professor Mary Becker expands on the justification behind legislation of this kind.

---

56 Davis, G. *et al.* (1999), above n.17.

57 Williams, G. (1989), 'Which of you did it?' *Modern Law Review* 52, 179.

58 Hayes, M. (2005), above n.30. For similar views from an American perspective see Rhein, R. (2003), 'Assessing criminal liability for the passive parent: Why New York should hold the passive parent criminally liable' *Cardozo Women's Law Journal* 9, 627.

> Adults in a household should be responsible for injury to the child if they knew or should have known about the abuse and could have taken steps to prevent the abuse by leaving with the children or reporting the abuse to the authorities. The assumption should be that the adult who was not literally a hostage – not literally coerced at every available second – could have acted to end abuse. Although the adult might have found herself or himself in circumstances such that protection of the child seemed impossible, the child is still a child. No matter how weak the mother, she is in a much better position than the child to prevent abuse and owes a duty of care to her children.[59]

The Home Office, when discussing the new offence, stated: 'The offence will only apply to a person who, because they were members of the household who had frequent contact with the victim, had a duty to protect the victim from harm. It is reasonable that a person in those circumstances should be expected to take some action if this is possible, not simply stand by and do nothing'.[60] The clear hope of the legislation is that it will provide a strong incentive to those living with children at risk of harm to ensure that the children are adequately protected.[61] Whether the existence of section 5 will affect the behaviour of people in that position remains to be seen. The evidence from other jurisdictions suggests that duty to rescue statutes generally,[62] and duty to protect children specifically, do not alter people's behaviour.[63]

There are many policy issues that could be raised concerning this offence. This chapter will focus on one particularly powerful set of concerns. These surround cases where a woman who is the victim of domestic violence is to be punished for failing to ensure protection for her children from the abuser who goes on to kill the children.[64] This is not to focus on a narrow band of cases. Where other jurisdictions have used 'failure to protect' statutes they are nearly always used against women and usually in cases where there has been a history of domestic violence.[65] There is, indeed, substantial evidence of the co-occurrence of child abuse and adult domestic

---

59 Becker, M. (1995), 'Double binds facing mothers in abusive families: Social support systems, custody outcomes and liability for acts of others' *University of Chicago Law School Roundtable* 2:13, 21.

60 *Home Office Circular 9/2005, The Domestic Violence, Crime and Victims Act 2004*, para. 12.

61 Tanck, N. (1987), 'Commendable or condemnable? Criminal liability for parents who fail to protect their children from abuse' *Wisconsin Law Review* 659; Peters-Baker, J. (1997), 'Punishing the passive parent: Ending a cycle of violence' *University of Missouri at Kansas City Law Review* 65, 1003.

62 Hyman, D. (2006), 'Rescue without law: An empirical perspective on the duty to rescue' *Texas Law Review* 84, 653.

63 Dunlap, J. (2004), 'Sometimes I feel like a motherless child: The error of pursuing battered mothers for failure to protect' *Loyola Law Review* 50, 565.

64 I use the term domestic violence here to indicate the intersection of violence, domesticity and structural inequality in the relationship, relying on the work of Dempsey, M. (2006), 'What counts as domestic violence? A conceptual analysis' *William and Mary Journal of Women and the Law* 12, 301.

65 Fugate, J. (2001), 'Who's failing whom? A critical look at failure-to-protect law' *New York University Law Review* 76, 272.

violence.[66] Estimates have suggested 40 per cent of child sexual abuse cases involve domestic violence and a third of child protection cases.[67]

It would be wrong to suggest that the killing of children is predominantly male. Child homicide is one of the few offences where women figure prominently as offenders.[68] In a Home Office review of statistics for England and Wales it was found that of killings of children under the age of one by natural parents, 47 per cent involved mothers and 53 per cent fathers.[69] When reading those figures it should be noted that children spend, generally, far more time with their mothers than their fathers.[70] Noticeably, looking at child killings by adults who are not natural parents, the vast majority are male. The topic of women killing their children is a very important one. It will not be dealt with here because it mainly occurs where women are caring for children alone.[71]

### *(i) Why domestic violence should be a defence to 'Failure to Protect'*

It will be argued that where the defendant has been the victim of domestic violence at the time of the killing it is inappropriate to charge her with failing to protect her children.[72] There are often good reasons why such defendants appear to 'fail to protect' their children. They may fear that an intervention will lead to further assaults. They may fear that seeking help will involve informing the police or social services and that may lead to the removal of their children. They may be convinced that there is nothing that can be done to protect the child. Mary Hayes argues that such reasons should not provide a defence. She explains:

> The message of the legislation is that parents and others are under a positive duty to take steps to protect children from significant risk. Their culpability lies in failing to take steps which a reasonable person would have taken. The defendant's reasons for his or her conduct are undoubtedly relevant but … not in relation to a finding of guilt.[73]

---

66 There is a substantial literature on this see, for example, Kruss Bell, M., Rivara, F. and Barnish, M. (2004), *Domestic Violence: A Literature Review* (HM Inspectorate of Probation); Kantor, G. and Little, L. (2003), 'Defining the Boundaries of Child Neglect: When Does Domestic Violence Equate With Parental Failure to Protect?' *Journal of Interpersonal Violence* 18, 338.

67 Humphreys, C. (2000), *Child Protection and Woman Protection: Links and Schisms. An Overview of the Research* (Women's Aid Federation of England); Mullender, A. (1996), *Rethinking Domestic Violence: The Social Work and Probation Response* (London: Routledge).

68 Alder, C. and Polk, K. (2001), *Child Victims of Homicide* (Cambridge: Cambridge University Press).

69 Brookman, F. and Maguire, M. (2003), *Reducing Homicide: a Review of the Possibilities* (London: Home Office).

70 *Ibid.*, 164.

71 *Ibid.*, 66–67.

72 Women's Aid Briefing Paper (2004), *The Domestic Violence, Crime and Victims Bill* (Bristol: Women's Aid).

73 Hayes, M. (2005), above n.30 at 317.

Rather than providing a defence, she suggests domestic violence might provide mitigation.

When considering the case of the victim of domestic violence, however, more thought needs to be given to the position the victim (now defendant) finds herself in. Andrea Dworkin writes of her experience as a domestic violence victim who failed to protect others from violence:

> Eventually I waited to die. I wanted to die. I hoped the next beating would kill me, or the one after that. When I would come to after being beaten unconscious, the first feeling I would have was an overwhelming sorrow that I was alive. I would ask God please to let me die now. My breasts were burned with lit cigarettes. He beat my legs with a heavy wood beam so that I couldn't walk. I was present when he did immoral things to other people; I was present when he hurt other people. I didn't help them.[74]

In her article she goes on to contrast the outpouring of concern that society feels towards the child harmed by the abuser with the lack of protection for the woman. She still feels a victim of domestic violence is culpable but sees the blame as resting with the absence of protection from violence that is offered by society. In short, can society legitimately punish a woman for failing to protect her child from violence when society itself has failed to protect her (and therefore the child) from violence as well?

We will return to those issues. For now we will look more precisely at why domestic violence against the defendant means that a section 5 charge should not be laid.

*(a) Mental condition defence* The offence fails to attach sufficient weight to the mental state of a woman suffering domestic violence.[75] Criminal lawyers have become familiar with the potential psychological impact of domestic violence through the debates that have surrounded women who have killed their abusers.[76] Of course, in that context it has been diminished responsibility or provocation which has been the source of the defence. For this offence those defences will not be available.[77] In her well-known book on battered women Leone Walker reports the effects that battering can have.

> Repeated batterings, like electrical shocks, diminish the woman's motivation to respond. She becomes passive. Secondly, her cognitive ability to perceive success is changed. She does not believe her response will result in a favourable outcome, whether or not it might

---

74 Dworkin, A. (1993), 'What battery really is' in Dworkin, A., *Letters From A War Zone Writings 1976–1989* (New York: Lawrence Hill Books) p.330.

75 Brown, G. (2005), 'When the bough breaks: traumatic paralysis – An affirmative defense for battered mothers' *William Mitchell Law Review* 189.

76 McColgan, A. (1993), 'In defence of battered women who kill' *Oxford Journal of Legal Studies* 13, 508.

77 Provocation and diminished responsibility are only defences to murder: Homicide Act 1957, ss.2 and 3.

> ... The learning ability is hampered and the repertoire of responses from which people can choose is narrowed. In this way, battered women become blind to their options.[78]

Battering has been linked to adverse psychological impacts on victims.[79] The impact of these can be that while in retrospect and from the outside, the death of the child may appear as an inevitable and foreseeable result of the abuse, that is not so for those trapped within the relationship.[80] For example, the complex effects of domestic violence can include 'traumatic bonding' whereby the victim becomes increasingly emotionally dependant on the abuser and is convinced that the violence has stopped or is about to stop.[81] The victim may regard herself as to blame for the violence and therefore believe that if she can modify her behaviour she and the children can be safe.[82] Another issue here concerns the unpredictability of abuse. Just when it appears the violence is about to stop it starts up again. All of these can restrict the victim's ability to see the need for protection. Indeed domestic violence by a man is often used precisely as a way of exercising control over his partner and robbing her of interaction with the outside world.[83]

Consider the following narrative from an American woman who suffered domestic violence and was subsequently charged for failing to protect her child:

> My husband started abusing my son when I wouldn't have sex. When he started hurting my son, I started trying to fight back and protect my son, but that only made things worse. He beat both of us worse than ever. He told me he would call my welfare worker and say I was the one hurting my son if I told the police. He sounded really convincing, and I believed him. He did things like burn my son with hot water in the bathtub while I was tied up on the bed. I lied to the neighbors sometimes, but I think they knew ... My welfare was cut off because I missed my face-to-face [meeting] because I was so badly beaten ... One day we were all hungry, and my son was crying. He beat him so badly I was really scared. He tied him up and made me have sex while my son was under the bed. When it was over, I rushed to get my son, but he wasn't breathing. He screamed, 'Look what you did, you killed him'. That's all I remember. I was crying and screaming for what seemed like a day ... When I threatened to tell the truth he went to my grandmother's house and beat her almost to death as a way to keep me quiet ...[84]

78 Walker, L. (1984), *The Battered Woman Syndrome* (New York: Springer) pp.48–49.

79 Humphreys, C. and Thiara, R. (2003), 'Mental health and domestic violence: I call it symptoms of abuse' *British Journal of Social Work* 33, 209.

80 Dunlap, J. (2004), above n.63.

81 Dutton, D. and Painter, S. (1993), 'Emotional Attachments in Abusive Relationships: A Test Of Traumatic Bonding Theory' *Violence & Victims* 8, 105 at 105.

82 Johnson, M. and Ferraro, K. (2000) 'Research on domestic violence in the 1990s, making distinctions' *Journal of Marriage and the Family* 62, 948 at 957.

83 *Ibid.*

84 Reported in Richie, B. (1996), *Compelled to Crime: Gender Entrapment of Battered Black Women* (New York; London: Routledge) pp.2–3.

As this indicates, violence distorts the perception of reality and saps the energy to do anything more than survive.[85] The violence will impact on the woman's awareness of the situation; the alternatives open to her; the risks to the children. The Home Office Circular recognises this:

> Domestic violence may seriously undermine the confidence of the victim and create an atmosphere of intimidation, shame and low self-esteem. It may not be easy for people to come forward if they are the victims of or witnesses to domestic violence or abuse. They may be very reluctant to admit that they are victims of domestic violence and therefore may not make clear their true circumstances, including any extenuating circumstances such as fear of the perpetrator. They may be afraid that they will be blamed for what has happened and that the family will be broken up and children will be taken into care.[86]

So, then, when considering what could be reasonably expected of the victim of domestic violence the effect of domestic violence on the victim must be taken into account. This may well require the jury to receive expert evidence.[87]

*(b) Reasons for not intervening* In some cases the mother has good reasons for not intervening. For a mother to intervene to protect her child by warning the relevant authority or restricting contact between the abuser and the child may be extremely dangerous. For a woman and her children to leave the abuser is often more dangerous than remaining with him.[88] It is easy from the outside to think of 'obvious' solutions for the woman, such as leaving the abuser or contacting the authorities, but these can be fraught with dangers. As Generva Brown notes:

> The paradigm of punishing battered mothers for the death of their own children places abused families in competing positions for protection and safety. If the mother is the last line of protection for abused children, who protects the mother? The tactics a battered mother uses to protect her child, she must also use to protect herself. When the levee breaks, when the battered mother's strategies no longer placate the batterer, the mother risks criminal prosecution and termination of her parental rights for not sufficiently protecting her child.[89]

The argument, then, is that extraordinary measures are expected of the 'reasonable mother'. Mothers do and are expected, to give up everything for the child, even to

---

85 Miccio, G. (1999), 'A reasonable battered mother? Redefining, reconstructing, and recreating the battered mother in child protective proceedings' *Harvard Women's Law Journal* 22, 89.

86 Home Office, *Home Office Circular 9/2005, Domestic Violence, Crime and Victims Act 2004*, para. 22.

87 Although see for concerns about the use of expert evidence, Kaganas, F. (2002), 'Domestic homicide, gender and the expert', in Bainham, A., Sclater, S. and Richards, M. (eds) (2002), *Body Lore and Laws* (Oxford: Hart Publishing).

88 Humphreys, C. and Thiara, R. (2003), 'Neither justice nor protection; women's experiences of post separation violence' *Journal of Social Welfare and Family Law* 25, 195.

89 Brown, G. (2005), above n.75.

the extent of endangering their own lives.[90] During the passage of the Bill, Baroness Scotland said: 'It is not an acceptable position for a parent – no matter how vulnerable or fearful they are for themselves – to do nothing for a child who is at risk'.[91] Where any attempt to protect children is likely to endanger her life or that of her children surely doing nothing is not only acceptable, but required.

What also may be so easily overlooked by juries and prosecutors, at least without expert assistance, are the myriad of ways that abused mothers do seek to protect their children: placing themselves as a buffer or alternative source for the abuser's violence; seeking to ensure that the child is alone with the abuser as little as possible; cutting back on working hours to be present with the child.[92] To some such protection or coping may appear feeble, but they may be the best that can be offered. Many writing in support of offences such as that in section 5 complain of the non-action of the mothers who are seen to be standing by while the abuse takes place. In fact non-action is rare. The kind of avoidance tactics, such as already mentioned, are often used, but are rarely given the attention they deserve.[93]

Women and children seeking to escape violence face dangers not only from the abuser. A woman fleeing from the violence with children will be risking the child with inadequate housing, financial insecurity and depriving the children of their relationship with their father.[94] These dangers too need to be weighed up against the risk posed by the abusive partner.

All of this means that the 'obvious' things that should be done by a woman and child to escape a violent situation are not necessarily safe or viable. In many cases it is a choice between the risk of violence in staying in the house or the risk of violence that will arise from seeking protection. An abused woman may well decide that for herself and her children the violence to which she has become accustomed is safer than the violence that may be provoked by an attempt to leave or seek assistance. Can we be confident that such an assessment is wrong?

*(c) The state's responsibility towards abused children* Under the Human Rights Act 1998 the state and public authorities have a special duty to protect children's rights.[95] If the authority fails to do all that could reasonably be expected of it to avoid a real and immediate risk to life of a child then the authority will have breached its

90 Jacobs, M. (1998), 'Requiring battered women die: Murder liability for mothers under failure to protect statutes' *Journal of Criminal Law and Criminology* 88, 579.

91 House of Lords, *Hansard*, 9 March 2004, Column 1163.

92 *Ibid.*

93 Magen, R. (1999), 'In the best interests of battered women: Reconceptualizing allegations of failure to protect' *Child Maltreatment* 4, 127.

94 Roberts, D. (1993), 'Motherhood and crime' *Iowa Law Review* 79, 95.

95 *R. (on the application of Plymouth City Council) v HM Coroner for Devon* [2005] 2 FCR 428. Law Commission (Law Com. No. 279) *Children: Their Non-Accidental Death Or Serious Injury (Criminal Trials) A Consultative Report* 2003 also refers to the right of the child to protection from violence that is enshrined in art.19 of the Convention on the Rights of the Child, although this is not technically binding on English courts.

duties to the child arising from the child's rights to life under article 2 of the ECHR.[96] Article 2 requires the state to intervene to protect children and vulnerable adults from serious violence of which the state is (or ought to have been) aware and also to ensure that the state enacts legislation to provide protection of children's rights. The point here is not to suggest that the legislation should have enabled the conviction of a local authority or its employees; but rather to make the point that where a child has been killed in a home a number of people may have failed to fulfil their legal responsibilities.

Let us consider a mother who is aware that her husband is being increasingly violent to the children. She has notified the local authority and they are aware of the risks, but fail to offer her or the child any protection. The mother does nothing more and the child is killed. While a jury might decide that informing the local authority was enough to meet her duty under section 5, it may well decide that she should have done more and a conviction is possible. But, is the mother any less to blame than the local authority in this case? Perhaps the obvious retort to this is that it has never been a defence to a criminal charge that someone else was also responsible for the harm to the victim.

However, particularly in the case where the mother is the victim of domestic violence the state's obligations to protect the children become heightened. There is a danger that the use of section 5 is an attempt to 'reprivatise' the responsibility for child abuse. The state should not claim to be satisfying its obligation to abused children by regarding mothers as having the role of protecting children and to punish them for failing to fulfil their obligations, when the state has likewise failed in its obligation towards children, without culpability.

*(d) The State's responsibilities towards the victim* If the State is to impose obligations on parents to care for children then it must provide the necessary assistance to do so.[97] Generally providing ready means of accessing help from the police and the social services to protect children will meet such an obligation. However, in the case where the defendant has suffered domestic violence this is not so. The provision of services for women seeking to escape violence are inadequate, especially given the vulnerable state they are in. There is still a desperate shortage of adequate shelters, financial help,[98] and wider social support for victims of domestic violence.[99] The current position where domestic violence cases are still not taken sufficiently

96 *E v UK* [2002] 3 FCR 700; *Z v UK* [2001] 2 FCR 246. See Choudhry, S. and Herring, J. (2006) 'Domestic violence and the Human Rights Act 1998: A new means of legal intervention?' *Public Law* 752 for a further discussion of this.

97 Kopels, S. and Sheridan, M. (2002), 'Adding Legal Insult to Injury: Battered Women, Their Children, and the Failure to Protect' *Affilia* 17, 9.

98 Melner, A. (1998), 'Rights of Abused Mothers Vs. Best Interest of Abused Children: Courts' Termination of Battered Women's Parental Rights Due to Failure to Protect Their Children From Abuse' *South California Review Law and Women's Studies* 7, 229.

99 Toren, A. (2004), *Survey of Domestic Violence Services* (Bristol: Women's Aid).

seriously by the police or the courts mean that the obligations imposed by section 5 become hard to justify.[100]

Not only that, but as a central part of the state's obligation to protect children is the obligation to protect their primary carers. Where the state fails to provide adequate protection from domestic violence it has failed the child and infringed the child's rights. For the state then to penalise the mother for the results of its own failure to protect is to penalise not the perpetrator of a crime but its victim.[101] As Kristian Miccio writes: 'Women are subjects of a system of familial terror, supported by state inaction where the veil of familial privacy shields the perpetrator and the state from accountability'.[102]

*(e) The division of primary carer and child* The standard presentation of the kind of wrong that we are faced with in these cases is that the child[103] (the victim) needs the protection of their mother (the defendant) from the abuser. Often the issues in this debate are presented as a clash between those who seek to promote the interests of battered women and those who seek to promote the interests of children.[104] The flaw in this presentation is that involves a separation of the child and the mother.[105] We cannot address protection of children in isolation from protection of their carers.[106] The interests of a child and her primary carer are intertwined.[107] To harm a primary carer is to harm the child; to harm the child is to harm the primary carer.[108] Protecting the child in these cases involves protecting the mother. When the mother is protecting herself she is protecting her child. One of the ironies of the law as it stands is that the more serious the abuse the mother has suffered the greater the threat that the abuser poses to her child and so the more blameworthy she is. The attempt by the law to prise apart the mother and child's interests by classifying one as the defendant and the other as the victim misrepresents the true position where their

100 See, for the tragic results of the state's failure to protect victims of domestic violence, *R (Mullane) v W. Berkshire Safer Communities Partnership* [2006] EWHC 2499.

101 Krane, J. (2003), *What's Mother Got To Do With It: Protecting Children From Sexual Abuse* (Toronto: University Of Toronto Press); Loder Clark, N. (1987), 'Crime Begins At Home: Let's Stop Punishing Victims and Perpetuating Violence' *William and Mary Law Review* 28, 263.

102 Miccio, G. (1999), above n.85.

103 Or vulnerable adult.

104 Buchbinder, E. and Wisikovits, Z. (2004), 'Reporting bad results: The ethical responsibility of presenting abused women's parenting practices in a negative light' *Child and Family Social Work* 9, 359.

105 Griffin, J. (2004), '"Which one of you did it?" Criminal liability for "causing or allowing" the death of a child' *Indiana International and Comparative Law Review* 15, 89.

106 Ahearn, K., Hodes, C., Holmes, L., Shapiro, L. and Witherspoon, I. (2000), 'Charging battered mothers with "failure to protect": Still blaming the victim' *Fordham Urban Law Journal* 27, 849.

107 Miccio, G. (2005), 'Exiled from the province of care: Domestic violence, duty and conceptions of state accountability' *Rutgers Law Journal* 37, 111.

108 Herring, J. (2005), 'Farewell welfare?' *Journal of Social Welfare and Family Law* 159.

interests are interdependent and both the mother and child are victims of the man's violence. Legal intervention should focus on the promotion of a just, non-violent relationship between carer and child, rather than seeking falsely to pit their interests against each other.[109]

*(f) The invisibility of the abuser*[110] The use of failure to protect offences such as section 5 can lead to a misfocusing of legal, professional and media presentation.[111] Somehow in these cases the responsibility of the abuser for what has happened is lost and it is the mother who is held up for public opprobrium.[112] The headlines in the media used to describe the recent cases involving the section 5 offence are revealing: 'Woman lets boyfriend kill her baby';[113] 'Mother allowed baby son's murder';[114] and 'Mother first to be convicted of failing to stop violent lover killing her baby'.[115] In one popular daily newspaper we read 'For her dereliction of the most basic motherly instinct, 23-year-old Hayley is now the first woman ever to be convicted of the new charge of familial homicide, or allowing the death of a child. And hurrah for that: frankly, if it were left to me, I'd throw away the key'.[116] Blogs and message boards on these cases contain similar vitriol against the mothers in these cases, with virtually nothing said against the men who have actually killed the children.[117]

This is also reflected in social work intervention in cases involving child abuse. The intervention nearly always focuses on the mother.[118] She is seen as the one amenable to change: pressure is put on her to protect the child; move out if necessary; ensure the child is never left alone with the abuse, and so on.[119] There often appears no pressure on the abuser to face up to his responsibilities for what he has done.

While not going that far, academics Laura Hoyano and Caroline Keenan are willing to say that there is 'a growing recognition in the law that in cases where an adult is a child's only hope of protection, the failure of that adult to effect an easy rescue of the child from the violence the child is suffering, can be as culpable as the person

109 Magen, R. (1999), above n.93.

110 Edleson, J. (1998), 'Responsible mothers and invisible men: Child protection in the case of adult domestic violence' 13 *Journal of Interpersonal Violence* 294; Dunlap, J. (2004), above n.63.

111 Edelson, L. (1998), *ibid.*

112 Clark, N. (1987), 'Crime begins at home: Let's stop punishing victims and perpetuating violence' *William and Mary Law Review* 28, 263.

113 *BBC Newsonline*, 'Woman let boyfriend kill her baby' 11 April 2006.

114 *BBC Newsonline*, 'Mother allowed baby son's murder' 13 March 2007.

115 Salkeld, L. (2006), 'Mother first to be convicted of failing to stop violent lover killing her baby' *Daily Mail*, 7 November 2006.

116 C. Sarler, 'Why is it NEVER a woman's fault?' *Daily Mail*, 24 January 2007.

117 See for example <www.crimelibrary.com/message_boards/index.html>; <http://eternalbachelor.blogspot.com/2006_11_01_archive.html>.

118 Scourfield, J. (2001), 'Constructing women in child protection work' *Child and Family Social Work* 6, 77; Davies, L. and Krane, J. (2006), 'Collaborate with caution: Protecting children, helping mothers' *Critical Social Policy* 26, 412.

119 Krane J. and Davies, L. (2000) 'Mothering and child protection practice: Rethinking risk assessment' *Child and Family Social Work* 5, 35.

who inflicts the blows which kill the child'.[120] To find those who fail to protect to be as blameworthy as those who actually kill the child seems extraordinary, especially in cases characterised by domestic violence. Even the courts are not immune from this. *Attorney General's Reference (No. 35 of 2005)*[121] is a striking case. The father admitted ill-treatment of the child which had involved bruises on various parts of her body, partial hair loss and a possible cigarette burn on her foot. He received a conditional discharge.[122] The mother (at a separate hearing) who admitted neglect on the basis that she had not sought medical attention for the injuries was given a six month prison sentence, albeit suspended for 18 months.

*(g) The glorification of motherhood* One of the difficulties with these kinds of cases is that in criminal law especially there is a tendency to separate out into clearly distinct categories the victim and the defendant. Victims can be idealised as innocent and lacking in agency; contrasting with the defendant who is a blameworthy and responsible person. The problem with such a dichotomy lies in cases where 'victims' do not accord with the idealised vision. This can be most apparent in rape trials where victims who are not church-attending, modestly dressed, sober women will be cast as the real 'causes of their own misfortune'.[123] There is a similar point here. Victims of domestic violence lose their victim status when regarded as responsible for the harm of the child. For once a child is killed we have the 'ideal victim': a 'blameless child'; and the status of the mother becomes ambiguous. Jacobs notes how easily the mother is blamed in cases like these:

> Although we can forgive or maybe excuse the mother for remaining in a violent relationship, on some level we may still view her as an implicit agent in her own abuse. We cannot forgive or excuse her for failing to prevent the abuse or death of her child. If forced to compete for the sympathies and interest of the public, a totally innocent child trumps a battered woman any day.[124]

How easily the abused become the abuser.

The contrast made between the truly non-autonomous/innocent child and the battered mother will mean that the battered mother will be regarded as the one with autonomy, the defendant. And she will be judged harshly.

Much of the writing in this area reflects the idealised vision of motherhood: the mother should be the provider, protector and nurturer.[125] It has been argued that much is expected of the 'good mother' and the slightest fall from grace is regarded in the

---

120 Hoyano, L. and Keenan, C. (2007), *Child Abuse* (Oxford: Oxford University Press) p.177.

121 [2006] EWCA Crim 378.

122 On appeal it was suggested a sentence of imprisonment should have been imposed although, given procedural problems it would not be in this case.

123 See for example, George, W. and Martinez, L. (2002), 'Victim blaming in rape' *Psychology of Women Quarterly* 22, 110.

124 Jacobs, M. (1998), above n.90.

125 Cahn, N. (2000), 'Policing women: Moral arguments and the dilemmas of criminalization' *DePaul Law Review* 49, 817.

harshest light;[126] while little is expected of the 'good father'. As long as he does not abuse the child or mother and pays his child support he is doing what he should. Dorothy Roberts notes:

> Mothers' crimes also include killing or abandoning their newborn babies. Fathers who abandon their children can escape criminal responsibility simply by leaving the children with their mother.[127]

Linda Panko argues that the blame that falls on mothers who fail to protect their children flows from such an idealised vision of motherhood. She writes:

> At the root of the belief that mothers who fail to protect their children are morally reprehensible, and thus criminally punishable, lies a condemnation not so much of their failure to perform acts of a physical nature but rather of their failure to perform acts of love – the way mothers should love their children. A mother's love for her child is the most-revered form of love, which knows no bounds; i.e., it overcomes all physical, financial, emotional, and moral obstacles. Where such obstacles actually do limit a woman's ability to protect her child, they are not recognized as 'obstacles' and are thus not considered relevant or legitimate factors in adjudicating guilt for failure-to-protect.[128]

Her point is, then, that the outrage that so often greets women who fail in their 'motherly duty' to protect their children, flows not so much from a sound assessment of their moral culpability but on an idealised vision of motherhood that requires them to sacrifice everything in the name of their children.

In the case of Sandra Sujuru[129] (discussed below) the judge emphasised how the baby died while the mother left the child alone with her partner while she went off to work. One cannot imagine the undertones of irresponsibility indicated by a mother working being applied to a father, who would be, of course, earning the 'family bread'. Jeanne Fugate,[130] looking at the use of failure to protect children statutes in the States, notes how in the rare cases that fathers are charged with failure to protect they are often able to claim that they did not notice the signs of abuse. However, mothers are always thought to notice any suspicious bruises and marks and appreciate the untruthfulness of any explanations offered by the father.[131]

When we say that parents ought to protect children from harm, where does this expectation come from? What standard of motherhood are these women departing from so far as to justify the intervention of the criminal law? Is this the standard of

---

126 Miccio, G. (1999), above, n.85; Neal. O. (1995), 'Myths and moms: Images of women and termination of parental rights' *Kansas Journal of Law and Public Policy* 5, 61.

127 Roberts, D. (1993), above, n.94.

128 Panko, L. (1995), 'Legal backlash: the expanding liability of women who fail to protect their children from their male partner's abuse' *Hastings Women's Law Journal* 67.

129 See n.138 below.

130 Fugate, J. (2001), above, n.65; see also Enos, P. (1996), 'Prosecuting Battered Mothers: State Laws' Failure to Protect Battered Women and Abused Children' *Harvard Women's Law Journal* 19, 229.

131 *Emma W* [2006] EWCA Crim 2723 where the court thought the mother could not really have been convinced by the father's explanations.

the ideal mother whose striving for their child knows no bounds and even extends to the lengths of sitting through interminable ballet performances given by their dears? Or is it the standard expected of a mother struggling under the oppression and dehumanising effect of abuse?

The idealisation of motherhood and the heightened expectations of mothers are readily apparent in the criminal law. In *R v Armer*[132] a mother was convicted of cruelty to her seven-week-old son Joel, after she took him to bed with her and 'overlay', killing him.[133] A 21-month sentence was imposed.[134] In discussing the case the Court of Appeal placed much weight on the fact that when she was discharged from hospital she was given a leaflet entitled 'Reduce the Risk of Cot Deaths'. Within the leaflet the dangers of sleeping with a baby were emphasised. With all respect, this is unrealistic. Does the Court of Appeal think that single mothers caring for newborn babies are able to read all the material they are given on discharge from hospital? Let alone remember and take it in. The Court of Appeal noted that there were no other signs of neglect or abuse; indeed the child was in good health. The case led to her other child being removed from her care. Too easily the explanation of what 'any reasonable mother' would do is based on white, middle-aged, middle-class expectations.[135] This case appears to indicate an extra-ordinarily high standard of care for the child. The father of the child goes unmentioned. His absence, his neglect, ignored, unpunished.

## V Cases Under the Act

The Home Office had suggested that there will only be a small number of charges under the new offence.[136] Nonetheless, we have already had several prosecutions under section 5.[137] These prosecutions indicate that the concerns raised above about the use of this offence in domestic violence cases are legitimate.

The first reported conviction concerned Sandra Mujuru, aged 21, who 'allowed' her partner, Jerry Stephens, to murder their four-year-old baby (Ayesha).[138] Ms Mujuru was sentenced to a two-year community order, while Mr Stephens received a life sentence for murder. Prior to sentencing while awaiting trial she had served the equivalent of more than a year in jail. The Court of Appeal justified her conviction in this way:

---

132 [2004] EWCA Crim 3437.

133 She was under the influence of drugs at the time.

134 This was reduced to 15 months on appeal.

135 Fugate, J. (2001), above, n.65; Panko, L. (1995), above, n.128.

136 Home Office, Home Office Circular 9/2005, *Domestic Violence Crime and Victims Act*. There were five prosecutions in 2005/6 and three in 2006/7 according to Nicholas, S., Kershaw, C. and Walker, A. (2007), *Crime in England and Wales 2006/7* (London: Home Office) p.36.

137 As well as the ones mentioned in the text, see also the convictions of Sumairia Parveen and Abid Ikram (*BBC Newsonline*, 'Couple jailed over baby torture', 7 September 2007).

138 *Stephens and Mujuru* [2007] EWCA Crim 1249.

> There was also evidence before the jury capable of supporting a finding that Miss M knew that S had broken A's arm, or had good reason to think that he might have done so, and that she was, or ought to have been, aware that there was a significant risk that he might deliberately harm A again. If they made those findings, the jury could go on to find that by leaving A in his care while she went to work Miss M failed to take such steps as she could reasonably have been expected to take to protect her.[139]

The CPS, justifying the decision to prosecute, noted that Ms Mujuru was aware of Stephens's potential for violence because she had visited him while he was serving time in prison for an attack on his previous girlfriend.

These explanations fail to give sufficient weight to the circumstances in which Ms Mujuru found herself. She was an asylum-seeker escaping violence in Zimbabwe. In sentencing her the judge commented that she was a 'decent young woman in a vulnerable position'. The judge noticed that Stephens was twice her age and was a 'self-centered and dangerous man with a dangerously short fuse'.[140] As a young asylum-seeker should she really have been expected to know from which authorities to seek advice and how to access the appropriate services? Could she have done this without endangering her child and herself by igniting her partner's 'dangerously short fuse'? On the day the child's body was found Stephens had assaulted his previous girlfriend, hitting her on the head with a frying pan and a vase. So, were her fears that she would be attacked if she sought help for her and her child really so ill-founded?

In May 2005 Rebecca Lewis, aged 21, was sentenced for failing to prevent the murder of her baby Aaron Gilbert, at the hands of her partner, Andrew Lloyd, with whom she had lived for six weeks.[141] She was sentenced to six years in prison. Lloyd was sentenced to 24 years in prison for murder. The court was told that Lewis was largely absent during Lloyd's attacks and was not present when he killed the baby. However, she knew that Lloyd had flicked Aaron's ears and feet when he cried; had picked him up by his ears and ankles; and had thrown him onto a bed. These the jury must have found indicated a risk of death or serious harm. In sentencing her the judge said 'You put your own interests first, above and beyond that of your vulnerable child. You could have stopped the violence that Lloyd was subjecting Aaron to. You could so easily have got the authorities to stop it'.[142] At the trial Lewis had explained that she did not summon help because Lloyd had said he would kill her if she left. For 'putting her interests first' she was given a sentence only a little shorter than the average given for rape.[143] In fact, the local social services had been warned about the child by Lewis's cousin. They responded to these concerns by writing a letter seeking

139 At [32].

140 At [35].

141 Eveleigh, R. (2006), 'My Beautiful Boy Was Murdered By His Mum's Evil Lover' *The Mirror*, 13 November 2006.

142 *BBC Newsonline*, 'Mother allowed baby son's murder', 15 December 2006.

143 The current average sentence for rape is 7 ½ years: Sentencing Guidance Council, *Sexual Offences Act 2003* (2006) p.18. Although the Council would like to see 5 years being the starting point.

to make an appointment, but it was sent to the wrong address.[144] It is noticeable that for Lewis's failure to protect her child due to threats to her life she received a lengthy prison sentence. For the authorities who failed to protect the same child, but who faced no such threat, no legal responsibility has been attached.

Hayley Kenny was jailed for four years for allowing the death of her son, Kieren.[145] Her former partner, Craig Pearce, was jailed for life for Kieren's murder. His death appeared to be caused by a very heavy blow. Ms Kenny told the court that when she returned from a shift working at a local supermarket she did not notice the child had been seriously injured. The prosecution case was that the boy had suffered numerous injuries in the weeks leading to his death and Ms Kenny must have known of what was being done. Ms Kenny accepted she was aware that the boy had bruises on the body, but put this down to Mr Pearce's rather heavy handedness in dealing with the child, rather than abuse.

The first case to reach the Court of Appeal was *R v Liu, R v Tan.*[146] It involved a man and his lover who had grossly mistreated the man's wife. She was kept as a slave and maltreated by both parties. Liu (the lover) was convicted of murder and the husband (Tan) under the section 5 offence. Tan was well aware of the gross mistreatment Liu was inflicting on his wife. Indeed, he was participating in it himself. He was not present on the day of the killing, but from the facts of the case it seems it was almost chance which of the many beatings the victim received would kill her. The use of the section 5 offence seemed unnecessary in such a case where the husband was shown to have committed grievous bodily harm.

## VI Conclusion

The offence in section 5 of the Domestic Violence, Crimes and Victims Act 2004 is a complex one. Many of its key requirements are ambiguous and apparently arbitrary distinctions are drawn. This is especially concerning because the offence includes liability for omissions. Where the criminal law does that it is particularly important that it is clear when the duty to act arises and what must be done to avoid criminal liability. These are not clear under the section 5 offence.

The motivation behind this offence is undoubtedly good. It is designed to protect children's rights. However, the offence must be viewed in the context within which it operates. Evidence from other jurisdictions indicates that it is primarily used against women who fail to protect their children from their violent male partners. This chapter has argued that its use in such cases is highly problematic. It tends to lead to prosecution of women who are themselves the victims of domestic violence. It assumes escape routes from the violence which are either not there or are not reasonable to expect the woman to take. Further, the offences are often based on a glamorised view of motherhood which regards the mother in an idealistic way

144 An official investigation subsequently accepted there had been failings in the way the case was handled by the authority: Swansea Safeguarding Children Board (2007), *Serious Cases Review Regarding Aaron Gilbert.*

145 *BBC Newsonline*, 'Mother jailed after baby's death', 16 January 2007.

146 [2006] EWCA Crim 3321.

as an all-knowing all-sacrificing protector. The prosecution of women who fail to live up to this image can lead to the focus of legal and public attention not being on the abuser but on the mother who 'left her children to die'. The offence also disguises the State's responsibility for abused and endangered children. The offence was promoted as the way of protecting children from abuse and violence. The way to do that is not section 5, but an effective and thorough raft of measures to protect women and children from violence. For the State to prosecute a mother who has been seeking to protect her children and herself from a violent man when the State has done so little to protect them cannot be justified. The time and effort in prosecuting abused women who fail to protect their children would be better spent on ensuring there was effective and adequate protection of women and children from violence.

## Chapter 8

# Medical Killing: Need for a Specific Offence?

Oliver Quick

How should criminal law appropriately respond to the following cases of fatal medical error?

i. A 71-year-old woman dies after a catastrophic blood loss during surgery to remove a cancerous liver tumour. On opening up the patient it is discovered that the tumour was twice the expected size, and situated near important blood vessels. The surgeon ignored the concerns of colleagues and continued with the procedure. He was alleged to have had his photo taken with the dissected liver during the operation.[1]

ii. A six-week-old baby boy dies after cardiac arrest during surgery for pyloric stenosis. Following the request of the surgeon to inflate the abdomen, the anaesthetist mistakenly injected air into a tube entering the patient's vein instead of the nasogastric tube.[2]

iii. A number of babies with cardiac abnormalities die following procedures which were carried out incompetently – despite the misgivings of nursing and anaesthetic staff and data suggesting poor technical performance of two surgeons.[3]

iv. Two junior doctors fail to diagnose a post-operative fatal infection in a 31-year-old man. They failed to respond adequately to classic signs of infection and did not chase up blood test results that would have indicated aggressive antibiotic treatment.[4]

v. A man dies during a routine eye operation following anaesthetic mismanagement. Although the anaesthetist checked a number of possible

---

1 'Doctor who killed patient on operating table escapes jail' *The Independent*, 24 June 2004 p.19.

2 'Doctor cleared' *The Times*, 19 May 2004 p.4.

3 For discussion of the 'Bristol heart babies affair' see Quick, O. (1999), 'Disaster at Bristol: Explanations and Implications of a Tragedy' *Journal of Social Welfare and Family Law* 21:4, 307–326.

4 *R v Misra* [2005] 1 Cr App R 21.

causes for the patient's deteriorating condition, he failed to check that the breathing tube had become disconnected.[5]

## I The Current Position

Currently, such cases are dealt with by the contentious and 'catch all' offence of gross negligence manslaughter (GNM). Although by no means unique as an example of objective criminal liability – crimes of negligence are on the increase[6] – its position near the apex of serious offences and the absence of a lesser charge or an inchoate crime renders this an unsatisfactory 'all or nothing' scenario, often hinging on moral luck[7] and prosecutorial performance in terms of the outcome. Although relatively rare, such prosecutions have risen markedly over the past 20 years,[8] causing much anxiety for the healthcare profession and inviting some academic inquiry.[9] Before considering the merits of a specific offence for medical killings, the question of whether such conduct should be criminal *at all* needs to be addressed. It is unlikely that many would argue for all such medical killing to fall outside the reach of criminal law; the task is thus to settle on a morally meaningful and fair framework for culpability. Given that this involves a wide range of conduct spanning the scale of culpability – from the blatantly reckless to the momentary slip – this is far from straightforward. For example, the case of the cavalier surgeon in case (i) above who causes death by undertaking unnecessarily dangerous procedures without patient consent and in the face of concerned colleagues, is properly classified as 'reckless killing'. However, it is in relation to the inadvertent and momentary slip, for example the misplaced injection of the anaesthetist in case (ii) that things get harder. Would things be easier – and better – with the creation of specific criminal offences applicable to the healthcare setting?

The question about the appropriateness of criminal negligence has largely exercised legal philosophers, who as Jerome Hall noted, found it an 'inordinately

5 *R v Adomako* [1994] 3 All ER 79.

6 For example, supplying intoxicating substances to the under aged (s.1(1) Intoxicating Substance (Supply) Act 1985); causing death by dangerous driving (s.1 Road Traffic Act 1988); insider trading (s.5292)(a) Criminal Justice Act 1993); harassment (ss.1(1) and 2(1) Protection of Harassment Act 1997); providing money or property for the purposes of terrorism (ss.15–18 of the Terrorism Act 2000); money laundering (s.330(2)(b) Proceeds of Crime Act 2002); and causing or allowing the death of a child or vulnerable adult (s.5 Domestic Violence, Crime and Victims Act 2004).

7 See Smith, J.C. (1971), 'The Element of chance in Criminal Liability' *Crim LR* 63 and Nagel, T. (1991), *Mortal Questions* (London: Canto).

8 Ferner, R. (2000), 'Medication errors that have led to manslaughter charges', *British Medical Journal*, 321, 1212–1216; Ferner, R. and McDowell, S. (2006), 'Doctors charged with manslaughter in the course of medical practice, 1795–2005: a literature review', *Journal of the Royal Society of Medicine* 99, 309–314, Quick, O. (2006), 'Prosecuting "Gross" Medical Negligence: Manslaughter, Discretion and the Crown Prosecution Service', *Journal of Law and Society* 33, 421–450.

9 Quick *ibid.*

troublesome' area.[10] Hall was responding (and rejecting) Hart's celebrated general theory of guilt in which he defended negligent criminal liability as part of a wider capacity theory of responsibility.[11] For Hall, the imposition of such liability loses sight of the notion of blame which is the proper foundation of criminal law. In terms of contemporary criminal law scholarship, Hart's view finds an echo in Ashworth's call to extend the use of negligence to other areas of criminal law.[12] And despite its general commitment to a subjectivist vision of criminal law, the Law Commission endorses criminal sanction for culpable inadvertence, albeit abandoning the label manslaughter for its favoured formulation of 'killing by gross carelessness'.[13] However, others have preferred Hall's objection to penalising negligence.[14] Yet amidst the arguments on the issue of principle, surely all would agree with Clarkson that the range of conduct and culpability encompassed by involuntary manslaughter is such that 'the crime label has become morally uninformative'.[15] Yet whilst there is a clear case for reform, there is less clarity on what this should be.

One option rests with creating a specific homicide offence for the healthcare context to replace or sit beneath GNM. This can be considered as part of the wider re-structuring of homicide and the more significant question about how much criminal law we need. This is an enduring debate, and one which has been largely based on questions about the 'general part' of criminal law.[16] Old concerns about the 'decline of guilt'[17] have continued with more recent critical comment about the problem of 'rampant over-criminalisation'[18] disconnected from moral blame. This has drawn attention to the appropriate scope and form of the special part of

10 Hall, J. (1972), 'Negligence and the General Problem of Criminal Responsibility' *Yale Law Journal* 81, 912 at p.952, and see also (1963) 'Negligent behaviour should be excluded from penal liability' *Columbia Law Review* 63:4, 632–644.

11 Hart, H.L A. (1968), 'Negligence, Mens Rea and Criminal Responsibility' pp.136–157, at p.147 in *Punishment and Responsibility: Essays in the Philosophy of Law* (Oxford: Oxford University Press).

12 See Ashworth, A. (2006), *Principles of Criminal Law*, 5th ed. (Oxford: Oxford University Press) p.194.

13 Involuntary Homicide Bill Clause 2(1): Law Commission (1996), *Legislating the Criminal Code: Involuntary Manslaughter* Law (Com. No. 237); and see Law Commission (2005), *A New Homicide Act for England and Wales?* (Consultation Paper 177).

14 McCall Smith, A. (1993), 'Criminal Negligence and the Incompetent Doctor' *Medical Law Review* 1 Autumn 336–349.

15 Clarkson, C.M V. (2000), 'Context and Culpability in Involuntary Manslaughter: Principle or Instinct?' (pp.133–165, at p.142) in Ashworth, A. and Mitchell, B. (eds), *Rethinking English Homicide Law* (Oxford: Oxford University Press). Clarkson persuasively argues for the creation of a more nuanced approach to involuntary manslaughter with the creation of separate offences, and in this context, favours the Law Commission's formulation of 'killing by gross carelessness'.

16 Duff, R.A. (ed.) (1989), *Philosophy and the Criminal Law: Principle and Critique* (Cambridge: Cambridge University Press).

17 Morris, H. (1988), 'The Decline of Guilt' *Ethics* 99:1, 62–76.

18 Husak, D. (2004), 'The Criminal Law as Last Resort' *Oxford Journal of Legal Studies* 24, 207 at 215.

criminal law.[19] In summarising the contribution of academic commentators, Husak accuses legal philosophers of being too quick to consider the reasons for, rather than against, criminalisation, and argues persuasively for a principle of criminal law and punishment as last resort, an approach which is adopted here in relation to considering the case for creating a specific offence/s for healthcare.

The issue most relevant to our present concern is whether the offence of GNM is specific and sensitive enough to reflect different levels of culpability for 'crime' committed in different contexts. Are medical cases sufficiently different to warrant labeling and prosecuting as a separate crime? What would be the merits and demerits of framing special criminal law for healthcare professionals? The key tension is between the need for fair labeling of offences and offenders against the risk of over-specificity and thus over-criminalisation, a very real risk in the fast moving world of criminal justice law and policy.[20] Before turning to the arguments for and against creating a specific offence, I will first evaluate the current scheme of liability and consider the options of re-conceptualising such cases, rejecting negligent criminal liability altogether as it applies to healthcare and of reviving recklessness as the sole basis of liability here.

## II How Should Criminal Law Respond to Blameworthy Fatal Medical Error?

### *(i) Re-conceptualising gross negligence?*

Some argue for a re-conceptualisation of such cases in line with a more philosophically satisfying theory of criminal responsibility. Thus Tadros would approach such cases in terms of the distinction he draws between non-moral and moral vices. This essentially boils down to analysing whether an individual is properly motivated by the interests of others.[21] This is part of a broader attempt to theorise a virtue jurisprudence of criminal liability – that is, connecting the conditions for criminal liability to particular vices.[22] As Duff explains, it is 'not just the fact that he committed a criminal action, but that in doing so he displayed a kind of civic vice, or serious lack of even minimal civic virtue, that makes him deserving of public condemnation'.[23] Duff also notes that this is essentially a daily task for courts when assessing defendants against the reasonable man standard: would a virtuous person have done as the defendant did? How would this apply to cases of alleged medical

19 Duff, R.A. and Green, S.P. (eds) (2005), *Defining Crimes: Essays on the Special Part of the Criminal Law* (Oxford: Oxford University Press) see pp.15–16, and see the British Academy organised series on 'Why Criminal Law?' <http://www.britac.ac.uk/events/2007/crimlaw2007/index.html> accessed on 5 November 2007.

20 See Sanders, A. and Young, R. (2007), *Criminal Justice* 3rd ed. (Oxford: Oxford University Press).

21 Tadros, V. (2005), *Criminal Responsibility* (Oxford: Oxford University Press) p.85.

22 See Duff, R.A. (2002), 'Virtue, Vice and Criminal Liability' *Buffalo Criminal Law Review* 6, 147.

23 Duff, R.A. (2007), 'The Virtues and Vices of Virtue Jurisprudence' in Chappell, T.D.J. (ed.), *Values and Virtues* (Oxford: Oxford University Press) pp.90–104 at p.98.

manslaughter? According to Tadros's conception of criminal responsibility, the doctors from case (iv) above are more culpable than the doctor in case (v) in that the former failed to carry out a number of checks despite warnings to the contrary, suggesting the vice of being insufficiently motivated by the patient's welfare, whereas the latter consciously checked a number of things but (unfortunately and inexplicably) not for the disconnected tube which actually caused the patient's death. Put another way, the latter failed in his duty whereas the former disregarded it.

This undoubtedly offers a pleasing philosophical model for classifying culpability in such cases. However, it is unclear whether such analytical classifications would assist prosecutors in practice; and as Duff notes, this approach is limited by the fact that 'virtue and vice are relatively lasting character-traits: we cannot have a virtue or a vice just for a day or a week'.[24] Cases of medical killings often involve seemingly virtuous professionals who have made astonishing yet isolated and uncharacteristic errors (for example, case (ii) above). But notwithstanding this, the available empirical research into medical manslaughter cases presents a strong case for going beyond analytical adjustments and abolishing the offence of GNM as it applies in the healthcare setting.

### *(ii) Rejecting gross negligence?*

There is nothing new in arguing against the imposition of negligent criminal liability in the medical setting.[25] However, such arguments have been based on a principled objection to the unfairness of this offence, and particularly as this applies to well intentioned professionals working in high risk (and often unsafe) systems. There has been little empirical investigation into the actual enforcement of this offence. A study by this author examining quantitative and qualitative data on medical manslaughter prosecutions observed that the offence is vague and vulnerable to the vagaries of discretion and discrimination, and concluded that it is incapable of clear and objective measurement and ought to be abolished.[26] Whilst it may be said that the malleability offered by the 'test' in Adomako is an advantage, in reality the offence is too broad for prosecutorial judgement to be consistently applied, and this translates into particular harshness for those operating in error-ridden activities who are exposed to risk of prosecution by virtue of their socially vital work, and often at the mercy of moral luck.[27] In mopping up a range of unintentional killings it also washes over issues of fair labeling. Although retaining the support of the Appeal courts and the Law Commission – albeit in its revised formulation of 'killing by gross carelessness' discussed below, several reasons of principle and practice point to its abolition. There *may* be sufficient cause to call for the complete abolition of GNM. However, the arguments presented here rest on research into its application to medical cases. Further research would be required to analyse its operation in other settings in terms of considering a complete abolition. This exemption of

24 *Ibid.* at 99.

25 For example, see McCall Smith above n.14.

26 This section summarises the findings from Quick above n.8

27 See Smith and Nagel above n.7.

GNM liability for healthcare professionals is open to the response that it leaves a wide gulf between reckless manslaughter and no criminal response, and in terms of criminalisation is thus even more 'all or nothing' than the status quo. It may also seem unfair in terms of undue protection for such professionals. However, healthcare is sufficiently 'special' compared with the other contexts under consideration in this collection, and if we accept, as I do, that the current position is unacceptable, then there are two choices: downgrade and probably prosecute more, or upgrade and narrow the focus on reckless killings as the business of criminal law and justice. For reasons that will be discussed below, I prefer the latter option.

An analysis of interviews with crown prosecutors at an office of the casework directorate of the CPS suggested that no real meaningful hierarchy of seriousness was adopted in relation to classifying errors as gross. Respondents struggled to pin down their understanding of the term gross, often initially relying on gut instinct, unhelpful as this is in analytical terms. Whilst there was some recognition of a distinction between tragic slips (excusable) and reckless mistakes (condemned), there was no reference to the developing literature on understanding the causes of medical mistakes, and the accepted classification of slips, errors and violations discussed below. In short, there was no obvious or objective system for classifying episodes as gross or not gross.

A closer analysis of the data, both statistical and qualitative, presents further reasons for abolishing this offence. The statistics reveal that a disproportionate number of non-white practitioners feature in medical manslaughter prosecutions – over 50 per cent – which is particularly high given that the number of non-white NHS hospital doctors is estimated to be around 25 per cent.[28] This is a troubling finding and one that may be understood with reference to a number of sociological explanations, such as the training and language skills of overseas trained doctors, as well as their ability to gain employment and superior supervision in better performing hospitals. The high number may also be related to racist attitudes that creep in to the decisions to complain about and consider investigating individuals in the first place. The notion of a principled, rational and just system of discretion is difficult when much depends on the possibly discriminatory decisions that inform the process of complaining and filtering such cases for investigation. Of course, there is no shortage of evidence of the effect of prejudicial attitudes within the criminal justice system[29] yet, coupled with the vagueness and seriousness of this offence category, the consequences may be particularly unfair.

The statistics also suggest a possible geography of prosecution, with unexplained regional variation of the number of prosecutions, with an increased number of prosecutions in the North, and particularly the North-West of England. Whilst the numbers are small, and *may* be explained by normal random distributions, it may

28 Cooke, L., Halford, S. and Leonard, P. (2003), *Racism in the Medical Profession: the Experience of UK Graduates* (British Medical Association).

29 For example see Fitzgerald, M. and Sibbitt, R. (1997), *Ethnic Monitoring in Police Forces: A Beginning* (Home Office Research Study 173) (London: Home Office), and Macpherson, Sir W. (1991), *The Stephen Lawrence Inquiry* Cm 4262I (London: Stationery Office).

also be a sign of increased prosecutorial confidence in certain regions which have 'got home' on *Adomako* and achieved a successful conviction, arguably significant given the overall low conviction rate.

Furthermore, the legal frame (in other words the measurement of 'gross negligence'), is effectively handed over to medical experts. The fact that expert evidence appears to effectively determine, as opposed to merely inform, what is a legal term of art, is inappropriate. Reflecting the difficult task of interpretation, expert discretion is itself an uncertain and fluctuating process of framing and re-framing, and something which we know little about. Finally, this study showed prosecutorial unease with the fairness of gross negligence, and the reality of prosecutors navigating around the *Adomako* test in search of subjective fault. The cases which are prosecuted, and certainly those which result in conviction, would be more appropriately accommodated within subjective recklessness.

Despite GNM surviving a human rights challenge in *Misra*, the issue of its compatibility with Articles 6 and 7 of the ECHR can not be considered settled.[30] The Court of Appeal's reasoning is unconvincing. Leaving aside the issue of the vagueness of GNM in terms of possible retrospective criminalisation under Article 7, it is the dismissal of the Article 6 argument which disappoints most. Article 6 entitles defendants to a 'fair and public hearing within a reasonable time by an independent and impartial tribunal established by law'. The jurisprudence surrounding Article 6 suggests that a fair hearing implies a reasoned decision, and it was argued by the defence that as juries here are effectively deciding a principle of law (that is, the meaning of the offence) and do not give reasons for their decisions, that this contravened Article 6. Although the Court of Appeal rejected this it is surely plausible that juries do accept that conduct *was* grossly negligent but decide against convicting the defendant of manslaughter. The relatively low conviction rate of around 39 per cent is evidence of jury reluctance to condemn doctors as guilty of manslaughter.[31] Why continue to struggle with the vagueness and vagaries of interpreting gross negligence when there is no consensus about what it actually means and whether it should be a crime? The argument for abolition is clear and compelling.

Arguably, these central problems would persist under the Law Commission's proposed replacement of GNM with 'killing by gross carelessness' (KGC). The current attempt to make sense of 'gross negligence' would be replaced by the similarly tricky task of assessing whether 'conduct falls far below what can reasonably be expected in the circumstances'.[32] This laudable aim of providing a clearer jury friendly formulation would surely fail. Whilst an improvement on paper, in practice it is difficult to imagine that this offence would not be beset by the same problems as GNM. Prosecutors (and their experts) would still struggle with what amounts to 'conduct falling far below reasonable expectations'. And the anxieties of judges and juries on seeing doctors in the dock would presumably continue. Furthermore, this reformulation is arguably broader than the current test for liability, and whilst surely not the intention of the Law Commission, this would likely lead to an increase of

30 Regrettably, leave for appeal to the House of Lords was rejected.

31 See Ferner and McDowell and Quick, above n.8.

32 Involuntary Homicide Bill, cl.2(1), above n.13.

prosecutions. On the whole, it is difficult to see that this tackles the fundamental objection to this type of liability, or that it would make much difference in practice. In short, it amounts to little more than an exercise in linguistic modernisation. The option of fleshing out this statutory formulation with reference to a notion such as 'extreme indifference', whilst purporting to promise greater clarity, would probably only cloud an already unclear task.[33]

### *(iii) Reviving recklessness?*

The easiest existing alternative would be to consider such cases within the category of subjective reckless manslaughter, which despite its lack of common law authority, appears well understood and uncontentious. The legal line drawing between subjective recklessness and gross negligence has always been at best blurry; as Horder points out, in the nineteenth century, judges were less concerned about committing to a subjective vision of criminal law and observing a neat separation between recklessness and negligence.[34] The quest for a strict separation of these related terms is a product of more modern criminal law scholarship and its pursuit of conceptual clarity.[35] And it is not entirely clear why the term 'gross' emerged as the dominant epithet, given that 'criminal' or 'wicked' would seem more closely connected with the idea of individual fault. Nevertheless, given that historically these terms have been used interchangeably, the current confusion is somewhat easier to understand. Arguably, it also makes it easier to justify abolishing gross negligence, and to place our trust in the concept of recklessness to work here.

Despite a series of convictions for GNM through the nineteenth and twentieth centuries, the decision in the infamous case of *Stone and Dobinson*[36] appeared to place the bar above GNM and resurrect recklessness by requiring 'reckless disregard of danger to the health and welfare … [and that] mere inadvertence is not enough. The defendant must be proved to have been indifferent to an obvious risk of injury to health, or actually to have foreseen the risk but to have determined nevertheless to run it'. In line with the prevailing *Caldwell*[37] recklessness of the day, the case of *Seymour*[38] seemed to suggest that recklessness replaced (or subsumed) negligent manslaughter. Although the House of Lords ditched *Caldwell* recklessness in favour of gross negligence in the leading case of *Adomako*, Lord Mackay muddied the waters somewhat by stating that:

33 See Clarkson, above n.15, at p.156. A similar criticism is made in relation to the factors for the jury to consider in assessing 'gross breach' contained in Section 8 of the Corporate Manslaughter and Corporate Homicide Act 2007, see Wells, C. (2006), 'Corporate Manslaughter: Why does reform matter?' *South African Law Journal* 122, 646–662.

34 Horder, J. (1997), 'Gross Negligence and Criminal Culpability' *University of Toronto Law Journal* 47, 495–521.

35 For example, the Law Commission's Codification project: Law Commission (1985), *Codification of the Criminal Law: A Report to the Law Commission* (Law Commission No. 143) (London: HMSO).

36 [1977] QB 354.

37 [1982] AC 341.

38 [1983] 2 All ER 1058.

> it is perfectly open to the trial judge to use the word 'reckless' in its ordinary meaning as part of his exposition of the law if he deems it appropriate in the circumstances of the particular case.[39]

The Law Commission has recently endorsed this by agreeing that:

> recklessness falling short of reckless indifference can really be regarded as a kind of gross negligence ... The fact that ... the defendant saw a risk and wrongly discounted it or stupidly thought it insignificant is simply compelling evidence of the grossness of his or her negligence.[40]

Putting it the other way around, perhaps the term gross negligence is really just recklessness in disguise? It is probably no accident that recklessness lurks in the background in judicial opinion about gross negligence. This reflects a sense of judicial reluctance with leaving liability at the lower level of gross negligence. A closer reading of recent reported medical cases confirms judicial support for incorporating subjective recklessness into the task of assessing gross negligence. The case of *Rowley* concerned an unsuccessful judicial review of a CPS decision not to prosecute following a death in a care home. The CPS argued, and the High Court agreed, that evidence (or lack of evidence) of subjective recklessness was relevant in determining gross negligence.[41] This was actually endorsed in *Misra* where whilst shielding GNM from a human rights challenge, the Court of Appeal stated that evidence of the defendant's state of mind is 'not irrelevant' to the issue of gross negligence, in fact, adding that it will often be a 'critical factor in the decision'.[42] This support for subjectivism was also apparent in its approval of the trial judge's direction that the jury should be satisfied that the doctors' conduct fell so far below the expected standard that 'it was something ... truly exceptionally bad, which showed ... indifference to an obviously serious risk to the life of the patient'.[43] Such comments suggest judicial unease with the potential unfairness of gross negligence, and demonstrate the alternative and arguably more appropriate liability based on subjective recklessness. Prosecutors also appear more comfortable working to the notion of recklessness, which whilst representing a tougher task of 'getting home' seems to correspond with some prosecutorial practice.[44] Certainly, the few cases which result in conviction would appear to be cases where the CPS could have proceeded on the basis of establishing subjective recklessness – for example, as in case (i) above where a doctor has continued with a dangerous operation despite the concerns of colleagues, or administered a large and lethal overdose which would have been obvious but for the refusal to look at the patient's medical history and current medication chart.[45] Given the recent rejection of objective recklessness in

39 *Adomako* above n.5, p.118.
40 Law Commission (2005), above n.13 at para. 3.182.
41 *R (Rowley) v DPP* [2003] EWHC 693.
42 *Misra*, above n.4 at para. 56.
43 *Ibid.* at para. 25.
44 Quick, above n.8.
45 'GP jailed for giving lethal morphine overdose' *The Guardian*, 6 April 2004.

criminal law,[46] framing the crime in terms of subjective recklessness would also benefit from conceptual coherence with other offence categories.

In their 1996 proposals, the Law Commission proposed to replace subjective reckless manslaughter with the offence of 'reckless killing' which would be committed when:

1) a person by his or her conduct causes the death of another;
2) he is aware of a risk that his conduct will cause death or serious injury;
3) it is unreasonable for him to take that risk, having regard to the circumstances as he believes them to be.

As Clarkson has noted, this is 'simply a clearer articulation of the one species of involuntary manslaughter that presently exists uncontroversially' and is thus difficult to criticise.[47] The situation would be somewhat different following the Law Commission's wider review of the law of homicide, whereby reckless killings could fall within 'second degree murder' ('Recklessly indifferent killing, where the offender realised that his or her conduct involved an unjustified risk of killing, but pressed on with that conduct without caring whether or not death would result') or manslaughter by 'Killing through an intentional act intended to cause injury or involving recklessness as to causing injury'.[48] The medical cases under investigation here are possibly captured by both of these, illustrating a worryingly wide 'murder two' category, although admittedly the Law Commission would envisage the worst cases of careless medical killing within its reformulated manslaughter framework.

The most important question then is whether we can place our trust in the concept of (subjective) recklessness to work here? For defenders of gross negligence liability, raising the bar to subjective recklessness risks removing cases which are currently prosecuted outside the reach of the criminal justice system. However, this is not necessarily the case in the context of medical treatment, where professionals would surely be aware of the risks of death associated with their work. Obviously this will differ depending on the circumstances such as the type of treatment or non-treatment, but the fear that prosecutors would be unable to present evidence suggesting subjective awareness of risk is an exaggerated one. For example, as Tadros suggests, where a doctor has special knowledge that certain types of procedures carry with them certain risks and fails to investigate that risk, then criminal responsibility might be properly attributed given that such conduct suggests the vice of being insufficiently motivated by the patient's interests.[49] Of course, as Yeo points out, this requires a reference to probability, given that all medical interventions leading to death must have carried some risk of fatal outcome. Yeo prefers to rest this on the basis of a high probability, but arguably the focus

46 *R v G* [2004] 1 AC 1034.

47 Clarkson, above n.15 at p.148.

48 Law Commission (2005), above n.13 at p.7.

49 Tadros, V. (2002), 'Recklessness and the Duty to Take Care' (pp.227–258 at 255) in Shute, S. and Simester, A.P. (eds), *Criminal Law Theory: Doctrines of the General Part* (Oxford: Oxford University Press). For further elaboration of this argument to criminal liability generally see Tadros, above n.21.

should be on culpability, that is, the recklessness of the conduct as opposed to just the probability of death/serious harm. A reckless disregard towards a small risk of death, perhaps because an individual couldn't care less, surely remains reckless. Tadros offers the following test for recklessness which represents a 'middle way' between subjective and objective requirements, and thus addresses the concerns over the ability to prosecute cases where establishing clear evidence of foresight of consequences *at the time* of action/inaction is difficult:

> (a) the action was of a kind that might carry risks with it according to the beliefs of the individual;
>
> and either
>
> (bi) given those beliefs the agent failed to fulfil his duty of investigating the risks; or
> (bii) the agent willfully blinded himself to the existence of the risks.[50]

This would arguably work well in the context of prosecuting medical manslaughter, and would be capable of capturing cases (i), (iii), (iv) and (v) above. Whilst predicting the practical effect in terms of numbers of prosecutions is difficult, committing to a form of subjective reckless liability would likely lead to a decrease in individual prosecutions. If the net effect of this change is to deter prosecutions in cases of momentary slips and lapses in concentration, then this should be welcomed rather than questioned. The two obvious arguments against this do not appear that strong. First, no one has persuasively argued that more prosecutions in the health setting would be a good thing. Secondly, there is the pragmatist argument that nothing would change in practice with the shift from gross negligence to recklessness, although in response, it would surely be surprising if this did not result in decisions not to proceed with dubious cases on the cusp.

## III Need for a Specific Offence?

The final option to consider is the creation of a separate offence or set of offences for cases falling below reckless killing. If we accept the argument for retaining (and renewing) the offence of reckless manslaughter, and for abolishing the offence of GNM, and are unconvinced by the promise of Law Commission proposals, do we need a new specific offence to supplement this? Of course, advocates of criminal law as last resort confront a significant problem in relation to fatalities caused by medical error in the sense that death demands an appropriate response.[51] My view about whether we need a specific offence is partly contingent upon whether it would end up replacing or co-existing with GNM. My lack of enthusiasm about the need and

50 Tadros (2002) above n.49, p.258.

51 This also translates into increased public pressure on prosecutors to respond: see Hoyano, A. *et al.* (1997), 'A Study of the Impact of the Revised Code for Crown Prosecutors' *Crim LR* 556.

likely effectiveness of a specific offence rests on the assumption that it would co-exist with the current offence of GNM – and thus create more criminal law. I would be more supportive should this be conceived as a replacement for GNM, although I am ultimately unconvinced that a compelling case exists. Whilst philosophical arguments which show an appreciation of responsibility in *this context* are persuasive (on the basis of fair labeling), practical questions and consequences point towards resisting this option. The separate argument for creating a specific defence (instead of an offence) misses the point that the conviction rate is already relatively low even in the absence of a relevant defence, that the process of prosecution is the punishment,[52] and that it is the basis of liability which needs re-assessing.

Calls for specific offences have been made in relation to a number of so-called problem areas of criminal justice. Unsurprisingly, given the drift towards a crime control model within the justice system,[53] coupled with a focus on the needs of victims',[54] most recent activity has considered the creation of specific offences from the perspective of providing justice to victims of domestic violence, sexual abuse, familial homicide, dangerous corporate conduct and anti-social behaviour. And the growth of the criminal justice system has been accompanied by academic analysis into its operation which sometimes results in the emergence of seemingly new 'specific' areas of interest.[55] There has been little focus on re-fashioning offences in terms of fairness to a class or classes of defendants, which I argue is the only persuasive argument for considering a downgraded specific offence here. As Ashworth has noted, issues of fair labelling and proportionality in the application of criminal law are particularly pertinent in relation to broad offences such as theft, criminal damage and robbery.[56] The law of involuntary manslaughter is an obvious addition to this list, and we must consider whether, in the context of fatal medical error, its rough edges need refining.

There are two standard objections to creating such offences: (i) it offends against the principle of minimalism and thus strays into over-criminalisation and (ii) it marginalises the offence, reduces its social stigma and dilutes its deterrent effect. However, these risks are less obvious here if this replaced the existing offence category of GNM and led to fairer rather than over-criminalisation. Similarly, the risk of marginalisation, which has informed debates about creating new specific offences for domestic violence and corporate killing, is less apparent where the rationale for reform is to reflect the *lesser* form of culpability in the context of providing healthcare treatment. However, any consideration of creating new offences for particular categories of conduct and their different contexts, must address the issue

---

52 Feeley, M. (1979), *The Process is the Punishment: Handling Cases in a Lower Criminal Court* (New York: Russell Sage).

53 See Sanders and Young, above n.20.

54 See Spalek, B. (2006), *Crime Victims: Theory, Policy and Practice* (Hampshire: Palgrave).

55 For example, Corbett, C. (2003), *Car Crime* (Cullompton: Willan); Hallsworth, S. (2005), *Street Crime* (Cullompton: Willan); Thomas, T. (2005), *Sex Crime* (Cullompton: Willan).

56 Ashworth, above n.12, p.89.

whether the differences are so great as to warrant reflection by substantive law.[57] In the context of involuntary manslaughter, Clarkson considered three candidates for differentiating substantive crimes on the basis of:

1) Culpability
2) Method of killing
3) Context of the killing

For Clarkson, only 1 and sometimes 3 should be relevant. The identity of the victim and defendant are rejected on the basis of over-specificity. In terms of context, Clarkson correctly discounts its relevance in relation to *reckless* killings (it being trumped by the level of culpability), but perhaps too readily rejects its significance in the context of 'careless killings'. The main objection is based on avoiding over-specificity, or what Horder has termed 'particularism'.[58] Yet, appreciation of different context has led to specific forms of liability (and calls for liability) in other settings. If we accept the argument that vehicular and familial homicide warrants separation from the emotive term manslaughter, it is difficult to deny similar context specific criminal law for deaths caused by careless medical treatment, where the context (discussed below) is marked by the pursuit of good intentions by the individual practitioner, and the high risk error ridden reality of healthcare. On one level, it is easier to attach moral blame to the speeding (and thus law breaking) driver than the inadvertently erring anaesthetist from case (ii) above. Compared with the National Express coach driver, charged with three counts of causing death by dangerous driving following a fatal motorway crash,[59] an anaesthetist who fatally misplaces an injection or momentarily loses concentration enjoys no such context specific investigation. They are stuck with the label manslaughter and its obviously stronger moral meanings. Even under the Law Commission proposals, the less emotive 'killing by gross carelessness', still seems worse than, for example, 'causing death through dangerous professional practice'. This raises an issue in terms of equality of law, and coupled with the rule of law and fair labeling objections to GNM and KGC, presents a plausible case for committing to a clearer offence category which better captures culpability in this context.

One option would be to create an offence applicable to those who kill by virtue of (mis)performing their work duties. The current law of GNM mainly applies to a motley crew of 'professional' defendants – doctors,[60] transport drivers,[61] electricians,[62]

57 Clarkson, above n.15, p.143.

58 Horder, J. (1994), 'Rethinking Non-Fatal Offences against the Person' *Oxford Journal of Legal Studies* 14, 335, at 341.

59 *The Times*, 4 January 2007.

60 *R v Adomako* and *R v Misra* above notes 4 and 5.

61 *R v Wacker* [2003] 1 Cr App R 329.

62 *R v Holloway (Stephen John)* [1993] 3 WLR 922.

architects,[63] school teachers,[64] prison officers[65] and other trained professionals managing risk as part of their work duties. Clarkson rejects this option on the grounds of over-specificity and further questions the validity of a different offence definition depending on employment. He cites the views of the US Twentieth Century Fund Task Force that 'if the legislature actually tried to anticipate every conceivable offence and offender variation, the result would be a penal law of enormous length and complexity, replete with hair splitting distinctions'.[66] For Clarkson, these cases are examples of 'great departures from expected standards' and thus there is no problem in classifying them as grossly careless, as in *Adomako*, and accommodating them within this broad category of homicide.[67] However, this does not adequately address the problem of an overly broad offence and its unfairly wide label. For example, the case of the anaesthetist's misplaced (and fatal) injection is a great departure from expected standards (surely most fatal errors would be so described), yet it does not necessarily follow that it is most appropriately classified and prosecuted as killing by gross carelessness, as opposed to some other context specific form of homicide.[68] The option of creating a new 'lesser' offence for those whose socially vital work places them at increased risk of causing death is a plausible alternative worthy of careful consideration. And it would seem to be a better option than the other candidates of creating a healthcare specific form of homicide such as 'causing death by medical negligence'[69] or endangerment offences such as 'endangering death by dangerous doctoring'. The former would run into the objection of providing special treatment for the medical profession, and of taking specificity too far, and would be at odds with the wider regulatory trend of getting tough with erring doctors. In terms of the latter, cautions against creating endangerment offences[70] are particularly well made in relation to the medical setting, where the high level of risk and potential harm could lead to an alarmingly high rate of prosecutions. Such offences would allow for

63 *R v Beckingham and Barrow Borough Council*. See Forlin, G. (2004), 'Directing Minds: caught in a trap' *New Law Journal*, 154/7118, 326–327.

64 'Teacher jailed over drowned boy', *BBC News Online* (published online 23 September 2003: <http://news.bbc.co.uk/1/hi/england/lancashire/3132102.stm> accessed on 23 September 2003.

65 'Prison officers cleared over death in cell' *The Times*, 3 April 2007.

66 (1976), *Report of the Twentieth-Century Fund Task Force on Criminal Sentencing, Fair and Certain Punishment* (New York: NY) p.18 cited in Clarkson, above n.15 at p.143.

67 Clarkson favours the Law Commission's 1996 formulation of 'killing by gross carelessness'.

68 Unless of course we were to unpack or subjectivise the element of 'expected' standards, which would surely be fraught with difficulties as applied to an increasingly specialised and multi-disciplinary health service.

69 Yeo's preference: Yeo, S. 'Manslaughter versus special homicide offences: An Australian perspective' in this volume.

70 Clarkson, C. (2005), 'General Endangerment Offences: The Way Forward?' *University of Western Australia Law Review* 32, 1–14.

too much discretion, would render it relatively easy to convict, but would be difficult to defend from a responsibility and justice perspective.[71]

So, what is the case for creating a specific offence or set of offences here? Broadly speaking, there are philosophical, practical and political arguments to consider. The last of these is the least convincing and so will be dealt with briefly here. In the ever changing world of criminal justice law and policy, there is much political expediency for government to demonstrate its response to a social problem with a new law, and of course, the ability to set targets and review performance for the enforcement of specific crime.[72] This is particularly true in the context of toughening up the regulation of the medical profession – a process which has gathered significant momentum over the last decade.[73] Passing new criminal law to 'crack down' on medical error would allow government to further demonstrate its commitment to improving patient safety – however misguided such an approach would be in view of the goals of error reduction strategies (discussed below). And as Ashworth correctly points out, the focus should surely be on what 'it is right to do, not about what it is politically prudent to do'.[74] And thus to the central question here: would enacting a context specific offence for healthcare be the right thing to do?

*(i) Philosophical arguments*

Framing criminal law on a clear and consistent notion of culpability is of critical importance. A closer understanding of the concept of responsibility is central to this. However, this is arguably where uniform theories of responsibility tend to be found wanting. There is no 'one size fits all' notion of responsibility which is meaningful for all contexts nor necessitating the same consequences.[75] A more sophisticated, nuanced and fair approach to designing criminal law thus calls for a context specific appreciation of responsibility. Contemporary scholars of criminal law have leant on particular understandings of responsibility to argue both for and against creating context specific offences. Victor Tadros has lamented the lost opportunity for a specific crime of domestic violence following recent legislative reform aimed at bolstering the application of, and relationship between, civil and criminal law.[76] Tadros searches for the different moral wrong of domestic violence and pursues a normative inquiry to sit alongside the substantial body of existing empirical

---

71 See Duff, R.A. (2005), 'Criminalizing Endangerment', in Duff and Green (eds), above n.19, pp.43–64.

72 See Ashworth, A. and Redmayne, M. (2005), *The Criminal Process* (Oxford: Oxford University Press) p.198.

73 For discussion see: Davies, A.C.L. (2000), 'Don't trust me I'm a Doctor: Medical Regulation and the 1999 NHS Reforms' *Oxford Journal of Legal Studies* 20, 437–456 and Chapter 8 in Newdick, C. (2004), *Who Should We Treat? Rights, Rationing and Resources in the NHS* (Oxford: Oxford University Press).

74 Ashworth, above n.12 at p.88.

75 Hall, above n.10.

76 Domestic Violence, Crime and Victims Act 2004.

research,[77] and concluding that the systematic denial of freedom and betrayal of trust entailed here justify the creation of a new offence, given the principal difference of the 'social context in which violence occurs'.[78] Accepting that there must be something different in kind rather than difference in degree, he argues that this is to be found in the diminished sense of freedom that such abuse entails. Creating a new offence is defended on the grounds of reflecting the normative wrong in question and also by its ability to contribute to the broader and sustained effort of tackling the social problem in question.[79]

In the context of the sexual transmission of HIV, Mathew Weait has argued against creating specific criminal law, calling instead for a different understanding of responsibility based on the *context* of sexual intercourse. According to Weait:

> Such a technical and decontextualized approach fosters the idea that crimes are simply the sum of their parts. Rather, I think that we should undertake a more critical dissection, one which involves an exploration of the broader concepts these elements represent – concepts such as harm, blame and responsibility. If, and only if, it is possible to establish that these are present, are manifest in the conduct, should we begin to think in terms of possible criminal liability and all that this entails.[80]

He concludes that 'it is precisely the context of transmission and the meaning of infection, which determine whether it is legitimate to think of it as a public wrong at all'.[81]

Likewise, the question of whether we need a specific offence for medical cases requires an understanding of the notion of responsibility for errors in the complex context of delivering healthcare treatment and services. This requires an appreciation of accepted understandings about the true toll and causes of error from the burgeoning literature on safety in healthcare. Errors are, as Everrett C. Hughes explained, a predictable property of work. In every occupation there is a calculus of the probability of making mistakes, and a certain amount of error remains normal and routine.[82] However, unlike some other industries, systematic attempts to investigate error-related harms in medicine did not emerge until the second half of the twentieth century, although studies of the relationships between healthcare

77 See for example, Hoyle, C. and Sanders, A. (2000), 'Police response to Domestic Violence: From Victim Choice to Victim Empowerment' *British Journal of Criminology* 40, 14–36, and Hoyle, C. (1998), *Negotiating Domestic Violence: Police, Criminal Justice and Victims* (Oxford: Oxford University Press).

78 Tadros, V. (2005), 'The Distinctiveness of Domestic Abuse: A Freedom Based Account' in Duff and Green (eds) above n.19 at p.122.

79 *Ibid.* at pp.141–142.

80 Weait, M. (2001), 'Taking the Blame: Criminal Law, Social Responsibility and the Sexual Transmission of HIV' *Journal of Social Welfare and Family Law* 23: 4, 441–457, at 448.

81 *Ibid.* at p.449 and for a fuller discussion see Weait, M. (2007) *Intimacy and Responsibility: The Criminalisation of HIV Transmission* (London: Routledge-Cavendish) (forthcoming).

82 Hughes, E.C. (1958), *Men and Their Work* (Connecticut: Greenwood Press).

interventions and outcomes had preceded these.[83] From the 1960s onwards, data started to accrue suggesting that a high proportion of hospital patients experienced potentially preventable iatrogenic harm. This attracted little attention until the 1990s, when the data were converted into estimates of the number of people in the USA who died each year from iatrogenic injury (180,000), and of what this equated to in terms of jumbo jet crashes (three every two days).[84] Media coverage of these estimates greatly raised public awareness of the scale of the problem.[85] These ideas were taken up in several initiatives to improve healthcare safety, and were moved into mainstream thinking about healthcare quality with the publication of the Institute of Medicine's report, *To Err is Human*[86] and the Department of Health's *Organisation with a Memory*.[87] These influential reports emphasised the scale of the problem of errors and harms in healthcare and the fact that these problems were for the most part attributable to features of healthcare delivery systems rather than individual health professionals. In line with this, most if not all medical manslaughter prosecutions, whilst concentrating on the acts/omissions of an individual, reveal problems of organisation, planning, design and communication. The case of *Misra* ((iv) above) is a good example of this and indeed the conviction and failed appeals of the doctors was followed by the conviction of the NHS trust for breaches of the Health and Safety at Work Act 1974.[88]

These reports also drew on research into the sociology and psychology of error to highlight the appropriate understanding and classification of error. Error is an essentially contested concept, particularly in complex and uncertain fields such as medicine. While all professions construct 'vocabularies of realism',[89] this is particularly well developed in medicine where risk and fatality are normal. This normalisation and even denial of mistakes has been demonstrated by a number of studies by medical sociologists.[90] Reflecting the increased awareness of the

83 Sharpe, V.A. and Faden, A.I. (1998), *Medical Harm: Historical, Conceptual and Ethical Dimensions of Iatrogenic Illness* (Cambridge: Cambridge University Press).

84 Leape, L.L. (1994), 'Error in Medicine' *Journal of the American Medical Association*, 272:23, 1851–1857.

85 Millenson, M.L. (2002), 'Pushing the profession: how the news media turned patient safety into a priority' *Quality and Safety in Health Care* 11: 1, 57–63.

86 Kohn, L., Corrigan, J. and Donaldson, M. (eds) (1999), *To Err is Human: Building a Safer Health System* (Washington: National Academy Press).

87 Department of Health (2000), *An Organisation with a Memory: Report of an Expert Group on Learning from Adverse Events in the NHS, Chaired by the Chief Medical Officer* (HMSO).

88 *R v Southampton University Hospital NHS Trust* [2006] EWCA Crim 2971. For discussion of the belated role of Health and Safety law in this context see Quick, O. (2007), 'Medical Manslaughter: the Rise and Replacement of a Contested Crime' in Erin, C. and Ost, S. (eds), *The Criminal Justice System and Health Care* (Oxford: Oxford University Press, forthcoming).

89 Stelling, J. and Bucher, R. (1973), 'Vocabularies of Realism in Professional Socialization' *Social Science and Medicine* 7, 661.

90 Freidson, E. (1975), *Doctoring Together: A Study of Professional Social Control* (New York: Elsevier); Bosk, C.L. (1979), *Forgive and Remember: Managing Medical Failure* (Chicago: University of Chicago Press); Millman, M. (1977), *The Unkindest Cut: Life in*

importance of improving patient safety, a number of doctors have publicly confronted their errors and those of their colleagues.[91] Much lies between the two extremes of blame-free accident and deliberate harm, and this is reflected by the myriad terms competing to describe the phenomenon of error in medicine: accidents, mishaps, mistakes, errors, negligence, failures, incompetence, misconduct, malpractice, deficient or substandard care, adverse or untoward events and iatrogenic harm all appear in the literature. Merry and McCall Smith have attempted to address the relationship between medical error and blame by conceptualising these events as errors or violations.[92] Errors are seldom intentional whereas violations are deliberate deviations from accepted rules, norms, or principles. This could also be classified as the difference between doing wrong and wrongdoing.[93] Administering the wrong drug or an anaesthetic mishap as in case (ii) above are errors as they are contrary to the intention to give the correct drug/injection. Whereas a decision to continue with surgery contrary to common practice and colleague concern (as in case (i) above) is clearly a violation. Errors are further divided into skill-based and technical errors. Skill-based errors are described as slips or lapses, such as the momentary loss of concentration/distraction which are not necessarily manifestations of carelessness as in case (ii) above. Technical errors are connected with variability in competency and performance which aptly describe the events in case (iii) above. Whilst this is a useful taxonomy of error, there is no evidence that this or other attempts to unpack error and responsibility have gained universal acceptance within healthcare.[94] And there is no evidence that this has filtered through to the reasoning of prosecutors handling such cases.[95] Designing a new criminal offence for this setting must surely in part depend on a well understood and accepted typology of error and the relationship between types of error and individual blame. Arguably, the study of medical error is at this time insufficiently well developed and understood to support the significant step of creating a new criminal offence. It might be argued that this is not the strongest objection to specificity: after all, we don't call for a similarly nuanced context-based analysis of driving errors. However, this misses the point that errors in healthcare, compared with those on the road, come in many more varieties and depend on variables which necessitate a closer concern with context.

---

*the Backrooms of Medicine* (New York: Morrow Quill); Paget, M.A. (1988), *The Unity of Mistakes: A Phenomenological Interpretation of Medical Work* (Philadelphia: Temple University Press); Rosenthal, M.M. (1995), *The Incompetent Doctor: Behind Closed Doors* (Buckingham: Open University Press).

91 Gawande, A. (2003), *Complications: A Surgeon's Notes on an Imperfect Science* (London: Profile) and (2007), *Better: A Surgeon's Notes on Performance* (London: Profile); Huyler, F. (1999), *The Blood of Strangers: True Stories from the Emergency Room* (London: Fourth Estate); Groopman, J. (2007), *How Doctors Think* (Boston: Houghton).

92 Merry, A. and McCall Smith, A. (2001), *Errors, Medicine and the Law* (Cambridge: Cambridge University Press).

93 Bosk found that doctors approached incidents as technical and normative errors, tolerating the former but not the latter, above n.90.

94 Editorial (2006), 'A research agenda for patient safety' *International Journal for Quality in Health Care* 18:1, 1–3.

95 See Quick, above n.8.

On the other hand, it could be argued that such a 'lesser' offence would be more appropriate and fairer on practitioners, compared with the vagueness and vagaries of GNM. In line with Tadros's account of the distinctiveness of domestic abuse, the central issues of context, betrayal of trust and repetition are usually shared by cases of medical error. However, surely framing of new criminal law requires agreement on a number of questions: is this conduct truly criminal? Can the broader aims of error reduction and professional accountability not be met in different ways? What would be the likely effect of a new offence in terms of number and type of prosecutions? Would more criminal law contribute to the goals of improving patient safety? Approaching this from the notion of law as last resort, I am sceptical of the need and likely effectiveness of more criminal law in this area. Consideration of these practical questions reveals too many uncertainties which point away from the creation of a new criminal offence.

### *(ii) Practical benefits?*

Those in favour of creating such offences must also accept that the logic extends to creating an offence of carelessly causing or endangering serious harm. This could be justified on the basis of mitigating the unfairness of the reality of moral luck and for offering coherence to the law. It would also reflect the communicative function of criminal law and the need for legal expression of the wrong which has occurred.[96] From a practical perspective, drafting specific offences provides the potential for improved clarity for those investigating and prosecuting crime. However, arguably we should step back from the pragmatic world of prosecution and ask more fundamental questions. For example, it is surely a pre-requisite for creating such offences that there exists a consensus that the conduct in question is clearly *criminal* and thus *worthy* of punishment. It is for those who argue in favour of liability beneath recklessness to convince that medical cases merit such criminalisation, yet persuasive arguments have not been forthcoming. Calls for new legislative offences should also be based on clear evidence that existing criminal law is failing to deliver on its aims. Unlike domestic/sexual violence or corporate killing, there is no such consensus upon which to build a new specific offence(s) for the healthcare setting.

A key question revolves around the purposes of obtaining convictions for any new offence. Consider the creation of offences of death by dangerous driving and careless driving – clearly the main rationale behind the relevant law and prosecution policy is to improve road safety. However, there are two reasons why this comparison does nothing to support the case for a new offence for healthcare. First, it does not compare like with like: driving is much simpler and with far fewer variables than doctoring. They are also separated by the issue of choice – most of us often have a choice not to drive in adverse conditions – an option which is not feasible for healthcare professionals operating at the sharp end. Secondly, criminal law is a blunt and ineffective tool for contributing to the broader goal of error reduction and safety in healthcare. The studies into medical error discussed above have showed that

96 See Feinberg, J. (1970), 'The Expressive Function of Punishment' in Feinberg, *Doing and Deserving* (Princeton: Princeton University Press) at 98.

creating a safety culture depends to a large extent about making people feel safe to talk about and report error – something which is inhibited by the prospect of criminal prosecution – even a morally diluted form of homicide. In terms of deterrence, whilst it is difficult to speak with confidence without the benefit of any directly relevant research, it would be somewhat surprising if creating a new offence did deliver a deterrent effect. It might be expected that lessons would be learnt from high profile prosecutions, but the fact that the same types of error tend to be repeated is no evidence of a deterrent effect of the current law of GNM (although admittedly this would be difficult to measure). Lacking the evidence for a valuable role of existing criminal law is hardly the platform from which to call for further offences.

And it is not as though the healthcare setting is short of alternative mechanisms of responding to medical error, whether through informal peer group control or more formal mechanisms of regulation and discipline, the latter being a particularly busy area of reform during the last decade. Looking ahead, we might anticipate greater roles for health and safety law and also the coroner in this context. Only where we feel confident that criminal law can do this better or make a meaningful contribution should we consider its possible use. The option of criminal law should only be used, as Peter Alldridge reminds, 'when all other methods of the legal regulation of the phenomenon in question have been canvassed and found wanting'.[97]

Even if one disagrees with these arguments there are further reasons to be sceptical about the promise of a specific offence. On a general level, there is something unduly optimistic, even naïve, behind the assumption that creating specific offences will alone fix problem areas of criminal law and justice. The evident failure of the Sexual Offences Act 2003 to effect any meaningful change in relation to prosecuting rape is a case in point.[98] Even if the point of principle for creating a specific offence is won, there is arguably little point in pursuing this unless practical issues of enforcement are addressed. For example, the Law Commission's 1996 offence of KGC would still envisage handing the question of measuring whether conduct 'falls far below reasonable expectations' over to experts, and to leaving much (arguably unnecessary) work for prosecutors and juries. Reform of substantive law, without similar thought to the uses (and abuses) of discretion in the criminal justice system, is always likely to disappoint.

How can we conclude then about the role of criminal law with regard to fatal medical error? In short, it does warrant a place within the ever widening range of response to medical error, although recourse to it should be the exception not the rule. Creation of a specific offence would likely lead to criminal charges becoming a normal response, yet an undesirable one in view of the arguments advanced here. Given the basic premise that we need less, not more, criminal law, the best option rests with abolishing GNM and relying on reckless killing liability as the most appropriate way of responding to cases which merit a criminal response. Writing in 1971, J.C. Smith cautioned that 'we should only have as much criminal law as we have to have.

97 Alldridge, P (2001), 'The crime of money laundering' *Buffalo Law Review* 5, 279, at 316.

98 See: Finch, E. and Munro, V. (2006), 'Breaking boundaries? Sexual consent in the jury room' *Legal Studies* 26:3, 303–320.

The enforcement of the criminal law, as such, benefits no one – except possibly the lawyers engaged in the case'.[99] Closer consideration of medical manslaughter cases suggests that this observation is apposite for the healthcare setting. There is no clear or strong case for additional specific offences beneath the level of recklessness. Reformist energies would be better applied to the task of replacing the harshness of GNM with the more appropriate, and suitably renovated, version of subjective recklessness.

---

99 Smith, above n.7.

## Chapter 9

# Dealing with Drug-induced Homicide

William Wilson

This chapter considers the desirability of creating a new offence to address the phenomenon of drug-induced homicide. The context for such an inquiry, if not necessarily support for a specialised offence, is clear. The House of Lords appeal in *Kennedy*[1] has recently been decided, providing important guidance in an area of law which has caused numerous problems for the past 30 years. Ever since *Cato*,[2] commentators have had cause to rue the cavalier fashion in which the law of manslaughter has been harnessed to fulfil a purpose for which it was not designed, namely to hold to account those who have given help or encouragement to someone whose death has been caused by taking a dangerous drug. There are other aspects of this context which are worth pointing out. The State in recent years has gradually changed its response to two superficially comparable social phenomena to that of drug supply, namely the sale and consumption of alcohol and tobacco. Increasingly, regulating the risk of harm rather than addressing the wrongfulness or otherwise of the relevant conduct is dictating State intervention. Alcohol and tobacco can kill. It can kill the individual consumer and it can kill others, either directly, as in passive smoking, or indirectly, as in alcohol induced violence, and it is this, notionally non-paternalistic, goal which seems to underpin the progressive ratcheting up of controls.[3] Tobacco consumption is no longer a matter of personal choice, since it has public consequences and so smoking in public places is prohibited. The marketing of both tobacco and alcohol is also subject to increasing control. At the same time the Home Office's expressed drugs strategy has drug treatment at the forefront, and yet the resources devoted to dealing with the problems posed by the misuse of drugs are dwarfed by those spent on enforcement.[4]

The final pieces in the contextual jigsaw are that the Law Commission has recently reported on homicide[5] and on complicity in crime[6] and if any further reform proposals were thought appropriate this is a good time for tabling them so that the legislature has the opportunity to examine the matter in the round and identify, if this

1 [2007] 3 WLR 612.

2 [1976] 1 WLR 110.

3 The latest such measure is the Children and Young Persons (Sale of Tobacco etc.) Order 2007, which raises the minimum age for the sale of tobacco products from 16 to 18.

4 Reuter, P. and Steven, A. (2007), *An Analysis of UK Drug Policy*: A Monograph Prepared for the UK Drug Policy Commission.

5 Law Commission (2006), *Murder, Manslaughter and Infanticide* (Law Com. No. 304).

6 Law Commission (2007), *Participating in Crime* (Law Com. No. 305).

is thought appropriate, exactly what it is which renders this form of complicity in self-harm a punishable wrong and how best to address it?

There are three possible approaches which may be advanced:

- The first is for those cases of drug-induced homicide which are presently subject to controversy to remain part of the law of manslaughter but to suffer clarification. This would satisfy those who believe that the risks to health posed by the consumption of drugs is a major reason for the criminalisation of supplying drugs and so a reason for holding suppliers accountable when they are closely implicated in their adminstration.
- The second is to drop altogether drug-induced homicide from the scope of manslaughter save for those uncontroversial cases where liability would be incurred on grounds other than the mere act of supply or administration. This approach chimes with the House of Lords' decision in *Kennedy* which reinstates the position that a person cannot be held responsible for the free and informed actions of another person. This would satisfy those who believe that drug consumption is a matter of personal choice, as are any personal consequences which may thereby ensue.
- The third is to create a special offence, either in addition to or as an alternative to the first option, which takes into account the fact of death. This would satisfy those who feel that drug-induced homicide is a special case which warrants criminalisation either because it poses problems for it to be charged as murder or is morally so different from manslaughter's paradigm cases as to warrant a specific label.

## I The First Option – Clarifying Existing Law

There is, of course, a core area of homicide doctrine into which drug-induced killing uncomplicatedly falls. Following *Kennedy* this core is wider and clearer and will now form the outer doctrinal limits governing accountability for drug-induced death. If A administers a lethal dose of heroin so as to kill B, and succeeds, they are guilty of murder. This is so irrespective of motive and the consent of the victim.[7] So if the administration is done in the knowledge that death will certainly occur in the ordinary course of events, unless the administration is an instance of justified clinically-sponsored palliative care or the jury, for some other reason, refuse to take the inference that death or grievous bodily harm was intended, such knowledge notwithstanding.[8] Otherwise, again, the motive of the administrator and consent of the victim does not affect the matter. If, without intending death, A foresees that V might die or suffer serious injury as a result of the administration and they die then this may be reckless manslaughter. This occurred in *Pike*, in which P administered a dose of carbon tetrachloride to their sexual partner to satisfy a sexual fetish for

7 *Cox* [1992] 12 BMLR 38.

8 *Adams* [1957] Crim LR 365; *Matthews and Alleyne* [2003] 2 Cr App R 30.

having sex with an unconscious person.[9] I say, 'may be reckless manslaughter' because, in principle, a good motive, say the urgent relief of pain, whether within a defined medical context or not, may contradict the lack of conscientiousness which recklessness implies.[10]

Gross negligence manslaughter may also uncontroversially be available for particularly bad cases of negligent administration. This may include medically sponsored administration as in *Prentice*[11] but is not restricted to such cases. In Australia, a mother, acting on medical advice given over the telephone, was convicted of manslaughter for mistakenly giving her six-year-old child a lethal overdose of a sedative.[12] Gross negligence manslaughter is also available for failures to intervene in omissions cases where a duty is owed. This can arise independently of an act of supply as in *Bonnyman* where a man was found responsible for the death of his drug addict wife for not seeking proper medical attention.[13] But it is particularly apt in cases where, having supplied or administered a drug to another, the defendant fails to respond appropriately to a resulting crisis. This happened in *Khan and Khan*, where the defendants supplied heroin to a young prostitute with no previous experience of taking heroin. When she fell unconscious they quit the flat rather than summoning medical help. Although a conviction for manslaughter was quashed, the Court of Appeal made the point that a conviction for gross negligence manslaughter would have been available if the jury had been directed properly on the question of duty.[14] Here it is possible that such a duty would arise on the authority of *Miller*.[15] It would be beneficial if this matter were settled once and for all.

Also tolerably clear is the position relating to mere acts of supply unattended by omissions liability. Here, as exemplified by *Dias*, the orthodox solution is that no liability arises due to the absence of any causal nexus between the illegal act of supply and the ensuing death.[16] It is in a fairly narrow band of cases that doctrinal problems arise, namely those where the defendant does not advert to the risk of death, and their act is not criminally negligent but they are nevertheless heavily implicated in the course of events leading to that death. The most directly implicated are those who personally inject the drug which causes death, as occurred in *Cato*.[17] Two drug addicts administered syringes of heroin to each other, a procedure which had passed without incident on numerous previous occasions. On this occasion, however, one of the parties died. The survivor was convicted of constructive manslaughter, which requires the act causing death to be criminally unlawful and also dangerous. The unlawful act grounding the conviction was section 23 Offences Against the Person Act 1861 which makes it an offence 'unlawfully and maliciously to administer, or cause to be administered to or taken by, any other person any poison or other

9 [1961] Crim LR 567.

10 Griew, E, 'Reckless Damage and Reckless Driving' [1981] *Crim LR* 743.

11 *Adomako; Prentice* [1994] 3 All ER 79.

12 *Taylor* (1983) 9 A Crim R 358.

13 *Bonnyman* (1942) 28 Cr App R 131.

14 *Khan* [1998] Crim LR 830.

15 *Miller* [1983] 1 All ER 978; *Commonwealth v Cali* 247 Mass 20, 141 NE 510 (1923).

16 *Dias* [2002] 2 Cr App R 5; *cf Dalby*[1982] 1 All ER 916 at 919 *per* Waller, L.J.

17 Above n.2.

destructive or noxious thing so as thereby to endanger the life of such person or so as thereby to inflict upon such person any grievous bodily harm'. On appeal, Lord Widgery, in the Court of Appeal, found as an alternative unlawful act the injecting of a substance of which the defendant was unlawfully in possession. This basis for conviction has been widely criticised, and rightly so, as liability for this form of manslaughter requires the act causing death to be unlawful, which here it was not. Certainly there was an unlawful act (possession) but this possession did not cause death.

In fact neither basis for the conviction is uncontroversial. The section 23 offence is probably the best bet here although it raises the vexed problem of whether one can consent to the administration of a noxious substance. On the basis of *Brown*[18] it might be thought that one cannot, except in the specific context of medical treatment, but the public interest concerns which police the boundary between the lawful and the unlawful are surely not exhausted by this context. There is an argument, for example, that a citizen administering drugs out of compassion for an addict suffering 'cold turkey', as a preliminary to seeking medical attention, is not acting unlawfully, either because the administration is not contrary to the public interest or because it is not malicious. The illegality of the administration of the noxious substance, upon which a conviction for manslaughter is based, depends upon it 'endangering life'. Clearly the administration in *Cato* did endanger the victim's life – it killed him – but, as Glanville Williams remarked, a conviction for the section 23 offence surely requires a 'mental element beyond the mere intention to administer heroin',[19] namely foresight of the risk of death, which in standard cases of heroin administration as this was would simply not be present. I would go further and suggest, on general principles, that the necessary malice would also not be present if any risk to which the defendant adverted was, in the circumstances known to him, reasonably taken. *Cato* was not doubted in *Kennedy* which was unfortunate, since the matters of doctrinal principle – voluntariness, autonomy, and choice – which so influenced their Lordships' decision are equally called into question in cases of direct administration.

More problematic still are those cases where there is some further act of involvement, or encouragement, in the lethal overdose falling short of actual injection, such as preparing the heroin mixture and handing it to the injecting user. The orthodox view is that such acts cannot form the basis of a conviction for unlawful act manslaughter. To establish this requires the relevant (unlawful) act to have caused the victim's death, or for the actor to be complicit in a principal offence. Where the victim self-injects of their own volition, first *Dalby*, and then *Dias*, ruled that the supplier's initial causal contribution is supplanted by the victim's own free chosen action. Domestic criminal law has long treated Othello rather than Iago as the cause of Desdemona's death. Although Iago is responsible for influencing Othello to kill Desdemona, he does not cause the death, which is all Othello's own.[20] The

18 [1993] 2 All ER 75.

19 Williams, G. (1983), *Textbook of Criminal Law*, 2nd ed. (London: Stevens & Sons) p.215.

20 As Williams puts it: 'What a person does (if he has reached adult years, is of sound mind and is not acting under mistake, intimidation or other similar pressure) is his own

classic statement is that of Hart and Honoré: 'The free, deliberate, and informed intervention of a second person, who intends to exploit the situation created by the first, but is not acting in concert with him, is normally held to relieve the first actor of criminal responsibility'.[21] Liability as an accomplice is also not possible. Where D prepares and hands a syringe containing heroin to P who self-injects and dies as a result, D is not criminally liable for P's death as a secondary party because P did not commit an offence by self-injecting.[22]

Prior to the House of Lords decision in *Kennedy* the Court of Appeal put these propositions in doubt in a number of cases, apparently as a means of delivering a conviction where to apply doctrinal orthodoxy would deny it. In *Finlay*, for example, the Court of Appeal held that the causal responsibility of the supplier of a filled syringe was not undone by the voluntary act of the donee in self-injecting himself.[23] The Court of Appeal relied on the authority of the *Empress Cars* case, where a company was held responsible for causing the release of polluted matter into a river although the release was in fact affected by a trespasser. Since they were placed under a duty to prevent such release and as such a duty was strict the company could not defend themselves by saying it was not their doing.[24] The Court of Appeal in *Finlay* boldly extrapolated from this that the supplier of the filled syringe caused its contents to be injected precisely because the act of supply was given for this purpose and was so used, in line with the parties' expectations.

In *Kennedy* the Court of Appeal accepted that there can be no question of K being an accomplice to the victim's own unlawful act of self injection in the absence of a principal offence.[25] If K is not an accessory the only way of convicting him is, therefore, upon the basis of his own unlawful act of supply. **If this causes** the death of the victim then unlawful act manslaughter is committed. The Court of Appeal so held on the basis that K had, by supplying the fully laden syringe, caused a noxious substance to be taken by V. Disregarding the *Empress* approach the problem of causation was obviated by the device of treating both supplier of the syringe and victim as parties to a single act of causing a noxious substance to be administered. In effect the supplier becomes the principal of the offence by dint of his participation in a single transaction leading to the injection. It was not, however, explained how D can illegally administer heroin to V by the same transaction by which V voluntarily (and legally) administers it to himself.[26] The House of Lords agreed that this made no sense and, approving the Hart and Honoré approach, allowed the appeal stating:

---

personal responsibility and is not to be regarded as having been caused by other people' (Williams, G. (1983), *ibid.*, p.39).

21 Hart, H.L.A. and Honoré, T. (1985), *Causation in the Law*, 2nd ed. (Oxford: Clarendon Press) p.326. This statement was expressly approved by the House of Lords in *Latif* [1996] 1 WLR 104.

22 *Dias* [2002] 2 Cr App R 5.

23 *Finlay* [2003] EWCA Crim 3868; *Rogers* [2003] EWCA Crim 945.

24 *Environment Agency v. Empress Car Co. (Abertillery) Ltd.* [1999] 2 AC 22.

25 *Kennedy* [2007] 3 WLR 612.

26 Ormerod, D. and Fortson, R. (2005), 'Drug Suppliers as Manslaughterers (Again)' *Crim LR* 819.

> It is possible to imagine factual scenarios in which two people could properly be regarded as acting together to administer an injection. But nothing of the kind was the case here. As in *R v Dalby* and *R v Dias* the appellant supplied the drug to the deceased, who then had a choice, knowing the facts, whether to inject himself or not. The heroin was, as the certified question correctly recognises, self-administered, not jointly administered. The appellant did not administer the drug. Nor, for reasons already given,[27] did the appellant cause the drug to be administered to or taken by the deceased.[28]

The conceptual challenge posed by cases such as *Kennedy* emphasises questions of attribution. The specific discussion outlined above takes the form of a proxy for what I have taken to be the more appropriate discussion, namely whether constructive manslaughter has any part to play where the accident of death shines its bright light upon the comings and goings of two participants in an all too common, but socially discreditable, enterprise. If it were simply a question of which causal test to apply I confess I would have no overwhelming objection to fashioning rules of attribution capable of justifying the conviction of the supplier of dangerous drugs. Unlike many commentators I am quite easy with the finding in *Empress* that, for the purpose of a strict liability offence designed to prevent the escape of pollutants into water courses, it is appropriate to assign causal responsibility to the controllers/possessors of the pollutant. The House of Lords in *Kennedy* takes a similar view:

> The House was not in that decision purporting to lay down general rules governing causation in criminal law. It was construing, with reference to the facts of the case before it, a statutory provision imposing strict criminal liability on those who cause pollution of controlled waters ... In the situation under consideration the act of the defendant could properly be held to have caused the pollution even though an ordinary act of a third party was the immediate cause of the diesel oil flowing into the river ... The committee would not wish to throw any doubt on the correctness of the *Empress Car* case. But the reasoning in that case cannot be applied to the wholly different context of causing a noxious thing to be administered to or taken by another person contrary to section 23 of the 1861 Act.[29]

I agree.

More generally, causal inquiries in the criminal law frequently face the difficulty of justifying holding an individual accountable for an event in the face of a broader contextual explanation of how that event came about. *Pagett* is a less controversial example of how context is relevant to the application of these tests.[30] P used his girlfriend as a hostage and human shield during a gun battle with police. The Court of Appeal found the defendant's conduct in using his girlfriend as a human shield and prompting the defensive fire of the police to be an operative cause of the death. Even if the police had acted improperly in returning fire[31] this causal contribution of P justified holding him accountable. It follows a standard course in criminal trials, requiring a special form of connection between the undesired event

27 That is because the injection was freely chosen and fully informed.

28 *Kennedy* [2007] 3 WLR 612 at [24].

29 *Ibid.* at [15], [16].

30 (1983) 76 Crim App R 279.

31 And there was some suggestion that they may have done.

and the defendant's conduct – the kind which elicits the response not merely that he participated in its occurrence but that it was his 'doing', or his 'fault'. On this there are clear similarities between *Pagett* and *Kennedy*. If we analyse both in terms of what they 'supplied', they supplied a dangerous context in which things could go badly wrong, and did. If Pagett, the supplier of a dangerous stand-off with armed police officers, is accountable, then why not the supplier of dangerous drugs? This is a bigger question than can be answered by a simple choice between tests.

All tests of causation, other than the free and intervening choice test, supply the necessary causal connection between Kennedy's act of supply and the victim's response. This includes the traditional reasonable foresight test articulated in The Draft Criminal Code Bill.[32] It also includes the more analytical 'within the risk' test. If the objective risk of V harming himself as a result of self-administration is one of the reasons why K should have guarded against supplying V with the drug then this affords grounds for attributing the consequence to K's act, as with any other unlawful and dangerous act. The fact that the individual concerned was an adult, knew what he was doing, and knew the risks of what he was doing, strongly supports the view that V must take responsibility for the consequences. But it is not a knock down argument against K *also* taking responsibility for the consequences by virtue of his critical intervention. Perhaps we are talking too loosely if we say K caused V to inject himself, but clearly his intervention was influential. Is this not enough to hold him to account?

As Stanley Yeo confirms in his chapter, the position taken in our jurisdiction in creating a hierarchy of causal tests in such cases is by no means the norm. We can single out Scotland and Australia as taking a more pragmatic approach. Moreover, a number of commentators have taken issue with the Hart/Honoré approach to the critical importance of intervening choices.[33] What counts ultimately is whether a given individual deserves to be held accountable for a given consequence.[34] If we convict someone of homicide the moral message conveyed is that the accused deserves to be associated with the fact of the victim's death and suffer condemnation and punishment for it. Treating, as some have done, the fact of intervening choice as conclusive of the matter is somewhat disingenuous in this respect. After all, what is 'free and voluntary' is itself contextually realised. In *Pagett* and *Kennedy*, for example, there are significant distinguishing features which, whether or not one is a proponent of the Hart and Honoré position, might be expected to bear upon the

32 Law Commission (1989), *A Criminal Code for England and Wales, Draft Criminal Code* (Law Com. No. 177), cl.17 provides that a person causes a result when '(1) ... (a) he does an act which makes a more than negligible contribution to its occurrence, or (b) he omits to do an act which might have prevented its occurrence and which he is under a duty to do according to the law relating to the offence. (2) A person does not cause a result where, after he does such an act or makes such an omission, an act or event occurs (a) which is the immediate and sufficient cause of the result; (b) which he did not foresee, and (c) which could not in the circumstances reasonably have been foreseen'.

33 Feinberg, J. (1970), *Doing and Deserving* (Princeton: Princeton University Press) pp.150–166; Jones, T. (2006), 'Causation, homicide and the supply of drugs' *Legal Studies* 26, 139–154.

34 See for example Norrie, A. (1991), 'A Critique of Criminal Causation' *MLR* 54, 685 at 694.

question of attribution. In *Pagett* the police's conduct, although sufficiently free and informed to have provided a plausible basis for convicting them of manslaughter had the boot been on the other foot,[35] was nevertheless by way of reaction to an external trigger. V's self-administration, on the other hand, was not triggered but deliberated. This is arguably enough to provoke the common sense judgement that Pagett is accountable for what the police did in a way that Kennedy was not, for what the deceased did. But we may not wish to reach this latter conclusion if the context were different, say the relationship between the parties was unequal or the deceased inexperienced.[36]

It would have been useful, for the short term at least, for the House of Lords in *Kennedy* to have provided guidance as to how to fit the more culpable cases of drug-induced killing within the existing architecture of homicide liability in a way which serves the twin objects of setting accountability and being faithful to existing legal values. It has not done so, preferring rather to restrict itself to reinstating the primacy of intervening choice. A good starting point, no doubt, but a starting point nevertheless. We should not generally expect criminal liability simply upon the basis of supply, with or without preparation. These are, as their Lordships insist, matters of personal choice and provide no cogent basis for the imputation of liability. A more comprehensive response, which would have addressed concerns over the adequacy of the law's overall response to drug-induced homicide, would be to bring within the explicit scope of manslaughter, victim's intervening choice notwithstanding, those cases where the context provides risks of specific dangers against which the supplier can be expected to guard.[37] In cases where D supplies V with the prepared syringe, for example, a duty of care could be made a matter of law which would necessitate reasonable efforts to ensure the suitability and quality of the drug administered to ensure the suitability of the dose for the donee, and to ensure D seeks medical attention for V where problems arise by dint of the administration.

## II The Second Option – Dropping Drug-induced Homicide from Manslaughter

Commentators are generally antagonistic to drug-induced killings being treated as constructive manslaughter.[38] This may be because of a general antipathy to constructive crime[39] or it may be because of the specific difficulty of imputing death to the supplier of drugs. Most of the argument against liability concentrates on specific doctrinal objections rather than deeper questions of principle, such as fair labelling.

---

35 Norrie, A. (1993), *Crime, Reason and History* (London: Wiedenfeld and Nicolson) p.145.

36 See discussion below at footnote 41.

37 Williams, R. (2005), 'Policy and Principle in Drugs Manslaughter Cases' *Cambridge Law Journal* 64, 66.

38 See for example Simester, A.P. and Sullivan, G.R. (2007), *Criminal Law: Theory and Doctrine*, 3rd ed. (Oxford and Portland, Oregon: Hart Publishing) pp.94–96; Ormerod D. and Fortson, R. (2005), above n.26 at 823; Ashworth, A. (2006), *Principles of Criminal Law*, 5th ed. (Oxford: Oxford University Press) p.129.

39 Ashworth, A. (2006), *ibid.*, pp.87–88.

Indeed, there is a strong argument in favour of drug-induced homicide dropping out of manslaughter altogether unless there is an independent basis for liability, such as absence of consent. The most compelling reason is that manslaughter is too serious a label, and that responsibility for death is already spread across too wide a spectrum. The fact of consent in the type of cases we are considering compounds the general problem of constructive liability and the lack of a foresight of harm requirement. The result is that manslaughter is too imprecise in what it signifies to have any value as a communicative medium and, given the absence of a strong correlation between drug supply and death, allows too much room for the operation of luck. This, then, as Tadros has suggested in his chapter, may be one of those cases 'towards the bottom limit of manslaughter that ought not to fall within the law of homicide at all'. The core of manslaughter, including gross negligence manslaughter, is quite robust enough to cope with the fact of death where the supplier truly makes his own bad luck.

We should disentangle two separate features which bear on the propriety of the approach taken to drug-induced homicide by the courts. The first feature, which is being dealt with now, is whether it is appropriate at all for the fact of death to be taken into account in the offence definition. At the level of general policy the argument against is that dealing in drugs is only nominally a crime and that the bad luck in which this involves users and suppliers should not be compounded by a finding of accountability for the ill-luck of death. Moreover, the maximum sentence for supplying drugs is already life imprisonment and judges can and do reflect the fact of death in their sentencing. More practically, holding suppliers to account for resulting death is a disincentive for those involved to summon assistance if things go wrong. There is every incentive built into existing law for suppliers to act as the defendants in *Khan* did, namely, to show more concern for their own skins than for that of the unfortunate victim.[40]

The second feature, which was dealt with above, is what the rules governing the attribution of that death should be, assuming it is appropriate. Should the supplier of drugs be subject to different rules of attribution than other killers? As has been explained, our response to this question may be driven by broader questions of context rather than the strict application of doctrinal tests, of which something more needs to be said. We may have in mind as our typical case *Khan and Khan* in which the defendants were professional drug dealers, careless whether the deceased, a 15-year-old girl with no experience of heroin, lived or died. But in fact, an equally, if not more typical case, involves the young small-time drug dealer who supplies drugs to a friend. In a recent unreported Scottish case,[41] the defendant, who was a small time dealer, supplied amphetamine to his 17-year-old friend, Jacqueline Gourlay, who suffered a fatal brain haemorrhage after a rare reaction to amphetamine. The defendant, who was 21, supplied both drugs and was convicted of culpable manslaughter. The two cases indicate that any impetus to differentiate the two cases in terms of the defendants' accountability for the death will be ill-served by asking the

40 Elliott, C. and de Than, C. (2006), 'Prosecuting the Drug Dealer When a Drug User Dies' *Modern Law Review* 69, 986–995. Significantly, they did show concern by returning the next day.

41 *Herald*, 16 May 2001.

question 'Did D's unlawful act cause V's death?' D's responsibility must be coaxed rather from the context within which he was operating which should emphasise not D's role as 'cause' of V's self administration but rather his moral responsibility for subjecting V to the risk of death.

*(i) The fact of death – The role of luck*

The sets of data provided in the tables below put the ratio of deaths to drug usage in some kind of perspective. The British Crime Survey gives us a snapshot of the amount and nature of drug use currently occurring (Table 9.1). The Office of National Statistics data gives us the total number of deaths involving comparable drugs, in England and Wales in 2005 (Table 9.2).

These statistics give no more than a blurred picture of the nature and extent of drug-induced homicide. The ONS data, for example, is not an authoritative census because there is no one organisation that collects information about drug-related deaths, for all of the UK, and there is no one definition of what we mean by drug-related deaths. The ONS data also does not indicate the number of deaths attributable, however loosely, to the involvement of another person. Elsewhere the ONS statistics tell us that the underlying cause of death was drug dependence or accidental poisoning/overdose in 60 per cent of these cases, which, one assumes, forms the main category out of which occasions of drug-induced homicide could be constructed. Three things come across fairly clearly, however, when looked at in conjunction with the British Crime Survey data. First, there is a lot of drug use going on, and this use is increasing. Secondly, in absolute terms, the statistics afford little evidence of special risks of death attributable to dangerous drugs. By this I mean dangers connected with the administration *per se*, with which the law of manslaughter is concerned, as opposed to the long-term effects of drug use which it is not. Thirdly, such dangers, including long-term dangers, as there are connected with dangerous drugs, are relatively insignificant as compared with alcohol and tobacco, where there is a high statistical correlation between use and death.[42]

Now what does this have to say about the propriety of building the fact of death into the criminal wrong associated with the supply of dangerous drugs? One of the arguments in favour of liability for drug-induced homicide is that there is a difference between unlucky outcomes over which one has control and those over which one has no control.[43] In one sense, at least, the drug supplier is in control in the sense that the possibility of something going awry is one of the reasons why he might be expected to have thought twice before handing over that syringe. In the Scottish case looked at above, Lord Wheatley, passing sentence on the young drug dealer, made the following remarks: 'It is accepted that you had no intention of causing the

---

42 Latest estimates for tobacco induced mortality are in the region of 110,000 deaths *per annum*. For further discussion see below.

43 See Nagel, T. (1979), 'Moral Luck' in *Mortal Questions* (Cambridge: Cambridge University Press) pp.24–38. Williams, B. (1982), 'Moral Luck' in *Moral Luck* (Cambridge: Cambridge University Press) pp.20–39.

death, but it's difficult to believe nowadays that anyone is unaware that drug use in general is dangerous. You were in the practice of supplying drugs to friends and acquaintances as a result of which a 17-year-old girl is dead. You pleaded guilty to a charge of culpable homicide and you have accepted that you are responsible for the death of another human being'.

**Table 9.1 Estimated numbers of 16- to 59-year-olds who have taken drugs**

| | Used ever | Used last year | Used last month |
|---|---|---|---|
| **Class A** | | | |
| Any cocaine | 2,310,000 | 776,000 | 376,000 |
| Cocaine powder | 2,273,000 | 769,000 | 368,000 |
| Crack cocaine | 270,000 | 53,000 | 25,000 |
| Ecstasy | 2,279,000 | 502,000 | 216,000 |
| Hallucinogens | 2,968,000 | 338,000 | 84,000 |
| LSD | 1,733,000 | 83,000 | 25,000 |
| Magic Mushrooms | 2,311,000 | 302,000 | 68,000 |
| Opiates | 272,000 | 47,000 | 35,000 |
| Heroin | 203,000 | 39,000 | 23,000 |
| Methadone | 149,000 | 33,000 | 24,000 |
| **Class A/B** | | | |
| Amphetamines | 3,655,000 | 426,000 | 176,000 |
| **Class B/C** | | | |
| Tranquillisers | 868,000 | 118,000 | 64,000 |
| **Class C** | | | |
| Anabolic steroids | 194,000 | 42,000 | 20,000 |
| Cannabis | 9,475,000 | 2,775,000 | 1,644,000 |
| **Total** | | | |
| Class A | **4,416,000** | **1,082,000** | **513,000** |
| Any Drug | **11,075,000** | **3,329,000** | **1,990,000** |

*Source*: 2005/06 British Crime Survey

However, we need more than control to justly holding an agent to account. The generous host who allows their guest to drink themselves into a stupour does no wrong that I am aware of, and if they die of asphyxiation as a result of inhaling their own vomit, the host is not accountable. They are not accountable because of the importance of intervening choice and also because the criminal law does not create this kind of accountability out of the supply of alcohol.[44] Given the very weak statistical correlation between drug use and death, particularly as alcohol consumption is far more potent in this respect, there are clearly grounds for questioning whether the supplier of dangerous drugs should be accountable for the ill luck of a resulting death, 'illegal' or 'dangerous' though they may be.[45] If we recognise that luck has selected these individuals to be the instruments of others' deaths it might be better to punish them for what we apprehend is their real wrong, namely that they have (culpably) endangered someone's life. Or we could be satisfied with a conviction for supplying Class A drugs which is, in any event, an implicit endangerment offence for which the sentence can and will take death into account. One advantage served by such an approach is that it solves at a stroke the major problem which, as has been seen, bedevils doctrine in this area, namely the production of coherent principles capable of distinguishing fairly between those to whom causal responsibility is assigned and those to whom it is not.

**Table 9.2 Number of deaths and percentage change compared to 1999 for specific substances involved in deaths related to drug misuse, England, 1999–2004**

| | 1999 | 2000 | 2001 | 2002 | 2003 | 2004 | Percentage change from 1999 to 2004 |
|---|---|---|---|---|---|---|---|
| Heroin and Morphine | 715 | 874 | 840 | 737 | 562 | 693 | -3 |
| Methadone | 286 | 226 | 199 | 205 | 167 | 194 | -32 |
| Benzodiazepines | 217 | 190 | 207 | 224 | 195 | 186 | -14 |
| Opiates (unspecified) | 141 | 163 | 154 | 132 | 80 | 106 | -25 |
| Dihydrocodeine | 114 | 98 | 107 | 95 | 77 | 73 | -36 |
| Cocaine | 85 | 76 | 86 | 131 | 107 | 139 | 64 |
| Amphetamines (excluding ecstasy) | 47 | 19 | 25 | 36 | 30 | 33 | -30 |
| MDMA/Ecstasy | 23 | 34 | 51 | 47 | 27 | 46 | 100 |
| Barbiturates | 23 | 16 | 28 | 14 | 18 | 14 | -39 |
| Codeine | 22 | 27 | 31 | 29 | 31 | 49 | 123 |

*Source*: Compiled by ONS, 2007

44 If he owed a duty of care to the guest he might be guilty of gross negligence manslaughter, as where a pharmacist is accountable if she does not take care over the correct dosage for the patient to self-inject but otherwise his power of control over a guest's behaviour does not render him accountable for the failures of so doing.

45 Ashworth, A. (1989), 'Belief, Intent and Criminal Liability' in Eekelaar, J. and Bell, J. (eds) (1989), *Oxford Essays in Jurisprudence* (3rd Series, Oxford: Oxford University Press); Ashworth, A. (1993), 'Taking the Consequences' in Shute, S, Gardner, J and Horder, J (eds), *Action and Value in Criminal Law* (Oxford: Clarendon Press).

Moreover, despite Lord Wheatley's salutary remark about 'drug use in general being dangerous' the paradigm of unlawful act manslaughter, and one which limits the role of luck, involves an act which is dangerous in the specific context rather than dangerous as a more general social phenomenon. The argument is not simply that death is not a reasonably foreseeable consequence of drug supply. It may be. It depends. It is rather that the risks against which policy is ranged and which therefore should inform the range of offences associated with it *do not emphasise the risk of death resulting from a single act of supply*. In 1998 the Runciman Inquiry recommended the following factors relevant to sentencing: the involvement of an organised criminal group; the use of violence or firearms; the use of children or young persons in trafficking activities; supply to minors; the commission of the offence in the vicinity of schools, psychiatric facilities or prisons; and public nuisance elements in the offence. Resulting death was not worth even a mention, although, of course, in practice it is a key matter for those sentenced.[46]

Leaving aside for a moment the general issue of the propriety of constructive crime, I would have thought it uncontroversial that it is inappropriate for a crime designed for one purpose – preventing future crime and promoting social cohesion – to be hijacked for another – holding someone to account for consequential death – particularly when the fatal result lies outside the reasonable scope of the risk created by the offence D was committing. In the cases of drug supply at least, quoting Ashworth, 'the gap between D's fault and the ultimate result is too wide'. I would go further. This is a case where we might be disposed to acknowledge that responsibility for the tragic results of drug misuse is shared with the society, whose policy failures regarding drugs, social exclusion, poverty and education makes drugs supply into the raging social problem it is. Responsibility for the death of individual actors in this context should not be easily limited to another of its victims. I shall return to this later.

I am one of the majority of commentators who, in general, believe that consequences should be built into the definitions of offences so long as it is fair to treat harmful events as the defendant's doing. Ignoring the fact of harmful outcomes as a focus for criminal liability is to ignore a major retributive concern, which is to allow society to put on record precisely how the victim has been wronged, and reflect the extent of the harm done in punishment. Side-stepping the issue of drug-induced homicide for one moment, it is appropriate and just that liability for homicide attends those cases where a person dies as a result of a beating. The wrong he commits is killing someone, not simply beating them.[47] There are, however, strong grounds for resisting this reasoning in cases of drug induced homicide. The first ground is to do with the nature of constructive manslaughter. The second is to do with broader questions of fair labelling.

---

46 Independent Inquiry into the Misuse of Drugs Act 1971 (2000), *Drugs and the Law: A Report* (London: Police Foundation).

47 Katz, L. (2000), 'Why the Successful Assassin is More Wicked than the Unsuccessful One' 88 *Caifornia Law Review* 791.

Accountability in constructive manslaughter follows a settled path. It belongs to a different family of crimes from that of gross negligence manslaughter, and drug-induced homicide fits uneasily within it for a number of reasons. In its paradigm form it is a crime of violence and, like murder, the paradigm unlawful killing, requires death to result from an attack. With murder the attack takes the form of unlawful conduct intended to cause death or grievous bodily harm. With manslaughter the attack takes the form of an attack in which the risk of harm is manifest and obvious or, under the most recent Law Commission proposals, the form of a criminal act by which the defendant intends to cause harm or is aware involves a serious risk of causing some injury.[48] Duff makes the case for distinguishing crimes of endangerment from crimes of attack particularly strongly in his chapter. 'These differences between attacks and negligent endangerment – the way in which in attacks success is the paradigm, whereas in endangerment it is the non-occurrence of harm that is the paradigm; differences in the extent to which we can or cannot assume that the agent would react with appropriate distress or relief to the occurrence or non-occurrence of harm – will in various ways condition the content and the tone of our responses to the agent'. We can add something extra to the ingredients in the case of constructive manslaughter, namely that the fact of attack changes the normative position of the attacker *vis à vis* unforeseen consequences. As Horder has argued, it is quite appropriate in unlawful act manslaughter that it should not be necessary for there to be a correspondence between fault and the result so long as the offence committed is in the same family of offence (here violence) as that occurring. By attacking the other he has disqualified himself from saying that any consequential harm suffered by the victim is down to luck. It is his bad luck and he must take responsibility for it.[49]

The problems facing the courts in the drugs cases are directly connected with this conceptual issue and only loosely connected to questions of attribution. But its relevance affects reasoning throughout the family of crimes with which constructive manslaughter is associated. It is this paradigm of attack, which drove Viscount Kilmuir in *Smith* and Hailsham in *Hyam* to use, as their distinguishing mark between murder and reckless manslaughter, an act which is aimed at the victim. This has been treated as a piece of throwaway nonsense. It is nonsense, if we take the statement at face value, but symbolically it is apt since it reduces to the accurate claim that the act in murder must be by way of an act of violence or other attack. The same device was used in *Dalby*. *Goodfellow*, nominally an endangerment case it should be noted, interpreted the 'directed at' requirement in *Dalby* to mean simply that the supplier must cause the victim's death, which it does not do if the victim self administers.[50] Again, this misses the point clamouring to be heard in *Dalby* that the essence of unlawful act manslaughter is an attack, for the purpose of describing the limits of accountability, and it was largely in furtherance of this point that the Court of Appeal quashed the conviction. A whole raft of cases has flirted with this idea that attack,

48 Law Commission (2006), *Murder, Manslaughter and Infanticide* (Law Com. No. 304).

49 Horder, J. (1997), 'Two Histories and Four Hidden Principles of *Mens Rea*' 113 *LQR* 95.

50 *Goodfellow* (1986), 83 Cr App R 23.

or in a related version, hostility, is central to offences against the person.[51] We know from *Brown* that a person cannot always escape liability for the consequences of an act of violence if harm was intended or foreseen. There are public interests at stake, which trump individual autonomy. But I wonder whether such considerations can possibly arise in cases like *Dalby* and *Kennedy* where not only is autonomy respected but the defendant does not even lay hands on the victim. Unlawful act manslaughter was held to be inapt when it resulted from extremely vigorous but consensual sex in *Slingsby*.[52] In both *Dica and Konzani* it was accepted that a person could consent, assuming fully informed, to sexual intercourse with a person who has HIV, a rather more dangerous activity, one might hazard, than administering Class A drugs.[53] One assumes that if death resulted there would be no question of liability for constructive manslaughter. What is distinctive about these cases is that where the victim chooses to subject themselves to risks and indeed may be the dominant partner in a commercial transaction or exchange of services there is no call for luck to redound to the supplier's discredit. This reasoning does not apply, it seems to me, in the paradigm of manslaughter by attack where the whole context is driven by what the attacker does and, because it involves relegating another's interests to one's own, rightly disables the defendant from passing the buck of responsibility by saying it was not my fault, or it was bad luck.

## III The Third Option: A Special Homicide Offence?

Does this conclusion leave any room for the enactment of a special homicide offence. I do not think so, but it would nevertheless be worthwhile considering the arguments of those in favour. There are two main strands: that the present law of manslaughter is not able to capture forms of drug-induced homicide where a finding of accountability is appropriate without so distorting doctrine as to destabilise manslaughter as a whole. The second argument is that the particular wrongdoing which drug-induced homicide represents is different in kind, and often in degree, from that which unites manslaughter in its various forms. It should be labelled differently to reflect different degree of involvement, to communicate effectively the moral structure of criminal homicide and to ensure an appropriate grading of seriousness.[54]

My reason for jibbing at the first argument should be clear. I think that the present law of manslaughter, particularly if finessed in the way I have suggested, captures all cases where a finding of accountability is appropriate. Drug-induced homicide is not comparable with other present or proposed special homicide offences, such as

51 See *Wilson v Pringle* [1986] 2 All ER 449.

52 [1995] Crim LR 570.

53 *Dica* [2004] QB 1257; *Konzani* [2005] EWCA Crim 706.

54 If it were simply a question of seriousness, a general offence such as that suggested by the Law Commission (1996) of 'culpable killing' with a lower maximum sentence than that of manslaughter is an alternative suggestion.

causing death by dangerous driving[55] or corporate killing.[56] With the former there is little controversy that those who kill while driving dangerously are rightly held accountable, ill-luck notwithstanding. The only issue that arises in this connection is why manslaughter is not the correct offence label. The commonly agreed answer is that the special offence is appropriate to ensure a conviction, and an adequate offence label, in a context where, desert notwithstanding, the jury are reluctant to convict. Requiring prosecutors to resort to general homicide offences could, therefore, result in undercharging. Regarding corporate killing there is, as Clarkson explains in this volume, an irresistible case for a special homicide offence. Here, unlike dangerous driving, it is the problems of attributing harm to individual actions which renders manslaughter unfit for purpose rather than the reluctance of the jury to convict. In this sense, at least, it invites comparison with the position with drug-induced homicide. However, unlike corporate killing where there is manifest wrongdoing but no really identifiable human subject to which the wrongdoing can be attributed, the problem faced in cases of drug-induced death is far less easy to manage. Here it seems to be the inability to justify a principled conviction of a defendant for a crime, rooted in the paradigm of attack, who, at worst, has no more than provided the victim with the means to harm himself.

Despite the view of successive courts, as illustrated in *Cato* and *Finlay*, that the injection of a Class A drug is something wrongful and dangerous and so something out of which can and should be constructed liability for homicide the doctrinal mechanisms for effecting this threaten to destabilise manslaughter as whole, and were rightly recognised by the House of Lords in *Kennedy*. However, we should not be blind to the fact that matters pertaining to the general part of the criminal law may not always fit the needs of the special part. The overwhelmingly hostile reaction to the various devices adopted by the courts to avoid the consequences of orthodox notions of attribution have tended to ignore the 'elephant in the room', which is the presence of a dead body. If we were to build a case for drug-induced homicide we would need, however, to be convinced first that what was wrong, if anything, with supplying dangerous drugs was of a nature to justify holding the supplier accountable for death. Peter Alldridge has argued that the supposed wrongs relevant for our purposes are controversial at best as a basis for criminalisation.[57] These are that drug dealers commit an inchoate offence against the person, that is that their involvement 'constitutes a step towards harming the eventual user'. Alternatively, they are complicit in self harm by the user. The former wrong is controversial because it ignores the relevance of victim's consent which, as I have argued, causes problems in the context of a charge of constructive manslaughter. The second, equally controversial, requires an acceptance that the criminal law's

55 Cunningham, S. (2001), 'The Reality of Vehicular Homicides: Convictions for Murder, Manslaughter and Causing Death by Dangerous Driving' *Crim LR* 679.

56 Clarkson, C. (2000), 'Context and Culpability in Involuntary Manslaughter: Principle or Instinct?' in Ashworth, A. and Mitchell, B., *Rethinking English Homicide Law* (Oxford: Oxford University Press) p.150.

57 'Dealing with Drug Dealing' in Simester, A.P. and Smith, A.T.H. (eds) (1996), *Harm and Culpability* (Oxford: Clarendon Press) p.239.

role here is a paternalistic one, based on the risks of physical harm, loss of autonomy and dependence which drug-taking generally and drug-addiction specifically brings. His radical conclusion is that in cases fit for criminalisation the real wrong in drug-dealing is that it involves a form of exploitation similar to blackmail, a wrong, one would assume, too far removed from the consequence of death to justify holding the exploiter to account. Assuming the inchoate offence or complicity in self-harm rationales were thought a sufficient basis for grounding a special homicide offence, what would be the justification for criminalising the resulting death? The answer has to be that the special features which distinguish constructive manslaughter from drug-induced homicide should be specifically built into the architecture of the offence so that the wrong is effectively communicated and understood the better to influence behaviour, while maintaining the communicative clarity which manslaughter currently enjoys. These special features are that the homicide is less serious, perhaps for the fact of consent or the absence of attack, or for the fact that the wrong targeted was in violation of the harm principle. Such an offence has been enacted in New Jersey and in Illinois. In Illinois the offence is known as 'Kelley's Law'. The specific problem posed by the law of causation, if not the principle which underlies it, is accommodated by severing any requirement of a causal link between the act of supply and the ensuing death. It is enough if a person to whom drugs have been sold or given dies from taking them. Section 9-3.3 is as follows:

> (a) A person who violates Section 401 of the Illinois Controlled Substances Act by unlawfully delivering a controlled substance to another, and any person's death is caused by the injection, inhalation or ingestion of any amount of that controlled substance, commits the offense of drug-induced homicide.

The first case prosecuted under this provision involved a 21-year-old on a charge of selling heroin to a 19-year-old who subsequently died of an overdose. This case, and the moniker attached to the offence, indicates the problems which arise when doctrine developed to honour and respect the rights and freedoms of the individual comes into conflict with the political ambition to allay concern about public safety and health, and promote social cohesion. The ways in which the Illinois offence can be committed in the absence of any significant connection between the defendant's act and the resulting death are startling in their breadth. Tim Jones tries to avoid this problem by tabling a proposal, with the specific aim of not impinging 'upon either the prevailing common law principles of causation or the law of manslaughter more generally'. By his proposal a provision could be inserted into the Misuse of Drugs Act 1971 creating an offence of 'causing the death of another person by the (production or) supply of a controlled drug' with the stipulation that 'it is not a defence ... that the deceased contributed to his own death by his voluntary (action) ... or by consenting to the administration of the controlled drug by another'.[58] If Jones manages to achieve his goal, it nevertheless leaves the question hanging as to why A should be liable for the death of B simply through having provided him with the means of harming himself.

---

58 Jones, T. (2006). 'Causation, Homicide and the Supply of Drugs' 26 *Legal Studies* 139 at 154.

One further feature may be tabled as supportive of a special homicide offence. Commentators have tended to limit discussion to the merits of the various methods of attribution adopted by the courts to address problems of accountability, but there are other elements which need to be accommodated by whatever scheme of liability we end up with. At a direct level these include matters such as the type of drug involved. The discussion has thus far centred on the specifics of drug injection, which no doubt falls nearer the paradigm of constructive manslaughter than, say, the supply of ecstasy tablets at a rave – but a coherent law must accommodate both. Of equally direct concern are matters relating to the reasons for the fatality: drug too pure; drug adulterated; drug overdose; drug admixed with other drugs; victim reaction, and so on, as well as issues such as the relative responsibility of victim/accomplice and other people in the supply chain for the production, preparation and administration of the drug.

The vagaries of context/culpability and accountability might make a specific crime more attractive, particularly when we look more closely at the issue of context. Responsibility for both drug supply and demand is arguably spread too broadly to justify atomising questions of responsibility in the fashion illustrated in *Kennedy*. In a typical case of death caused by heroin overdose this context may muddy the waters of accountability in a more telling fashion than is usual. We can start with a farmer in Afghanistan who returns to farming opium poppies, following State sponsored invasion to remove the Taliban under whose governance it was banned. Following its removal he restores links with a local distributor, who in turn restores his links with an international distributor. We can continue down the supply line to the organisations who prepare the pure heroin, cut it for onward transmission to wholesalers and retailers, including those small retailers who form part of the alienated community of people to whom the drug has such attraction. Where does responsibility lie here? And who is accountable? Given that taking class A drugs of the nature of heroin is a dangerous pastime, and that all those implicated in supplying people with such drugs bear some responsibility for the consequences if those turn out to be fatal, is there any reason to limit accountability to the person most directly associated with the end user? It is certainly arguable that the special transactional context requires us to abandon the premise that causation should be an all or nothing element in liability and embrace the idea that causal responsibility can be apportioned. This would arguably enable the construction of offence labels with appropriately proportioned punishments to reflect the realities of the defendant's causal contribution.[59] Elliot and de Than's suggested offence only partly reflects this analysis:

> 1 (a) A person is liable for an offence if he or she knowingly and unlawfully supplies to the victim a Category A controlled drug, or is an accessory to the supply of the controlled drug or is part of a conspiracy to supply the controlled drug, and the person's conduct causes the death of the victim.
> (b) A person will be held to have caused the death of the victim when:
> (i) he or she does an act which makes a more than merely negligible contribution to its occurrence

59 Hassett, P. (1987), 'Absolutism in Causation' *Syracuse Law Review* 38, 683.

or
(ii) he or she omits to do an act which might have prevented its occurrence
(c) A person does not cause a result where, after he or she does such an act or makes such an omission, an act or event occurs
(i) which is the immediate and sufficient cause of the result;
(ii) which he or she did not foresee, and
(iii) which could not in the circumstances reasonably have been foreseen.
(d) A defence to this offence will apply where the defendant has attempted to seek medical assistance for the victim within a reasonable time.[60]

The voluntariness of the deceased's conduct in self administering the drug is air-brushed out of this account, so also the broader context within which individual acts of supply take place. It makes accountability simply a function of the contribution made to the events leading up to the death of the victim by being associated with an act of supply. Although it would spread the net of accountability wider than at present its weakness lies precisely in its failure to acknowledge that responsibility for the harms engendered by the supply of dangerous drugs stretches too far to justify singling out individual suppliers and their associates for liability where death occurs.

## IV Conclusion: The Fourth Option

Much of the discussion relating to the propriety of holding actors to account for the fatal consequences of self-administration of dangerous drugs emphasises questions of attribution and doctrinal analysis. Commentators, as has been seen, seem predominantly concerned to reorder criminal doctrine for acts of supply leading to death by sidelining the critical fact of the victim's own involvement. If it were simply a matter of reconciling doctrine and social policy in a tidy way, a simpler mechanism would be to make self-injection a criminal offence, a proposal which is rumoured to be under consideration by the Home Office. This would enable the conviction of suppliers and other parties to the transaction by virtue of the rules governing accessories. This, like the other proposals considered above, is an answer to the question, 'How can we hold the supplier to account for the victim's death?' The more compelling question, however, is 'Why should we want to?' We live, it seems, in a society in which increasing numbers of people use psychoactive drugs as a routine mechanism for managing the life experience, or, as it is termed, 'self medication'. Some of these drugs are lawful, some are not and questions of legality are not settled by reference to the dangerousness of the individual substance. In 2000 there were 114,000 deaths attributable to smoking, representing one fifth of all deaths in that year.[61] The number of alcohol-related deaths more than doubled in the period 1991–2005, from 4,144 to 8,386, far more if we take into account deaths attributable to intoxication such as accidents in the home, at work and while

60 Elliot and de Than, above, n.40.

61 British Heart Foundation Statistics Database, 2004.

driving.[62] During a similar period, 1993–2002, the number of prescription items for all anti-depressants in England increased two and a half fold between from about 10 to 26 million prescription items per year, accounting for over 400 deaths per year, amounting to 18 per cent of all drug poisoning deaths, including opiates at around 600 per year.[63]

Not only are the physical risks associated with the consumption of illegal drugs relatively small but also, by contrast with anti-depressants, alcohol and tobacco consumption, they tend to concern not so much the nature of the drug and its tendency to do harm but the absence of quality control, compounded by fear of intervention when crisis strikes, the absence of effective treatment centres, needle exchange and supervised injecting facilities. In short, there is little wrong with the law relating to drug-induced killings which the decriminalisation of drug possession and supply would not put right. As Husak[64] has argued, criminalisation is a very serious matter. It requires the State not only to have good reason to restrict a person's freedom of action but also good reason to censure and punish people who, rightly or wrongly, reject that reason as a reason to comply with the law. There is widespread concern that this particular element in the equation is absent in respect of the possession and consumption of drugs. Even assuming that the State is justified in restricting citizens' freedom to supply, possess and consume controlled drugs, when no such restriction occurs in the case of other more dangerous psycho-active substances, the reasonableness of punishing those who fail, or refuse, to comply is controversial at best. The Home Office's drug stategy, which is to prevent young people from becoming drug misusers; reduce the supply of illegal drugs; increase the number of individuals accessing effective drug treatment; and reduce drug-related crime bears witness to this.[65] If its primary reason for criminalising the use and supply of dangerous drugs is to restrict its prevalence and to reduce the associated social problems it is clear from the British Crime Survey statistics that this strategy is not working. Significantly, current research tells us that neither do drug treatment programmes. Although the number of dependent drug users entering treatment has increased, from 85,000 in 1998 to 181,000 in 2004/5, research has shown that, while beneficial to the individuals concerned and their families, this is unlikely to have any noticeable effect on either drug use or associated crime.[66]

The Home Office's strategy is also dangerously compromised by the emphasis on enforcement rather than prevention. In 2002 this was implicitly acknowledged in an official Government report:

---

62 This corresponds to an alcohol-related death rate in the UK increasing from 6.9 per 100,000 population in 1991 to 12.9 in 2005 (Office for National Statistics, General Register Office for Scotland, Northern Ireland Statistics and Research Agency 7 November 2006).

63 *Fatal Toxicity of Anti-depressants in England and Wales,* 1993–2002 ONS 2004. The Information Centre, Lifestyles Statistics.

64 Husak, D. (2002), 'Limitations on Criminalisation and the General Part of the Criminal Law' in Shute, S. and Simester, A. (2002), *Criminal Law Theory: Doctrines of the General Part* (Oxford: Oxford University Press) pp.22–23.

65 Home Office (2004), *Tackling Drugs; Changing Lives* (London: Home Office).

66 Reuter, P. and Stevens, A. (2007), *An Analysis of UK Drug Policy: A Monograph Prepared for the UK Drug Policy Commission* (London: UKPDC).

> The strong evidence is that chaotic or problematic drug-users give rise to 99% of the economic and social costs of drug misuse and that heroin, crack and cocaine users are responsible for 50% of acquisitive crime such as burglary, shoplifting and car crime. Preventing young people from becoming problematic drug users, bringing problematic drug users into effective treatment and supporting them in that treatment is at the heart of the Governments drug strategy. Evidence from the NTORS demonstrates that for every £1 spent on treatment £3 is saved on criminal justice and other public and private costs (the so-called 'victim costs' of crime).[67]

Since then, matters have changed very little with the best estimates still suggesting that despite increased investment in treatment, 'the majority of government spending on responding to illegal drugs is still devoted to enforcing drug laws'.

Commenting on a similar phenomenon in Canada, David Roy has made a plea for the State to make virtue of the moral necessity to turn its attention from enforcement to the protection and welfare of those who, for one reason of another, are the victims of drugs or drug related crime. He claims that:

> it is *ethically* wrong to continue criminalizing approaches to the control of drug use when these strategies: fail to achieve the goals for which they were designed; create evils equal to or greater than those they purport to prevent; intensify the marginalization of vulnerable people; and stimulate the rise to power of socially destructive and violent empires ... ignore the more immediately commanding urgency of reducing the suffering of drug users and assuring their survival, their health, and their growth into liberty and dignity.[68]

Ian Malkin explicitly adopts this call to arms, suggesting that the emphasis on enforcement rather than treatment, specifically, supervised injecting facilities, may be a breach of Australia's international human rights obligations under the International Convention on Economic Social and Cultural Rights and the International Convention on Civil and Political Rights, specifically article 12(1) relating to the right to health.[69] The UK is a signatory to both these treaties.[70]

Whether or not we are likely to see a formal challenge to the UK's approach to dealing with the problem remains to be seen, but it is hard to resist the conclusion that its present emphasis in favour of enforcement rather than treatment smacks of bad faith at the very least. How can it be justified to punish alienated individuals for succumbing to the very risks which a socially and economically fractured

---

67 The Government reply to the Third Report from the Home Affairs Committee Session 2001-2 HC 318, *The Government Drugs Policy: Is it Working?* CM 5573, July 2002.

68 *Injection Drug Use and HIV/AIDS: Legal and Ethical Issues*, Canadian HIV/AIDS Legal Network, 24 November 1999.

69 The Economic and Social Council's General Comment 14 notes that 'the right to health must be understood as a right to the enjoyment of a variety of facilities, goods, services and conditions necessary for the realization of the highest attainable standard of health', which necessitates the following [T]he establishment of prevention and education programmes for behaviour-related health concerns such as sexually transmitted diseases, in particular HIV/AIDS ... and the promotion of social determinants of good health, such as ... education'. See Malkin, I. (2001), 'Establishing Supervised Injecting Facilities: A Responsible Way to Help Minimise Harm' *Melbourne University Law Review* 25, 680 at para. 173.

70 Malkin, I. (2001), *ibid.*

society engenders through its failure to put all its citizens' welfare at the forefront of its planning? Returning to the focus of this chapter, in a context such as this, responsibility for death should not be attributed to suppliers and other associates. As Peter Cane puts it:

> it would be unwise to assume that causal principles developed for the purpose of allocating responsibility for past bad outcomes would serve well as recipes for preventing bad outcomes in the future. If the aim of punishment is to minimise the incidence of bad outcomes in the future there is reason to think that in targeting those who have caused bad outcomes in the past may be a second best technique, whether in law or in morality.[71]

I agree. It is inappropriate to exploit rules developed to prevent future harms for the purpose of punishing past bad outcomes given that (i) the risk of that outcome is remote, (ii) the sentencing parameters of the offence already take into account that it is a dangerous activity, and (iii) a substantial proportion of responsibility lies with failed state policies concerning the control of, and treatment available for, drug misuse. Punishing someone who may himself be a victim of that context is not just. Rather it compounds injustice.

71 See Cane, P. (2002), *Responsibility in Law and Morality* (Oxford: Oxford University Press) pp.139–140.

Chapter 10

# Manslaughter Versus Special Homicide Offences: An Australian Perspective

Stanley Yeo[1]

## I Introduction

Each state and territory of Australia has its own criminal law[2] as does the Commonwealth of Australia.[3] Furthermore, some of these are governed by the common law while others are contained in codes.[4] As such, it would not be prudent to attempt a comprehensive coverage of what each Australian jurisdiction has to say about each of the five areas[5] covered by this book. Instead, I shall concentrate on selected developments of Australian law which, when compared with English law, might promote reflection and debate.

This chapter commences with a brief description of the Australian law of manslaughter. Next, an explanation is offered for why special homicide offences may be needed for some or all of the selected areas. The groundwork will then have been laid to discuss Australian perspectives on each of these areas. Following this discussion, some ideas of tackling, in a general way, the problems encountered in those areas will drawn from Australian law.

## II The Australian Law of Manslaughter

All Australian jurisdictions recognise that a person who causes the death of another by gross negligence is guilty of manslaughter. In the common law jurisdictions of New South Wales, South Australia and Victoria, the degree of negligence required involves:

---

1 This project was partially funded by the Singapore Ministry of Education's Academic Research Fund Tier 1 (WBS No R-241-000-050-112).

2 There are six states and two territories. The states are New South Wales, Queensland, South Australia, Tasmania, Western Australia and Victoria. The territories are the Australian Capital Territory and the Northern Territory.

3 That is, the Federal jurisdiction covering crimes against the Commonwealth. See further note 18.

4 New South Wales, South Australia and Victoria are common law jurisdictions while the remainder have criminal codes.

5 Namely, corporate killing, supply of illegal drugs leading to death, child neglect leading to death, vehicular killing and medical killing.

> such a great falling short of the standard of care which a reasonable man would have exercised and which involves such a high risk that death or grievous bodily harm would follow that the doing of the act merited criminal punishment.[6]

This common law definition has been expressly adopted by the criminal codes of the Australian Capital Territory, the Northern Territory and the Commonwealth.[7] In Queensland, Tasmania and Western Australia, a killing resulting from the breach of a statutory duty to avoid danger or to preserve life will constitute manslaughter if the breach was grossly negligent. Since the codes of these jurisdictions are silent on what gross negligence amounts to, the courts have given it the same meaning as found in the common law.[8]

In sum, the test of gross negligence for manslaughter is the same for all Australian jurisdictions. It is also similar to the English test of gross negligence except for two matters. First, while the English law confines the type of harm risked to death alone, the Australian law extends it to grievous bodily harm. Secondly, while the English law recognises certain characteristics of the accused which have the effect of lowering the standard of care expected of a reasonable person, the Australian law has not been prepared to do so. These differences should be borne in mind in any comparison between the English and Australian laws of negligent manslaughter.[9]

Australian common law also recognises that a person who causes death by an unlawful and dangerous act is guilty of manslaughter. The act is 'unlawful' if it constituted a crime as opposed to a civil wrong, and provided it involved positive conduct as opposed to an omission. Additionally, crimes of negligence such as careless driving are excluded. The accused's conduct is 'dangerous' if 'from the standpoint of a reasonable person [it was] an act carrying with it an appreciable risk of serious injury to the deceased'.[10] The Australian codes do not expressly set out this type of manslaughter. However, the provisions relating to unlawful killings in the Queensland, Tasmanian and Western Australian codes have been judicially interpreted as recognising a type of manslaughter which is akin to unlawful and dangerous act manslaughter at common law.[11]

The Australian law of unlawful and dangerous act manslaughter is similar to the English law save for one major difference. Under Australian law, the type of harm risked must be of serious injury whereas English law allows for any harm that was not of a trivial nature. Thus, this form of manslaughter is narrower in scope under Australian law compared to the English law.[12]

---

6 *Nydam v The Queen* [1977] VR 430 at 445 and approved of by the High Court in *Wilson v The Queen* (1992) 174 CLR 313 and *R v Lavender* (2005) 222 CLR 67.

7 Criminal Code 2002 (ACT), s.21; Criminal Code (NT), s.43AL; Criminal Code 1995 (Cth), s.5.5.

8 *Callaghan v The Queen* (1952) 87 CLR 115 at 124.

9 See further, Yeo, S. (1997), *Fault in Homicide* (Annadale, NSW: Federation Press) pp.211–212.

10 *Wilson v The Queen* (1992) 174 CLR 313 at 335.

11 *Pemble v The Queen* (1971) 124 CLR 107 at 122; *Boughey v The Queen* (1986) 161 CLR 10 at 40.

12 See further Yeo, above, n.9, pp.228–232.

## III The Need for Special Homicide Offences

A simple explanation can be offered for the perceived need to introduce special homicide offences. For some areas, the explanation lies in the fact that the requirements for manslaughter have not been met, but it is thought that the accused should be made criminally responsible for causing death. For other areas, it may lie with the reluctance of society to convict and punish the offender for manslaughter even though the requirements of that offence have been made out. In both of these sorts of areas, whether special homicide offences have been introduced in a particular jurisdiction largely depends on the extent to which legislators have been prepared to account for and implement the views of the community. While the interplay between politics and law is a significant consideration, it is beyond the scope of this chapter to appraise why, say, the English legislators have been very active in seeking to implement a special offence of corporate manslaughter while many of their Australian counterparts have been diametrically opposed to doing so.

### *1 Corporate killing*

The obstacles to convicting corporations for manslaughter are the same for England and Australia. The root problem lies with the law of manslaughter not having been created to deal with the conduct of non-natural persons such as corporations. The common law solution of an 'identification doctrine'[13] has proven to be largely ineffective since it still requires individual persons who are the 'guiding minds' of the corporation whose conduct was grossly negligent to be found. In practice, it is very difficult to trace such negligence to specific individuals. In the words of the New South Wales Law Reform Commission, 'the present law ... does not seem to take into account adequately the complexity of processes in corporations where decisions are made by a number of individuals at different levels of management'.[14]

The predominant legislative response in Australia to deaths caused by corporations has been to widen the scope of liability and to increase the penalties under occupational health and safety legislation.[15] Only in the two territories which, on account of their small populations are minor players in comparison to the states, has a crime of corporate manslaughter been introduced.[16] Efforts at doing the same in the states have failed because the view has been taken that occupational health and safety offences are to be preferred for being proactive in preventing deaths in the workplace, as opposed to a corporate manslaughter offence which is reactive to death that has occurred. Additionally, the deterrent effect of corporate manslaughter

13 Devised by the House of Lords in *Tesco Supermarkets Ltd v Nattrass* [1972] AC 153 and followed in Australia, for example, in *Hamilton v Whitehead* (1988) 63 ALJR 80.

14 NSWLRC Report 102 (2003), *Sentencing: Corporate Offenders*, p.9.

15 For an example of legislation increasing the scope of liability, see Occupational Health and Safety Act 2000 (NSW), s.32A, which creates a new offence of reckless conduct causing death at a workplace by a person with occupational health and safety duties.

16 See generally, Wheelwright, K. (2004), 'Prosecuting corporations and officers for industrial manslaughter – recent Australian developments' 32 *Australian Business Law Review* 239.

has not been tested.[17] Whether these reasons carry as much weight in England will be left for others to comment on.

Assuming that the legislature is determined to enact an offence of corporate manslaughter, what form should it take? Both the Australian Capital Territory (ACT) and Northern Territory (NT) formulations have been modeled after the part of the Commonwealth Criminal Code 1995 dealing with corporate responsibility.[18] The ACT offence will be mainly described here since it is the more detailed of the two.[19] The offence is called 'industrial manslaughter' and covers cases where a worker (as opposed to a member of the public) has been killed by the criminal conduct of his or her employer. The offence appears as section 49C of the Crimes Act 1900 (ACT) and reads as follows:

> An employer commits an offence if:
> (a) a worker of the employer
> (i) dies in the course of employment by, or providing services to, or in relation to, the employer; or
> (ii) is injured in the course of employment by, or providing services to, or in relation to, the employer and later dies; and
> (b) the employer's conduct causes the death of the worker; and
> (c) the employer is –
> (i) reckless about causing serious harm to the worker, or any other worker of the employer, by the conduct; or
> (ii) negligent about causing the death of the worker, or any other worker of the employer, by the conduct.

The key concepts of 'conduct', 'reckless' and 'negligent' contained in this provision are spelt out in the Criminal Code 2002 (ACT). These will be dealt with in turn.

*(a) The conduct element of manslaughter by a corporation* Beginning with 'conduct' the ACT code specifies that 'conduct is taken to be committed by a corporation if it is committed by an employee, agent or officer of the corporation acting within the actual or apparent scope of his or her employment or within his or

17 See Sarre, R. and Richards, J. (2005) 'Responding to Culpable Corporate Behaviour – Current Developments in the Industrial Manslaughter Debate' 8 *Flinders Journal of Law Reform* 93 at 101–105, 110–111.

18 Part 2.5. The Commonwealth code was devised by the Model Criminal Code Officers Committee in an attempt to codify the general principles of criminal responsibility for all the criminal laws of Australia. It is left to the states and territories to decide whether or not to adopt the provisions of the Commonwealth Code. Thus far, only the territories have done so. It is also noteworthy that, by virtue of the Australian Constitution, the offence of manslaughter falls outside the jurisdiction of the Commonwealth.

19 The NT offence came into being in 2005 by virtue of amendments to the NT code which incorporated Part 2.5 of the Commonwealth code as well as enacting a crime of manslaughter under s.163. However, s.163 simply declares that 'a person who unlawfully kills another under such circumstances as not to constitute murder is guilty of manslaughter'. Accordingly, the fault elements for manslaughter have been left to the NT courts to decide and it is as yet uncertain how they will treat corporate manslaughter.

her actual or apparent authority'.[20] Working on the principle of vicarious liability, the conduct element of the ACT offence is relatively straightforward and easily satisfied. The definition of conduct is not exhaustive and acts or omissions may be attributed directly to a corporation without the need to identify an individual or set of individuals whose conduct has caused a worker's death. The conduct element of the offence is made simple to assist with prosecution in an area which is notorious for its complexity. A corporation's criminal liability depends primarily on proving that it possessed the fault element of the offence, namely, recklessness or negligence as defined by the code.

At this juncture, it would be useful to make some observations about the conduct element of the English offence of corporate manslaughter.[21] In contrast to the simplicity of the ACT provision, the conduct element of the English offence is described in terms of 'the way in which [an organisation's] activities are managed or organized by its senior management is a substantial element in the breach of [its duty of care]'.[22] The English formulation is made more complicated than the ACT one by requiring the court to determine whether the individuals concerned were 'senior managers', what constitutes 'substantial', and whether the organisation did owe a duty of care to the deceased in respect of the activities in question.

*(b) Corporate negligence* The ACT and English offences have in common 'gross negligence' as a basis for criminal responsibility. The ACT formulation states that conduct is negligent for the purposes of industrial manslaughter if it involved:

> (a) such a great falling short of the standard of care that a reasonable [corporation] would exercise in the circumstances; and (b) such a high risk that [the death of a worker] exists or will exist.[23]

Furthermore, the fault element of negligence may exist for a corporation 'when viewed as a whole that is, by aggregating the conduct of a number of its employees, agents or officers'.[24] Of course, it is also possible for negligence by an individual employee, agent or officer of whatever station to be attributed to the corporation.

The concept of negligence under the English offence shares many of the features of the ACT offence. However, there are significant differences. Reference has already been made to the restriction concerning senior managers imposed by the English but not the ACT offence. Another notable difference is that, unlike the ACT formulation, the English offence does not expressly require for there to have been a high (that is, likely or probable) risk of death.[25] This appears to be a material oversight and

20 S.50.

21 Corporate Manslaughter and Corporate Homicide Act 2007.

22 *Ibid.*, s.1(3).

23 Crimes Act 1900 (ACT), s.49C(c)(ii) read with Criminal Code 2002 (ACT), s.21.

24 Criminal Code 2002 (ACT), s.52(2). The English formulation incorporates this concept of aggregate negligence in s.1(3) where it speaks of 'the way in which [the organisation's] activities are managed or organised by its senior management'.

25 Although s.8(2) refers to 'risk of death', it is not stating that the offence requires the corporation's negligence to have involved a high risk of death.

one which lays the English offence open to the charge that its fault element fails to adequately reflect the fatal consequence that underscores the crime of manslaughter. This oversight is made more glaring when it is noted that the conventional definition of gross negligence manslaughter under English law imposes this requirement.[26]

Another difference between the ACT and English provisions is that only the latter specifies criteria for determining whether a corporation had fallen far below the standard of care expected of it in the circumstances. The English stance is to be preferred for instructing the jury that they must assess the corporation's alleged breach of duty by reference to whether there was a serious failure and how much of a risk of death it posed.[27] There is also an English provision which permits the jury to 'consider the extent to which the evidence shows that there were attitudes, policies, systems or accepted practices within the organisation that were likely to have encouraged any such failure'.[28] This introduces the concept of corporate culture and appears to have been borrowed from the ACT provision on corporate recklessness, to be discussed below. For now, it may be observed that this English provision is comparable to the clause in the NT legislation which reads:

> Negligence may be evidenced by the fact that the prohibited conduct was substantially attributable to
>
> (a) inadequate corporate management, control or supervision of the conduct of one or more its employees, agents or officers; or
>
> (b) failure to provide adequate systems for conveying relevant information to relevant persons in the body corporate.[29]

*(c) Corporate recklessness* The ACT offence may also be established by proving that the corporation was 'reckless about causing serious harm[30] to the worker ... by the conduct' which caused death.[31] To overcome the conceptual difficulty of a corporation possessing the subjective mental state of recklessness, the ACT offence treats express, tacit or implied authorisation or permission of the commission of the offence as equivalent to recklessness.[32] This occurs if the corporation's board of directors or a high managerial agent intentionally, knowingly or recklessly engaged in the relevant conduct, or expressly, tacitly or impliedly authorised or permitted

26 *R v Adomako* [1994] 3 All ER 79.

27 Corporate Manslaughter and Corporate Homicide Act 2007, s.8(2).

28 *Ibid.*, s.8(3).

29 Criminal Code (NT), s.43BN(4), which is borrowed directly from s.12.4(3) of the Commonwealth code. It is unclear why the ACT legislature chose not to adopt this clause.

30 The alternative fault element of negligence recognised under s.49C(c)(ii) refers to the causing of death alone. The difference in the type of harm seeks to create an equivalence of blameworthiness between recklessness (which being subjective, comprises a higher degree of blameworthiness and therefore requires only serious harm) and negligence (which being objective, comprises a lower degree of blameworthiness and therefore requires the harm to be death).

31 Crimes Act 1900 (ACT), s.49C(c)(i).

32 Criminal Code 2002 (ACT), s.51(1). The whole section is reproduced in the Appendix.

the commission of the offence.[33] The cases envisaged here are 'one-off situations where it cannot be said that there is any ongoing authorization of the conduct'.[34] In practice, prosecutors are more likely to focus on the conduct of a high managerial agent who is defined as 'an employee, agent or officer of the body corporate whose conduct may fairly be assumed to represent the corporation's policy because of the level of responsibility of his or her duties'.[35] The corporation may escape liability by showing that it exercised due diligence to prevent the conduct, authorisation or permission of the high managerial agent.[36]

A further way of proving that the corporation authorised or permitted the commission of industrial manslaughter is by showing that a corporate culture existed within the body corporate which directed, encouraged, tolerated or led to non-compliance with the contravened law.[37] Alternatively, the prosecution could show that the corporation failed to create and maintain a corporate culture requiring compliance with the contravened law.[38] 'Corporate culture' is defined as 'an attitude, policy, rule, course of conduct or practice existing within the corporation generally or in the part of the corporation where the relevant conduct happens'.[39]

Corporate culture may be proven by showing that authority to commit an offence of the same or similar character had been given by a high managerial agent of the corporation.[40] It may also be proven by showing that the employee, agent or officer of the corporation who committed the offence reasonably believed or had a reasonable expectation that a high managerial agent of the corporation would have authorised or permitted the commission of the offence.[41] Thus, corporations will be caught whose corporate policy ostensibly prohibits the relevant conduct but which is in fact encouraged by management. The concept of corporate culture is the most innovative feature of the ACT offence and marks a considerable shift from conventional principles of criminal responsibility. The application of the concept to real life corporate criminal conduct has yet to be tested in the courts.[42]

The English offence does not recognise this unique form of fault involving corporate recklessness. While gross negligence may be able to cover many cases of corporate wrongdoing causing death, there will be circumstances when negligence may be inappropriate or difficult to prove against the erring corporation. The concept of corporate culture operating within the fault element of corporate recklessness

---

33 *Ibid.*, s.51(2)(a) and (b).

34 Model Criminal Code Officers Committee (1992), *General Principles of Criminal Responsibility*, p.111.

35 Criminal Code 2002 (ACT) s.51(6).

36 *Ibid.*, s.51(3).

37 *Ibid.*, s.51(2)(c).

38 *Ibid.*, s.51(2)(d).

39 *Ibid.*, s.51(6).

40 *Ibid.*, s.51(4)(a).

41 *Ibid.*, s.51(4)(b).

42 For possible difficulties with applying the concept, see Clough, J. and Mulhern, C. (2002), *The Prosecution of Corporations* (Oxford; New York: Oxford University Press) pp.146–147.

would, if it could be successfully applied in practice, go to the heart of corporate blameworthiness.

*(d) Penalties* Regarding penalties for industrial manslaughter in the ACT, a corporation could be fined up to a maximum of $1 million.[43] This amount is viewed as sufficient to deter large corporations. In addition to a fine, a court may order the guilty corporation to publicise the offence, the consequences of its conduct (such as the deaths or serious injuries) and any penalties imposed or orders made because of the offence.[44] Additionally, the court may order the corporation to undertake stated tasks, or establish or carry out a specified project for the public benefit even if the project is unrelated to the offence.[45] In making the order, the court must take into account the financial circumstances of the corporation and the burden that compliance with the order will impose.[46] Should the corporation fail without reasonable excuse to comply with the order, the court may authorise the commissioner for occupational health and safety to do anything that is necessary or convenient to carry out any remaining action to be done under the order.[47] The commissioner is also authorised to publicise the corporation's failure to comply with the order. The reasonable cost incurred by the commissioner is regarded as a debt owing to the ACT by the corporation.[48]

*(e) Manslaughter by a senior officer* Besides industrial manslaughter by an employer, the ACT legislation provides for an offence of industrial manslaughter by a senior officer.[49] This offence occurs when the officer's own negligent or reckless conduct has caused the death of a worker of the corporation. Accordingly, the officer is not held responsible for the negligent or reckless conduct of others, or for the failure of the corporation's systems to prevent the death of a worker. No other Australian jurisdiction has such an offence and it is rare for an officer of a corporation to be charged with manslaughter.

A much more radical proposal in respect of the criminal liability of senior officers was made in the Crimes (Workplace Deaths and Injuries) Bill 2001 of Victoria. As with the ACT offence, the Victorian bill proposed establishing the offence of industrial manslaughter, under which a corporation's conduct could be examined as a whole to determine if it was grossly negligent.[50] Where the corporation was found guilty of the offence, a senior officer could then be held criminally liable, or 'organisationally responsible' for the conduct of the corporation which resulted in the death or serious injury, and who had materially contributed to its commission.[51] Hence, unlike the ACT offence, the proposed Victorian offence does not require proof that the senior officer's own conduct caused a worker's death. The Bill

43 Crimes Act 1900 (ACT) s.49C.
44 *Ibid.*, s.49E(2)(a).
45 *Ibid.*, s.49E(2)(c).
46 *Ibid.*, s.49E(5).
47 *Ibid.*, s.49E(7).
48 *Ibid.*, s.49E(10).
49 Crimes Act 1900 (ACT) s.49D.
50 Crimes (Workplace Deaths and Injuries) Bill 2001 (Vic), ss.12–13.
51 *Ibid.*, s.14C.

was defeated and it appears unlikely that Victoria will again consider introducing industrial manslaughter legislation in the near future. By way of comparison, it is noted that the English Act does not create any offence whatsoever in respect of senior managers of a corporation.

### *2 Supply of illegal drugs leading to death*

This section will commence with an examination of the conventional tests for causation under Australian law and their application to the case of a drug user who dies after self-administering a drug supplied by a dealer. The liability of the dealer for manslaughter in such a case depends largely on whether he or she could be said to have caused the user's death. Since the answer under English law is a 'no', the call has been made in that jurisdiction to create a special homicide offence against the dealer. It could well be that the answer is a 'yes' under Australian law enabling manslaughter to be made out and thereby dispelling the need for a special offence.

The discussion continues with an examination of a provision in the Queensland and Western Australian codes which handles the issue of causation for such cases in a special way. This will be followed by a description of an emerging Australian common law development which situates causal responsibility by the drug dealer in a quite different context.

*(a) Invoking the conventional tests of causation* Rather surprisingly, the courts in the Australian common law jurisdictions have yet to consider the issue of whether a drug dealer could be said to have caused the death of the user who self-administered the drug. What follows is therefore speculative of how the courts would treat the issue when it does arise.

At common law, several alternative tests for causation were propounded in the High Court of Australia case of *Royall v The Queen*.[52] The first of these asks the jury to apply their commonsense to determine whether the accused's conduct had caused the victim's death, with a reminder of the significance of their decision to criminal liability. A second test involves looking backwards from the death to ascertain whether, in the light of all that transpired, the accused's conduct substantially contributed to the death. A third test involves looking forward from the accused's conduct to ascertain whether the death was a reasonably foreseeable consequence of that conduct.

It is observed that each one of these tests requires the jury to consider *all* the relevant circumstances involving the accused's conduct and the victim's death. Hence, the supply of the drug by the dealer would be only one factor or circumstance to be considered in the causal inquiry. The same may be said of the self-administration by the user. Other relevant factors would be the quality of the drug supplied, the user's tolerance to it, and the dealer's actual or constructive knowledge of these matters. The jury will be asked to consider all that happened when deciding the ultimate issue of whether the dealer's conduct of supplying the drug had caused the user's

52 (1991) 172 CLR 378. See further Arenson, K. (1996), 'Causation in the Criminal Law: A Search for Doctrinal Consistency' *Criminal Law Journal* 20, 189.

death. The point that is being made here is that the tests of commonsense, substantial contribution and reasonable foreseeability do not single out one factor for attention such as the fact that the victim had self-administered the drug. It is conceivable that the application of all three tests for causation under Australian common law could result in a finding of causation against the dealer even where the user had 'voluntarily intervened'.[53] This more holistic line of inquiry is in marked contrast to the approach taken by the English courts with regard to the principle of voluntary intervention.[54]

The Australian common law of causation has also devised special tests for intervening acts. These tests assist juries to ascertain whether a subsequent causal act or event was so significant as to constitute a *novus actus interveniens*, that is, an intervening act which breaks the causal connection between the accused's conduct and the victim's death. It may well be that an Australian court will treat a case of drug supply and self-administration leading to death as involving an intervening act. Consequently, the court will apply the tests for intervening acts instead of the common sense, substantial contribution and reasonable foreseeability tests mentioned previously.

At the outset, it is noted that there is no Australian common law case authority which expressly subscribes to the principle of voluntary intervention.[55] Hence, this principle is not among the tests formulated by the Australian courts for assisting with the determination of intervening acts. The High Court in *Royall* propounded various tests to determine whether the act of V in jumping out of a window of a high rise building to escape D's violent attack amounted to a *novus actus interveniens*. For the purposes of this discussion, the relevant ones are the 'natural consequence' test, 'the reasonable act' test and the 'reasonable foreseeability' test.[56] These tests share the underlying premise that V's conduct constitutes a *novus actus interveniens* if it could be described as abnormal or a coincidence. When applied to a case of drug supply, it is difficult to conclude otherwise than that the drug user's conduct of self-administration was normal or to be expected. Using the determinative concepts underlying the various tests, it could be said that the user's self-administration was

---

53 Simply stated, the principle of voluntary intervention declares that the free, deliberate and informed conduct of a third party or the victim (such as self-injection by a drug user) breaks the causal connection between the accused's conduct and the proscribed consequence (such as the dealer's act of supply and the user's death). For a discussion of the principle and its application by the English courts, see Jones, T. (2006), 'Causation, homicide and the supply of drugs' 26 *Legal Studies* 139 at 140–150.

54 *Kennedy* [2007] 3 WLR 612.

55 The judicial pronouncement which comes closest to adopting the principle of voluntary intervention appears in the South Australian case of *R v Hallett* [1969] SASR 141 where the court found that D had caused V's death by leaving him unconscious on a beach resulting in his drowning when the tide rose. The court opined (at p.149) that '[o]nly if [V] consciously entered the water would it in our view be even arguable that the chain of causation had been broken'.

56 Other tests such as that involving reasonable apprehension by V, and whether V's act was a reasonably proportionate response are, by their nature, only relevant to self-preservation or 'fright' cases such as *Royall*.

a natural consequence of being supplied the drug, such self-administration of the drug was a reasonable act for him or her to have done, and that act was reasonably foreseeable by the dealer.[57] Consequently, the causal connection linking the dealer's act of supply to the user's death remains intact.

This same outcome occurs in the Northern Territory, Queensland and Western Australia by virtue of their codes providing that 'any person who causes the death of another, directly or indirectly, by any means whatever, is deemed to have killed that other person'.[58] Therefore, in these jurisdictions, it would not matter that the user had died as a result of self-administering the drug (an indirect act) supplied to him or her by the dealer. That said, the courts of these jurisdictions have adopted the more general tests of causation propounded by the common law.[59] Accordingly, in such a case, the jury would be instructed to apply their commonsense when deciding whether the dealer has caused the user's death, or else to ascertain whether the dealer's act of supply substantially contributed to the user's death, or that the death was a reasonably foreseeable consequence of supplying the drug to him or her. The earlier suggestion that these tests could result in a finding of causation against the dealer is therefore equally pertinent to these code jurisdictions.

Of course, a finding of causation against a drug dealer does not automatically result in his or her conviction for manslaughter. For this to happen, the prosecution must prove either gross negligence on the dealer's part or that the act of supply constituted an unlawful and dangerous act. These forms of fault for manslaughter are by no means readily satisfied even when dangerous drugs are involved. For negligent manslaughter, the dealer's conduct must have involved a great falling short of the standard of care expected of a reasonable person in the circumstances, and also have involved a high risk of death or grievous bodily harm. Thus, simple negligence or the risk of some harm would be insufficient to establish criminal liability. With regard to unlawful and dangerous act manslaughter, the requirement of 'unlawful act' would presumably be readily satisfied on account of drug supply being an offence under Australian drug legislation. However, the prosecution must also prove that the supply of drug involved an appreciable risk of serious bodily harm to the drug user. Whether this requirement is met in a given case will depend on factors such as the quality and amount of the drug supplied, the tolerance of the user to it, and the dealer's actual or constructive knowledge of these matters.

*(b) A code innovation: a duty of care over dangerous things* The criminal codes of the Northern Territory, Queensland and Western Australia have a provision which

57 It is observed that the law here focuses on the victim's conduct and not its consequence, that is, of death. On the other hand, the more general tests of commonsense, substantial contribution and reasonable foreseeability do focus on that consequence.

58 Criminal Code (NT) s.157: Criminal Code 1899 (Qld), s.293; Criminal Code 1913 (WA), s.270. The Tasmanian Criminal Code Act 1924 (s.153(2)) requires proof that the victim's death was 'directly and immediately connected' with the accused's conduct, so as to impose a more restrictive test than the common law.

59 See Colvin, E., Linden, S. and McKechnie, J. (2005), *Criminal Law in Queensland and Western Australia* (Chatswood, NSW: Butterworths) pp.32–34.

deals with the issue of causation under consideration in a unique way.[60] The provision was derived from the English Criminal Code Bill of 1879[61] and reads:

> It is the duty of every person who has in the person's charge or under the person's control anything, whether living or inanimate, and whether moving or stationery, of such a nature that, in the absence of care or precaution in its use or management the life, safety or health of any person may be endangered, to use reasonable care and take reasonable precautions to avoid such danger, and the person is held to have caused any consequence which results to the life or health of any person by reason of any omission to perform that duty.

The provision imposes a duty of care in relation to the use or management of a dangerous thing under one's charge or control. Its effect is to deem the person to have caused any injury resulting from a failure to discharge that duty. Hence, there is no need to enquire whether the accused's conduct was a substantial cause of the proscribed harm. Not being an offence-creating provision, it has to be read with one. Where death has occurred, the offence would most likely be manslaughter based on a gross failure to exercise reasonable care or take reasonable precautions.

The Queensland Court of Appeal case of *R v Stott & Van Embden*[62] concerned the application of this provision to the type of case under consideration.[63] On one version of the facts, the accused had given the deceased an injection containing a strong dose of heroin after the deceased had complained that the heroin he had already consumed was not having any effect on him. The deceased had then self-injected the heroin and died alone in the accused's flat from an overdose. The accused were charged and convicted of manslaughter based on a finding of gross negligence and the operation of section 289 of the Queensland Code (that is, the duty provision being discussed). On appeal, Atkinson J summarised what the prosecution had to prove in such a case:

> In my view, the evidence given at this trial was also consistent with criminal negligence. In such a case the prosecution is obliged to prove that:

60 Criminal Code (NT), s.151 read with s.153; Criminal Code 1899 (Qld), s.289; Criminal Code 1913 (WA), s.266.

61 This was based primarily on the 1878 draft criminal code of Sir James Stephen. The Bill was withdrawn from Parliament and revised by a Royal Commission of Judges. It was reintroduced in Parliament in 1880 but was never enacted.

62 [2002] 2 Qd R 313.

63 For a different set of circumstances where the provision applied, see the Queensland case of *R v Hodgetts & Jackson* [1990] 1 Qd R 456 where the accused had, for a prank, placed poison in a can of soft drink for a vagrant to consume.

1. the strong dose of heroin in the possession of the accused was a dangerous thing;
2. the heroin was in his charge or under his control;
3. the absence of care or precaution in the use or management of the heroin might endanger the life, health or safety of another; [and]
4. the accused failed to use reasonable care and take reasonable precautions to avoid such danger.[64]

Atkinson J held that all these elements were proven. However, McPherson JA and Muir J disagreed on the ground that the accused no longer had the charge or control of the heroin once they had delivered it to the deceased. By contrast, Atkinson J was of the view that the relevant time when the accused had to exercise care or take precautions was when they were in possession of the heroin. This latter view is to be preferred for being more in accord with a straight reading of section 289. It also better achieves the objective of the provision of holding people blameworthy for any injury, however indirectly caused, that results from their failure to manage a dangerous thing under their control. Thus, in *Stott & Van Embden*, it mattered not that the deceased had self-injected the fatal dose of heroin so long as his death was the result of the accused's omission to exercise reasonable care in supplying the heroin to him. Factors supporting a finding of such a failure to exercise reasonable care would have included the accused's knowledge of the strength of heroin supplied to the deceased, their knowledge that he had already consumed heroin, and the fact that the deceased had self-injected and died in their flat.

*(c) A common law innovation: a duty of care to preserve life endangered by the accused* Like the English law, the Australian common law of homicide restricts criminal liability for omissions to situations where there was a legal duty to preserve the life of another. One such duty which is directly pertinent to cases of drug supply leading to death was pronounced by the South Australian Court of Criminal Appeal in *R v Lawford & Van de Weil*.[65] The accused had beaten her victim senseless with a steel bar, strangled him and left him lying on the floor where he died from blood loss and shock. The court ruled that:

> [If the accused] was responsible for the deceased being rendered unconscious and placed in a dangerous situation as a consequence, a duty to take positive action to render assistance would arise.[66]

The court also accepted the trial judge's direction to the jury that:

> [For the duty to arise, the accused] must have appreciated that there was an obvious, serious and immediate risk that the [deceased] might die unless he initiated such steps as were in his power … by seeking help from others to lead to his resuscitation …[67]

64 [2002] 2 Qd R 313 at 324.

65 (1993) 69 A Crim R 115.

66 *Ibid.*, at 121 per Duggan J.

67 *Ibid.*

This pronouncement was subsequently endorsed by the ACT Supreme Court in *R v Rao*.[68] In that case, the prosecution alleged that the accused had supplied a drug to her friend S knowing that she was going to use it to kill the deceased. The court affirmed the above stated ruling in *Lawford & Van de Weil* but held that it did not apply to the case at hand because there was insufficient evidence that the accused was responsible for rendering the deceased unconscious.

Based on these case authorities, it may be stated that Australian common law imposes a duty on a drug dealer to render assistance to a drug user provided (i) the user was rendered unconscious by the drug supplied, and (ii) the dealer knew of this and of the serious risk that the user might die unless the dealer provided or sought assistance. Of course, for a manslaughter charge to succeed, the prosecution would need to prove further that the dealer had breached the duty of care as a result of being grossly negligent and that the breach caused the user's death.[69] It is submitted that the combined effect of these requirements is to impose criminal liability for culpable homicide on drug dealers only in the most deserving cases.

In *Rao* the prosecution had also submitted that where 'the accused had unconsciously placed [the deceased] in danger by her conduct, she had a duty to remove him from that danger when she became aware or ought to have become aware of it'.[70] The prosecution contended that this proposition was supported by the House of Lords case of *R v Miller*.[71] The ACT Supreme Court rejected this proposition after noting that *Miller* was a case involving arson, not manslaughter, and that care was needed in transposing principles from one area of the law to another. The court concluded that, while the current authorities dealing with the crime of manslaughter did not appear to recognise such a principle, it was prepared to wholeheartedly endorse the principle 'as a matter of general morality'.[72] It is submitted that there is no strong reason why the law should not also impose such a duty to provide assistance on a drug dealer who had, without necessarily rendering the drug user unconscious, (i) placed him or her in danger of death, and (ii) knew of that danger. This would be a slight and logical extension of the duty propounded in *Lawford & Van de Weil*.[73]

---

68 [1999] ACTSC 132.

69 Compare this with the proposal made by Williams, R. (2005), 'Policy and Principle in Drugs Manslaughter Cases' 64 *Cambridge Law Journal* 66 at 76–78.

70 [1999] ACTSC 132 at para. [144].

71 (1983) 1 All ER 978.

72 [1999] ACTSC 132 at para. [144]. On further appeal, the Federal Court of Australia in *R v MR* [2000] FCA 1127 noted the lower court's opinion but did not feel the need to comment on it for procedural reasons.

73 Whether the prosecution's submission that the duty is also owed where the accused ought to have known of the danger is much more controversial.

### *3 Child neglect leading to death*

The criminal law has long acknowledged that dependent children are especially vulnerable and frequently exposed to serious physical danger. The law's response has been to impose a legal duty on the carers of these children to protect them from such danger. However, this duty has not prevented some wrongdoers from escaping criminal liability because the prosecution cannot prove that they had caused the proscribed harm. This could occur in two circumstances. First, the prosecution may be unable to prove that the carer's breach of duty had caused the child's death. Secondly, the prosecution may be unable to identify the person who had caused the death. The Queensland code contains a provision which largely overcomes the problem of proving causation under the first circumstance, while the South Australian Criminal Law Consolidation Act 1935 has a provision tackling the problem posed by the second circumstance.

*(a) A legal duty to protect children against danger* Section 286 of the Queensland Criminal Code states as follows:

> (1) It is the duty of every person who has care of a child under 16 years to
> (a) provide the necessaries of life for the child; and
> (b) take precautions that are reasonable in all the circumstances to avoid danger to the child's life, health or safety; and
> (c) take the action that is reasonable in all the circumstances to remove the child from any such danger;
> and he or she is held to have caused any consequences that result to the life and health of the child because of any omission to perform that duty, whether the child is helpless or not.[74]

Section 286 belongs to a set of duty provisions which are not offence-creating as such.[75] Where a child has died as a result of its carer's omission to perform their duty under section 286, the prosecution may bring a charge of manslaughter which is satisfied upon proof of gross negligence in failing to discharge the duty. The people who owe a duty under the provision are 'a parent, foster parent, step parent, guardian or other adult in charge of the child, whether or not the person has lawful custody of the child'.[76] The function of section 286 is to make it easier for the prosecution to prove causation against the accused. Once it is shown that the carer had failed to take reasonable precautions to avoid danger to the child's life or take reasonable action to remove the child from any such danger, they will be deemed to have caused *any* consequences to the child's life and health arising from such failure. Causation

74 See also the Criminal Code (NT) s.149. The Criminal Code 1913 (WA), s.263, only imposes a duty to provide necessaries of life for the child.

75 In the previous section on drug supply leading to death, one other such provision was discussed, namely, s.289 of the Queensland code which is also shared by the Northern Territory and Western Australia.

76 S.286(2).

would be made out even if it could be shown that someone else had caused the injury to the child or that the child could have itself avoided the danger.

To illustrate, D drives V, his 15-year-old daughter, to school without ensuring that V has secured her seatbelt. A negligent driver collides into D's car resulting in V being flung out of the car and suffering fatal injuries. Evidence shows that V would not have died if she had her seatbelt on. In these circumstances, section 286 will deem D to have caused V's death even if it is shown that the collision was entirely the other driver's fault and that V was capable of securing her own seatbelt. Of course, for D to be convicted of manslaughter, he would need to have been grossly negligent in failing to ensure that V had her seatbelt on.

*(b) An offence of criminal neglect* Turning now to the South Australian provision, section 14 of the Criminal Law Consolidation Act 1935 creates the offence of criminal neglect.[77] Introduced in 2005, the offence is loosely modelled on the crime of 'causing or allowing the death of a child or vulnerable adult' contained in the Domestic Violence, Crime and Victims Act 2004 (UK).[78] To be guilty of the South Australian offence, the prosecution would need to prove that:

- a child under 16 years or a vulnerable adult[79] (the victim) had died or suffered serious harm as a result of an unlawful act;[80]
- the accused had, at the time of the unlawful act, a duty of care to the victim;[81]
- the accused was, or ought to have been, aware that there was an appreciable risk that serious harm would be caused to the victim by the unlawful act; [82]
- the accused failed to take steps which he or she could reasonably be expected to have taken in the circumstances to protect the victim from harm;[83] and
- the accused's failure to do so was, in the circumstances, so serious that a criminal penalty was warranted.[84]

The provision stipulates that persons having a duty of care to the victim are 'a parent or guardian of the victim, or has assumed responsibility for the victim's care'.[85] An act (which may comprise an omission or a course of conduct) is 'unlawful' for the purposes of the offence if 'it constitutes an offence or would constitute an offence if committed by an adult of full legal capacity'.[86] The penalty is a maximum of 15

77 The provision is reproduced in full in the Appendix.

78 S.5.

79 Defined in s.14(4) as 'a person aged 16 years or above whose ability to protect himself or herself from an unlawful act is significantly impaired through physical or mental disability, illness or infirmity'.

80 S.14(1)(a).

81 S.14(1)(b).

82 S.14(1)(c).

83 S.14(1)(d).

84 S.14(1)(d).

85 S.14(3).

86 S.14(4).

years' imprisonment in the event that the victim died, and 5 years' imprisonment where they suffered serious harm.

This offence is a lesser charge than manslaughter and may be used in circumstances where it is unclear who caused the death or serious harm to a child or vulnerable adult. The offence was introduced to counter cases where it was clear that at least one of the carers of the victim was responsible, but proving that it was one carer rather than the other was extremely difficult because both accused each other, or else both denied that they were responsible. The carers may both be charged with the offence of criminal neglect in these circumstances since the offence does not require proof of who caused the death or serious harm, the emphasis being instead on the fact that an unlawful act had occurred and insufficient protection had been provided by the carers.

The offence is based on the assumption that the unlawful act which killed or seriously harmed the victim was committed by someone other than the accused. To prevent the perverse outcome of an accused escaping conviction by saying that they, and not someone else, had killed or harmed the victim, s14(2) provides that the jury may find the accused guilty of the offence 'even though of the opinion that the unlawful act may have been the act of the accused'.

The fault element of this offence adopts aspects of the fault element for unlawful and dangerous act manslaughter and for negligent manslaughter under Australian common law.[87] Thus, the requirements of 'unlawful act' and 'appreciable risk of serious harm' stem from the law of unlawful and dangerous act; and the failure to take reasonable steps which failure warrants punishment is derived from the law of negligent manslaughter.

At this juncture, it would be useful to point out the main differences between the South Australian offence and its English counterpart. First, the South Australian offence covers death or serious harm while the English offence is confined to death. Extending the scope of the offence to cases of serious harm is to be preferred for increasing the protection afforded to children and vulnerable adults.

Secondly, the South Australian offence expressly refers to a duty of care and spells out when it exists. Apart from parents and guardians, only persons who have assumed responsibility for a child or vulnerable adult will owe a duty of care. In this way, the offence acknowledges that there may be people sharing a household with a child or vulnerable adult who have not assumed responsibility for them. By contrast, the English offence does not overtly refer to a duty of care but implies it in respect of a person who was a member of the same household as the child or vulnerable adult and had frequent contact with them. It is contended that the South Australian formulation is the more attractive for recognising that merely sharing a household and having frequent contact do not automatically signify that a person had assumed responsibility for the welfare of the child or vulnerable adult. For instance, a person may have shared a household for only a short period or for a limited purpose.

A third difference is that the South Australian offence includes relationships beyond households by contemplating a duty of care arising from an assumption of responsibility. Thus, the offence may lie against, say, an adult who has assumed

87 Described at the beginning of this chapter.

responsibility for the day in respect of their child's school friend, and that child dies or suffers serious harm while in the adult's care. On the other hand, the English offence is restricted to domestic or household relationships. Again, the wider scope of the South Australian offence is to be preferred for affording more protection to children and vulnerable adults.

Fourthly, unlike the English offence, the South Australian offence does not require the unlawful act 'to have occurred in circumstances of the kind that D foresaw or ought to have foreseen'.[88] It is debatable whether this additional requirement is strictly necessary. Arguably, the South Australian offence sufficiently connects the carer's duty of care with the unlawful act by requiring that he or she 'was, or ought to have been, aware that there was an appreciable risk that serious harm would be caused to the victim by the unlawful act'.[89]

A final difference is that the South Australian offence, but not the English one, requires the jury to decide whether the accused's failure to take reasonable steps to protect the victim 'was, in the circumstances, so serious that a criminal penalty is warranted'.[90] This additional requirement is attractive for instructing the jury to convict the accused only if their failure amounted to negligence of a high degree.

A deficiency of both the South Australian and English provisions is that they do not expressly state that the physical and mental capacity of the accused is to be taken into account when applying the elements of the offence. For instance, what if the accused was a 15-year-old parent[91] or suffered from a mild intellectual disability? While it may be argued that such characteristics of the accused are impliedly recognised through the concept of 'reasonableness' appearing in the provisions,[92] it would be much better if the provisions were to state so explicitly. Having such a clause would also align the English provision with the reformulation of manslaughter proposed by the Law Commission.[93]

### *4 Vehicular killing*

Following England's lead, all Australian jurisdictions have enacted vehicular homicide offences. The offence was introduced in the 1950s to counter the perceived

---

88 Domestic Violence, Crime and Victims Act 2004 (UK), s.5(1)(d)(iii).

89 Criminal Law Consolidation Act 1935 (SA), s.14(1)(c). The English legislation has a closely similar requirement: see s.5(1)(c) read with s.5(1)(d)(i).

90 S.14(1)(d).

91 Note, however, that s.5(3)(b) of the Domestic Violence, Crime and Victims Act 2004 (UK) provides that D, who is not a parent of V, will only be required to have taken any reasonable steps expected of a person aged 16 years and above to protect V from the risk. There is no equivalent clause in the South Australian provision.

92 Criminal Law Consolidation Act 1935 (SA), s.14(1)(d); Domestic Violence, Crime and Victims Act 2004 (UK), s.5(1)(d)(ii).

93 Consultation Paper No. 177 (2005), *A New Homicide Act for England and Wales? An Overview*, para. 6.10, the relevant part of which states that 'the accused had the capacity to appreciate the risk and the accused's conduct fell far below what could reasonably be expected in the circumstances'. For a similar proposal, see the Victorian Law Reform Commission, Report No. 40 (1991), *Homicide*, para. 270.

reluctance of juries to convict drivers of manslaughter, and in the hope of placing a check on the all too frequent incident of negligent driving causing death.[94] This special homicide offence lies between the more serious crime of manslaughter and less serious offences such as dangerous driving causing grievous bodily harm and negligent driving.

Australian law reform bodies and legislators have long been preoccupied with identifying the appropriate type of fault for this type of offence. The Australian experience has produced the following types of fault: (i) negligence of the same degree as required for manslaughter; (ii) negligence of a lower degree than for manslaughter but of a higher degree than for civil negligence; and (iii) driving in a dangerous manner without a reasonable excuse for so driving. Each of these types of fault will be considered in turn.

*(a) The same degree of negligence as for manslaughter* Australian jurisdictions which have adopted this form of fault for vehicular homicide regard as merely cosmetic the problem of jury reluctance to convict negligent drivers for manslaughter. In their view, the degree of negligence should be the same as for manslaughter with only the offence label requiring alteration. The offence of culpable driving causing death under section 318 of the Crimes Act 1958 (Vic) is a good example. Previously, the penalty prescribed for this offence was much lower than for manslaughter,[95] prompting the Victorian Law Reform Commission to retort:

> Why should it make any difference that a death occurs in the context of the use of a motor vehicle rather than in the context of the use of firearms or drugs? What justifies the disparity of penalties?[96]

In response, the Victorian legislature has increased the penalty for culpable driving causing death to the same as for manslaughter.[97] This development largely removes the complaint that the difference in penalties between manslaughter and the vehicular homicide offence lacks any principled justification so long as proof of the same degree of fault is needed for both offences. However, the issue remains of whether there is a need to have a different label for this type of homicide.

There appears to be a discernible shift in public opinion since the 1950s away from regarding vehicular homicide as something different to manslaughter. For example, in a community attitude survey organised by the Victorian Law Reform

---

94 See Law Reform Commission of Victoria, Discussion Paper No. 21 (1991), *Death Caused by Dangerous Driving* at para. 21; Western Australian Law Reform Commission, Report No. 17 (1970), *Final Report on Motor Car Manslaughter* at para. 14. For judicial observations, see *Callaghan v The Queen* (1952) 87 CLR 115 at 120; *Attorney-General v Bindoff* (1953) 53 SR (NSW) 489 at 490; *Giorgianni v The Queen* (1985) 2 MVR 97 at 109.

95 It was originally set at a maximum of 7 years' imprisonment compared to 20 years for manslaughter.

96 Law Reform Commission of Victoria, Discussion Paper No. 21 (1991), *Death Caused by Dangerous Driving*, para. 22.

97 The penalty was increased to 10 years in 1991, 15 years in 1992 and finally 20 years in 1997.

Commission in 1992, a large majority of respondents believed that a drunk driver who had knocked down and killed someone on a pedestrian crossing should be convicted of manslaughter rather than a lesser offence.[98] Likewise, for a motorist who crossed double lines to overtake a car near the crest of a hill and hit an oncoming car killing its driver.

A similar view has been expressed by some judges. In the Victorian Court of Criminal Appeal case of *R v O'Connor*, Winneke J opined that:

> If there is still a residual opinion existing in this community that the offence of culpable driving is not to be treated like other criminal offences because it is 'a tragedy for all concerned' … then, in my view, the time has come for such views to be dispelled. Offences of culpable driving are commonly committed by persons of good character, but it must be understood that the community will not tolerate the taking of human life by acts of gross negligence of the sort that has occurred in this case. The offence is a species of involuntary manslaughter, and it must be treated as such.[99]

An even stronger comment was made by the New South Wales Court of Criminal Appeal in *R v Vukic*[100] in respect of the offence of driving in a dangerous manner causing death.[101] After referring to the reason for introducing the offence, Adams J said:

> There has, I think, been a considerable change in public attitudes to serious death inflicted by wrongful driving since 1951 and there can be little doubt that the reason for [introducing the special homicide offence] no longer holds. This is not to say that the provision is not appropriate in many cases, but I do not think that it can now be justified upon the basis that juries would be unjustifiably reluctant to convict reckless drivers of manslaughter in defiance of their oaths.[102]

Adams J went on to encourage prosecutors to be mindful of this change in public attitude when deciding on the appropriate charge. In this regard, the operation of the new charging regime operating in the English criminal justice system should be of interest to Australian prosecutors.[103]

---

98 Law Reform Commission of Victoria Report No. 45 (1992), *Death Caused by Dangerous Driving*, Appendix 3.

99 [1999] VSCA 55 (3 May 1999), at para. 19.

100 [2003] NSWCCA 13 (27 February 2003).

101 Crimes Act 1900 (NSW) s.52A, which reads in part: 'A person is guilty of the offence of dangerous driving occasioning death if the vehicle driven by the person is involved in an impact occasioning the death of another person and the driver was, at the time of the impact, driving the vehicle … in a manner dangerous to another person or persons'.

102 [2003] NSWCCA 13 (27 February 2003), at para. 10.

103 The regime was introduced by the Criminal Justice Act 2003 (UK). See further Brownlee, I. (20004), 'The Statutory Charging Scheme in England and Wales: Towards a Unified Prosecution System?' *Crim LR* 896; Cunningham, S. (2005), 'The Unique Nature of Prosecutions in Cases of Fatal Road Traffic Collisions' *Crim LR* 934.

*(b) An intermediate level of negligence* Several Australian jurisdictions have an offence of driving in a dangerous manner causing death.[104] For a while, the courts interpreted this offence as having a fault element comprising something more than mere carelessness but falling short of gross negligence required for manslaughter.[105] However, none of these decisions clearly explained the nature of this intermediate level of negligence. This line of case authorities was subsequently overruled by the High Court of Australia in *Jiminez v The Queen* which held that the fault element for the offence was not based on negligence.[106]

The Victorian Law Reform Commission in its 1991 report also proposed an intermediate level of negligence for the offence of dangerous driving causing death.[107] The Commission provided a model direction to juries which reads as follows:

> Clearly, it is not always easy to distinguish between driving which is so bad as to constitute manslaughter, that which is bad enough to make the accused guilty of the lesser offence of dangerous driving causing death, and that which is merely careless. However, it will help you to make up your mind to think of a scale. At the bottom of this scale are cases of momentary carelessness – the kind of driving errors which most of us make from time to time, when we are not concentrating as carefully as we should. At the top of the scale is driving which we would agree is totally unacceptable. Driving of the kind required to prove manslaughter belongs near the top end of this scale – it is a gross departure from what we would expect of a careful and competent driver. Dangerous driving is driving which falls more towards the middle of the scale. It is driving which we would all agree is unacceptable and deserves to be punished, but is not so bad as to warrant that person being convicted for manslaughter. On the other hand, it involves considerably more than just a momentary, perhaps excusable, mistake or error of judgment.[108]

The use of a scale to explain the intermediate level of negligence required for the offence has not really clarified the position. As the Victorian Court of Appeal observed, '[w]hat is the jury to be told if they ask when negligence ceases to be merely serious and becomes gross?'[109] The practical difficulty of formulating a coherent description of such a middling type of negligence was also noted by the Model Criminal Code Officers Committee.[110] In sum, efforts to devise an intermediate level of negligence for vehicular homicide have not met with success and do not currently form part of Australian law.

104 See, for example, Crimes Act 1900 (NSW) s.52A; Criminal Law Consolidation Act 1935 (SA) s.319; Crimes Act 1958 (Vic) s.319; Criminal Code 1899 (Qld) s.328A; Criminal Code 1913 (WA) s.59.

105 For example, see *R v Kroon* (1990) 52 A Crim R 15; *R v Buttsworth* [1983] 1 NSWLR 658.

106 (1992) 173 CLR 572. This form of fault is discussed below.

107 Law Reform Commission of Victoria, Discussion Paper No. 21 (1991), *Death Caused by Dangerous Driving*, para. 33.

108 *Ibid.*, at para. 34. This jury direction attempts to paraphrase concisely the discussion in *R v Buttsworth* [1983] 1 NSWLR 658 at 684–687.

109 *R v Shields* [1981] VR 717 at 718.

110 Discussion Paper (1998), *Fatal Offences against the Person*, p.169.

*(c) Driving in a dangerous manner* As mentioned previously, the High Court in *Jiminez* restated the law on the offence found in several Australian jurisdictions of driving in a dangerous manner causing death.[111] The court held that the critical element of the offence was the serious potentiality of danger to others, whether realised by the accused or not, that was occasioned by the manner of driving. Negligent driving does not invariably constitute dangerous driving. The offence of driving in a dangerous manner causing death requires proof of a 'serious breach of the proper conduct of the vehicle' as opposed to the deviation from the standard of care expected of a careful driver.[112] The High Court in the earlier case of *McBride v The Queen* described the task of the prosecution as follows:

> It is essential to define what is charged as the manner of driving, so that when that has been found, the two succeeding questions can be dealt with, namely, was that manner of driving in itself or in its circumstances so dangerous to the public and, did the impact which caused the death or injury occur whilst the vehicle was being so driven. Of all these matters the jury are to be satisfied beyond all reasonable doubt.[113]

Dangerous driving falls within the category of offences under Australian law called strict liability offences. For such offences, the prosecution need only prove a physical (or conduct) element, there being no fault requirement. Thereafter, the accused is liable unless they can successfully plead the defence of reasonable mistake of fact.[114] It has been observed that the distinction may be tenuous between a strict liability offence where an accused pleads reasonable mistake of fact and an offence requiring proof of negligence.[115] However, the distinction is real since an unreasonable mistake need not involve a gross departure from acceptable standards of care.[116]

Presently, Australian prosecutors mostly rely on this offence to charge culpable drivers who have caused death. The most advanced formulation of this form of offence is section 328A of the Queensland Criminal Code which was revised in 1997.[117] It differs from other dangerous driving offences in using the term 'operates' which includes managing, using as well as keeping a machine working. Furthermore, the offence covers 'interfering' with the operation of a vehicle which may not involve driving the vehicle. Given the potentially dangerous nature of motor vehicles, these extensions are warranted in seeking to reduce the number of deaths and serious injuries caused by the poor condition of these vehicles. Section 328A also helpfully provides the following non-exhaustive list of circumstances which the court should

---

111 An example of a provision specifying such an offence is reproduced in n.101.

112 *McBride v The Queen* (1966) 115 CLR 44 at 50 per Barwick CJ.

113 *Ibid.*, at 51.

114 See further, Fairall, P. and Yeo, S. (2005), *Criminal Defences in Australia* (Chatswood, NSW: Lexis/Nexis Butterworths) ch.2. English law does not recognise this type of offence, only 'absolute liability' offences where the accused has no recourse to a defence of reasonable mistake of fact.

115 Fisse, B. (1990), *Howard's Criminal Law* (North Ryde: Law Book Co) p.512.

116 *NSW Sugar Milling Co-operative Ltd v Environmental Protection Authority* (1992) 59 A Crim R 6. See further Leader-Elliott, I. (1993), 'Case note on *Jiminez*' 17 *Criminal Law Journal* 61 at 65.

117 The full provision is reproduced in the Appendix.

consider when determining whether an accused person had operated or interfered with the operation of a vehicle dangerously:

(a) the nature, condition and use of the place [in which the incident occurred];
(b) the nature and condition of the vehicle;
(c) the number of persons, vehicles or other objects that are, or might reasonably be expected to be, in the place;
(d) the concentration of alcohol in the operator's blood; and
(e) the presence of any other substance in the operator's body.

The offence of driving in a dangerous manner causing death has been criticised notwithstanding its conceptual coherence.[118] One criticism is that, as a matter of principle, the imposition of a severe penalty[119] for an offence which dispenses with the need for proof of fault is difficult to justify. By way of rebuttal, a relatively high degree of culpability of the offender is shown by the dangerous manner of their driving and the absence of a reasonable mistake of fact. Another criticism is that the ease of proving the offence encourages the prosecution not to charge the accused with a more serious offence such as manslaughter which is commensurate with the accused's serious wrongdoing. While this problem is real, it can be overcome by requiring the prosecution to lay a manslaughter charge, and permitting the offence of driving in a dangerous manner causing death to serve as an alternative lesser charge.[120]

*5 Medical killing*

Unlike in England, it has been rare in Australia for criminal charges to be brought against a medical practitioner for the death of a patient. In the few cases where a manslaughter charge was brought, the jury acquitted the accused of that offence and convicted them of a lesser offence.[121]

*(a) The position at common law* In Australian common law jurisdictions, the explanation for this reluctance to prosecute or to convict medical practitioners of manslaughter is certainly not due to the law of manslaughter itself. Indeed, if anything, some features of the test for gross negligence under Australian law work unduly against medical practitioners by failing to take sufficient account of the nature of their work. One such feature is that the test sets the degree of risk at 'high', that is, 'probable'.[122] In many medical negligence cases, the treatment rendered would by its

118 See Model Criminal Code Officers Committee (1998), Discussion Paper, *Fatal Offences Against the Person*, pp.169–171.

119 The penalties differ from jurisdiction to jurisdiction and range from 4 years' imprisonment in Western Australia to 10 years in NSW.

120 While there is currently no statutory imperative to lay a manslaughter charge, some statutes provide for alternative verdicts. For example, see the Criminal Law Consolidation Act (SA) s.19B.

121 For a recent example, see *R v Sood* [2006] NSWSC 1141 (31 October 2006).

122 See the quotation from *Nydam* reproduced in the main text accompanying n.6.

very nature involve a probable risk of death or grievous bodily harm either because of the attendant risks of the treatment given, the already weakened condition of the patient, or a combination of the two. Accordingly, the requirement of 'probable risk' would be easily satisfied even where no negligence was committed by the medical practitioner. An argument could therefore be made that, in respect of medical practitioners, the risk should be one of 'highly probable' for a manslaughter conviction to lie.

Another feature of the test that works against medical practitioners is that it includes both death as well as grievous bodily harm for the type of harm risked.[123] Arguably, the inclusion of grievous bodily harm extends the criminal liability of medical practitioners to an unacceptable degree. In particular, it could result in the conviction of a medical practitioner for the manslaughter of a patient whose pre-existing condition heightened the risk of grievous bodily harm in the first place. A strong case could therefore be made for restricting the type of harm risked to death alone insofar as medical practitioners are concerned.

A third feature is the largely objective nature of the 'reasonable person' concept found in the test. While the concept permits a consideration of the particular circumstances in which the accused medical practitioner was placed, the law will not invest any of their personal characteristics which has the effect of lowering the standard of care expected of the reasonable medical practitioner in those circumstances. Thus, a characteristic such as inexperience will not be recognised even when it was beyond the control of the particular accused.[124] This appears to be unduly harsh. While the strictly objective reasonable person test may be appropriate for civil negligence, being concerned as it were with compensation, the task of the criminal law is to decide whether the accused is deserving of society's condemnation and punishment.

*(b) The position in the Code jurisdictions* In relation to the Code jurisdictions, since the test for gross negligence is the same, the above concerns are equally relevant there. Additionally, the Northern Territory, Queensland and Western Australian codes have a provision which simplifies the prosecutor's task of proving causation against medical practitioners charged with manslaughter.[125] The provision reads in part as follows:

> It is the duty of every person who, except in a case of necessity, undertakes to administer surgical or medical treatment to any other person …, to have reasonable skill and to use reasonable care in doing such act, and the person is held to have caused any consequences which result to the life or health of any person by reason of any omission to observe or perform that duty.

123 Unlike under English law where the type of harm is confined to death alone: see *R v Adomako* [1994] 3 All ER 79 at 87.

124 Unlike under English law where such inexperience is recognised for the purposes of the reasonable person test: see *R v Prentice* [1993] 4 All ER 935 at 949.

125 Criminal Code (NT), s.150 read with s.153; Criminal Code 1899 (Qld) s.288; Criminal Code 1913 (WA) s.265.

The effect of the provision is to deem the medical practitioner to have caused *any* consequence, however indirectly, upon proof that he or she had failed to observe or perform the stated duty.[126]

The combined effect of this provision and the features of the test for gross negligence which work against medical practitioners, is that it is relatively easy for them to be convicted of manslaughter. However, countering this effect is the following code provision:

> A person is not criminally responsible for performing in good faith and with reasonable care and skill a surgical operation upon any person for the patient's benefit ... if the performance of the operation is reasonable, having regard to the patient's state at the time and to all the circumstances of the case.[127]

What constitutes 'reasonable care and skill' will depend on the status of the accused and the particular circumstances of the case. Where there is some evidence supporting this provision, the onus is on the prosecution to negative its operation.[128]

*(c) The need for a special medical homicide offence* In spite of the relative ease of securing a conviction for manslaughter, this has not been the path chosen by Australian prosecutors in both common law and code jurisdictions. One possible explanation is that prosecutors themselves believe that the manslaughter label is inappropriate for a medical practitioner whose gross negligence has caused the death of a patient. Another is the view that blame for the patient's death lies primarily with the relevant health departments in failing to provide or maintain adequate healthcare services.[129]

These explanations do not, however, dispel the need to punish some medical practitioners whose negligence in causing death is deserving of social condemnation. Both the deterrent and retributive aims of punishment support this proposition. If the offence of manslaughter has not been used to achieve these aims, a strong case may be made for introducing a special medical homicide offence. Thus far, however, there have been no serious moves to do so in any Australian jurisdiction. The likely reason is that incidents of medical homicide are rare by comparison to the other forms of homicide discussed in this chapter (such as corporate homicide, child neglect leading to death and vehicular homicide) so as not to gain the attention of legislators. But once again, the small number of incidents of medical homicide

126 This paper has previously examined similar duty provisions in relation to cases of drug supply and child neglect leading to death.

127 Criminal Code 1899 (Qld) s.282; Criminal Code 1913 (WA) s.259. See further O'Regan, R.S. (1990), 'Surgery and Criminal Responsibility under the Queensland Criminal Code' 14 *Criminal Law Journal* 73.

128 *R v Ross, McCarthy and McCarthy* [1955] St R Qd 48.

129 For example, see the thrust of the discussion in Wilson, R., Harrison, B., Gibberd R. and Hamilton, J. (1999), 'An Analysis of the Causes of Adverse Events from the Quality in Australian Health Care Study' 170 *Medical Journal of Australia* 411. The issue of corporate homicide is relevant here: see further Hor, M. (1997), 'Medical Negligence: The Contours of Criminality and the Role of the Coroner' *Singapore Journal of Legal Studies* 86 at 104–106.

is insufficient a reason for not introducing a special offence to deal with cases of serious wrongdoing.

It is submitted that a special offence of medical homicide should be enacted in Australia. For it to be a viable alternative to manslaughter, the offence would need to overcome those features of the test of gross negligence, identified previously, which fail to pay sufficient regard to the nature of the work performed by medical practitioners and their working environment. I have suggested elsewhere[130] that the offence could be named 'medical negligence causing death' and read as follows:

> (1) Any medical practitioner who, by the negligent provision of medical diagnosis or treatment, causes the death of another person, is guilty of an offence under this section.
> (2) 'Negligence' in this section is established where the act or omission causing death involved:
>   (a) a great falling short of the standard of care required of a reasonable practitioner; and
>   (b) a highly probable risk that death would result; and
>   was so serious that a criminal penalty was warranted.
> (3) In deciding whether the accused was negligent for the purposes of this section, the jury shall have regard to all the surrounding circumstances, including the urgency of the situation and the availability of resources and equipment.
> (4) A 'reasonable practitioner' in s.2(a) means a reasonable medical practitioner with the same skill, experience and training as the accused.

The penalty for this proposed offence may be the same as that currently prescribed for manslaughter or some lesser penalty. What really matters is the label used to describe the criminal negligence of medical practitioners and the wide discretion to be given to the sentencing court to enable it to select a penalty which fits the particular circumstances of the case.

## IV Further Australian Perspectives

Besides the law attending the five areas discussed in this chapter, there are two Australian developments worth describing which cut across many of these areas. The first is a proposal by the Australian Model Criminal Code Officers Committee, and the second is a unique offence contained in the Northern Territory Criminal Code. Each will be considered in turn.

130 Callahan, R. and Yeo, S. (1999), 'Negligence in Medical Manslaughter Cases' 6 *Journal of Law and Medicine* 253 at 268.

### *1 Abolishing negligent manslaughter*

The Model Criminal Code Officers Committee has recommended a major restructuring of the fault elements for manslaughter.[131] Under its proposed scheme, (i) manslaughter would require a subjective fault element, (ii) what is now negligent manslaughter would form a new offence called 'dangerous conduct causing death', and (iii) unlawful and dangerous act manslaughter would be abolished. The Committee proposed the following two offences for homicide other than murder:

> *Manslaughter*
> A person (a) whose conduct causes the death of another person; and (b) who intends[132] to cause, or is reckless[133] about causing, serious harm[134] to that or any other person by that conduct, is guilty of an offence.
> Maximum penalty: Imprisonment for 25 years.
> *Dangerous conduct causing death*
> A person (a) whose conduct causes the death of another person; and (b) who is negligent[135] about causing the death of that or any other person by that conduct, is guilty of an offence.
> Maximum penalty: Imprisonment for 25 years.

The Committee considered incorporating negligence into the offence of manslaughter but ultimately decided to reserve the manslaughter offence to cases where death resulted from conduct which was known to involve a risk of serious harm. The Committee thought that this was necessary because cases of negligent conduct causing death usually involved less wrongdoing than cases of reckless conduct causing death. Having two separate offences supported the Committee's approach that 'where meaningful distinctions can be made in the degree of fault attaching to

131 See its Discussion Paper (1998), *Fatal Offences against the Person*, pp.145–155, for the Committee's reasons for the changes. The Committee defined murder (in cl.5.1.9) as follows: 'A person (a) whose conduct causes the death of another person; and (b) who intends to cause, or is reckless as to causing, the death of that or any other person by that conduct is guilty of [murder]'.

132 This and other types of fault elements are defined in the Model Criminal Code accompanying the Committee's *Final Report, Chapter 2. General Principles of Criminal Responsibility* (1992). S.203.1 defines 'intention' in part as follows: 'A person has intention in respect to a result when he or she means to bring it about or is aware that it will occur in the ordinary course of events'.

133 The Model Criminal Code, s.203.3, defines this in part as follows: 'A person is reckless with respect to a result when he or she is aware of a substantial risk that it will occur and it is, having regard to the circumstances known to him or her, unjustifiable to take the risk'.

134 Under the Committee's proposal, murder requires the accused to have intended or been reckless in causing death alone.

135 The Model Criminal Code, s.203.4, defines this as follows: 'A person is negligent with respect to a physical element when his or her conduct involves such a great falling short of the standard of care which a reasonable person would exercise in the circumstances; and such a high risk that the element exists or will exist that the conduct merits criminal punishment for the offence in issue'.

conduct, it is a matter appropriate for jury determination rather than relegation to the sentencing stage of the trial'.[136] Another reason given by the Committee was its recognition that juries appeared reluctant to convict accused persons of manslaughter on proof of negligence, particularly in respect of criminally negligent conduct causing death on the road and in the workplace. Based on our discussion of medical killing, a medical practitioner's negligent conduct causing the death of a patient could be added to this list. The Committee felt that a distinct offence of 'dangerous conduct causing death' would better express the degree of societal condemnation in such cases compared to manslaughter.

If implemented, the Committee's proposal to change the label of negligent manslaughter to dangerous conduct causing death would assist in the prosecution and punishment of persons for vehicular and medical killing, as well as company officers whose negligence had caused death in the workplace. It is observed that this outcome would not feature under the English Law Commission's scheme for manslaughter since it retains negligence as a form of fault for that offence.[137]

### *2 Introducing a 'failure to rescue' offence*

The Northern Territory Criminal Code contains a provision which is unique to Australia and rare for common law jurisdictions.[138] It imposes a duty to rescue in certain circumstances, a failure of which results in conviction for the offence. The offence appears as section 155 and reads:

> Any person who, being able to provide rescue, resuscitation, medical treatment, first aid or succour of any kind to a person urgently in need of it and whose life may be endangered if it is not provided, callously fails to do so is guilty of a crime and is liable to imprisonment for 7 years.

Although not a homicide offence, section 155 is relevant to our discussion because it provides an alternative form of criminal liability for many of the areas considered in this chapter.[139] In this regard, the Northern Territory Supreme Court in *R v Salmon* noted that the provision could involve 'motorists and others who fail to assist victims of accidents, doctors who fail to make home visits to sick or injured persons, and

136 MCCOC Discussion Paper (1998), *Fatal Offences Against the Person*, p.155.

137 The Law Commission, Consultation Paper No. 177 (2005), *A New Homicide Act for England and Wales? An Overview* (TSO), para. 5.45. The Commission's other form of fault for manslaughter based on recklessness (see para. 5.50) is closely similar to that proposed by the Australian Model Criminal Code Officers Committee.

138 In contrast, many criminal codes of civil law jurisdictions have such a 'failure to rescue' offence. For examples, see Feldbrugge, F.J.M. (1966), 'Good and Bad Samaritans' 14 *American Journal of Comparative Law* 630 at 655–657.

139 For a detailed discussion of this offence and its theoretical underpinnings, see Kift, S. (1997), 'Criminal Liability and the Bad Samaritan: Failure to Rescue Provisions in the Criminal Law' 1 *Macquarie Law Review* 212; 258.

parents who fail to summon medical attention for their sick children'.[140] To these may be added dealers who fail to assist users of drugs supplied by them.

Unlike homicide offences where liability is contingent on a result, section 155 is a conduct offence so that problems of causation do not arise. Accordingly, cases of drug supply or child neglect leading to death which pose difficulties over proof of causation could alternatively be dealt with under this provision.

The elements of section 155 may be briefly stated. The duty to rescue is imposed on everyone and arises when life is in immediate danger and the victim is in urgent need of assistance. The accused is obliged to do one of five things – to rescue, resuscitate, treat, administer first aid or provide succour – the failure of which satisfies the conduct element of the offence.[141] The fault element comprises a 'callous failure' which the court in *Salmon* interpreted as having both a subjective and an objective component. The former comprises 'a deliberate and conscious choice by an informed accused not to provide aid or assistance to the victim' while the latter involves 'proof that the accused's failure was such as to offend common standards of respect, decency and kindness in the sense that a reasonable person would regard the accused's failure to act as callous'.[142]

This is not the place to canvass fully the deficiencies of section 155 but two may be mentioned. One is that the detailed prescription of what actions the rescuer is required to take is too limiting. In particular, there is no allowance for informing others such as ambulance or police services which could provide better aid to the victim. Another weakness of the provision is its failure to release the accused from the duty even where there is a risk of life or serious injury to the accused or to others. These weaknesses are absent in the following formulation of the 'duty to rescue' offence proposed by the Canadian Law Reform Commission:

> (1) Every one commits a crime who, realizing that a person is in immediate danger of death or serious harm, omits to take reasonable steps to aid that person.
> (2) Subsection (1) does not apply to a person who cannot render aid without incurring a risk of death or serious harm to [himself or herself] or another person or for any other valid reason.[143]

As an overarching reform proposal which has relevance to the 'manslaughter versus special homicide offence' debate, consideration could be given to introducing an English 'duty to rescue' offence such as the one found in the Northern Territory or, better still, that proposed by the Canadian Law Reform Commission.

140 (1994) 70 A Crim R 536 at 551 per Kearney, J.

141 It has been suggested that the further option should be provided of informing the relevant authorities: see Kift, above n.139 at 273.

142 (1994) 70 A Crim R 536 at 557.

143 Report No. 31 (1987), *Recodifying Criminal Law*, cl.54 of the draft code.

## V Conclusion

This study of the five areas where the 'manslaughter versus special homicide offence' debate occurs shows that a pragmatic view is taken of the issues by Australian lawmakers. Special homicide offences have been enacted where there is a perception that juries will not convict for manslaughter but would be prepared to convict for a lesser crime or one bearing another label. The vehicular homicide offences found in all Australian jurisdictions are prime examples. Special homicide offences have also been created where a manslaughter charge will fail because a particular offence element is missing or difficult to prove and it is thought that the accused should nevertheless be made criminally responsible for the death. An example of this is the South Australian offence of criminal neglect of children leading to death which overcomes the problem encountered in some cases of having to prove who caused the child's death. Another example is the ACT offence of industrial manslaughter which circumvents the problem of a corporation being a non-natural person by embracing novel principles of corporate criminal responsibility. The pragmatism of the State legislators, however, is shown by their refusal to introduce such an offence, preferring instead to increase the scope and penalties for offences dealing with occupational health and safety.

In respect of the supply of illegal drugs leading to death, it appears that the Australian laws on causation (judge-made and codified) do not present the same problems as encountered under English common law. Accordingly, there has not been any proposal to introduce a special homicide offence for this area. With regard to medical killing, the absence of any move to enact a special homicide offence may be due to the perception, rightly or wrongly, that incidences are so small that there is no need to create such an offence. Another explanation may be that the lawmakers view the problem as lying with the healthcare system and not with individual medical practitioners. Again, their pragmatism is evident in seeking to reduce the incidents of medical killing by improving the healthcare systems and services rather than invoking the criminal law.

Besides the pragmatic stance of Australian legislators, the only other noticeable common theme among the five areas pertains to the formulation of negligence. It is that the test of gross negligence developed by the Australian courts for manslaughter has been adopted for all special homicide offences which have negligence as their fault element. This is so in respect of the ACT offence of industrial manslaughter, the Victorian offence of culpable driving causing death and, with some modifications, the South Australian offence of criminal neglect of children.

The test for gross negligence could be altered to suit the particular circumstances of homicide in question. For example, the concept of 'aggregate negligence' has been incorporated into the ACT offence of industrial manslaughter. The suggestion has also been made for the test of gross negligence to be modified to take into account the working conditions of medical practitioners.

Finally, mention should be made of the set of duty provisions found in various Australian criminal codes, several of which have been discussed in this chapter. The attractiveness of these provisions is attested to by their continued existence in the Queensland and Western Australian codes for over a century, and their incorporation into the much newer Northern Territory code. Certainly, these provisions have been a boon to prosecutors in overcoming problems of proving causation. Might it not be time for the English legislature to enact these provisions which first appeared in the English Criminal Code Bill of 1879?

## Appendix

*Corporate recklessness*

### Criminal Code 2002 (ACT)

*Corporation – fault elements other than negligence*

S.51(1) In deciding whether the fault element of intention, knowledge or recklessness exists for an offence in relation to a corporation, the fault element is taken to exist if the corporation expressly, tacitly or impliedly authorises or permits the commission of the offence.

(2) The ways in which authorisation or permission may be established include:

(a) proving that the corporation's board of directors intentionally, knowingly or recklessly engaged in the conduct or expressly, tacitly or impliedly authorised or permitted the commission of the offence; or

(b) proving that a high managerial agent of the corporation intentionally, knowingly or recklessly engaged in the conduct or expressly, tacitly or impliedly authorised or permitted the commission of the offence; or

(c) proving that a corporate culture existed within the corporation that directed, encouraged, tolerated or led to noncompliance with the contravened law; or

(d) proving that the corporation failed to create and maintain a corporate culture requiring compliance with the contravened law.

(3) Subsection (2) (b) does not apply if the corporation proves that it exercised appropriate diligence to prevent the conduct, or the authorisation or permission.

(4) Factors relevant to subsection (2) (c) and (d) include:

(a) whether authority to commit an offence of the same or a similar character had been given by a high managerial agent of the corporation; and

(b) whether the employee, agent or officer of the corporation who committed the offence reasonably believed, or had a reasonable expectation, that a high managerial agent of the corporation would have authorised or permitted the commission of the offence.

(5) If recklessness is not a fault element for a physical element of an offence, subsection (2) does not enable the fault element to be proved by proving that the board of directors, or a high managerial agent, of the corporation recklessly engaged in the conduct or recklessly authorised or permitted the commission of the offence.

(6) In this section:

'board of directors', of a corporation, means the body exercising the corporation's executive authority, whether or not the body is called the board of directors.

'corporate culture', for a corporation, means an attitude, policy, rule, course of conduct or practice existing within the corporation generally or in the part of the corporation where the relevant conduct happens.

'high managerial agent', of a corporation, means an employee, agent or officer of the corporation whose conduct may fairly be assumed to represent the corporation's policy because of the level of responsibility of his or her duties.

*Criminal neglect of a child or vulnerable adult*

**Criminal Law Consolidation Act 1935 (SA)**
*Criminal liability for neglect where death or serious harm results from unlawful act*

S.14(1) A person (the 'defendant') is guilty of the offence of criminal neglect if:
(a) a child or a vulnerable adult (the 'victim') dies or suffers serious harm as a result of an unlawful act; and
(b) the defendant had, at the time of the act, a duty of care to the victim; and
(c) the defendant was, or ought to have been, aware that there was an appreciable risk that serious harm would be caused to the victim by the unlawful act; and
(d) the defendant failed to take steps that they could reasonably be expected to have taken in the circumstances to protect the victim from harm and the defendant's failure to do so was, in the circumstances, so serious that a criminal penalty is warranted.

Maximum penalty:
(a) where the victim dies – imprisonment for 15 years; or
(b) where the victim suffers serious harm – imprisonment for 5 years.

(2) If a jury considering a charge of criminal neglect against a defendant finds that:
(a) there is reasonable doubt as to the identity of the person who committed the unlawful act that caused the victim's death or serious harm; but
(b) the unlawful act can only have been the act of the defendant or some other person who, on the evidence, may have committed the unlawful act, the jury may find the defendant guilty of the charge of criminal neglect even though of the opinion that the unlawful act may have been the act of the defendant.

(3) For the purposes of this section, the defendant has a duty of care to the victim if the defendant is a parent or guardian of the victim or has assumed responsibility for the victim's care.

(4) In this section:
'act' includes:
(a) an omission; and
(b) a course of conduct;
'child' means a person under 16 years of age;
'serious harm' means:
(a) harm that endangers, or is likely to endanger, a person's life; or
(b) harm that consists of, or is likely to result in, loss of, or serious and protracted impairment of, a part of the body or a physical or mental function; or
(c) harm that consists of, or is likely to result in, serious disfigurement;
'unlawful' – an act is unlawful if it:
(a) constitutes an offence; or
(b) would constitute an offence if committed by an adult of full legal capacity;
'vulnerable adult' means a person aged 16 years or above whose ability to protect themselves from an unlawful act is significantly impaired through physical or mental disability, illness or infirmity.

*Dangerous operation of vehicle causing death*

**Criminal Code 1899 (Qld)**
*Dangerous operation of a vehicle*

S.328A (1) A person who operates, or in any way interferes with the operation of, a vehicle dangerously in any place commits a misdemeanour.
Maximum penalty – 200 penalty units or 3 years' imprisonment.
(2) If the offender:
(a) at the time of committing the offence is adversely affected by an intoxicating substance; or
(b) has been previously convicted either upon indictment or summarily of an offence against this section; the person commits a crime.
Maximum penalty – 400 penalty units or 5 years' imprisonment.
(3) If the offender has been:
(a) previously convicted either upon indictment or summarily of an offence against this section committed while the offender was adversely affected by an intoxicating substance; or
(b) twice previously convicted either upon indictment or summarily (or once upon indictment and once summarily) of the same prescribed offence or different prescribed offences;
the court or justices shall, upon conviction, impose as the whole or part of the punishment, imprisonment.
(4) A person who operates, or in any way interferes with the operation of, a vehicle dangerously in any place and causes the death of or grievous bodily harm to another person commits a crime and is liable upon conviction upon indictment to imprisonment for 7 years unless at the time of committing the offence the offender is adversely affected by an intoxicating substance in which case they are liable upon conviction upon indictment:
(a) to imprisonment for 10 years; or
(b) if the intoxicating substance is alcohol and the offender was, at that time, over the high alcohol limit – to imprisonment for 14 years.
(5) In this section:
'high alcohol limit' see the Transport Operations (Road Use Management) Act 1995, section 79A.
'operates, or in any way interferes with the operation of, a vehicle dangerously' means operate, or in any way interfere with the operation of, a vehicle at a speed or in a way that is dangerous to the public, having regard to all the circumstances, including:
(a) the nature, condition and use of the place; and
(b) the nature and condition of the vehicle; and
(c) the number of persons, vehicles or other objects that are, or might reasonably be expected to be, in the place; and
(d) the concentration of alcohol in the operator's blood or breath; and
(e) the presence of any other substance in the operator's body.
'prescribed offence' means:

(a) an offence against this section; or
(b) an offence charged on indictment involving the driving or operation of a vehicle at a speed causing or likely to cause injury to anyone; or
(c) an offence against the Transport Operations (Road Use Management) Act 1995, section 79(1), (2), (2A), (2B), (2D) or (2J).
'place' does not include a place being used to race or test vehicles and from which other traffic is excluded at the time.
'the public' includes passengers in a vehicle whether in a public or private place.

(6) The offender may be arrested without warrant.

## Chapter 11

# 'Manslaughter': Generic or Nominate Offences?

Andrew Ashworth

From many points of view the current English law of homicide looks untidy and unprincipled, a picture of piecemeal pragmatism. The clinical approach of the 1980s' criminal code team was only able to present the law in a reasonably structured manner (albeit with infanticide and manslaughter by suicide pact bolted on) because some important aspects were simply excluded, most controversially the offence of causing death by dangerous driving.[1] The reform proposals of the 1990s raised doubts about the reach of the law of manslaughter itself, with the Law Commission's 1996 report recommending both a contraction (abolishing manslaughter by unlawful act) and an extension (a new offence of corporate killing).[2] The present government has moved away from the first, and the second of those proposals has appeared in legislation only in diluted form in the Corporate Manslaughter and Corporate Homicide Act 2007. In the meantime Parliament has extended the law of homicide on another front – two new offences of causing death on the roads, introduced by the Road Safety Act 2006.

In this chapter I will take up, at a general level, four of the many themes that emerge from the other contributions to this book. First, what should be the threshold of fault for liability for a homicide offence? Secondly, and connected with the first question, under what circumstances might the commission of a certain wrong resulting in death justify conviction for a homicide offence? Thirdly, should the structure of this part of English law be based around one or more general offences, or should the primary approach be to create nominate offences for different circumstances of causing death? And fourthly, how should a re-shaped law of 'manslaughter' be enforced?

Before starting on that journey, I should state that this chapter defines homicide in the largest sense, so as to encompass any offence that includes 'causing death' or 'killing' or similar words in its label. Homicide, after all, is bringing about the death of a human being. So this would exclude endangerment offences and others that do not require the causing of a death – for example, the offences against health and safety regulations in sections 2, 3 and 33 of the Health and Safety at Work Act

1 Law Commission for England and Wales (1989), *A Criminal Code for England and Wales* (Law Com. No. 177).

2 Law Commission for England and Wales (1996), *Legislating the Criminal Code: Involuntary Manslaughter* (Law Com. No. 237).

1974 – but would include infanticide, causing death by driving while disqualified, unlicensed or uninsured, corporate manslaughter, and so forth.

## I The Threshold of Fault for Homicide Offences

The first question to be explored concerns the lower threshold of fault for homicide liability. My submission is that, in principle, the minimum fault requirement in relation to death should be the same across all homicide offences. Good reasons ought to be produced if one offence is to have a lower threshold than others, or a higher threshold. From this starting point, which will be discussed further below, we should examine possible fault requirements. We can begin with the usual culpability ladder, running from intention through recklessness to negligence and beneath. In this volume we are not dealing with the intentional causing of death, but that does not mean that we can exclude intention from all our discussions – it will re-appear in the next section below. The two key points, however, are the appropriateness of gross negligence as the lower threshold, and the appropriate reference point for whatever degree of fault is selected.

The assumption of English criminal law is that, for offences of any seriousness, the appropriate fault requirements are intention and recklessness, and therefore that advertence is needed. But English law departs from this principle in respect of homicide, presumably because the causing of death is so tragic an event that liability for inadvertent killing is thought appropriate when there is a high degree of inadvertent fault (gross negligence). Other legal systems, some of them common law systems, provide for convictions for lesser offences (such as causing injury) on the basis of gross negligence; but English law has always rejected that, and has continued to regard homicide liability as exceptional in this respect. Mere negligence, of the kind sufficient to found liability in tort, is considered not to be demanding enough for conviction of a homicide offence, and so the tendency has been to require a higher degree of fault. In his chapter Oliver Quick calls for a reconsideration of the ingredients of this standard of liability, and his arguments deserve careful attention. The debate spills over into the kind of advertence/inadvertence arguments that were generated by the *Caldwell* decision[3] and which survive its demise. Those arguments become particularly poignant when linked to the question of the appropriate reference point for gross negligence.

Can it be argued that gross negligence as to death, defined (say) as conduct falling not merely below but grossly below the standard to be expected of a reasonable citizen, is on a roughly equivalent level to recklessness as to causing serious injury, defined as awareness that an activity carried a risk of serious injury to someone but not that there was a risk of death? If we take it that the grossly negligent actor failed to realise the risk of death (culpably so, because he should have realised), whereas the reckless actor realised the risk of serious injury and no more, we might regard the latter as more culpable because of the advertence, and we might go further and

3 [1982] AC 341; for discussion and references, see Ashworth, A. (2006), *Principles of Criminal Law*, 5th ed. (Oxford: Oxford University Press) pp.185–195.

question the circumstances in which anyone who recognises a risk of serious injury can be sufficiently sure that death is not a possibility. What about the comparison between the person who was grossly negligent as to death, and someone who was reckless as to a risk of (non-serious) injury arising from the activity? We are being driven towards the *Caldwell* point that, at some stage, we should be able to say that the failure to recognise a risk that most people would have foreseen is as culpable as some forms of advertence to risk: where the risk that a person culpably failed to recognise was one of death ensuing, it is surely plausible to argue that that is morally worse, *ceteris paribus*, than knowingly taking the risk of causing a non-serious injury to someone.[4] Thus it seems to me that we cannot simply rank all cases of (advertent) recklessness as more culpable than all cases of (inadvertent) gross negligence, and we therefore have to embrace the greater complications entailed by overlapping culpability categories.

At common law it is now settled that the proper reference point for the gross negligence required for conviction of manslaughter is the causing of death: in assessing whether the negligence was gross, a court should have regard 'to the risk of death involved'.[5] A risk of injury, not death, would be insufficient. That can be defended by reference to the correspondence principle that the referential point of the fault should be on the same level as the harm specified as the outcome of the offence.[6] What is strange about the development of the English law of homicide is that the fault element in similar homicide offences, apart from manslaughter, is defined differently. Thus the law on causing death by dangerous driving refers to the degree of deviation from the standard to be expected of a competent driver ('the way he drives falls far below what would be expected of a competent and careful driver'), and the term 'dangerous' is defined as referring to 'danger either of injury to any person or of serious damage to property'.[7] The primary standard, 'falling far below' the appropriate standard of driving, appears to be close to gross negligence; but the danger specified – the referential point, in the terminology used here – is not death or even serious injury, but merely injury or serious damage to property. It is interesting to speculate what effect it might have if the fault element for causing death by dangerous driving were changed to gross negligence as to (a) death or (b) death or serious injury. Some might say that either of those tests would have no significant effect on verdicts, since they are more or less equivalent to the test now applied. In practice, who can distinguish meaningfully between a risk of death and a risk of death or serious injury? The position is a little clearer for the offence of corporate manslaughter, the definition of which specifies 'a gross breach of the

4 I am leaving aside those cases where both propositions are true – D knowingly risked causing a non-serious injury, and was also grossly negligent as to the risk of death.

5 *Adomako* [1995] 1 AC 171, at 187.

6 This is not the place for separate discussion of this principle. See further Horder, J. (1995) 'A Critique of the Correspondence Principle' *Crim LR* 759; Mitchell, B. (1999), 'In Defence of the Correspondence Principle' *Crim LR* 195; Horder, J. (1999), 'A Reply' *Crim LR* 206; and Simester, A.P. and Sullivan, G.R. (2007), *Criminal Law: Theory and Doctrine*, 3rd ed. (Oxford: Hart) pp.186–191.

7 Road Traffic Act 1988, s.2(1)(a) and s.2(3).

duty of care owed by the organisation to the deceased'.[8] Unlike the definition of causing death by dangerous driving, there is nothing in the definition relating to the referential point of the danger. However, section 8(2)(b) of the 2007 Act makes it clear that one of the matters that a jury must consider when determining whether the breach of the relevant duty of care was 'gross' is 'how much of a risk of death it posed'. This falls short of requiring gross negligence (or its equivalent) as to death as part of the definition, although it draws both the degree and the magnitude of the risk into the assessment of 'grossness'.

The question is different for intentional offences, such as murder, where it is possible for a person to intend to break another's arm or leg and yet not intend to endanger their life: that is part of the reasoning behind the Law Commission's latest formulation of the fault element for first degree murder, which includes an intention to kill or to cause serious injury in the awareness that life is thereby being endangered.[9] Thus, one question to be faced in refashioning the law of manslaughter is whether gross negligence, or gross carelessness (if preferred), should be as to death, or as to death or serious injury. It should not be sufficient that the fault is as to injury or property damage (as in causing death by dangerous driving); and the test for the new offence of corporate manslaughter should be more explicit.

This line of argument should lead us to question the propriety of the new offence of causing death by careless driving.[10] There is an obvious argument that the offence of careless driving is directly connected to road safety and so it is both defensible and right to hold the careless driver liable for a homicide offence where death happens to result. However, this line of argument is only plausible because of the elasticity of the term 'road safety'. In reality, most offences of careless driving that come to the notice of the police are not even prosecuted, and those that are prosecuted are thought (by the legislature, which set the maximum penalty) not to be so serious that anything more than a fine is called for. So the road safety policy that underlies the offence of careless driving is not really one about saving lives, and is rather a matter of preserving people from injury and preserving property. All that an offence of careless driving requires is driving that falls below the standard to be expected of a competent and careful driver, and there is no reference to a risk of injury, let alone serious injury or death. Perhaps an offence of causing injury by careless driving might be justifiable (as lying within the scope of the risk), but an offence of causing death is certainly not.

In conclusion, it has been proposed that the minimum threshold of fault applicable to homicide offences should be the same, unless there are powerful arguments for a lower or higher threshold. Whether the general standard is set at gross negligence

8 Corporate Manslaughter and Corporate Homicide Act 2007, s.1(1)(b).

9 Law Commission for England and Wales (2006), *Murder, Manslaughter and Infanticide* (Law Com. No. 304) on which see Ashworth, A. (2007), 'Principles, Pragmatism and the Law Commission's Recommendations on Homicide Law Reform' *Crim LR* 333, and Taylor, R. (2007), 'The Nature of "Partial Defences" and the Coherence of (Second Degree) Murder' *Crim LR* 345.

10 Road Traffic Act 1988, s.2B (inserted by the Road Safety Act 2006); see the chapter by Sally Cunningham in the present volume, and Cunningham, S. (2007), 'Punishing Drivers Who Kill: Putting Road Safety First?' *Legal Studies* 27:2, 288.

or elsewhere (perhaps gross carelessness), it should in principle be a standard of gross negligence as to death. There seems to be no adequate justification for the offence of causing death by dangerous driving to refer only to the danger of injury or serious property damage; and no adequate justification (save that of appeasing public opinion, which seems doubtful) for creating an offence of causing death by careless driving when the fault requirement is so very low.

## II The Threshold of Wrongs for Homicide Offences

The discussion above started from the proposition that, in principle, the minimum fault requirement in relation to death should be the same across all homicide offences. Good reasons ought to be produced if one offence is to have a lower threshold than others, or a higher threshold. We should now examine another application of that principle: whereas above we looked at forms of homicide offence that turn on the existence of fault of a certain degree (gross negligence, gross breach of duty, and so on), we now consider whether it is justifiable to create homicide offences that require something less than that level of fault, in that they turn on the commission of an originating wrong that can be connected to the death.

Where a person causes the death of another, it is usually fair to say that he or she is responsible for that death. But responsibility in that wide ascriptive sense is merely a necessary condition of legal liability. If the victim's family wishes to pursue an action for compensation, then it must prove that there was sufficient fault to ground liability in tort, or under another heading of civil liability. If there is a criminal prosecution, simple causal responsibility is likewise necessary but not sufficient. More must be proved, and that may be either fault to a given degree (gross negligence) or an originating wrong. Now there are various kinds of situation in which an originating wrong has been put forward as a sufficient basis for a manslaughter conviction – cases of supply of illegal drugs leading to death, cases of driving while disqualified, and of course unlawful act manslaughter itself. In each of these situations there are different factors at work, but for me the key question is the relationship of the defendant's fault to the fatal result. Unlawful act manslaughter raises the question sharply: why should a minor but unlawful act, done in circumstances where there is no gross negligence as to death (that is, a reasonable person would not have taken precautions against death resulting), be converted into a serious crime when by mischance death results? One justification, advanced by John Gardner[11] and by others including Chris Clarkson,[12] is that by intentionally committing an assault or other unlawful act D changes their normative position vis-à-vis the victim and it is therefore fair to hold them responsible for the death that ensues, however unforeseeable that was in the circumstances. I have subjected the

11 Gardner, J. (1998), 'On the General Part of the Criminal Law', in Duff (ed.), *Philosophy and the Criminal Law* (Cambridge: Cambridge University Press).

12 Clarkson, C.M.V. (2000), 'Context and Culpability in Involuntary Manslaughter: Principle of Instinct?' in Ashworth and Mitchell (eds), *Reforming the English Law of Homicide* (Oxford: Oxford University Press).

'change of normative position' idea to criticism elsewhere:[13] in essence it is nothing more than an assertion which awaits justification, at least in relation to liability for an unexpected outcome such as death in our example. John Gardner has now conceded that his use of the phrase 'changing one's normative position' was not intended as a substantive moral justification of constructive liability: it was an attempt 'to present the law as morally intelligible but not necessarily as morally acceptable',[14] and the latter argument is still to be made. Good reasons need to be advanced to explain why the commission of an originating wrong (of a certain type) should lead to constructive liability, and a simple reference to 'change of normative position' is unhelpful and inadequate. Moreover, even if one were to concede that committing a crime amounts to a relevant change of normative position, this does not entail that a person who intends a minor assault should be liable for manslaughter – certain limiting principles might properly come into play. Thus, as one of the doctrine's supporters accepts, there is too great a moral distance between the assault intended and the serious offence of manslaughter to justify conviction of that offence.[15]

Another justification for basing homicide liability on an originating wrong might build on the notion of attack developed by Antony Duff, in his chapter above and elsewhere. For him, attacks are worse than endangerment because the attacker wants to succeed and is disappointed by failure, whereas the endangerer may be relieved if no serious harm results from the activity. But the question for us is whether an attack that amounts to nothing more than a minor assault should render the attacker liable for a serious homicide offence if, by a highly unusual sequence of events, death results. Note that this is not the desired result for the attacker, and that they may well feel genuine regret that this unwanted consequence has ensued – unlike the attacker who was trying to bring about the result that occurred. (In other words, on the emotional level stressed by Antony Duff when distinguishing between attackers and endangerers, this places this particular attacker closer to the endangerers.) I am not disputing that there is a sense in which D can be said to be responsible for V's death. But the question is whether D should be held criminally liable for a homicide offence when that was not the desired result of the attack and was so statistically unlikely an outcome that no reasonable person would regard it as coming within the scope of the risk created by a single punch. For me, echoing the position formerly held by the Law Commission[16] and before that by the Criminal Law Revision Committee,[17] the defendant's fault falls too far short of the unlucky result.

A third justification is now more prominent, particularly in government circles, and it seems to mix a causal argument with the element of unlawfulness and a

13 Ashworth, A. (2008), 'A Change of Normative Position: Determining the Contours of Culpability in Criminal Law' *New Criminal Law Review* 11 (forthcoming).

14 Gardner, J. (2007), *Offences and Defences: Selected Essays in the Criminal Law* (Oxford: Oxford University Press) p.331.

15 Horder (1995), above n.6, at p.769.

16 See above, n.2.

17 Criminal Law Revision Committee (1980), *Offences Against the Person* (14th Report), para. 120.

broad concept of the scope of risk. Thus the government proposed[18] (and the Law Commission now recommends)[19] that unlawful act manslaughter should be replaced by a narrower offence of causing death by a crime of violence involving intention to cause injury or recklessness as to causing injury. This would, rightly, remove from manslaughter those cases where liability is based on an act of criminal damage, or even a minor assault, which does not reach the level of recklessness as to causing injury. However, it still assumes that, when it comes to deliberately or knowingly injuring someone, the risk of death is so much greater than it would be for a minor assault that it is sufficient to trigger manslaughter liability. However, there is a strong counter-argument that this goes too far, since only non-serious injury is in issue, and that lies a long way short of death. Nonetheless, a similar style of argument has been used to support the new offence (created by the Road Safety Act 2006) of causing death by driving while disqualified, uninsured or unlicensed. The causal argument is there – V would not have been killed if D had not been on the road when they should not have been – and the element of unlawfulness or originating wrong is also present. D defied the criminal law, and this is the result. The argument is said to be strengthened by two other factors. The first is that the purpose of the driver licensing system, and of disqualification from driving, is to keep dangerous people off the roads. In particular, a driver would only be disqualified for good road safety reasons. Secondly, the risk of involvement in accidents is much higher for unlicensed drivers. Now the difference between this group of offences and those in the gross negligence category described above is thought to reside in the factors of unlawfulness and deliberate defiance of the law. The person who kills through gross negligence is typically engaged in a lawful activity, but without taking the amount of care that we would expect of other citizens in that position. For these new driving offences the facts that D was behaving unlawfully, and that this was a deliberate defiance of a safety requirement, are said to combine to establish a direct link to the result that has occurred, and so there is every reason to hold D liable for it.

My argument thus far, therefore, is that the justifications offered for creating a lower level of homicide offences, beneath gross negligence, are less than compelling. Those lines of argument that place their emphasis either on the 'change of normative position' allegedly inherent in an assault, or on the fact that one person made an 'attack' on another, are not capable of supplying a convincing ground for holding the person liable for a homicide offence, a strong counter-argument being that the result was outside the realistic scope of the risk. The challenge to those who support offences such as unlawful act manslaughter and causing death by driving while disqualified is to produce a good reason for bringing these unexpected deaths within a homicide offence, rather than accepting that the outcome was unforeseeable and convicting the defendant of the non-homicide offence constituted by their conduct.[20] This is not to deny that D was responsible for the death, since that is an attribution

18 Home Office (2000), *Reforming the Law on Involuntary Manslaughter: the Government's Proposals*.

19 Law Com. No. 304 (above, n.9) pp.61–62.

20 Supporters of the offence of causing or allowing the death of a child or vulnerable adult, introduced by s.5 of the Domestic Violence, Crime and Victims Act 2004, believe that

of authorship which (we assume) is not in dispute. But, if we are not to be governed by the law of deodand or by a raging constructivism, we should have the courage to refuse to label such cases as homicide offences. It is wrong to be so influenced by the fact that D was committing an offence by doing the act that caused death, as to turn the offence into homicide even when the fatal result lies outside the scope of the foreseeable risk created by the offence D was committing (assault, driving while disqualified, and so on). The gap between D's fault and the ultimate result is too wide or, to borrow Jeremy Horder's phrase, the moral distance is too great. Supporters of the new offences introduced by the Road Safety Act 2006 may claim that driving whilst disqualified is different: drivers are disqualified for good road safety reasons, and a disqualified driver who takes a car on to the road is intentionally defying a command addressed specifically to them. But we have already noted that the phrase 'good road safety reasons' refers to any possibility of a collision and not necessary to a threat to life, and intentional defiance of the law (however objectionable in itself) should not be fault enough for conviction of a homicide offence.

## III General or Particular Offences?

Is it better to shape the law around one or more generic homicide offences, or do the arguments favour the creation of a number of nominate offences? Murder, or (in the Law Commission's recommendations)[21] first degree murder, will be left out of the calculation here. But what the Law Commission now casts as murder in the second degree, as well as what the Commission classifies as manslaughter, will be taken to fall within the scope of our discussion. We should not assume that there should only be a single offence beneath murder, however. There may be arguments in favour of two or even three generic homicide offences to cover the ground adequately. One approach to the creation of generic homicide offences would be to track the culpability distinctions proposed earlier, at least to an extent. One generic offence below murder might be reckless manslaughter, based on a definition restricted to knowledge or realisation that conduct carried a risk of causing death. This would be a serious offence, sometimes only slightly below murder. One question would be whether such a generic offence should be confined to awareness of the risk of causing death, or extended to cases of awareness of a risk of causing serious injury: the Law Commission's recommendation for second degree murder confines the 'reckless killing' category to cases of awareness of the risk of death, albeit coupled with an intention to cause injury or fear of injury.[22] This proposed offence would cover all forms of advertent recklessness beneath knowledge of virtual certainty, which would remain as a form of oblique intent taking the offence into murder. A second generic

---

the previous difficulty of obtaining any conviction in some such cases is a justification for the creation of that offence; but see the critique by Jonathan Herring in this volume.

21 See above, n.9.

22 Interestingly this straddles Antony Duff's two categories of endangerment and attack: the intent to cause injury or fear of injury seems to amount to an attack, albeit at a lesser level, but the known risk to the victim's life places what, in my view, is the most important aspect of the offence in the endangerment camp.

offence might be termed culpable homicide, and the essence would be causing death by gross negligence.[23] The definition would require gross negligence as to death, and might also cover the ground currently occupied by causing death by dangerous driving and by corporate manslaughter. We have also given consideration to a generic offence of homicide based on an originating wrong: it was argued above that this would not be justifiable, but the official English view favours such a category.

If nominate offences are to be considered, what should the denominators be? Two possibilities will be mentioned briefly but not pursued. The first would be to distinguish offences by the method of killing – poisoning, shooting, sharp instrument, and so forth. One reason for rejecting this is that there is no necessary link between the chosen method and the level of culpability. Such a description might help to communicate with citizens, but the method of killing is usually reported as widely as the conviction itself and so nominalism of this kind is hardly needed. A second approach to categorisation would be to distinguish offences by the status of the victim or by the victim's relationship to the offender. This might bring separate offences of homicide of a law enforcement officer, or more broadly homicide of a public official on duty, and it might also bring offences such as parricide, matricide and so forth. One problem here is that the connection between the categories and culpability is not always sharp enough: these matters can be taken into account when sentencing, insofar as they bear on culpability, but if they were relevant at the liability stage then it might be necessary to create many nominate offences in order to avoid leaving out certain types of victim. That difficulty may be illustrated by the one offence of this kind in the existing law, infanticide, where the drawing of the definitional line (only applicable in respect of the killing of a child under 12 months) has long been the source of claims of injustice.

Taking those two arguments for nominate offences no further, we must now confront the question whether the law should be structured around generic homicide offences or nominate offences. Three arguments in favour of nominalism stand out – that it is much more communicative, thereby emphasising the special duties of citizens in certain roles or positions; that the circumstances of some types of case are so unlike others that a separate category is a more accurate label; and that, if there were not a nominate offence for certain conduct, the law might be misapplied by juries. One argument against nominate offences is that their creation may convey the impression, however wrongly, that they are regarded as less serious than manslaughter because they are labelled separately and differently. Another counter-argument raises questions about the deliberate mis-labelling of certain homicides in order to avoid controversy.

The first argument in favour of a separate named offence would be that this helps in publicising the duty imposed on people in a given type of situation, and the consequences of breaching that duty. This is not advanced as a rationale based on general deterrence: it is difficult to believe that having a special offence for drivers, or for doctors, or for companies, will have a greater deterrent effect than

23 There are some who would like to see cases in which a partial defence to murder is successfully pleaded (provocation, diminished responsibility) placed in this category too, together with any cases of reckless manslaughter where such a partial defence might apply.

a generic offence of manslaughter – a term of some solemnity – if it were applied regularly in those situations.[24] It is more a matter of communicating the duty and its breach to more people, including potential offenders, victims' families and potential victims, and so forth. The special label would be more specific and less mysterious than manslaughter. Infanticide, whatever one thinks of the current definition, is an example of this form of communication. A separate communicative label may be thought necessary when the offence creates a specially extended duty for a class of persons, such as the additional duties on 'members of the same household' created by the Domestic Violence, Crime and Victims Act offence.[25] Chris Clarkson argues that the communicative rationale should extend to the manner in which a nominate offence is drafted: just because it applies only to a particular group of cases, this does not mean that we should mince words. Thus he argues that the law should have an offence of corporate killing, not corporate manslaughter, because the former is a more arresting label and is needed to underscore the seriousness of the offence. Similarly, the arguments for having an offence of vehicular homicide, rather than causing death by dangerous driving, might be that this is not only more appropriate in one sense (extending the offence from road traffic cases to other modes of transport such as rail) but also less euphemistic, exchanging 'homicide' for 'causing death'. Some may wish to argue for or against particular labels and what they imply, but the underlying point is clear. However, there are counter-arguments here. Would not full-page advertisements in the newspapers be more effective in communicating duties to particular categories of people, such as drivers, company executives, electricians, and so forth? Perhaps it would, but it might not satisfy victims' families and other members of the public. Yet we do not know whether such people would be more satisfied with a nominate offence than with a generic homicide offence.

An overlapping but slightly different argument is that fair and representative labelling requires us to create special offences for certain kinds of situation or conduct. The offence of corporate manslaughter might be an example: it could be argued that the circumstances of such offences are so different from homicides by individuals, whatever form of corporate responsibility is used, that it would be inappropriate simply to include them in a generic offence. Whether that would be a compelling argument if there were no other nominate offences is an interesting question: are corporate offences really so different, if it is granted that the fault element ought to be the same as for one of the generic offences of manslaughter? There are many non-homicide offences that can be committed by companies without any change of label; and corporate liability could be brought within the general law of manslaughter by procedural means.[26] Turning to driving offences, could it

24 In relation to companies, one approach would have been to provide that a company may be convicted of the general offence of manslaughter if certain conditions were fulfilled – those conditions being along the same lines as the provisions of the Corporate Manslaughter and Corporate Homicide Act 2007. See, however, the chapter by Chris Clarkson in this volume.

25 Not to mention the ambiguities surrounding the duty and other unsatisfactory features identified in Jonathan Herring's chapter.

26 See above, n.24.

be said that their circumstances are so different from the ordinary run of cases that they require a special label? This calls for careful analysis: as argued above, no good reason has been produced for having a standard or threshold of liability for the dangerous driving offence that differs from the standard for the appropriate generic manslaughter offence, and if the special circumstances are simply that most of us are involved in driving cars and occasionally make errors of judgement, that is more about the difficulty of convicting people than the circumstances of the offending. What might be said, however, is that offences now classified as causing death by dangerous driving stem from doing a lawful act (driving, usually on the roads but perhaps on the rails) with a degree of negligence that is unlawful. The existing law of manslaughter fails to separate those cases from the other group of cases that stem from an originating unlawful act, such as assault (or, in the driving context perhaps, driving while disqualified). That is a distinction that should be drawn, but it argues for separate generic offences, not for a plethora of nominate offences.

A further argument, the risk of jury nullification, surfaces in various parts of English criminal law, such as prosecutions of police officers and prosecutions for breach of the Official Secrets Acts. In homicide its main application has been thought to be in motoring cases. One of the reasons for creating the nominate offence of causing death by dangerous driving in 1956 was that juries would not convict of manslaughter in such cases. However, to sustain this argument in the twenty-first century we really need to know whether, if presented with good evidence that a driver (of a car, bus, lorry or train) falls far below the standard to be expected and so could be described as grossly negligent – or whatever generic standard we decide upon – juries would be unlikely to convict of manslaughter if there were no nominate offence of causing death by dangerous driving available. Do we have any information on this? Barry Mitchell's small survey suggests that public attitudes have changed significantly since 1956.[27] Yet only a few of the very worst driving cases are now prosecuted as gross negligence manslaughter,[28] and one or two might be prosecuted as reckless manslaughter (or 'murder in the second degree') if such a category were available. One reason for prosecutorial reluctance to charge manslaughter is that sentencing practices have changed dramatically since 1956. Juries may not know it (although prosecutors certainly do), but conviction for causing death by dangerous driving may lead to a substantial prison term that may be no shorter than would have resulted from a manslaughter verdict. The raising of the maximum penalty to 14 years for causing death by dangerous driving, and for causing death by careless driving while intoxicated, means that long prison sentences will be handed down in some such cases.[29] But it remains unclear how sentence length interacts with labelling, and whether English law should be so bold as to go beyond the terms 'murder' and 'manslaughter' and to embrace other terms, such as 'culpable homicide' or 'homicide in the second degree', as suitable for a lesser generic category of homicide.

27 Mitchell, B. (2000), 'Further Evidence of the Relationship between Legal and Public Opinion on the Law of Homicide' *Crim LR* 814, at p.824.

28 For example, *Ballard* [2005] 2 Cr App R (S) 186.

29 See further *Richardson* [2007] 2 Cr App R (S) 211, and Sentencing Guidelines Council (2008), *Causing Death by Driving: Definitive Guideline*.

Perhaps the problem of jury nullification, if it exists, is more a question of convicting a defendant who has hitherto lived a blameless life, an apparently upstanding member of the community who has made a single but egregious driving error that resulted in death. This problem takes us towards the character theory of liability, and to broader arguments about the proper approach to out-of-character errors by people whose everyday lives involve dealing with serious risks. Oliver Quick raises this argument in the context of doctors, and suggests that we should consider focusing liability on culpable indifference to those risks and not allowing momentary slips to lead to homicide liability.[30] Setting aside the possible difficulty of distinguishing between a course of conduct and a single act or manoeuvre, one might just as well argue that this ought to apply to electricians and to drivers on the roads or the rails and to police firearms officers, who also deal with serious risks in their everyday activities. The sentencing guidelines applicable to causing death by dangerous driving distinguish between a course of bad driving and a single act of misjudgement,[31] and we might try to reflect such a distinction at the liability stage. This might enable us to deal directly with the 'problem' by refining the law, and creating one or more lesser offences (such as an offence of endangerment)[32] for the doctor, the electrician, or the owner of an activity centre who has no history of such misjudgements. Obviously the collection and presentation of evidence in such cases would require prosecutors to take a different approach, but the question for discussion is whether this would be a morally supportable and practically viable way of handling these cases. Two related arguments – fairness to those who generally conduct themselves safely, and the avoidance of jury nullification – must be scrutinised if such proposals are to merit serious consideration.

One general argument against nominate offences is that they may amount to a down-grading of the offence. Classifying the offences as manslaughter or culpable homicide would be an appropriate signification of the degree of wrongdoing, but a nominate offence (perhaps using the less censuring term, 'causing death by …') may not be a proper valuation. In order to grapple with this we need to separate the label from the essence. Applying a separate label to an offence (causing death by dangerous driving, infanticide) may lead people to believe – and this would be an empirical question – that certain forms of wrongdoing are being taken less seriously. But then there is the further and arguably more important question of whether that amounts to a real under-valuation, that is, whether the 'valuation' consists not merely of the label attached but also of the level of sentence imposed. That, too, would be an empirical question. As intimated above, this question is rendered complex by the increasing levels of sentencing for causing death by dangerous driving in recent years, sentences that are often higher than those for manslaughter by gross negligence

30 Quick (chapter in this volume).

31 *Cooksley* [2004] 1 Cr App R (S) 1.

32 Conviction for a non-homicide offence where death has been caused is not unusual, and may be justifiable if the level of the offender's fault is not sufficiently high to warrant a homicide conviction. This may be true of some or many of the cases brought under the Health and Safety at Work Act 1974 when a death has been caused.

and unlawful act manslaughter, and sometimes higher than for manslaughter upon provocation (where the considerations are, of course, very different).[33]

A further argument against nominalism, though limited in its scope, draws our attention back to the political context in which proposals for homicide law have to be assessed. Any proposal explicitly to reduce the censuring of homicides resulting from assisted suicide, suicide pacts and mercy killing tends to stir up formidable political opposition. Fears about the effects of such opposition led the Law Commission to leave these cases out of its final report in 2006. Some will decry this as cowardice, but the pragmatic truth is that recommendations that were viewed as relaxations of the law in those areas might well undermine all the other proposals in a package of reforms, so strong is the feeling among some religious groups and others. The tendency is therefore to leave these difficult cases aside, consigning them to a twilight world in which other doctrines (notably diminished responsibility) are stretched to accommodate such cases but only if sympathetic medical witnesses can be found. This is an unusual face of nominalism: there seems to be less controversy and greater public acceptance to be gained through mislabelling these cases, often as manslaughter by reason of diminished responsibility, than through using a clear and representative label that draws attention to the circumstances.

## IV Enforcing a New Law of Homicide

Throughout the discussions above I have put forward the principle that the law of homicide (not to say the criminal law as a whole) should aim to ensure the equal treatment of offences of equal seriousness. In the first section of this chapter, the principle was used to urge an alignment of the culpability requirements for homicide offences, in the absence of strong reasons to the contrary. In the second section of the chapter, the principle was one of various arguments invoked against lowering the threshold of homicide liability in cases where an originating wrong led to the victim's death. In the third section, these arguments were applied, with others, to the more political question of how homicide offences should most appropriately be labelled, and in particular whether the general approach should be through nominate or generic offences. It is my view, following on from the general principle, that even if nominate offences are thought advisable for some types of homicide, the thresholds of liability for such offences should be the same. This line of reasoning should be maintained notwithstanding the outcome of the debate about whether to raise the threshold of fault for homicide liability in cases of those who make a momentary error of judgement.[34]

The principle of equal treatment of offences of equal seriousness also has another, more practical dimension. This is that offences of equal seriousness should be investigated and prosecuted on the same principles and, so far as possible, by the same agencies. It is well known that some of the regulatory agencies, including the Health and Safety Executive, have a general policy of enforcement that gives

33 Sentencing Guidelines Council (2005), *Manslaughter by Reason of Provocation: Definitive Guideline*.

34 See the argument in Oliver Quick's chapter in this volume, for example.

priority to ensuring compliance with the law and regards criminal prosecution as a last resort. Whether or not this policy applies to cases where death has resulted, there is no good reason why the approach to investigating and prosecuting such cases should be any different from that in the general run of homicide cases with which the police and Crown Prosecution Service deal. There are now protocols to ensure that corporate manslaughter cases are handed over to the CPS. The same general principle should apply across all forms of homicide, whether caused on the roads, in the home, to young children, or whatever. Unless there are compelling reasons, the approach to homicide should be one of equal treatment across the board.

One of the important points about enforcement to emerge from the book, and a fitting point on which to conclude, is that the prevention of homicide – a goal to which we would all subscribe, surely – calls for broader social policies and initiatives. Efforts to counteract the widespread availability of guns and to displace the 'gun culture' seize the headlines, but no less important are policies of support for the mothers of young children, for women and children in the home who live in fear of violence, and for those addicted to drugs or alcohol. As William Wilson rightly argues in his chapter, we should look closely at the medical and social response to drugs before suggesting that the law of manslaughter needs tightening in respect of drug-induced homicide. The shape of the law of homicide is highly unlikely to have any effect on the day-to-day behaviour of individuals. Proper social and medical policies, appropriately implemented, are needed for that. The law should aim to respond in a fair, equal and measured way to the tragic incidents in which death is caused, labelling as homicide only those that cross the appropriate threshold of fault, and responding in some lesser way to cases where the fault falls below that threshold.

# Index

For Product Safety Concerns and Information please contact our EU
representative GPSR@taylorandfrancis.com
Taylor & Francis Verlag GmbH, Kaufingerstraße 24, 80331 München, Germany

www.ingramcontent.com/pod-product-compliance
Ingram Content Group UK Ltd.
Pitfield, Milton Keynes, MK11 3LW, UK
UKHW010959180926
475701UK00004B/454